1 MONTH OF FREE READING

at

www.ForgottenBooks.com

By purchasing this book you are eligible for one month membership to ForgottenBooks.com, giving you unlimited access to our entire collection of over 1,000,000 titles via our web site and mobile apps.

To claim your free month visit:
www.forgottenbooks.com/free918690

* Offer is valid for 45 days from date of purchase. Terms and conditions apply.

ISBN 978-0-266-97938-8
PIBN 10918690

This book is a reproduction of an important historical work. Forgotten Books uses state-of-the-art technology to digitally reconstruct the work, preserving the original format whilst repairing imperfections present in the aged copy. In rare cases, an imperfection in the original, such as a blemish or missing page, may be replicated in our edition. We do, however, repair the vast majority of imperfections successfully; any imperfections that remain are intentionally left to preserve the state of such historical works.

Forgotten Books is a registered trademark of FB &c Ltd.
Copyright © 2018 FB &c Ltd.
FB &c Ltd, Dalton House, 60 Windsor Avenue, London, SW19 2RR.
Company number 08720141. Registered in England and Wales.

For support please visit www.forgottenbooks.com

A LIBRARY

OF

NATIONAL ANTIQUITIES.

A SERIES OF VOLUMES,

ILLUSTRATING

THE GENERAL ARCHÆOLOGY AND HISTORY OF OUR COUNTRY.

Published under the direction and at the expense of

JOSEPH MAYER, ESQ., F.S.A., ETC.,

HONORARY CURATOR OF THE HISTORIC SOCIETY OF LANCASHIRE AND CHESHIRE.

A VOLUME OF VOCABULARIES.

EDITED BY

THOMAS WRIGHT, ESQ., M.A., F.S.A., ETC.

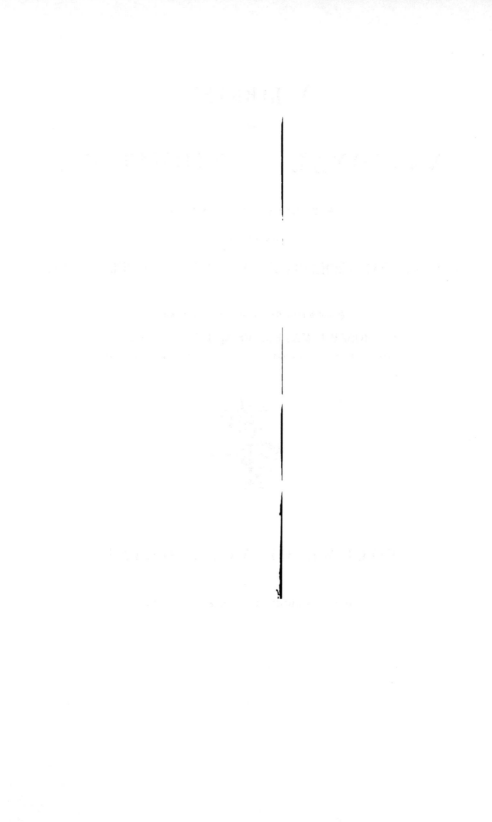

A VOLUME

OF

VOCABULARIES,

ILLUSTRATING

THE CONDITION AND MANNERS OF OUR FOREFATHERS, AS WELL
AS THE HISTORY OF THE FORMS OF ELEMENTARY
EDUCATION AND OF THE LANGUAGES
SPOKEN IN THIS ISLAND,

FROM THE TENTH CENTURY TO THE FIFTEENTH.

EDITED,

from MSS. in Public and Private Collections,

BY

THOMAS WRIGHT, ESQ., M.A., F.S.A., HON. M.R.S.L., ETC.,
CORRESPONDING MEMBER OF THE INSTITUTE OF FRANCE.
(ACADÉMIE DES INSCRIPTIONS ET BELLES LETTRES.)

PRIVATELY PRINTED.
MDCCCLVII.

PREFACE.

The Public is indebted for the following volume to the liberality and public spirit of Mr. Joseph Mayer, whose name is now so well known to all who interest themselves in the Archæology of this country. Its design originated in a social conversation between Mr. Mayer and myself, and we have endeavoured in it to make available to labourers in the field of antiquarian research and investigation a class of documents which, though they have been hitherto almost overlooked, form a rich treasury of information on almost every subject connected with the Archæology of the Middle Ages. They have been furnished by a number of contemporary manuscripts, scattered through various libraries in this country and abroad. Of one of the most valuable of the later vocabularies here printed, the original is preserved in Mr. Mayer's own collection; and for the communication and permission to print another—the curious and interesting pictorial vocabulary which closes the series—we owe our sincere thanks to the Lord Londesborough, of whose collection the manuscript forms a part. As far as regards my own labours, I will only say, that I have endeavoured to make the texts, which are arranged in strict chronological order, as nearly as is consistent with the duty of an editor, fac-similes of those of the original manuscripts. In fact, their very errors and corruptions form no unimportant facts in the history of education and knowledge, and they have been carefully preserved as, under these circumstances, an integral part of the text itself. Nevertheless, whenever I have been able to meet with several copies of the same tract, I have collated them, and made use of any additional matter they furnished, without interfering with the text of that which I have chosen as the best. It will be quite evident to anybody who glances at the contents of the present volume, that it is susceptible of annotations which might be made to swell out several such volumes. I therefore beg to state that I have had no intention of loading the volume with elaborate annotations; but I have hoped that a few explanatory and illustrative notes would make the work more popular, and would render it more useful to the general reader, and their pretensions go no further.

THOMAS WRIGHT.

BROMPTON, LONDON,
September, 1857.

INTRODUCTION.

THE Treatises which form the present volume are interesting in several points of view. Their importance in a philological sense, as monuments of the languages which prevailed at different periods in this island, is evident at the first glance, and need not be dilated upon. They are curious records of the history of Education; and, above all, they are filled with invaluable materials for illustrating the conditions and manners of our forefathers at various periods of their history, as well as the Antiquities of the Middle Ages in general. The history of Education is a subject which is now deservedly attracting more attention than was formerly given to it. It is certainly not uninteresting to trace the various efforts which were made, at all periods of the middle ages, to simplify and render popular the forms of elementary instruction, and the several modifications which these forms underwent.

The groundwork of all school-learning was the knowledge of the Latin language; and the first tasks of the young scholar were to learn the elements of the Latin grammar, to commit to memory words and their meanings, and to practise conversation in the Latin tongue. It was this practical application of the language which contributed very largely to its corruption, for the scholar began by making himself acquainted not with the pure Latin diction of classical books, but with a nomenclature of words—many of them extremely barbarous—which it had then become customary to apply to objects of ordinary use and occurrence. The lessons were given by word of mouth, as boys could not in those times be accommodated with books; but they had slates, or roughly made tablets (*tabulæ*), on which they wrote down the lesson in grammar, or the portion of vocabulary, from the lips of the master, and, after committing it to memory, erased the writing, to make place for another. The teacher had necessarily his own written exemplar of an elementary Latin grammar, as well as his own written vocabulary of words, from which he read, interpreted, and explained. The old illuminations of manuscripts give us not unfrequently pictures of the interior of the school, in which we see the scholars arranged, with their tablets, before or round the teacher, who is dictating to them. In the earlier periods of Christianity among the Anglo-

Saxons, the study of the Latin language was pursued with extraordinary zeal and proportionate success, and our island was celebrated for its learned men; but as time passed on, various circumstances combined to produce a general neglect of learning, so that king Alfred complained, in the latter part of the ninth century, that very few of his subjects could translate from Latin into their mother tongue. "So clean," he said, was teaching "ruined among the English people, that there were very few even of the ecclesiastical order, southward of the Humber, who could understand their service in English, or declare forth an epistle out of Latin into English; and I think there were not many beyond Humber." It may be observed, that in the earlier period, the Northumbrian kingdom was the great seat of learning. "So few such there were," Alfred adds, "that I cannot think of a single instance to the south of the Thames when I began to reign. To God Almighty be thanks that we now have any teacher in stall."[1]

Some of the causes of this decadence in the study of Latin among the Anglo-Saxons belonged probably to a change which had taken place in the social condition of the country, and were not to be overcome. Our great-minded Anglo-Saxon king intimates that his countrymen began to prefer books translated into or compiled in their own language to Latin compositions, and his own example in labouring upon such translations, or causing others to labour upon them, contributed no doubt to give permanence to this very natural taste. Nevertheless, the study of Latin was revived in England with some success during the tenth century, and it was increased by the intercourse between the English and continental scholars. Still this study was by no means general, and at the end of this century and beginning of the next, the labours of the two Alfrics in translating and compiling in English show sufficiently the neglect of the study of Latin even among the English clergy, which is confirmed by the complaints of the Norman ecclesiastics after the conquest. It is to these two distinguished scholars that we owe the first elementary school-books that are known to have existed in the English language—a Latin grammar (compiled and translated from Donatus and Priscian) and Latin-English vocabularies.

It is singular how soon our forefathers began to exercise their ingenuity in arranging their elementary books — and more especially the vocabularies —

[1] Swa clæne heo wæs oðfeallen on Angelcynne þæt swiðe feawa wæron beheonan Humbre þe hira þenunge cuðon understandan on Englisc, oððe furðon an ærend-gewrit of Ledene on Englisc areccan; and ic wene þæt naht monige begeondan Humbre næron. Swa feawa heora wæron, þæt ic furþon anne ænlepne ne mæg geþencan, be suðan Thamise þa þa ic to rice feng. Gode ælmigtigum sy þanc, þæt we nu ænigne an steal habbað lareowa."—*King Alfred's Preface to the Translation of Gregory's Pastorale.*

in forms calculated to be most attractive to the learner, or to enable him more easily to commit them to memory. The first of the treatises printed in the present volume, which had passed successively through the hands of the two Alfrics, the archbishop and his disciple, is compiled in the form of an interesting and very amusing dialogue, so contrived as to embody a large number of the words of common occurrence in the ordinary relations of life. It is written in Latin, but accompanied with a continuous interlinear gloss in Anglo-Saxon, precisely on the plan of the modern elementary books of the Hamiltonian system of teaching, to which it has been more than once compared; but it possessed one striking difference, which must not be overlooked—that the old Anglo-Saxon treatise was glossed for the assistance of the teacher, and not, as in the modern books of this description, for the learner. In fact, it is evident that at this time the schoolmasters themselves were very imperfectly acquainted with the Latin language, and that they found it necessary to have books in which the English meaning was written above or beside the Latin word, to enable them to explain it to their scholars. It was this same ignorance which rendered it necessary to have vocabularies, or lists of Latin words, with the translation attached to them—such as those which form the bulk of the present volume. In the earlier and better period, no doubt the teacher had such lists merely in Latin, or glossed only in cases of difficulty, and he was sufficiently learned in the language to explain them himself; but now the schoolmaster required to be reminded himself of the meaning of the Latin word. Nor was this all; for, besides the very incorrect and corrupt manner in which the words are frequently written in these manuscript vocabularies, in many instances the Latin word is wrongly interpreted. Several instances of such blunders may be pointed out in Alfric's "Colloquy;"[1] and others occur frequently in the Anglo-Saxon vocabularies, some of which are indicated in the notes.

These vocabularies appear to have been numerous during the later Anglo-Saxon period, and those which remain differ considerably from each other. I have included in the present volume all that are now known to exist. The last of them brings us down to at least the middle of the twelfth century, after which we lose sight of similar vocabularies, until we reach the fifteenth century.

---

[1] Some of these are curious. At p. 7, occurs the adverb *solum*, which the glossator has translated as an adjective, instead of an adverb. Towards the bottom of the next page, the merchant speaks of selling his merchandise *carius*, dearer, than he bought it; but the Anglo-Saxon interpreter has translated as though it meant more beloved, evidently not understanding the phrase to which it belongs. Again, on p. 5, speaking of the fisherman's art, he evidently did not know whether the Latin *hamus* meant the hook or the bait.

The Anglo-Norman period presents us with a new description of vocabulary, in which the words, still kept together in their different classes, are collected into a sort of continuous discourse. Of these, the earliest, and in many respects the most curious, is that by the celebrated scholar, Alexander Neckam, in which the principal operations and professions of life are enumerated and described in a familiar style. Neckam, singularly enough for an ecclesiastic, begins with the kitchen, describes its furniture and implements and their several uses, and treats of the articles of food and of the methods of cooking them. He then turns to the possessor of the house, describes his dress and accoutrements, when remaining at home or when riding abroad, and introduces us in the sequel to his chamber and to its furniture. The chamber-maid is next introduced to us, with her household employments; and we are taken to the poultry-yard, with a chapter on the cooking of poultry and fish, and on the characteristics of good wine. We are next taught how to build a feudal castle, to fortify it, to store and to defend it; and this leads us naturally to the subject of war in general, and to arms, armour, and soldiers. From this we return to matters of a more domestic character—to the barn, the poultry-yard, and the stable, and to that important occupation of mediæval domestic life, weaving. The occupations of the country follow, and the author explains the construction of carts and waggons, the process of building an ordinary house, and its parts, the various implements and operations of farming, and the construction and use of the plough. We turn rather abruptly from agriculture to navigation, and are instructed in the different sorts of ships, and in their parts and the articles with which they were usually stored. The tools, qualifications, and duties of the mediæval scribe, the operations of the goldsmith, and a copious enumeration of ecclesiastical furniture, complete this curious treatise.

The similar treatise of John de Garlande, composed in the earlier half of the following century, differs very much from its predecessor in details and arrangement. Its author occupies himself more with the objects which meet the eye in the interior of a great city (Paris), than with feudal or agricultural life. After giving, by way of introduction, a description of the human body and its various parts and members, he proceeds with a long list of trades and manufactures, and the various articles made or sold, such as the hawker who carried shoes and other articles of leather for sale on a pole, the girdle-makers, saddlers, shield-makers, buckle-makers, dealers in needles and other such articles, makers of bridles, hucksters, frobishers (or furbishers), the shop-keepers of the Grand-Pont, glovers, hatters, bowyers, makers of brooches and clasps, bell-makers, coblers, cordwainers, furriers, street criers, menders of cups, itinerant dealers in wine, sellers of cakes, regraters, bakers, pie-makers, cooks, changers, minters, goldsmiths, clothiers, linen-drapers, apothecaries, carpenters, wheelwrights, cart-makers, millers, armourers, fullers, dyers, tanners, smiths. At this point, John de Garlande interrupts his list of trades, to describe the house of a citizen *(probus homo)* and its furniture, which is followed by the different implements necessary to a scholar, or clerk. John de Garlande then proceeds to give the learner a list of his own wardrobe. A rather quaint account of the ecclesiastical library of a priest follows, with his apparel, and the implements belonging to the service of the church. We return from the church very abruptly to the stable, and then we have a list of the various domestic implements belonging to the mistress of the house, with descriptions of the occupations and employments peculiar to women—weaving, needlework, &c. The account of a poultry-shop in the Parvis of Notre Dame furnishes an occasion for giving a list of domestic fowls; that of the fowler, for an enumeration of wild fowls; and that of the fisherman, for a list of fish. In the chapters following, John de Garlande enumerates the domestic animals he had seen in the fields, the wild ones he had met with in the king's forest, the plants and herbs which grew in his own garden, the fruits in his orchard, and the shrubs in his grove; he gives a description of his own hall, an enumeration of the ships he had seen at sea, of the various tortures of the martyrs which were suggested to his mind by the fear of shipwreck, of the jongleurs, minstrels, dancing girls, &c., who performed at the feasts of the rich, of the punishments reserved for sinners, and of the joys of the blessed.

The close of the thirteenth century introduces us to a document of a novel character, although still similar in plan. It is written in verse, no doubt that it might be more easily carried in the memory, and, instead of being intended to teach the Latin language, its purpose was to teach French to the children of the English nobility and gentry. Accordingly, the text is written in French, with an interlinear gloss in English. This "treatise," as it is called, which was written by a man evidently of aristocratic blood, named Walter de Biblesworth, marks a very important period in the history of the English language, as it shows that before the end of the thirteenth century, and perhaps subsequently to the barons' wars, that language had already become the mother tongue of the children of the Anglo-Norman nobility, and that they learnt it before they were taught French.[1]

---

[1] I may perhaps be allowed to repeat here the remarks on this subject made in a paper on the History of the English Language, read before the Historic Society of Lancashire and Cheshire, and printed in their Transactions, vol. ix, p. 150, 1857. I there said, "It was not only as the language of the Normans, but as that peculiarly of the feudal aristocracy in

The subjects in this treatise are arranged in an order which seems to have been considered most suitable to the class for which they were intended. Walter de Biblesworth begins with the child when new-born, tells how it is to be nursed and fed, and then proceeds to the description of the human body. In this and in other parts, the author labours to impress upon the learner the nice distinctions between words of nearly similar meaning, and the different meanings of words which are similar in sound, as well as the distinction of genders, which even then appears to have presented a difficulty to the young beginner in the French language. The description of the body itself is followed by the process of clothing it, and by an enumeration of the various articles of apparel. The author then returns again to the manners of the child, and describes its proper diet. After some rather curious instructions for the proper and distinctive use of certain classes of words, we are taken to the barn, and the teacher describes the processes of thrashing, of converting corn into meal, of baking, of the cultivation of flax, and the various stages through which it went before it is converted into linen cloth, and of brewing, as well as of the character and effects of good ale. The scholar is next taken a-fishing, and the various characteristics of the country, with the phases of the weather, and the changes of season, are pointed out to him. The fine weather offers the occasion of another rural excursion, with a description of the flowers, the fruit and other trees, the birds, and the animals which are supposed to present themselves to his view. Rural occupations are next introduced, with full descriptions of a cart and a plough. Then we witness the building of a house, and the arrangements of its different parts, the domestic processes of lighting

general, that French was introduced into England under William the Conqueror; and it was in that character that it continued to be the language of the aristocracy until feudalism itself was broken down. It had ceased, however, to be exclusively their language in the thirteenth century. In the latter years of that century, a tract or treatise was written in French or Anglo-Norman verse, forming a sort of vocabulary of that language, and designed expressly for the purpose of teaching it to children. The number of copies of this tract still preserved in MS. show that it was a popular elementary book, and that it was in extensive use. The compiler was Walter de Biblesworth, a man known elsewhere as a writer of French verse, and apparently belonging himself to the aristocratic class; he was a friend of the great statesman of the reign of Edward I., Henry de Lacy, earl of Lincoln and Salisbury, and compiled the treatise we are speaking of at the request of the lady Dionysia de Monchensey. Thus all the relations of the author and of his book were of an aristocratic character. Now, Walter de Biblesworth states his object to be to instruct the rising generation in the proper use of the words of the French language, and especially in the correct application of the genders: and the French words are explained in English, implying thus that the learner was acquainted with the English language before he began to learn French. We thus ascertain the very important fact, that, before the end of the thirteenth century, the children of the aristocracy of England learnt English before they were instructed in any other language—or, in other words, that English had become their mother tongue."

the fire, cooking the food, and placing it on the table, and the various articles of food and their arrangement. The whole closes with the description of a great feast. The notion of composing such vocabularies in verse was applied to Latin, as well as to French, an example of which will be found also in the present volume.

During the fourteenth century, school teaching seems to have fallen greatly into neglect in this country, and we hardly find any manuscripts of these educational treatises between those of the thirteenth century and those of the fifteenth. In the latter century, however, a great movement took place,—it was the age, especially, of founding grammar-schools, so many of which were re-founded at the dissolution of papal colleges under Edward VI. A similar degradation, in fact, had taken place to that which we have remarked under the Anglo-Saxons, though the causes were not entirely the same. The influence of the great development of learning in the twelfth century, and the example of the able and elegant Latin writers whom that age had produced, extended over at least a portion of the thirteenth century; but before the end of that century, the priest was already gaining the victory over the schoolmaster, and the power of the universities was yielding to that of the Popish church. During the two following centuries, learning was reduced almost to its lowest degree; and this became so apparent, that an effort was made to raise it by striking at what was supposed to be the root of the evil—the want or the inefficiency of the elementary schools. Those who undertook the task of reformers, however, mistook the cause of the evil, and did not understand that the Middle Ages were approaching their end, and that there was no remedy for the restoration of forms and principles which were expiring from their own exhaustion. Nevertheless, the effort seems to have been made with earnestness, and caused, in the fifteenth century, a considerable extension in the lower grades of scholastic education. The manuscripts of grammatical treatises—of school-books, in fact—now become extremely numerous. Latin-English vocabularies are also not uncommon during this period, and I have given three in the present volume—one from a manuscript in the British Museum, and the two others from private collections. The last of these, and apparently the latest in date—but it is not very easy to distinguish nicely the distinctive dates of this particular class of manuscripts during the fifteenth century—presents a new peculiarity,—it is illustrated with rude pen-and-ink drawings in the margin of many of the articles enumerated in the text of the vocabulary. These illustrations, we should imagine, were designed to assist in fixing the attention of the scholar on his task, and it thus, as the latest of these attempts at improvement, forms an appropriate conclusion to our volume. It shows us, moreover, how little of novelty there is in most of the plans for simplifying school teaching in more modern times, for in these mediæval treatises we meet with the prototypes of almost every scheme that has been proposed, from the more recent Hamiltonian system to the *Orbis Sensualium Pictus* of Comenius, which made so much noise by its novelty of plan in the earlier part of the seventeenth century.

It can hardly be doubted that the manuscripts of these vocabularies of the fifteenth century were written by schoolmasters for their own use; and we cannot help being struck by the large proportion of barbarous Latin words which are introduced into them, and by the gross blunders with which they abound, especially in their orthography. Many of the Latin words are so disguised and corrupted, that we can hardly recognise them; and in some instances, the schoolmaster has actually mistaken the genders. It is thus clear that the schoolmasters of the fifteenth century were very imperfect scholars themselves, and we can easily understand how the Latinists of the old school fell into that barbarous style of writing which drew upon them the ridicule of the classical scholars after the revival of learning, as well as their hostility to that new light which exposed their defects. These vocabularies of the fifteenth century differ so entirely from each other, both in their general arrangement and in the words introduced under each head, that there seems little room for doubt that each schoolmaster compiled his own book. This circumstance has added extremely to their philological value, as the English words in each vocabulary may be supposed to present some, at least, of the peculiarities of the dialect in which it was written. Through the preceding ages, the schoolmasters seem to have laboured under a difference of opinion as to the subject which had a claim to precedence of the others, and therefore ought to be placed at the head of the vocabulary. Archbishop Alfric gave the palm to agriculture, expressly in the Colloquy, and practically in his Vocabulary.[1] The vocabulary from the Brussels manuscript,[2] and that printed as the appendix to the present volume from the Cottonian MS,[3] begin with birds, for which it would be difficult to assign any reason. The Anglo-Saxon glossary of the other Cottonian manuscript,[4] with the semi-Saxon vocabulary abridged from it,[5] first present the more natural order of commencing with the Deity and with the human body and its parts. Alexander Neckam, as already stated, begins with the kitchen; but John de Garlande returns to the more natural order, beginning with man and the human body, which

---

[1] See pp. 2, 11, and 15 of the present volume.
[2] P. 62 of the present volume.
[3] See p. 280.
[4] P. 70.
[5] P. 87.

is adopted also in principle by Walter de Biblesworth. The vocabularies of the fifteenth century adopt, I think, invariably the human body as the leading subject, but they arrange the subjects which follow very diversely. Some of them, too, divide and subdivide these subjects under more numerous heads, or titles, than others.

It is this circumstance of grouping the words under different heads which gives these vocabularies their value as illustrations of the conditions and manners of society. It is evident that the compiler gave, in each case, the names of all such things as habitually presented themselves to his view, or, in other words, that he presents us with an exact list and description of all the objects which were in use at the time he wrote, and no more. We have, therefore, in each a sort of measure of the fashions, and comforts, and utilities of contemporary life, as well as in some cases of its sentiments. Thus, to begin with a man's habitation, his house—the words which describe the parts of the Anglo-Saxon house are few in number, a *heal* or hall, a *bur* or bedroom, and in some cases a *cicen* or kitchen, and the materials are chiefly beams of wood, laths, and plaister.[1] But when we come to the vocabularies of the Anglo-Norman period, we soon find traces of that ostentation in domestic buildings which William of Malmsbury assures us that the Normans introduced into this island; the house becomes more massive, and the rooms more numerous, and more diversified in their purposes. When we look at the furniture of the house, the difference is still more apparent. The description given by Alexander Neckam of the hall, the chambers, the kitchen, and the other departments of the ordinary domestic establishment in the twelfth century, and the furniture of each, almost brings them before our eyes,[2] and nothing could be more curious than the account which the same writer gives us of the process of building and storing a castle.[3] The bare lists of names in the vocabularies of the fifteenth century are hardly less expressive. Thus, in the earliest of these vocabularies, we have the baronial hall furnished with its board and trestles, with which the table was laid out when wanted; the table dormant, or permanent table, which was probably even then an article of rarer occurrence; benches, as the ordinary seats; a long-settle to draw up to the fire, or to place on the dais, behind the high table; a chair, for ceremonious occasions, and a stool; a cushion for the chair; bankers and dossers, or carpets to lay over the principal seats; a screen; a basin and laver, for washing the hands of the guests; andirons to support the fire, tongs to arrange it, and bellows to raise it into a flame.[4] So again, in the subject of costume, we have the

[1] See pp. 26, 57, 58, and 80.
[2] See pp. 96, 98, 100, 101, 109, 110.
[3] See pp. 103, 104.
[4] See p. 197.

names of different articles of wearing apparel in use at successive periods, from the tenth century to the end of the thirteenth, and again during the fifteenth centuries. The same thing may be said of the weapons of war. Some of these documents, and especially the *Dictionarius* of John de Garlande, throw an interesting light upon the trades and manufactures of the middle ages. Others show us the progress — or rather the want of progress — of our forefathers in the practice of agriculture. In fact, there is hardly any subject connected with mediæval life which does not receive some light from the tracts which are printed in the present volume. We here see our forefathers in all their positions of relationship, position, and occupation, from infancy to old age; we are introduced to the child in the nursery, and to the boy at his school; we see him in the clothes he wore, and with the arms that he carried to those constant wars which absorbed so much of mediæval life; we learn in minute detail how he lived, what was his food and how it was prepared, and what he drank; we see the industrious housewife attending to her domestic cares, or busied in her usual occupations of spinning and weaving; we witness the games and amusements of the different stages of life; and we even penetrate into the retired study of the scholar.

Again, in these vocabularies the Archæologist will find the only means of identifying by their proper names a multitude of utensils, which are elsewhere named without description, or of which he is acquainted with the forms, but knows not what to call them. This is especially the case with a class of articles which have been during the last few years much more studied by antiquaries than formerly, such as mediæval pottery, and vessels for the table of glass and metal, as well as articles of jewellery and other ornaments of the person. We even gain instructive glances at notions which show us the progress of science, and at implements of various kinds which reveal to us important facts in the history of modern inventions.

None of these, perhaps, is of more importance than the curious early allusion to the use of the mariner's compass by the navigators of the western seas.[1] It is well known to all readers that this invaluable invention has been formerly supposed to have been brought from the East, and not to have been known in the West until the fourteenth century, when it was used by the Italian mariners. Allusions to it have, however, been discovered by the students of mediæval literature in works which date as far back as the thirteenth century. In the following pages, we find this invention not only alluded to in the twelfth century, but described in such a manner as to show that it was then absolutely in its infancy, and to leave little doubt of its having originated

[1] See p. 114.

in the west. Alexander Neckam, in his treatise *de Utensilibus*, enumerates, among the ship's stores, a needle which was placed on a pivot, and when turned round and left to take its own position in repose, taught the sailors their way when the polar star was concealed from them by clouds or tempest. I have discovered and printed in the note to this passage, a passage in another of Neckam's works, the inedited treatise *de Naturis Rerum*, which gives a more distinct account of this invention. " Mariners at sea," he says, " when through cloudy weather in the day which hides the sun, or through the darkness of the night, they lose the knowledge of the quarter of the world to which they are sailing, touch a needle with the magnet, which will turn round till, on its motion ceasing, its point will be directed towards the north." A comparison of these two passages seems to shew pretty clearly that at this time the navigators had no regular box for the compass, but that they merely carried with them a needle which had been touched with the magnet (perhaps sometimes they carried the magnet also, and touched the needle for the occasion), and that when they had to use it, they merely placed it upon some point, or pivot, on which it could turn with tolerable freedom, and then gave it a motion, and waited until it ceased moving. This mode of using the needle was, it must be confessed, rude enough. The passage in the treatise *de Utensilibus* contains one particular which is very obscure, as Neckam informs us that when the needle ceased moving it pointed towards the east *(donec cuspis acus respiciat orientem);* and as all the manuscripts agree in this reading, and it is glossed by *est,* this must be the intention of the writer. I know no way of explaining this, unless it be by the supposition that, as in the twelfth century the East was the grand object of most voyages from this part of the world, an attempt had been made to improve the magnetic needle by adding to it a limb at right angles, which should point to the east when the needle itself pointed to the north; and that this was what Neckam calls the *cuspis acus*. Between this time and the date — whatever it may be — of the poem, also quoted in my note on the passage of Neckam, which contains the first allusion to the mariner's compass in the thirteenth century, an attempt had been made to facilitate its use.[1] This was done by thrusting the needle through some substance which would not sink, and placing it upon the surface of water. Guiot de Provins, the author of the poem alluded to, calls this substance a *festu*, a stick or straw (the Latin *festuca*). The mariners, he tells us, have a contrivance depending on the

---

[1] In this interval, we meet with another slight but very curious allusion to the use of the magnetic needle for purposes of navigation. Jacques de Vitri, one of the historians of the crusades, who wrote about the year 1218, says, (Hist. Hier. cap. 89,) "Acus ferrea, postquam adamantem contigerit, ad stellam septentrionalem, quae velut axis firmamenti aliis vergentibus non movetur, semper convertitur; unde valde necessarius est navigantibus in mari."

xviii.

qualities of the magnet, which cannot fail. The magnet, he adds, is an ugly brownish stone, to which iron is attracted. "After they have caused a needle to touch it, and placed it in a stick, they put it in the water, without anything more, and the stick keeps it on the surface. Then it turns its point towards the star with such certainty, that no man will ever have any doubt of it, nor will it ever for anything go false. When the sea is dark and hazy, that they can neither see star nor moon, they place a light by the needle, and then they have no fear of going wrong; towards the star goes the point, whereby the mariners have the knowledge to keep the right way. It is an art which cannot fail." According to another poet, the substance through which the needle was usually thrust was cork. He tells us that "the mariners who went to Friesland, or to Greece, or Acre, or Venice," were guided in their route by the polar star; but when at night, or in obscure weather, it was invisible, they discovered its position by the following contrivance:—"They thrust a needle of iron through a piece of cork, so that it is almost buried in it, and then touch it with the loadstone; then they place it in a vessel full of water, so that no one pushes it out until the water is calm, for in whatever direction the point aims, there without doubt is the polar star." The MS. in which this latter poem was found is undoubtedly of the fourteenth century; but the poem itself is evidently of somewhat older date— of the beginning of that century, or not improbably of the century preceding. It is possible, therefore, that this rudely constructed mariner's compass may have continued unimproved until the fourteenth century.[1]

---

[1] This very curious poem, a sort of song, is preserved in a manuscript formerly in the collection of M. Barrois, of Paris, and now in that of Lord Ashburnham. It was first pointed out by M. Fr. Michel, who printed the portion relating to the mariner's compass in the preface to his *Lais inédits*, Paris, 1836. As this is now a rare book, I have thought it desirable to give here the whole passage, as a complement to the extracts given in the note on p. 114 of the present volume. It is as follows:—

La tresmontaine est de tel guise,
Qu'ele est el firmament assise
Où ele luist et resilambie.
Li maronier qui vont en Frise,
En Gresse, en Acre, ou en Venise,
Sevent par li toute la voie;
Pour nule riens ne se desvoie,
Tout jours se tient en une moie.
Tant est de li grans li servisse,
Se la mers est enflée ou koie
Jà ne sera c'ou ne le voie,
Ne pour galerne ne pour bise.

Pour bise ne pour autre afaire
Ne laist sen dout servise à faire
La tresmontaigne clere et pure;
Les maroniers par son esclaire
Jete souvent hors de contraire,
Et de chemin les asseure.
Et quant la nuis est trop oscure,
S'est ele encor de tel nature,
C'à l'amant fait le fer traire,
Si que par forche et par droiture,
Et par nulle qui tous jours dure,
Sevent le liu de son repaire.

Son repaire sevent à route,
Quant li tans n'a de clarté goute,
Tout chil qui font cest maistrise,
Qui une aguille de fer boute
Si qu'ele pert presque toute
En .i. poi de liége, et l'atise
A la pierre d'aimant bise;
S'en .i. vaissel plain d' yave est mise,
Si que nus hors ne la deboute,
Si tost com l'iave s'aserise;
Car dons quel part la pointe vise,
La tresmontaigne est là sans doute.

The philologist will appreciate the tracts printed in the following pages as a continuous series of very valuable monuments of the languages spoken in our island during the Middle Ages. It is these vocabularies alone which have preserved from oblivion a very considerable and interesting portion of the Anglo-Saxon tongue, and without their assistance our Anglo-Saxon dictionaries would be far more imperfect than they are. I have endeavoured to collect together in the present volume all the Anglo-Saxon vocabularies that are known to exist, not only on account of their diversity, but because I believe that their individual utility will be increased by thus presenting them in a collective form. They represent the Anglo-Saxon language as it existed in the tenth and eleventh centuries; and, as written no doubt in different places, they may possibly present some traces of the local dialects of that period. The curious semi-Saxon vocabulary is chiefly interesting as representing the Anglo-Saxon in its period of transition, when it was in a state of rapid decadence. The interlinear gloss to Alexander Neckam, and the commentary on John de Garlande, are most important monuments of the language which for a while usurped among our forefathers the place of the Anglo-Saxon, and which we know by the name of the Anglo-Norman. In the partial vocabulary of the names of plants, which follows them, we have the two languages in juxta-position, the Anglo-Saxon having then emerged from that state which has been termed semi-Saxon, and become early English. We are again introduced to the English language more generally by Walter de Biblesworth, the interlinear gloss to whose treatise represents no doubt the English of the beginning of the fourteenth century. All the subsequent vocabularies given here belong, as far as the language is concerned, to the fifteenth century. As written in different parts of the country, they bear evident marks of dialect; one of them—the vocabulary in Latin verse—is a very curious relic of the dialect of the West of England at a period of which such remains are extremely rare.

ERRATA.

P. 29. In note 6 on this page, the explanation of the A.-S. *scric*, by *shrike*, has crept in by a mere oversight: it should be " the missel-thrush, still called in some parts of England a *screech*.'

P. 93. In the second column of the note, a line has been accidentally misplaced—what is here the 16th line from the top of the column, should follow the 20th line.

CONTENTS.

	PAGE.
I. THE COLLOQUY OF ARCHBISHOP ALFRIC. 10TH CENTURY	1

From MS. Cotton. Tiberius A III. Found also in MS. Col. S. Johan, Oxford. Printed in Thorpe's Analecta Anglo-Saxonica.

II. ARCHBISHOP ALFRIC'S VOCABULARY. 10TH CENTURY 15

From a MS. now lost, belonging to Rubens, the painter. A transcript among the MSS. of Junius in the Bodleian Lib. at Oxford. Printed at the end of Somner's Anglo-Saxon Dictionary, 1659, now a rare book.

III. SUPPLEMENT TO ALFRIC'S VOCABULARY. 11TH CENTURY . . . 49

From the same MS.

IV. ANGLO-SAXON VOCABULARY. 11TH CENTURY 62

From a MS. at Brussels. Printed in Mr. Purton Cooper's Appendix B. to the Report of Record Commission, which was suppressed.

V. ANGLO-SAXON VOCABULARY. 11TH CENTURY 70

From MS. Cotton. Julius A. II. Found also in a MS. in St John's College, Oxford.

VI. SEMI-SAXON VOCABULARY. 12TH CENTURY 87

From a MS. in the archives of Worcester Cathedral. Printed privately by Sir Thomas Phillipps, Bart.

VII. THE TREATISE DE UTENSILIBUS OF ALEXANDER NECKAM. 12TH CENTURY 96

From MS. Cotton. Titus D. XX. Collated with two MSS. in the Imperial Library, Paris

VIII. THE DICTIONARIUS OF JOHN DE GARLANDE. FIRST HALF OF 13TH CENTURY 121

From MS. Cotton. Titus D. XX. Collated with another and later copy preserved in MS. Harl. 1002, and with an edition from three Paris MSS. printed in *Paris sous Philippe le-Bel*, by M. Gérard.

IX. VOCABULARY OF THE NAMES OF PLANTS. MIDDLE OF 13TH CENTURY 139

From MS. Harl. No 978.

X. THE TREATISE OF WALTER DE BIBLESWORTH. CLOSE OF 13TH CENTURY 142

From MS. Arundel, No. 220 (Brit. Mus.). Collated with MS. Sloane, No. 809, and partially with a MS. in the library of the University of Cambridge.

XI. METRICAL VOCABULARY. PERHAPS OF THE 14TH CENTURY . . 175
   From MS. Harl., No. 1002.

XII. NAMES OF THE PARTS OF THE HUMAN BODY. SAME DATE AS
   PRECEDING 183
   From MS. Harl., No. 1002.

XIII. ENGLISH VOCABULARY. 15TH CENTURY 185
   From MS. Reg. 17 C. XVII. (Brit. Mus.)

XIV. A NOMINALE. 15TH CENTURY 206
   From a MS. in the collection of Joseph Mayer, Esq.

XV. A PICTORIAL VOCABULARY. 15TH CENTURY 244
   From a MS. in the collection of the Lord Londesborough.

APPENDIX.

XVI. ANGLO-SAXON VOCABULARY. 10TH OR 11TH CENTURY 280
   From MS. Cotton Cleop. A. III. Overlooked in its place in the earlier part of the volume.

TABLE OF SUBJECTS.

(This Table is intended to facilitate the reference to the following pages to the Archæologist, by furnishing him with an index of the general heads under which words relating to each subject will be found grouped together. It is not, however, intended to include a reference to miscellaneous words, or to words belonging to these subjects which occur singly. The numbers refer, of course, to the pages of the book.)

THE HUMAN BODY, AND ITS PARTS, 42, 64, 70, 87, 121, 144, 179, 183, 185, 200, 244, 282.
AFFECTIONS OF THE BODY; DISEASES AND THEIR REMEDIES, 19, 45, 75, 89, 224, 267.
NURTURE OF INFANCY, 143, 203.
THE SCHOOL, 6, 13.
COSTUME, 25, 39, 81, 98, 99, 100, 133, 149, 182, 196, 238, 259.
ORNAMENTS OF THE PERSON, 16, 40, 74, 89.
THE TABLE, DIFFERENT ARTICLES OF FOOD, 26, 27, 41, 82, 93, 97, 102, 150, 172, 173, 174, 178, 198, 200, 240, 241, 258, 266, 290.
DRINKS OF DIFFERENT KINDS, 27, 98, 102, 103, 178, 198, 232, 233, 257, 290.
HOUSES AND OTHER BUILDINGS, AND THEIR PARTS, 26, 57, 58, 80, 81, 82, 83, 86, 92, 93, 94, 109, 110, 137, 169, 170, 178, 203, 204, 235, 260, 273, 274, 289.
    THE HALL, 109, 137, 197.
    THE CHAMBERS, 100, 190, 242, 259, 284.
    THE BUTTERY, 257.
    THE DAIRY, 202.
    THE PANTRY, 258.
    THE NURSERY, 203.
    THE KITCHEN AND COOKERY, 96, 97, 102, 132, 199, 256.
FURNITURE OF HOUSES, 25, 81, 100, 132, 170, 178, 199, 232, 256, 250, 284.
HOUSEHOLD OCCUPATIONS, 66, 101, 134, 268, 269.
IMPLEMENTS USED BY WOMEN — SPINNING AND WEAVING, 59, 66, 82, 93, 106, 107, 134, 135, 156, 157, 180, 203, 217, 269, 281.
EARTHENWARE AND OTHER VESSELS, 24, 41, 82, 83, 92, 98, 132, 176, 178, 233, 257.
MALTING AND BREWING, 157, 158, 200, 276.

RANKS AND DIGNITIES OF MEN, 17, 18, 41, 42, 72, 88, 182, 210, 211, 262.
RANKS OF WOMEN, 215, 268.
OFFICERS OF THE HOUSEHOLD AND SERVANTS, 28, 72, 73, 173, 176, 211, 212.
DEGREES OF CONSANGUINITY, 50, 51, 52, 72, 87, 205, 214.
ECCLESIASTICAL DIGNITIES, 42, 71, 182, 209, 261.
ECCLESIASTICAL FURNITURE, ETC., 28, 59, 81, 119, 133, 134, 193, 230, 248.
POPULAR MYTHOLOGY AND HEATHENDOM, 17, 22, 36, 60, 74, 89, 273.
TRADES, MANUFACTURES, AND OCCUPATIONS, 19, 74, 88, 181, 194, 212, 213, 216.
    THE MERCHANT, 8.
    GIRDLERS, 123.
    SADDLERS, 123.
    SHIELD-MAKERS, 123.
    BUCKLE-MAKERS, 123.
    LORIMERS, 123.
    HUCKSTERS, 123.
    FROBISHERS, 124.
    GLOVERS, 124.
    HATTERS, 124.
    BOWYERS, 124.
    BROOCH-MAKERS, 125.
    BELL-FOUNDERS, 125.
    COBLERS, 125, 181.
    CORDWAINERS, 125.
    FURRIERS, 125.
    STREET-CRIERS, 126.
    CUP-MENDERS, 126.
    CRIERS OF WINE, 126.
    SELLERS OF CAKES, 126.
    REGRATERS, 126.

BAKERS, 34, 83, 93, 127, 155, 197, 201, 233, 276.
MISCELLANEOUS DEALERS, 122, 123, 124.
PIE-MAKERS, 127.
COOKS, 10, 127.
CHANGERS, 128.
MINTERS, 128.
COLDSMITHS, 117, 118, 128.
CLOTHIERS, 128.
LINEN DRAPERS, 129.
APOTHECARIES, OR DRUGGISTS, 129.
  SPICES AND DRUGS, 227.
CARPENTERS, 11, 129.
WHEELWRIGHTS, 129.
CARTERS; CARTS AND WAGGONS, 66, 83, 84, 85, 107, 108, 129, 166, 167, 180, 181, 202, 277, 278, 284.
COOPERS, 275.
MILLERS, 34, 130, 180, 233.
SALTERS, 9.
FULLERS, 131.
DYERS, 131.
TANNERS, 131.
SMITHS, 11, 131, 180.
DIKERS, 277.
THATCHERS, 277.
CARDERS OF WOOL, 135.
POULTRY-DEALERS, 135.
HUNTERS AND FOWLERS, 4, 7, 100, 135, 27, 278.
FORESTERS, 278.
FISHERMEN, 5, 135, 153, 158.
MISCELLANEOUS IMPLEMENTS, 34, 38, 180, 181, 233, 234, 235, 276.
AGRICULTURE, 2, 11, 15, 30, 74, 84, 110, 111, 112, 113, 154, 218, 277, 278.
  THE PLOUGH, 169, 180.
THE COUNTRY IN GENERAL, 37, 53, 54, 58, 80, 92, 159, 161, 195, 239, 270, 271, 272.
GARDENING, 38, 39, 111, 136, 277.

THE VINEYARD, 38, 39, 240.
KINDS OF CORN, 38, 106, 201, 233, 264, 287.
THE STABLE, 106, 134.
  THE HORSE, AND HIS CAPARISON, 99, 108, 180, 234.
WAR, AND THINGS PERTAINING TO IT, 18, 103, 104, 105.
ARMS, 35, 84, 94, 104, 130, 181, 195, 263, 278.
THE CASTLE, 103.
NAVAL AFFAIRS, AND SHIPS, 47, 48, 56, 63, 73, 88, 113, 114, 115, 137, 239, 274.
TOWN AFFAIRS, 18, 34, 36, 84, 94.
GAMES AND AMUSEMENTS, MUSIC, 39, 60, 61, 66, 73, 88, 137, 179, 202, 216, 217, 240, 284.
LITERATURE, AND LEARNING; THE CLERK AND THE SCRIBE, 46, 75, 80, 89, 116, 117, 132, 210.
DISCREDITABLE PROFESSIONS, 216, 217, 275.
LAWS AND THE STATE, 20, 59, 60.
CRIMES AND PUNISHMENTS, 21, 74, 85, 86, 95, 105, 137.
ART; COLOURS, &c., 46, 47, 76.
ANIMALS; FOUR-FOOTED BEASTS, 22, 77, 90, 136, 166, 177, 187, 204, 218, 219, 250, 251, 286, 287.
  PARTS OF ANIMALS, 221, 251, 253, 286.
BIRDS, 29, 62, 77, 90, 100, 106, 135, 151, 163, 164, 165, 177, 188, 220, 252, 280.
FISHES, 55, 65, 77, 90, 97, 98, 136, 177, 189, 222, 253, 254, 281.
INSECTS AND REPTILES, 23, 77, 78, 90, 91, 137, 177, 190, 204, 222, 223, 254, 255, 281.
PLANTS, 30, 66, 78, 91, 136, 139, 161, 162, 190, 225, 264, 265, 286.
TREES, 32, 79, 91, 136, 162, 163, 181, 191, 192, 227, 228, 229, 285.
METALS, 34, 85, 94, 195, 255, 286.
STONES, ETC., 37, 38, 85, 94, 256.
THE ELEMENTS, SEASONS, ETC., 21, 41, 52, 70, 76, 89, 138, 160, 201, 205, 238, 239, 271, 272, 273, 284.

THE COLLOQUY OF
ARCHBISHOP ALFRIC.[1]

(OF THE TENTH CENTURY)

Colloquium ad pueros linguæ Latinæ locutione exercendos, ab Ælfrico primum compilatum, et deinde ab Ælfrico Bata, ejus discipulo, auctum, Latine et Saxonice.

        we   cildra   biddaþ   þe cala lareow þæt þu tæce us sprecan
D. Nos pueri rogamus te, magister, ut doceas nos loqui Latialiter
[rihte] forþam ungelærede we syndon and gewæmmodlice we sprecaþ
recte, quia idiote sumus, et corrupte loquimur.

        hwæt wille ge sprecan
M. Quid vultis loqui?

       hwæt   rece we   hwæt we sprecan buton hit riht spræc sy, and behefe
D. Quid curamus quid loquamur, nisi recta locutio sit, et utilis,
næs idel oþþe fracod
non anilis, aut turpis?

       wille [ge beon] beswungen on leornunge
M. Vultis   flagellari   in discendo?

---

[1] Alfric of Canterbury, by whom this Colloquy was compiled, was commonly known by the title of Alfric the Grammarian, from the active part he took in the educational movement of his time. He was for a short time bishop of Wilton, and in 995 succeeded Sigeric as archbishop of Canterbury. He died on the 16th of November, 1006. The colloquy was probably composed in the earlier period of his life, when he was a monk of Winchester. It was, as stated in the Latin title, enlarged and republished by Alfric Bata, a scholar under the archbishop when he taught in the schools at Winchester, and who is supposed to have died about the middle of the eleventh century. On both these writers, see my Biographia Britannica Literaria, Anglo-Saxon period. The enlarged edition of the colloquy, by Alfric Bata, seems to have so entirely superseded the original, that it appears to be the only one now preserved. It is here printed from a manuscript in the British Museum, MS. Cotton. Tiberius A. III., fol. 58, v°, contemporary with Alfric Bata. The only other copy known is preserved in a MS. in the Library of St. John's College, Oxford, in which the title, or rubric, is, *Hanc sententiam Latini sermonis olim Ælfricus abbas composuit, qui meus fuit magister, sed tamen ego Ælfric Bata multas postea huic addidi appendices.* Some additional words from the Oxford MS. are here printed within brackets. It will not escape remark, how much superior the sentiment which pervades this Anglo-Saxon tract is to that of the later mediæval treatises of the same description. It is impossible now to say which were the additions made by Alfric Bata to the original tract, but we may reasonably consider the whole as belonging to the tenth century.

COLLOQUY OF ARCHBISHOP ALFRIC.

    leofre ys us beon beswungen for lare þænne hit ne cunnan ac
D. Carius est nobis flagellari pro doctrina, quam nescire; sed
we witan þe bilewitne wesan and nellan onbeleden swincgla us buton þu bi to-genydd
scimus te mansuetum esse, et nolle inferre plagas nobis, nisi cogaris
fram us
a nobis.

    ic axie þe hwæt   spryest þu hwæt hæfst þu weorkes
M. Interrogo te quid mihi loqueris? quid habes operis?

    ic eom geanwyrde monuc and ic sincge ælce dæg seofon tida mid
D. Professus sum monachum, et psallam omni die septem sinaxes[1] cum
gebroþrum and ic eom bysgod [on rædinga] and on sange ac þeah-hwæþere ic wolde
fratribus, et occupatus sum lectionibus et cantu; sed tamen vellem
betwenan leornian sprecan on Leden gereorde
interim discere sermocinari Latina lingua.

    hwæt cunnon þas þine geferan
M. Quid sciunt isti tui socii?

    sume synt yrþlincgas, sume scephyrdas sume oxanhyrdas sume eac swylce
D. Alii sunt aratores, alii opiliones, quidam bubulci, quidam etiam
huntan sume fisceras sume fugeleras sume cyp-menn sume see-wyrhtan
venatores, alii piscatores, alii aucupes, quidam mercatores, quidam sutores,
    sealteras   bæceras.
quidam salinatores, quidam pistores loci.

    hwæt sægest þu yrþlinge hu begæst þu weorc þin
M. Quid dicis tu, arator,[2] quomodo exerces opus tuum?

    eala leof hlaford þearle ic deorfe ic ga ut on dægræd þywende oxon to
A. O mi domine, nimium laboro; exeo diluculo, minando boves ad
felda and jugie lng to syl nys hyt swa stearc winter þæt ic durre
campum, et jungo eos ad aratrum; non est tam aspera hiemps ut audeam
lutian æt ham for ege hlafordes mines ac gemkodan oxan and gefæstnodon
latere domi, pre timore domini mei; sed junctis bobus, et confirmato
sceare and cultre mit þare syl ælce dæg ic sceal erian fulne æþer[3] oþþe mare
vomere et cultro aratro, omni die debeo arare integrum agrum, aut plus.

    hæfst þu ænigne geferan
M. Habes aliquem socium?

    ic habbe sumne cnapan þywende oxan mid gad-isene þe eac swilce
A. Habeo quendam puerum minantem boves cum stimulo,[4] qui etiam
nu has ys for cylde and hreame
modo raucus est, pre frigore et clamatione.

---

[1] *Septem synaxes*, the seven canonical hours, or, more literally according to the meaning of the word, the assemblies of the monks at those hours for the several services which belonged to them. It is from this practice that the old Catholic service-books are called *Hours (horæ, heures)*, as containing the forms of service for the canonical hours of the day. (See further on.)

[2] The Anglo-Saxon sentiment which gave the first rank in worth and utility to the practice of agriculture, is curiously illustrated by implication here, where it is taken first in order of the occupations of men, and more directly further on, where its excellence is made the subject of discussion. It probably arose from the circumstance that the more purely Anglo-Saxon portion of the population were the possessors of the land, while the inhabitants of the towns, and those occupied in arts and manufactures, represented the older Roman population.

[3] The MS. reads distinctly *æþer*, which is no doubt an error for *ǽcer*.

[4] It is a curious circumstance, as showing how little the practice of agriculture had changed in

COLLOQUY OF ARCHBISHOP ALFRIC.

        hwæt   mare   dest þu on dæg
M. Quid amplius facis in die?
     gewyslice þænne mare ic do   ic sceal   fyllan   binnan   oxan mid hig and
A. Certe adhuc plus facio. Debeo implere presepia boum feno, et
wæterian hig and scearn heora   beran   ut
adaquare eos, et fimum eorum portare foras.
       hig hig   micel   gedeorf ys hyt
M. O, O, magnus labor est!
     ge leof   micel gedeorf hit ys forþam ic neom   freoh.
A. Etiam, magnus labor est, quia non sum liber.[1]
     [hwæt segst þu] sceaphyrde hæfst þu ænig gedeorf.
M. Quid dicis tu, opilio? Habes tu aliquem laborem?
    gea leof ic hæbbe on forewerdne morgen ic drife sceap mine to heora læse and
O. Etiam habeo; in primo mane mino oves meas ad pascua, et
stande ofer hig on hæte and on cyle mid hundum þe læs wulfas forswelgen hig
sto super eas, in estu et frigore, cum canibus, ne lupi[2] devorent eas,
and ic agenlæde hig to heora loca and melke hig tweowa on dæg and heora loca
et reduco eas ad caulas, et mulgeo eas bis in die, et caulas earum
ic hæbbe on þærto and cyse and buteran ic do and ic eom getrywe hlaforde minon
moveo insuper, et caseum et butirum facio, et fidelis sum domino meo.[3]
    eala oxanhyrde hwæt   wyrst   þu
M. O bubulce, quid operaris tu?
    eala hlaford min   micel ic gedeorfe þænne se yrþlinge unsceþ þa oxan
B. O domine mi, multum laboro. Quando arator disjungit boves,
ic læde hig to læse and ealle niht ic stande ofer hig waciende for
ego duco eos ad pascua, et tota nocte sto super eos vigilando propter
þeofan and eft   on ærne mergen ic betæce hig þam yrþlinege wel gefylde and gewæterode
fures,[4] et iterum primo mane adsigno eos aratori, bene pastos et adaquatos.
      ys þæs of þinum geferum
M. Est iste ex tuis sociis?

---

this country through many centuries, that the illuminations of manuscripts, down to a late period, represent the oxen yoked to the plough, driven by the ploughman, with the boy who carries the *goad* [*gad-iserne*], to urge them on.

[1] The agricultural labourer, among the Anglo-Saxons, was a serf (a *þeow*), and belonged to the lord of the land as much as the land itself, to which, in fact, he was attached. This passage of Alfric's Colloquy is a curious illustration of the feeling of commiseration for the condition of the servile class, which prevailed among the Anglo-Saxon clergy, and which disappeared at the time of the Norman conquest, when feudalism, which inculcated a profound contempt for the unnoble classes of society, was introduced into our island.

[2] Wolves appear still at this time to have been common in England.

[3] It would appear from this passage that ewes' milk was that used principally by the Anglo Saxons; and that it was the business of the shepherd to furnish the household with milk, butter, and cheese.

[4] Cattle were the great objects of plunder in the predatory excursions of the middle ages—and the care of the cattle at night was a duty of great importance among the Anglo-Saxons; hence the herdsman was a person of more consideration than the agricultural labourer. His duties, as intimated in our text, are illustrated by what Bede tells us with regard to the poet Cædmon, in the seventh century — Quod dum tempore quodam faceret, et relicta domo convivii, egressus est ad stabula jumentorum, quorum ei custodia nocte illa erat delegata. Bedæ Hist. Eccles. lib. iv. c. 24. In king Alfred's Anglo Saxon version this passage is rendered—to neata scypene, ðær heorde him wæs ðære mihte beboden.

D. Etiam est. [gea he ys]

M. Scis tu aliquid? [canst þu ænig þing]

V. Unam artem scio. [ænne cræft ic cann]

M. Quale est? [hwylcne ys]

V. Venator sum. [hunta ic eom]

M. Cujus? [hwæs]

V. Regis. [cincges]

M. Quomodo exerces artem tuam? [hu begæst þu cræft þinne]

V. Plecto mihi retia, et pono ea in loco apto, et instigo canes meos ut feras persequantur, usque quo perveniunt ad retia improvise, et sic inretientur, et ego jugulo eos in retibus.[1]
[ic brede me max and sette hig on stowe gehæppre and getihte hundas mine þæt wildeor hig ehton oþ þat hig þe cuman to þam nettan unforsceawodlice and þæt hig swa beon begrynode and ic ofslea hig on þam maxum sic inretientur]

M. Nescis venare nisi cum retibus? [ne canst þu huntian buton mid nettum]

V. Etiam, sine retibus venare possum. [gea butan nettum huntian ic mæg]

M. Quomodo? [hu]

V. Cum velocibus canibus insequor feras. [mid swiftum hundum ic betæce wildeor]

M. Quales feras maxime capis? [hwylce wildeor swyþost gefehst þu]

V. Capio cervos, et apros, et dammas, et capreos, et aliquando lepores. [ic gefeo heortas and baras and rann and rægan and hwilon haran]

M. Fuisti hodie in venatione? [wære þu to dæg on huntnoþe]

V. Non fui, quia dominicus dies est, sed heri fui in venatione. [ic næs forþam sunnan-dæg ys, ac gyrstan-dæg ic wæs on huntunge]

M. Quid cepisti? [hwæt gelæhtest þu]

V. Duos cervos et unum aprum. [twegen heortas and ænne bar]

M. Quomodo cepisti eos? [hu gefencge þu hig]

---

[1] The hunter of the Anglo-Saxons appears to have answered nearly to our gamekeeper, and his method of taking the game militates rather against our ordinary notions of the mediæval passion for the chase. But the Anglo-Saxons do not appear to have been, in general, great hunters, in the sense of the word as it was taken by the Anglo-Normans, for hawking appears to have been the more favourite diversion with them.

COLLOQUY OF ARCHBISHOP ALFRIC.

    heortas ic gefenge on nettum and bar ic ofsloh
V. Cervos cepi in retibus, et aprum jugulavi.

    hu wære þu dyrstig ofstikian bar
M. Quomodo fuisti ausus jugulare aprum?

    hundas bedrifon hyne to me and ic þær togeanes standende færlice
V. Canes perduxerunt eum ad me, et ego e contra stans subito
ofstikode hyne
jugulavi eum.

    swyþe þryste þu wære þa
M. Valde audax fuisti tunc.

    ne sceal hunta forhtfull wesan forþam mislice wildeor wuniað
V. Non debet venator formidolosus esse, quia varie bestie morantur
on wudum
in silvis.

    hwæt dest þu be þinre huntunge
M. Quid facis de tua venatione?

    ic sylle cync swa hwæt swa ic gefo forþam ic eom hunta hys
V. Ego do regi quicquid capio, quia sum venator ejus.

    hwæt sylþ he þe
M. Quid dat ipse tibi?

    he scryt me wel and fett and hwilon sylþ me hors oþþe
V. Vestit me bene et pascit, aliquando dat mihi equum, aut
beah þæt þe lustlicor cræft minne ic begancge
armillam, ut libentius artem meam exerceam.

    hwylcne cræft canst þu
M. Qualem artem scis tu?

    ic eom fiscere
P. Ego sum piscator.

    hwæt begyst þu of þinum cræfte
M. Quid adquiris de tua arte?

    bigleofan and scrud and feoh
P. Victum et vestitum et pecuniam.[1]

    hu gefehst þu fixas
M. Quomodo capis pisces?

    ic astigie min scyp and wyrpe max mine on ea and ancgil rel æs[2] ic wyrpe
P. Ascendo navem, et pono retia mea in amne, et hamum projicio
and spyrtan and swa hwæt swa hig gehæftað ic genime
et sportas, et quicquid ceperint sumo.

    hwæt gif hit unclæne beoþ fixas
M. Quid si inmundi fuerint pisces?

    ic ut-wyrpe þa unclænan ut and genime me clæne to mete
P. Ego projiciam immundos foras, et sumo mihi mundos in escam.

    hwær cypst þu fixas þine
M. Ubi vendis pisces tuos?

---

[1] The hunter was a man in the employ of another; his occupation was an office, or service. The fisherman worked for himself.

[2] The glossator appears to have been doubtful of the meaning of *hamus*. The word *æs* means a bait; *angil*, which means a hook, is of course the origin of our term *angling*, given to the process of fishing with the line and hook.

COLLOQUY OF ARCHBISHOP ALFRIC.

          on   ceastre
P. In civitate.

         hwa bigþ hi
M. Quis emit illos?

       ceasterwara   ic ne mæg   swa fela [gefon] swa fela swa ic mæg   geayllan
P. Cives. Non possum tot capere quot possum vendere.

       hwilce fixas gefehst þu
M. Quales pisces capis?

       ælas   and hacodas mynas and æleputan   sceotan and lampredan
P. Anguillas, et lucios, menas, et capitones, tructos,[1] et murenas,
and swa wylce swa on wætere swymmaþ sprote
et qualescunque in amne natant saliu.

       for hwi ne   fixast þu on sæ
M. Cur non piscaris in mari?

       hwilon   ic do ac seldon forþam micel   rewyt   me ys to sæ
P. Aliquando facio, sed raro, quia magnum navigium mihi est ad mare.

       hwæt fehst þu on sæ
M. Quid capis in mari?

       hærincgas and leaxas mere-swyn and stirian   ostran and crabban   muslan
P. Alleces et isicios, delfinos et sturias, ostreas et cancros, musculas,
pinewinclan sæ-coccas   fage and   floc and lopystran and fela swylces
torniculi, neptigalli, platesia, et platissa, et polipodes, et similia.[2]

       wilt þu fon   sumne   hwæl
M. Vis capere aliquem cetum?

       nic
P. Nolo.

       forhwi
M. Quare?

       forhwan plyhtlic þingc hit ys gefon   hwæl   gebeorhtlicre ys me faran to
P. Quia periculosa res est capere cetum. Tutius est mihi ire ad
 ea   mid   scype mynan þænne faran mid manegum scypum on   huntunge
amnem cum nave mea, quam ire cum multis navibus in venationem
hranes
ballene.

       forhwi swa
M. Cur sic?

       forþam leofre ys   me   gefon   fisc þæne ic mæg ofslean þe
P. Quia carius est mihi capere piscem quem possim occidere, qui

---

[1] The list of river fish is not very large; and it is not easy to explain the absence of several which must have been in common use among our Anglo-Saxon forefathers, especially if *mynas* signify minnows, as it has been interpreted, but I suspect wrongly. *Eel-pout* is still the name for a small kind of eel.

[2] Herrings come first in the list of sea-fish, because they were more extensively used than any other kind of fish throughout the middle ages. Red-herrings figure largely in the mediæval household acounts. The Anglo-Saxon name for the salmon, called in old English *lax*, had not been quite displaced by the Anglo-Norman one in the fourteenth century. The *mere-swyn* was probably the porpoise, which was supposed to answer to the Latin *delphinus*. The sturgeon (*stiria*) is now no more eaten than the porpoise; the *fage* and *floc* were probably plaice and soles; the *sæ-coccas* were no doubt cockles.

M. … na þæt an me ac eac swylce mine geferan mid anum slege he mæg besencean oþþe gecwylman
non solum me sed etiam meos socios uno ictu potest mergere aut mortificare.

M. and þeah mænige gefoþ hwælas and ætberstaþ frecnysse and micelne sceat þanon begytaþ
Et tamen multi capiunt cetos,[1] et evadunt pericula, et magnum pretium inde adquirunt.

P. soþ þu segst ac ic ne geþristige for modes mines nytenysse
Verum dicis, sed ego non audeo, propter mentis meæ ignaviam.

M. hwæt segst þu fugelere hu beswicst þu fugelas
Quid dicis tu, auceps? quomodo decipis aves?

A. on feala wisan ic beswice fugelas hwilon mid netom mid grinum mid lime mit hwistlunge mid hafoce mid treppan
Multis modis decipio aves; aliquando retibus, aliquando laqueis, aliquando glutino, aliquando sibilo, aliquando accipitre, aliquando decipula.

M. hæfst þu hafoc
Habes accipitrem?

A. ic hæbbe
Habeo.

M. canst þu temian hig
Scis domitare eos?

A. gea ic cann hwæt sceoldon hig me buton ic cuþe temian hig
Etiam scio. Quid deberent mihi, nisi scirem domitare eos?

V. syle me ænne hafoc
Da mihi unum accipitrem.

A. ic sylle lustlice gyf þu sylst me ænne swyftne hund
Dabo libenter, si dederis mihi unum velocem canem. hwilcne hafoc wilt þu habban þone maran hwæþer þe þone læssan
Qualem accipitrem vis habere, majorem aut minorem?

V. syle me þæne maran
Da mihi majorem.

M. hu afest þu hafocas þine
Quomodo pascis accipitres tuos?

A. hig fedaþ hig sylfe and me on wintra and on lenegten ic læte hig ætwindan to wuda and genyme me briddas on hærfæste and temige hig
Ipsi pascunt se et me in hieme, et in vere dimitto eos avolare ad silvam, et capio mihi pullos in autumno, et domito eos.

M. and forhwi forlætst þu þa getemedon ætwindan fram þe
Et cur permittis tu domitos avolare a te?

A. forþam ic nelle fedan hig on sumera forþam þe hig þearle etaþ
Quia nolo pascere eos in estate, eo quod nimium comedunt.

M. and manige fedaþ þa getemedon ofer sumor þæt eft hig habban gearuwe
Et multi pascunt domitos super estatem, ut iterum habeant paratos.

---

[1] There are many reasons for believing that the whale trade was carried on to a considerable extent by the Anglo-Saxons, as well as by the northern nations. The walrus was an object of value then, on account of its teeth, which, under the name of whales'-bone, were used in place of ivory, and form the substance of many ornamental objects in our cabinets.

A.
             gea   swa hig doþ   ac   ic   nelle oþ þæt an   deorfan   ofer   hig
A. Etiam sic faciunt, sed ego nolo in tantum laborare super eos,
forþam ic can oþre   na   þet   ænne   ac eac swilce manige   gefon
quia scio alios non solum unum sed etiam plures capere.

         hwæt sægst þu   mancgere¹
M. Quid dicis tu, mercator?

          ic secge þæt   behefe ic eom ge cinge and ealdormannum and weligum
MER. Ego dico quod utilis sum et regi et ducibus et divitibus
and eallum   folce
et omni populo.

         and   hu
M. Et uomodo?

           ic astige min scyp mid hlæstum minum and rowe   ofer   sælice
MER. Ego ascendo navem cum mercibus meis, et navigo ultra marinas
dælas   and   cype   mine þinge and biege þincg dyrwyrðe   þa   on þisum lande ne
partes et vendo meas res, et emo res pretiosas quæ in hac terra non
beoþ acennede and ic hit to gelæde   eow   hider mid micclan   plihte   ofer   sæ   and
nascuntur, et adduco vobis huc, cum magno periculo super mare, et
     hwylon   forlidenesse   ic þolie mid   lyre   ealra   þinga   minra   uneaþe
aliquando naufragium patior, cum jactura omnium rerum mearum, vix
cwic ætberstende
vivus evadens.

         hwylce þinc geladst þu   us
M. Quales res adduces nobis?

            pællas   and   sidan   deorwyrþe gymmas and   gold   seleuþe reaf
MER. Purpurum, et sericum, pretiosas gemmas, et aurum, varias vestes,
and wyrtgemange   win   and   ele   ylpes ban and   mæstlinge   ar   and   tin
et pigmenta, vinum, et oleum, ebur, et auricalcum, æs, et stagnum,
swefel and   glæs   and þyleces   fela
sulfur, et vitrum, et his similia.²

           wilt þu syllan þinge þine   her cal swa þu hi gebohtest   þær
M. Vis vendere res tuas hic, sicut emisti illic?

           ic nelle hwæt þenne me fremode gedeorf min   ac ic wille heora cypen
MER. Nolo. Quid tunc mihi proficit labor meus? Sed volo vendere
her lufticor þonne [ic gebiege þær þæt   sum   gestreon me   ic begyte þanon ic me
hic carius quam emi illic ut aliquod lucrum mihi adquiram, unde me
afede   and   min wif and minne sunu
pascam et uxorem et filios.

          þu sceo wyrhta hwæt   wyrest þu   us   nytwyrþnesse
M. Tu, sutor, quid operaris nobis utilitatis?

---

¹ It is a curious instance of the degradation through which words go, that what was in the Saxon period the designation for the most elevated description of merchant, *mancgere*, is now only a term for small dealers, and principally in petty wares, *monger*.

² We must no doubt consider this as a list of the most valuable articles imported into this country under the Anglo-Saxons. *Purpura*, or, as it is translated in Anglo-Saxon, *pællas*, was a sort of rich stuff brought from the east, and is coupled with silk. *Pigmenta*, explained by *wyrtgemange*, appears to have been a general term for perfumes. Glass appears to have been little made in England during the Saxon period; and the enumeration of the metals would seem to show that the great mining operations of the Romans had ceased after the Saxon invasion.

COLLOQUY OF ARCHBISHOP ALFRIC.

       ys witodlice crœft min behefe þearle eow and neodþearf
S. Est quidem ars mea utilis valde vobis et necessaria.

      hu
M. Quomodo?

      ic bicge hyda and fell and gearkie hig mid crœfte minon and wyrce of
S. Ego emo cutes et pelles, et preparo eas arte mea, et facio ex
him gescy mistlices cynnes swyftleras and sceos leþer-hosa and butericas
eis calciamenta diversi generis, subtalares, et ficones, coligas et utres,
bridel-þwancgas and geneda flaxan vel pinnan¹ and higdifatu spur-leþera and hælftra pusan
frenos et falera, flascones et calidilia, calcaria et chamos, peras
and fætelsas and nan eower nele oferwintran buton minon crœfte
et marsupia, et nemo vestrum vult hiemare sine mea arte.

      sealtera hwæt us fremaþ crœft þin
M. O salinator, quid nobis proficit ars tua?

     þearle fremaþ crœft min eow eallum nan eower blisse bryc𐌸
S. Multum prodest ars mea omnibus, nemo vestrum gaudio fruitur
on gererduncge oþþe mete buton crœft min gistliþe him beo
in prandio aut cena nisi ars mea hospita ei fuerit.²

      hu
M. Quomodo?

     hwylc manna þurh werodum³ þurhbrycþ mettum buton swœcce sealtes hwa
S. Quis hominum dulcibus perfruitur cibis sine sapore salis? Quis
gefylþ cleafan his oþþe heddærna buton crœfte minon efne buter-geþweor
repplet cellaria sua sive promptuaria sine arte mea? Ecce butirum
œlc and cys-gerunn losaþ eow buton ic hyrde ætwese eow þe ne furþon an wyrtum
omne et caseum perit vobis, nisi ego custos adsim, qui nec saltem oleribus
eowrum butan me brucaþ
vestris sine me utimini.

    [hwæt segst þu] bæcere hwam fremaþ [crœft þin] oþþe hwæþer we butan þe
M. Quid dicis tu, pistor? Cui prodest ars tua, aut si sine te
magon lif adreogan
possimus vitam ducere?

     ge magon þurh sum fæc butan [minon crœfte lif adreogan
P. Potestis quidem per aliquod spatium sine arte mea vitam ducere,
ac] na lancge ne to wel soþlice butan crœfte minon œlc beod æmtig
sed non diu, nec adeo bene; nam sine arte mea omnis mensa vacua

---

¹ It will be seen by this enumeration of articles, that the business of the Anglo-Saxon shoewright was much more extensive than that of the modern shoemaker; in fact, all articles made of leather came within his province. Among these were leathern flasks, and various other vessels, as well as leather bags and purses (pusan and fætelsas).

² The importance of the salter is better understood when we consider that, as the produce of the land was in the middle ages almost entirely consumed on the spot, and it was not easy to get supplies of provisions from a distance, immense quantities of victuals of all kinds were salted, in order that they might keep during the whole year round, and were preserved in vast larders and storehouses. This habit of eating so much salt meat, would cause meats eaten without salt to be considered insipid. In fact, the quantity of salt used in the middle ages must have been enormous; and to it, probably, we must ascribe the prevalence of those diseases which excited so much horror under the name of leprosy.

³ Sic MS. But the word þurh before werodum is perhaps a mere error of the scribe.

10   COLLOQUY OF ARCHBISHOP ALFRIC.

byþ gesewen and buton hlafe ælc mete to wlættan byþ gehwyrfed ic heortan
videtur esse, et sine pane omnis cibus in nausium convertitur. Ego cor
mannes gestrangie ic mægen wera and furþon litlinegas nellaþ for-
hominis confirmo, ego robur virorum sum, et nec parvuli volunt præ-
bigean me
terire me.

           [hwæt secgaþ we be cocce] hwæþer we beþurfon on ænigon cræfte
M. Quid dicimus de coco, si indigemus in aliquo arte ejus?

           gif ge me ut-adrifaþ fram eowrum geferscype ge etaþ wyrta
Dicit cocus. Si me expellitis a vestro collegio, manducabitis holera
eowre grene and flæsc-mettas eowre hreawe and furþon fætt broþ
vestra viridia, et carnes vestras crudas, et nec saltem pingue jus
ge magon [butan cræfte minon habban]
potestis sine arte mea habere.

          we ne reccaþ [be cræfte þinon] ne he us neodþearf ys forþam we sylfe
M. Non curamus de arte tua, nec nobis necessaria est, quia nos ipsi
magon seoþan þa þinge þe to seoþenne synd and brædan þa þinge þe to brædene synd
possumus cocere quæ coquenda sunt et assare quæ assanda sunt.[1]

          gif ge forþy me fram-adryfaþ þæt ge þus don þonne beo ge ealle
Dicit cocus: Si ideo me expellitis, ut sic faciatis, tunc eritis omnes
þrælas and nan eower ne biþ hlaford and þeah-hwæþere buton [cræfte minon] ge
servi,[2] et nullus vestrum erit dominus; et tamen sine arte mea non
ne etaþ
manducatis.

       eala munuc þe me to-spycst efne ic hæbbe afandod þe habban gode
M. O monache qui mihi locutus es, ecce probavi te habere bonos
geferan and þearle neodþearfe and ic ahsie þa
socios, et valde necessarios; qui sunt illi?

       ic hæbbe smiþas isene-smiþas gold-smiþ seolofor-smiþ ar-smiþ treow-wyrhtan
D. Habeo fabros, ferrarium, aurificem, argentarium, ærarium, lignarium,
and manegra oþre mistlicra cræfta biggenceras
et multos alios variarum artium operatores.[3]

       hæfst ænigne wisne geþeahtan
M. Habes aliquem sapientem consiliarium?

       gewislice ic hæbbe [hu mæg] ure gegaderunge buton geþeahtynde
D. Certe habeo. Quomodo potest nostra congregatio sine conciliario
beon wissod
regi?

       [hwæt segst þu] wisa hwilc cræft þe geþuht betwux þas furþra wesan
M. Quid dicis tu, sapiens? que ars tibi videtur inter istas prior esse?

---

[1] The writer of the colloquy is here expressing the feeling of the more strictly sober part of the community, against the extravagance of the table, which seems to have been increasing very much during the latter part of the Anglo-Saxon period.

[2] The MS., by an evident error, has coci.

[3] *Smith* was the general term for a worker in metals, and *wright* for one who worked in wood, and other materials. Hence, in the later English period, *smith* (which, in Anglo-Saxon, when used without any characteristic addition, was understood as applying more particularly to the worker in iron,) became the particular name of a blacksmith, and *wright* of a carpenter, as it is still in Scotland. The iron-smith (*isene-smið*) of the Anglo-Saxons was our blacksmith and whitesmith combined.

[ic secge þe] me ys gebuht Godes þeowdum betweoh þas cræftas ealdorscype
C. Dico tibi, mihi videtur servitium Dei inter istas artes primatum
healdan swa swa hit [ys] gerad on godspelle fyrmest seceað rice Godes and
tenere, sicut legitur in evangelio, Primum querite regnum Dei et
rihtwisnesse hys and þas þinge ealle beoþ to-geh}hte eow
justitiam ejus, et hæc omnia adjicientur vobis.
and hwilc þe geþuht betwux cræftas woruld[1] heoldan ealdordom
M. Et quales tibi videtur inter artes seculares retinere primatum?
eorþ-tilþ forþam se yrþling us ealle fett
C. Agricultura, quia arator nos omnes pascit.[2]
se smiþ secgð hwanon [þam yrþlinge] sylan-scear oþþe culter þe na gade
Ferrarius dicit: Unde aratori vomer aut culter, qui nec stimulum
hæfþ buton of cræfte minon hwanon fiscere ancgel oþþe sceo-wyrhton æl oþþe
habet nisi ex arte mea? Unde piscatori hamus, aut sutori subula, aut
seamere nædl nis hit of minon geweorce
sartori acus? nonne ex meo opere?
se geþeahtend andsweraþ soþ witodlice sægst þu ac eallum us leofre
Consiliarius respondit: Verum quidem dicis; sed omnibus nobis carius
ys wikian mid þam yrþlincge þonne mid þe forþam se yrþling sylð us hlaf
est hospitari apud aratorem quam apud te; quia arator dat nobis panem
and drenc þu hwæt sylst us on smiþþan þinre buton iscnne fyr-spearcan and
et potum; tu quid das nobis in officina tua, nisi ferreas scinctillas et
swegincga beatendra sleegea and blawendra byliga
sonitus tundentium malleorum et flantium follium?
se treow-wyrhta segð hwilc eower ne notaþ cræfte minon þonne hus and
Lignarius dicit: Quis vestrum non utitur arte mea, cum domos, et
mistlice fata and scypa eow eallum ic wyrce
diversa vasa, et naves, omnibus fabrico?
se smiþ andwyrt eala tryw-wyrta forhwi swa spryest þu þonne ne furþon
Ferrarius respondit: O lignarie, cur sic loqueris, cum nec saltem
an þyrl [buton cræfte minon] þu ne miht don
unum foramen sine arte mea vales facere?
se geþeahtend sægþ eala geferan and gode wyrhtan uton towurpon hwæðeor þas
Conciliarius dicit: O socii et boni operarii, dissolvamus citius has
geflitu and sy sibb and geþwærnyss betweoh us and framige urum gehwylcum
contentiones, et sit pax et concordia inter nos, et prosit unusquisque
oþron on cræfte hys and gedwærian symble mid þam yrþlinge þær we bicleofan
alteri in arte sua, et conveniamus semper apud aratorem, ubi victum
us and foddor horsum urum habbaþ and þis geþeaht ic sylle eallum
nobis et pabula equis nostris habemus; et hoc consilium do omnibus
wyrhtum þæt anra gehwylc cræft his geornlice begange forþam se þe cræft
operariis, ut unusquisque artem suam diligenter exerceat; quia qui artem
his forlæt he byþ forlæten fram þam cræfte swa hwæðer þu sy swa mæsse prest
suam dimiserit, ipse dimittatur ab arte. Sive sis sacerdos,

---

[1] *Sic MS.* for *woruld-cræftas.*
[2] This notion of the pre-eminence of agriculture above all other crafts, has been noticed before. It is no less curious to remark, at this very early period, the sort of antagonism between the agricultural and the trading and manufacturing portion of the community, which seems to have existed in all ages in modern times. The artizans who are introduced in the colloquy, rise up indignantly to protest against the superiority which the "wise man" ascribes to agriculture.

swa munuc swa ceorl swa kempa bega þe sylfne on þisum and beo
sive monachus, seu laicus, seu miles, exerce temet ipsum in hoc; et esto
þæt þu eart forþam micel hynð and sceamu hyt is menn nelle wesan
quod es, quia magnum dampnum et verecundia est homini nolle esse
þæt þæt he ys and þæt þe he wesan sceal
quod est et quod esse debet.

eala cild hu ⋅ eow licaþ þeos spræc
M. O pueri, quomodo vobis placet ista locutio?

wel heo licaþ us ac þearle deoplice sprycst and ofer
D. Bene quidem placet nobis, sed valde profunde loqueris, et ultra
maþe ure þu forþtyht spræce ac sprec us æfter urum
etatem nostram protrahis sermonem; sed loquere nobis juxta nostrum
andgyte þæt we magon understandan þa þing þe þu specst
intellectum, ut possimus intelligere que loqueris?

ic ahsige eow forhwi swa geornlice leornige ge
M. Interrogo vos cur tam diligenter discitis.

forþam we nellaþ wesan swa stunte nytenu þa nan þing witaþ buton
D. Quia nolumus esse sicut bruta animalia, quæ nihil sciunt nisi
gærs and wæter
herbam et aquam.

and hwæt wille ge
M. Et quid vultis vos?

we wyllaþ wesan wise
D. Volumus esse sapientes.

on whilcon wisdome wille ge beon prættige oþþe þusenthiwe on lea-
M. Qua sapientia? Vultis esse versipelles, aut milleformes, in men-
sungum lytige on spræcum gleawlice hindergepe wel sprecende and yfele þencende
daciis vafri,[1] in loquelis astuti, versuti, bene loquentes et male cogitantes,
swæsum wordum underþeodde fan[2] wiðinnan tyddriende swa swa bergyls metton
dulcibus verbis dediti, dolum intus alentes, sicut sepulchrum depicto
ofergeweorke wiþinnan full stence
mausoleo intus plenum fetore?

we nellaþ swa wesan wise forþam he nys wis þe mid dydrunge
D. Nolumus sic esse sapientes, quia non est sapiens qui simulatione
hyne sylfne beswicð
semet ipsum decipit.

ac hu wille ge
M. Sed quomodo vultis?

we wyllaþ beon bylewite butan licetunge and wise þæt we bugon
D. Volumus esse simplices sine hipochrisi, et sapientes ut declinemus
ram yfele and don goda gyt þeah-hwæþere deoplicor mid us þu smeagst
a malo et faciamus bona; adhuc tamen profundius nobiscum disputas
þonne yld ure onfon mæge ac sprec us æfter uron gewunon næs
quam ætas nostra capere possit; sed loquere nobis nostro more, non
swa deoplice
tam profunde.

and ic do eal swa ge biddaþ þu cnapa hwæt dydest [to- dæg
M. Et ego faciam sicut rogatis. Tu, puer, quid fecisti hodie?

[1] The Cotton. MS. has *astuti* for *vafri*. [2] For *facn*, guile

COLLOQUY OF ARCHBISHOP ALFRIC.

manega þing ic dyde on þisse niht   þa þa   cnyll ic gehyrde   ic aras   on
Multas res feci. Hac nocte, quando signum audivi, surrexi de
lde and eode to cyrcean and sang uht-sang mid gebroþrum
ɔ et exivi ad ecclesiam, et cantavi nocturnam cum fratribus;
we sungon be eallum halgum and dægredlice lof-sanges æfter þysum
cantavimus de omnibus sanctis et matutinales laudes; post hæc,
and seofon seolmas mid letanian and capitol mæssan syþþan
et vii. psalmos, cum letaniis, et primam missam; deinde
and dydon mæssan be dæge æfter þisum we sungon middæg and
et fecimus missam de die; post hæc cantavimus sextam, et
n and druncon and slepon and eft we arison and
ivimus, et bibimus, et dormivimus, et iterum surreximus, et
non and nu we synd her ætforan þe gearuwe gehyran hwæt
ius nonam, et modo sumus hic coram te, parati audire quid
ꞅege [1]
ixeris.

hwænne wylle ge syngan æfen oþþe niht-sange
    Quando vultis cantare vesperum aut completorium? [2]
þonne hyt tima byþ
    Quando tempus erit.

wære þu to-dæg beswuncgen
M. **Fuisti hodie verberatus?**
ic næs forþam wærlice ic me heold
D. **Non fui, quia caute me tenui.**
and hu þine geferan
M. **Et quomodo tui socii?**
hwæt me ahsast be þam ic ne dear yppan þe digla
D. **Quid me interrogas de hoc? Non audeo pandere tibi secreta**
ure anra gehwylc wæt gif he beswuncgen wæs oþþe na
nostra. Unusquisque scit si flagellatus erat an non.

hwæt ytst þu on dæg
M. **Quid manducas in die?**
gyt flæsc-mettum ic bruce forðam cild ic eom under gyrda drohtniende
D. **Adhuc carnibus vescor,**[3] **quia puer sum sub virga degens.**
hwæt mare ytst þu
M. **Quid plus manducas?**

---

[1] The account here given of the regular occupations of the young monk, during a part of the day, is very curious. The *uht-sang*, or *nocturn*, called at a later period *matutina*, or *matins*, began at three o'clock in the morning, at which the monk was called from his bed by the ringing of the church bell. The service of *prime* followed, at six o'clock; after which came *underntide*, or *tierce*, at about nine o'clock—and *middæg*, or *sext*, at noon. It appears that the monks had no meal until after the mid-day service; and that after it they retired to sleep, from which they were roused to perform the service of *none*, about two o'clock. It appears not to have been till after this latter service that they were properly at liberty to attend to other business; and the boys, or younger members of the community, then went to school.

[2] The evening service, or vespers, commenced at four o'clock, and *niht-sang*, or compline, at seven, which finished the canonical service of the day.

[3] There would seem to be an error here, for the child evidently means to say, not that he eat meat, but that he did not eat mean, because he was as yet too young.

             wyrta and ægra   fisc and   cyse   buteran and beana and   ealle
    D. Holera et ova, pisces et caseum, butirum et fabas, et omnia
clæne þingc   ic ete   mid   micelre   þancunge
munda manduco, cum gratiarum actione.

         swyþe waxgeorn eart þu þonne   þu ealle þingc etst   þe   þe toforan [gesette synd]
    M. Valde edax es, cum omnia manducas que tibi apponuntur.

         ic ne eom swa micel swelgere þæt ic ealle   cynn   metta on anre gereordinge
    D. Non sum tam vorax ut omnia genera ciborum in una refectione
etan   mæge
edere possum.

       ac   hu
    M. Sed quomodo?

       ic bruce   hwilon   þisum mettum and   oþrum mid   syfernysse
    D. Vescor aliquando his cibis, et aliquando aliis, cum sobrietate,
swa swa dafnað   munuce   næs mid oferhropse forþam ic eom nan gluto
sicut decet monachum, non cum voracitate, quia non sum gluto.

       and hwæt drincst þu
    M. Et quid bibis?

        eala   gif ic hæbbe oþþe   wæter gif ic næbbe   ealu
    D. Cervisam, si habeo, vel aquam, si non habeo cervisam.

       ne drincst þu   win
    M. Nonne bibis vinum?

       ic ne eom   swa   spedig þæt ic mæge bicgean me   win and   win
    D. Non sum tam dives ut possim emere mihi vinum; et vinum
nys   drenc   cilda   ne   dysegra   ac   ealdra and   wisra
non est potus puerorum sive stultorum, sed senum et sapientum.

       hwær   slæpst
    M. Ubi dormis?

       on   slæpern   mid gebroþrum
    D. In dormitorio cum fratribus.

       hwa   awecþ   þe to   uht-sancge
    M. Quis excitat te ad nocturnos?

       hwilon   ic gehyre   cnyll   and   ic arise   hwilon   lareow   min
    D. Aliquando audio signum, et surgo; aliquando magister meus
awecþ   me   stiþlice   mid   gyrde
excitat me duriter cum virga.

       eala ge [gode] cildra   and wynsume leorneras   eow   manaþ   eower   lareow
    M. O probi pueri, et venusti mathites, vos hortatur vester eruditor
þæt ge hyrsumian godcundum   larum   and þæt ge healdan eow sylfe   ænlice   on a'lcere
ut pareatis divinis disciplinis, et observatis vosmet eleganter ubique
    stowe   gaþ   þeawlice   þonne   ge gebyran   cyricean   bellan   and
locorum. Inceditis morigerate, cum auscultaveritis ecclesie campanas, et
    gaþ   into   cyrcean   and   abugaþ   eadmodlice   to halgum wefodum and standaþ
ingredimini in oratorium, et inclinate suppliciter ad almas aras, et state
    þeawlice   and   singaþ   anmodlice and gebiddaþ   for eowrum   synnum
disciplinabiliter, et concinite unanimiter, et intervenite pro vestris erratibus,
and   gaþ ut   butan   hygeleaste   to   claustre   oþþe to   leorninge
et egredimini sine scirilitatem in claustrum vel in gimnasium.

ARCHBISHOP ALFRIC'S VOCABULARY,

(OF THE TENTH CENTURY.)[1]

DE INSTRUMENTIS AGRICOLARUM.

Vomer, vel vomis, scear.
Aratrum, sulh.[2]
Aratio, eriung.
Buris, sulh-beam.
Stercoratio, dingiung.
Fimus, dinig.
Dentale, cipp.
Stiba, sulh-handla.
Occatio, egegung.
Rastrum, vel rastellum, raca.
Traha, ciþe.
Runcatio, weodung.
Tragum, dræg-net, *vel* dræge.
Stimulus, ga[d].
Aculeus, sticel, *vel* gad-isen.
Veractum, lcncgten-erðe.
Sulcus, furh.
Circus, vel circulus, wiððe.
Funiculus, vel funis, rap.
Proscissio, land-bræce.
Ovile, sceapa-hus.
Bucetum, hryðra fald.
Bovile stabulum, scepen steal *vel* fald.
Vitularius, cealfa hus.

[1] The vocabulary, or glossary, of archbishop Alfric, is the oldest monument of this description of the English language now extant. It is printed from one of the manuscripts of Junius, in the Bodleian Library at Oxford; it usually follows Alfric's Anglo-Saxon translation from the Latin Grammar of Priscian, which was the favourite class-book of the medieval schools. It was transcribed, not always correctly, by or for Junius, from a MS. in the possession of Reubens the painter, which is no longer known to exist. This manuscript, from an apparent reference to king Cnut, seems to be not older than the eleventh century, when Alfric's original vocabulary was perhaps considerably modified, and this no doubt gave it the irregular character it here presents. The following lines were prefixed to it in the MS.:

    Præsulis hic redolent Elfrici lypsana summi,
    Qui rector patriæ perstitit Anglgeusæ.
    Inter pontifices rutilans ceu mystica lampas,
    Defensor regni, necne salus populi.

    Heu nostram fera mors extinxit nempe lucernam,
    Heu nostri cecidit fons quoque consilii.
    Hunc sexta decimaque kalendas namque Decembris,
    Assumpsit Michahel, seu dedit Emanuhel.

The object of these vocabularies was chiefly twofold; first, to interpret Latin words to the Anglo-Saxon scholar, and secondly, to furnish him with the Latin words for the common objects of life. The vocabulary of Alfric would seem to have been originally arranged with a view to the latter object; but we find the plan often broken into, by the introduction of words which have nothing to do with those which they immediately follow, and which appear, in some instances, to have been taken almost at hazard from an alphabetical dictionary. In accordance with the character given to the science of agriculture, in the colloquy, it takes the precedence of all other subjects in the vocabulary.

[2] A plough is still called a *sull,* in the dialects of the West of England.

ARCHBISHOP ALFRIC'S VOCABULARY.

Bobellum, falt.
Subula, æl.
Repagulum, salpanra.
Acrum, seencen.
Scops, bisme.
Caule, sceapa locu.
Æquiale, hors-ern.
Vanga, spada.
Conjuncla, þristra.
Turminosus, fortogen.
Sarculus, wingeardes screadung-isen.
Terebrum, navegar.[1]
Pastinatum, plant-sticca.
Fossorium, costere, *vel* delf-isen, *vel* spadu, *vel* pal.
Ligo, becca, *vel palus*, *vel fustis*.
Falcastrum, siðe, *vel* bill.
Serula, saga, *vel* snide.
Ferrarius, isern-wyrhte.
Plaustrum, *vel carrum*, wæn.
Rota, hweol.
Cantus, felga.
Modiolus, naveþa.
Radii, spacan.
Temo, *vel arctoes*, þisl.
Hircipes, *vel tribula*, egþa.
Spadatus, *vel enuchizatus*, belisnod.[2]
Sarcina, seam, *vel* berþen.
Propolim, *vel pertica*, stod.
Scudicia, *vel fossorium*, spad.
Jugum, ioc.
Jugalis, ioc-tema.
Artena, boga.
Obicula, ioc-sticca.
Rotabulum, myx-force, *vel* ofen-raca

Capistorium, corn-troh.
Tritorium, þerscel.[3]
Cybutum, *vel cistella*, cest, *vel* earc.
Mozytia, *vel arcula*, tæg.
Sitarchia, mete-fætels, *vel* sceat-cod.
Astraba, fotbret.
Saccus, bigerdel.
Arpax, geara feng, *vel lupus*.
Arpago, *vel palum*, hooc.
Columbar, sceacul, *vel* bend.
Limes, fot-sid-gerif.
Scrupulum, ynca.
Manuliatus, *vel manicatus*, geslefed.
Pigrus, *vel lentus*, sleac, *vel* slaw.

Epiphania, ætewung.[4]
Scenophegia, getimbra halgung, *vel* geteld wurþung.
Neomenia, niwe-mona.
Encenia, niwe-circ-halgung.
Sinagoga, gegaderung.
Cerimonia, *vel orgia, g*.[5] geldagas, þæt sind halige.
Heresis, kyre, *vel* gedwelo-æfterfelgund
Palla, cyrtel, *vel* ofer-brædels.
Murenula, *vel torques*, swur-beh.
Redimicula, kævinge.
Reticulum, feax-net.
Monilia, menas.
Inaures, ear-preonas, *vel* ear-hringas.
Lunula, bend.
Tenia, tæppan, *vel* dol-smeltas.
Catelle, swur-racenteh.
Vitta, snod.
Rigula, feax-net.

---

[1] *Nauegar*, an auger. Alfric introduces, in his enumeration, tools necessary or useful to the agriculturist, which are not absolutely agricultural instruments.

[2] This word is no doubt introduced here as applied to animals, and records one of the operations in farming.

[3] A flail, still called in Lancashire a *threshell*.

[4] Quitting entirely the subject of agriculture, the compiler of the vocabulary introduces abruptly a number of words belonging to ecclesiastical affairs, which are oddly enough mixed with a few words of a different description.

[5] The *g* stands no doubt for *Græcè*, meaning that the preceding word is Greek, and not Latin.

ARCHBISHOP ALFRIC'S VOCABULARY.

Ricinum, winpel, *vel* orl.
Discriminalia, uplegene, *vel* feax-preonas.
Orarium, vel ciclas, orl.
Calamistrum, feax-nædel.
Menstruum opus, monþes weorc.
Vomex, vel vomens, spiwere.
Stipes, stipitis, treowwes-steb.
Stips, stipis, wist, *vel* anleofa, *vel* ælmesse.
Superstitio, superfluitas, ofer-flowencs.
Gimnosophista, nacod plegere.
Ariolus, wigbed-wiglere.
Aruspex, dægmel-sceawere.[1]
Augur, vel auspex, fugel-weohlere.
Astrologus, vel magus, vel mathematicus, tungel-witega, gebyrd-wiglære.
Scinodens, twisel-toðe.
Puerperium, hyse-berðlinge.
Puerpera, cildiung-wif.
Virago, ceorl-strang fæmne.
Portentum, vel prodigium, vel ostentum, fortacen.
Satiri, vel fauni, vel sehni, vel fauni ficarii, unfæle men, wude-wasan, unfæle wihtu.[2]
Veredus, cræte-hors.
Mannus, vel brunnicus, geþracen hors.

Burdo, hors of steden, *vel* of asrennc.
Alfa, i. initium, angin.[3]
Abra, i. ancilla, þinen, wyln.
Acha, i. virtus, strengð.
Acer, i. vehemens, strang.
Achor, i. conturbatio, drefing,
Actionator, folc-gerefa.
Acisculum, pic.
Asscopa, flaxe oððe cylle.
Agape, ælmesse.
Altanus, þoden.
Anastasis, dygelnyssum [4]
Angiportus, i. refrigerium navium, hyð.
Ardamo, i. gusto, ic gesmecge.
Andreporesis, i. homo utriusque generis, bæddel.
Centaurus, vel ippocentaurus, healf man and healf hors.
Onocentaurus, healf mann and healf assa.
Agrestis, wilde.
Brunda, heortes heafod.
Orbis, vel firmamentum, ymbhwerft.
Rotella, vel orbiculus, lytel ymbhweorft.

NOMINA OMNIUM HOMINUM COMMUNITER.[5]

Imperator, Cæsar, vel Augustus, casere.
Basileus, kyning.
Regillus, under-cyning.

---

[1] The compiler has singularly misunderstood the Latin word *aruspex*. Dægmæl-sceawere signifies literally one who announces or proclaims the hours of the day.

[2] Somner conjectures, perhaps rightly, that *sehni* is a corruption of *obsceni*.

[3] This, and the words which follow, were evidently taken from an alphabetical glossary. It may perhaps be well to observe, with regard to them, as well as to many Latin words in this vocabulary, that the Anglo-Saxon scholars did not take their standard of Latin from the good classical writers, but they sought their words in the *Origines* of Isidore, and in writings of that class; and they affected, especially, barbarous compounds from the Greek. The words, here given in alphabetical order, belong chiefly to these two classes. From this circumstance, also, it appears that there are Anglo-Saxon words in the vocabulary, at the meaning of which we can only guess, on account of the obscurity or corruptness of the Latin equivalents.

[4] It is evident that the compiler of this part of the vocabulary mistook entirely the meaning of the Latin word, and imagined it to be *anastrus,* or something of that kind, meaning *without stars.* It is hardly necessary to say that *dygelnyssum* means *in secrecy,* or *in darkness.*

[5] It will be seen at once that, in the list of political terms which follow, the compiler has sought to explain the words in use in the Roman empire by their nearest Anglo-Saxon equi-

Diadema, kyne-gerd.
Sceptrum, cyne-gerd.
Ducatus, ealdordom.
Consul, gerefa.
Proconsul, under-gerefa.
Monarces, an-walda.
Prætor, vel præfectus, vel præpositus, vel quæstor, burh-gerefa.
Tribunus, manna ealdor.
Millenarius, þusend-rica.
Ciliarcus, þusendes ealdor.
Preses, scir-gerefa.
Centurio, hundredes ealdor.
Quinquagenarius, vel pentecontarcus, fiftiga ealdor.
Cohors, fif hund cempena ealdor.
Emeritus, alæten cempa.
Tyro, iung-wiga.
Optiones, gecorene cempan.
Sinmistes, vel consecretalis, gehala, *vel* geruna.
Rebellio, wiðer-cwyda.
Excubiæ, dæg-wæccan.
Excubitor, vigil, dæg-weard.
Vigiliæ, niht-wæccan.
Veltes, swifte ærendracan.
Turma, þrittig rid-wigena.
Legio, feþu.
Acies, geræerud feða.
Manipulus, twa hund cempna.
Castrum, fyrd.
Castra, fyrd-wic.
Exercitus, here.
Cuneus, getrimmed feða.
Alæ, fedes.

Nodus, getrum.
Agmen, gangend feða.
Cives, burhwara.
Oppidanus, burhseta.
Vulgus, vel plebs, heanra burhwered.
Senatus, ealdermanna duguð.
Censores, vel judices, vel arbitri, deman.
Proceres, vel primores, vel primarii, yldest burhwara.
Municeps, port-gerefa, *vel* burhwita.
Curiales, vel decuriales, burh-gerefa.
Commentariensis, gerefa.
Exactor, hæcewol.
Collegiati, replinge-weardes.
Mercedarii, hyne-gildan.
Publicanus, wic-gerefa.
Villicus, vel actor, vel curator, vel procurator, vel rector, tun-gerefa.
Colonus, oðres eardes land-seta.[1]
Inquilinus, tun-gebur.
Indigena, inlenda.
Vernaculus, inbirding.
Vernula, fostorling.
Ædilis, hof-weard, *vel* byri-weard, *vel* botl-weard.
Libertus, freo-læta.
Libertinus, freo-lætan sunu.
Titirus, scyphyred.
Canum servitor, hund-wealh.
Pirata, vel piraticus, vel cilix, wicing, *vel* scegðman.
Archipirata, yldest wicing.
Vappa, awerde.
Vafer, vel fatuus, vel socors, abroten, *vel* dwæs.

valents, and not to give the Latin to the terms in use under the Anglo-Saxon government. Nevertheless, some of them are extremely curious, as helping us to understand the real import of the Anglo-Saxon words.

[1] This is one of several instances which occur in the course of the vocabulary, of the mistaking, by the Anglo-Saxon translator, of the real meaning of the Latin word: *colonus* was no doubt, from the other words in connexion with it, intended to be taken in its original sense of a husbandman, whereas the translator seems to have taken it in its secondary meaning of a colonist. A little further down, the name so familiar to the readers of Virgil, *Tityrus,* is given as a general word for a shepherd.

Cernuus, pronus, vel inclinatus, hnitol, vel eadmod.
Himeneas, hæmeða.
Æquævus, vel coætaneus, efn-eald.
Clivosus, clifig, to-hyld.
Coturnus, ofer-mod.
Pabulator, hors-hyrde, *vel* fodder-brytta.
Agressor, strudere, *vel* reafere.
Sarcitector, vel tignarius, hrof-wyrhta.
Carpentarius, wæn-wyrhta.
Lignarius, treow-wyrhta.
Opifex, cræftiga.
Fullones, fulleres.
Navicularius, scip-wyrhta.
Architectus, yldest-wyrhta.[1]
Cimentarius, weal-wyrhta.
Latomi, stan-wyrhta.
Lapidicina, vel lapidicedum, stan-hywet.

Pestilentia, vel contagium, vel lues, cwealm.[2]
Carbunculus, spring, *vel* angset, *vel pustula*, cwydele, *vel pustella*, swelca.
Scottomia, swinglung.
Spasmos, hramma, *vel* swiung.
Titanus, ofer-bæc-geteung.
Telum, i. dolor lateris, stic-wærc, stic-adl.
Yleos, hrif-wirc, *vel* hrig-teung.
Ydrofobam, vel limphatici, wæter-firhtnys.
Epilepsia, vel caduca, vel larvatio, vel commitialis, bræc-coðu, fylle-seoc.
Reuma, bræc.

Coriza, neb-gebræc.
Branchos, hræc-gebræc.
Tipus, lengten-adl.
Pleuriticus, on sidan lama, *vel* sid-adl.
Raucedo, hasnys.
Arteriasis, sweor-coþu.
Suspirium, hriung, *vel* siccetung.
Apostema, swyle.
Enpus, ingeswel.
Peripleumonia, blot-hræcung.
Emoptois, blot-spiung.
Phtisis, wyrs-hræcing, *vel* wyrs-ut-spiung.
Ypaticus, lifer-adl.
Lienosus, milte-seoc.
Nefresis, lenden-wyrc.
Cacexia, yfel-adl.
Atrophia, mete-afliung.
Sciascis, hip-werc.
Vertibulum, hwyrf-ban.
Artericus, vel artriticus, lið-adl.
Caucalus, cysel-stan.
Disuria, vel stranguria, earfoð læte micga.
Strictura, gebynd.
Saturiasis, synwrennys, *vel* galscipe.
Diarria, ut-siht.
Dissenteria, blodig ut-siht.
Lienteria, mete ut-siht.
Colum, hrop.[3]
Colica, hrop-wyrc.
Orificium, ælces kynnes muð *vel* ðyr.
Alopecia, feax-feallung.

---

[1] Here, again, the translator has mistaken the meaning of his word rather singularly, for he supposed that the import of the first member of the compound word was the same in *architectus* as in *archepiscopus*, and words of that class.

[2] We now have a list of diseases, which no doubt includes all those that were known to the Saxon physicians, commencing with the most fearful of all—the plague. In *stic-wærc* and *stic-adl* we have a term which is still preserved in the popular word *stitch*, applied to a pain in the side. One of the names for the epilepsy, *fylle-seoc*, was preserved in the later term, the falling sickness. *Swyle*, for an aposteme, is preserved in the provincial word *swail*: and *wild-fire* is, I think, still in some parts used for the *erysipelas*. But in general the Anglo-Saxon names for diseases, which were mostly popular expressions or translations of the Latin, have been lost in the English language.

[3] This word still exists in the provincial name *ropes*, for bowels. *Colum* is the Greek χῶλον.

Parotides, car-coðu, *ota, g.* ear.
Inpetigo, teter.
Erisipilas, wylde-fyr.
Serpedo, pytful wyrmses.
Prurigo, emertung.
Pruritus, gicþa.
Verruca, wearte.
Nictalmus, niht-ege.
Satiriasis, weartene heap.
Elephanticus, vel hicteris, vel artuatus, syd-mycle-adl.
Ordeolus, stigend.
Furunculus, vel antrax. angseta.
Oscedo, muð-coþu.
Frenus, muð-berstinge.
Ulcus, rotung.
Tabes, gemolsnad flæsc, *vel* forrotad.
Pharmacia, sealf-læcung.
Ligatura, sar-clað.
Picra, biter-wyrt-drenc.
Tiriaca, drenc wyð attre.
Catartica, i. purgatoria, wyrt-drenc.
Catapodia, swylfende drenc.
Diamoron, berig-drenc.
Colliria, eag-sealfe.
Girba, se ealra mæsta mortere.
Pilurus, vel pistor, se þe pilað, *vel* tribulað.
Tipsane, beren-gebered corn.
Stacten, stor þe bið of-gewringe.

Fax, Godes riht.[1]
Jus, manisc riht.
Jus naturale, gecynde riht.
Solempnitas, þeaw, *vel* wise.
Stipendium, scipe, *vel* bigleofa.
Pragma, æbod, *vel* intinga.
Pragmatica negotia, æbodas, *vel* ceapunge.
Hereditas, yrfeweardnes.

Legatum, gewriten yrfe.
Legatum testamentum, heah gerefan gesetnysse.
Legatarius, yrfeweard-writere.
Testator, yrfe-writend.
Intestata hereditas, ungewriten yrfe.
Ruptum testamentum, uncwedene yrfe-bec. [yrfe-bec.
Suppressum testamentum, forswiged
Cretio, yrfe-fyrt.
Nuncupatio, underne yrfe-bec.
Jus liberorum, sam-hiwna yrfe-bec.
Familiæ, erciscundæ, yrfe-gedal.
Mandatum, hand-festnung.
Satura lex, mænibræde-dom.
Rodia lex, scip-manna riht.
Cirographum, ræding-gewrit, *vel* hand-gewrit.
Donatio, forgifung.
Dos, morgen-gifu.
Conditio, geewide, *vel* gewyrd.
Stipulatio, gehat.
Sacramentum, að-wed, *vel* aðe-gehat.
Res, æht, *vel* þinc.
Jus, decretum, vel lex, andweald.
Peculium, heanra man, *vel* ceorlic æhta.
Locatio, behiring, *vel* gehyred feoh.
Conduco, ic ahyre.
Congressio, gefeoht.
Jus publicum, ealdormanna riht.
Jus quiritum, weala sunder riht.
Plebisscita, medrica gesetnyssa.
Senatus consultum, ricera gesetnes.
Constitutio, kyninga gesetnysse.
Responsa, geaxode domas.
Jurisconsultus, vel jurisperitus, riht-scrifendom.
Res credita, gelened feoh, *vel* on borh-geseald.
Usura, wæmst-sceat.

[1] Here we commence another series of terms, belonging to the Roman law, which appears to be quite out of its place, and was perhaps an addition to the original vocabulary

Commodum, læn.
Precarium, landes læn.
Mutuum, wrixlung.
Depositum, to healdenne, *vel* ædfæst tæht, *vel* becwyddod.
Pignus, wed, *vel* alæned feoh.
Arra, gylden wed, *vel* feoh.
Arrabona, vel arrabo, wed, *vel* wedlac.
Fiducia, forweddad feoh.
Ypotheca, feoh-lænung butan borge.
Parricidii actio, mæg-morþres witnung.
Inficiatio, vel abjuratio, borges andsæc.
Ambitus judicium, gebohtre scire-witnung.
Majestatis reus, wið cyning forwyrt.
Compedes, fot-fetera.
Nervi, boia, fot-copsa, *vel* sweor-scacul.
Anguilla, vel scutica, swipa.
Scorpio, ostig gyrd, *vel* tindig.
Eculeus, unhela þrepel.
Ignominia, scande.
Infamia, unhlisa.
Exilium, wræcsið.
Postliminium, edcyr of spræc-sið c.
Relegatus, to wite asend mid unsehte.
Patibulum, galga.[1]
Culleum, ælces cynnes witnung.
Fabe frese, vel pilate, gepunede-beane.
Facinus, scæð-dæd.
Vis potestatis, riccra manna nced.
Calumnia, hol-tihte, *vel* teone.
Seditio, folc-slite *vel* æswicung, sacu, ceast.
Sacrilegium, godes fees ðeof.
Stuprum, raptum, wifa nydnimung.
Adulterium, cwena geligr, *vel* unriht hæmed.

Balus, isern feter.
Bagula, bridel, *i. frenum.*
Momentum, to hwile læn.
Instrumentum, tool.
Instrumentum, gewroht.
Usus, nittung, *vel* notu, *vel* eorð-wæstm, cess, to æte alyfed.
Merces, cepe-þingc.
Comercium, cepena ðinga gewrixle.
Bicoca, hæfer-blæte, *vel* pun.[2]
Bobla, flod.
Bargina, boccfel.
Bulge, leþer-coddas.
Bacharus, mere-swyn.
Burdus, seamere.
Bases, tredelas, *vel* stæpas.
Crepusculum, glomung.[3]
Conticinium, cwyl-tid, *vel* gebed-giht.
Aupicium, initium, angin.
Vibrissæ, nosterla hær.
Zenia, gifu.
Sales, wynsum gamen.
Stiria, stillicidia, ises gicel.
Olimpias, fifwintra fæc.
Lustrum quinquennium, fif wintra fæc.
Bimus, vel biennis, vel bimulus, twi-winter. [winter.
Trinus, vel triennis, vel trimulus, þri-
Ævum, vel ætas perpetua, widerfeorlic, *vel* ece.
Prestigium, scinhiw.
Arpa, æren-geat.
Lotium, hlom, *vel* micga.
Submanicatus, be slifan gebunden.
Comitia, wyrd-sciras.
Draconarii, vel vexillarii, vel signiferi, segn-boran, tacn-boran.

[1] *Galga,* the gallows, appears to have been the usual form of capital punishment among the Anglo-Saxons, and is represented not uncommonly in the early illuminated manuscripts.

[2] The extracts from the alphabetical glossary, now in the letter B, recommence here. Neither the Latin words, nor their Anglo-Saxon equivalents, are always intelligible.

[3] The Anglo-Saxon word for twilight is still preserved in the Scottish *gloming.* The words which follow, are of a very miscellaneous character.

Purulentus, wurmsihtig.
Vermiculus, corn-wurma.
Melinum, vel croceum, geolu.
Centumpellio, feleferð.
Lithologia, stan-lesung.
Lithostratos, stan-bricge.
Taberna, boc-cest.
Glarea, glitis, vel samia, sand.
Flebotomus, blod-sex.
Flebotomarius, blod-lætere.
Fiscus, vel saccus publicus, biggyrdel.
Rudera, vel ruina, geswapa, *vel* meox.
Quisquiliæ, æppel-screada, *vel* corn-æsceda.
Capreoli, wingeard-bogas.
Quitinas, g. caducas, milsore treowa blosman.
Subacta coria, vel medicata, vel confecta, getannede hyd.
Feriatus, reste-dæg.
Jaculum, vel funda, widnyt, *vel* fla.
Coragium, mædena bergen.
Aquagium, wæter-þeote.
Hostimentum, wiðer-riht, *vel* edlean.
Idolothytum, idelgild offrung.
Galerus, vel pileus, fellen hæt.
Annicto, vel annuto, ic wincie.
Camilema, leaces sex.
Subplaudo, ic gilpe.
Repatrio, ic ham-siþie.
Obunco, ic ymbclipe.
Obrigesco, ic stifie.
Oppando oppansus, ic aþenige.
Infesto, ic ehtige.
Expertus, i. multum peritus, þurhlæred, *vel* gleaw.
Expers, indoctus, dæl-leas, *vel* cræft-leas.

NOMINA FERARUM.

Animal, ælc cuce þinc, *vel* nyhten.
Pecus, jumentum, ælces kynnes nyten.
Fera, wild-deor.
Bellua, reðe-deor.
Elephans, ylp.
Promuscida, ylpes bile, *vel* wrot.
Unicornis, vel monoceros, vel rinoceros, an-hyrne deor.
Griffes, eow, fiðerfote fugel.
Urus, wesend.
Bubalus, wilde-oxa.
Fiber, castor, ponticus, befer.
Raturus, ræt.
Lutria, otor.
Netila, hearma.
Ferunca, vel ferunculus, mearð.
Scirra, aquilinus, sciurus, acwern.
Taxus, vel melos, cuniculus, broc.
Bromus marinus, seolh.
Linx, lox.
Glis, sise-mus.
Mustela, wesle.
Camelus, vel dromeda, olfend.
Simia, vel spinx, apa.
Talpa, vel palpo, wande-wurpe.
Licos, wulf.
Lepus, vel lagos, g., hara.
Cervus, vel eripes, heort, buc.
Cerva, hind.
Damula, vel caprea, vel dorcas, g., hræge.
Capreus, rah-deor.
Hinnulus, hind-cealf.
Vulpes, fox.
Porcastor, foor.
Aper, wilde bar.
Verres, tam bar.
Magalis, bearh.
Scrofa, sugu.
Sus, swyn.
Suilla, vel sucula, gilte.
Suilli, vel porcelli, vel nefrendes, fearas.
Caper, vel hircus, vel tragos, bucca.
Capra ægida, gat-buccan hyrde.

Hedus, ticcen.
Ibix, firing-gat.
Sonipes, hors.
Equifer, wilde cynnes hors.
Agaso, hors-þen.
Jumentum, hryofif.
Equa, mere.
Canterius, hengst.
Faussarius, steþa.
Equartium, stood.
Poledrus, fola.
Sugma, seam-sadol.
Sugmarius equus, seam-hors.
Antela, forð-gyrd.
Postela, æfter-ræpe.
Subligar, þearm-gyrd.
Scansile, stirap.
Corbus, sadul-boga.
Sella, sadul.
Centrum, vel filtrum, felt.
Frenum, vel lupatum, midl.
Chamus, bridles midl.
Bagula, salivare, brydel.
Ducale, latteh.
Mulus, mul.
Asinus, assa.
Onager, wilde assa.
Ursus, bera.
Ursa, byrene.
Muriceps, vel musio, murilegus, catt.
Sorex, mus.
Canis, hund.
Canicula, bicge.
Millus, vel collarium, sweor-teh.
Molossus, ryðða.
Inutilis canis, hroð-hund.
Cinomia, hundes-fleoge.
Ricinus, hundes-fleoge.
Bos, oxa.
Vacca, vel bucula, cu.

Anniculus, vel trio, steor-oxa.
Vitulus, cealf.
Juvencus, vel vitula, steor.
Annicula, vel vaccula, heahfore.
Juniculus, iung hryþer.
Juvenca, iung cu.
Unus, oxa on þam forman teame.
Binus, on þam æfteran teame
Mutinus, gadinca, *vel* hnoc.
Altilium, fæt heahfore.
Altile, fedels.
Aries, ramm.
Triennis, þry-winter, sumer gildeto.
Ovis, vel mandritis, g. scep.
Mandra, vel ovile, locc.
Vervex, vel manto, weþer.
Agnus cinist, (*sic*) lamb.
Magnicaper, ormæte-buccan.

DE NOMINIBUS INSECTORUM.

Musca, fleoge.
Chosdrus, vel castros, beo-moder.
Fucus, dran.
Crabro, hyrnet.
Oestrum, beaw-hyrnette.
Blatta, niht-buttor-fleoge.
Vespa, wæps.
Apis, vel melle, beo
Atticus, vel burdo, dora.
Scarabeus, scearn-fifel.
Papilio, buttor-fleoge.
Locusta, astaco, gærstapa.
Bruchus, ceafor.
Cinomya, hundes-fleoge.
Bibiones, vel mustiones, musc-fleotan, *vel* wurma sinite.
Culex, stut.[1]
Cicindela, se glisigenda wibba.[2]
Formica, æmete.

A gnat is still called a *stut* in Somersetshire. [2] The glittering worm, no doubt the glow-worm.

Loppe, fleonde næddre, *vel* attor-coppe.[1]
Gurgulu, cawel wurm.
Scinifes, vel tudo, gnæt.
Limax, snægl.
Testudo, gehused snægl.
Bombyx, syd-wyrm, *vel* seolc-wyrm.
Eruca, mælscæafa.
Termes, vel teredo, wyrm þe borað treow.
Sanguisuga, vel hirudo, læce.
Pulex, fleo.
Pediculus, vel sexpes, lus.
Lens, vel lendix, hnitu.
Cimex, maþu.
Tippula, wæter-buca, *vel* gat.
Tinea, moððe.
Tomus, maða, mite.
Culus, micge.
Mordiculus, bitela.
Botrax, vel botraca, yce.
Rana, frogga.[2]
Buffo, tadige.
Lacerta, vel stilio, efete.
Emigranus, flæsc-maþu.
Blatta, eor-wicga.
Stellio, sla-wyrm.
Tauri, eorð-caferas.
Spalangius, sla-wyrm
Surio, vel briensis, vel sirineus, hand-wyrm.
Musaraneus, screawa.
Istrix, se mara igil.

Lumbricus, ren-wyrm, *vel* angeltwicce.
Chelio, testudo, vel marina gagalia, sæ-snæl, *vel* pinewinclan.
Ricinus, hundes wyrm.
Usia, swines lus.
Buprestis, twin-wyrm.

NOMINA VASORUM.[3]

Amfora, sester.
Cantarus, win-cester.
Crater, vel canna, canne.
Patera, mele.
Alabastrum, stænen ele-fæt.
Cocula, olfata.
Karchesia, melas.
Caupus, vel obba, cuppe.
Fiala, vel scala, bledu.
Cratera, earde fæt.
Ciatus, hnæp.
Anthlia, hnæp.
Dolium, cyf.
Fundum, byden botm.
Hauritorium, hlæden.
Patella, panne.
Colatorium, scohhe.
Cribrum, syfe.
Cupa, tunne.
Tympanum, tunne-botm.
Cistella, vel cartallum, windel.
Corbis, vel qualus, tænel.
Batus, amber.

---

[1] The word *atter-coppa* is generally explained as signifying a spider, and it continued to be used apparently in that sense in English until the fifteenth century; yet in some cases this meaning appears to be doubtful. In an A.-S. MS in the Cottonian library, Vitel. C. III., we have drawings of the *atter-coppa* of that period, which by no means agree with the notion of its being a spider. One of them is engraved in my Archæological Album, p. 182.

[2] It is curious that in the eyes of the Anglo-Saxon naturalists, the frog, the toad, the lizard or eft (*efete*), and other reptiles, were usually placed under the head of insects; and this odd classification was preserved to rather a late period. Here we have the shrew-mouse (*screawe*), and the hedgehog (*istrix, igil*), as well as the slow-worm (*slaw-wyrm*), and the periwinkle (*pinewincla, or sæ-snæl*), placed in the same category.

[3] This chapter, and what follows, appear to have been accidentally displaced, and so interposed between the list of insects and the list of birds.

ARCHBISHOP ALFRIC'S VOCABULARY.

Sartago, vel frixorium, dyrsting panne.
Canistrum, vel alvearium, hyf.
Cophinus, wilige.
Orca, orc.
Enophorum, win-fæt.
Quasillus, litel tænel.
Flaxa, flaxe.
Lagena, æscen.
Anfora, crocca.
Situla, stoppa.[1]
Ansa, sal.
Ydria, vel soriscula, wæter-fæt.
Mulctrale, vel sinum, vel mulctrum, meolc-fæt.
Uter, byt.
Scortia, leðren-fæt.
Flasco, buteruc.
Lenticula, æren-byt.
Sciffus, lævel.
Emicudium, ele-fæt.
Urseus, vel in mansiterna, cenc.
Acetabulum, æced-fæt.
Emistis, andrece-fæt, *vel trapetum*.
Cucuma, cyperen-hwer.
Lebes, hwer, *vel* cytel.
Cacabus, cytel.
Gillo, wægel.
Malluviæ, hand-þweales fæt.
Pelluviæ, fot-þweales fæt.
Paropsis, vel catinus, læpeldre fæt.
Trisilis, þri-fotad fæt.
Patena, husel-disc.
Cimbia, scip-fæt.[2]
Lagena, læmen-fæt.

Sartago, isen panne.
Arula, vel batilla, fyr-panne.
Pixis, bixen-box.

Domus, vel lar, hus.[3]
Supellex, yddisc.
Cubiculum, bed-cofa, *vel* bur.
Cubicularius, bur-þen.
Camerarius, bed-þen.
Culcites, feþer-bed.
Plumacius, bed-bolster.
Capitale, heafd-bolster.
Cervical, wangere.
Stragula, wæstling.
Sindo, scyte.
Pulvillus, lytel pile.
Fulcrum, cal bed-reaf.
Vestis, clamis, scrud.
Sagum, hwitel.
Cunabulum, cradel.
Cune, vel crepundie, cild-claðes.
Planeta, cæppe.
Penula, gerenod cæppe.
Pretexta, cildes scrud.
Manualis, hand-lin.
Mantium, glof.
Zona, gyrdel.
Colobium, smoc, *vel* syrc.
Tubroces, vel brace, strapulus.
Perizomata, vel campestria, vel succinctoria, wæd-brec.
Manicæ, vel brachila, slyfa.
Toral, rooc.
Amphibalum, ruh-hrægel.

[1] The modern word *stoop*.
[2] Perhaps the *nef* of later times.
[3] From the list of vessels of different kinds, the vocabulary goes on to describe the house, with its parts and contents, beginning with the chamber, because probably it was the room in which, being less public, most of the articles of any value were kept, and which had most furniture. Of the names here given to the chamber, the first, *bed cofa*, means literally a bed-recess, or bed-closet; for the bed-room was probably, in earlier times and in the ordinary houses, only a recess from the room in which the family lived. *Bur* is the *bower* of a later period, when it was used as the poetical term for the lady's room. The enumeration of articles of dress is also introduced here in the sequel, as they were usually kept in the bed chamber.

Anabala, winpel.
Pedula, meo.
Commissura, clut.
Glomus, clypen.
Vitta, snod.
Limbus, stemning, *vel* hem.
Fascia, winingc.
Fascia, nostle.
Vallegias, wyncgas.
Instita, þræs.
Callicula, rocc.
Stigmentum, full maal on rægel.
Textrinum opus, towlic weorc.
Colus, distæf.
Fusus, spinl.
Cernui, fot-leaste, læs-hosum.
Fico, sco.
Solear, solen.
Subtalares, swiftelcnres.
Baxear, wifes sceos.
Coturnus, triwen sceo [1]
Caligarius, læst-weorhta.
Talares, unhege sceos.
Ocrea, *vel musticula*, læste.
Obstrigilli, rifelingos.[2]
Nebris, sceat, *vel* heortes hyd.
Bulga, hydig fæt.
Polimita, *vel oculata*, bring-fegh.
Orbiculata, lig-rægel.
Sigillum, *vel bulla*, insegel.
Arcus, forbigels.
Columna, swer.
Excussorium, flor on huse.
Tectum, þecen. *vel* rof.

Valva, hlid-gata.
Patronus, stapul.
Ascensorium, stæger.
Destina, vel postis, vel fulcimen, stipere.
Secessus, digle-hus.
Tignum, ræfter.
Asseres, lætta.[3]
Laquear, fyrst.
Cleta, cratis, hyrdel.
Vectis, steng.
Paxillus, cyrfel, *vel* litel stigul.
Sardanium, butere.
Taxea, spic.
Palestra, gewin-stow.
Arca, *vel scrinium*, scrin.
Convocatio, gelaðung.
Altar, *vel ara*, weofod.
Crux, *vel staurus*, rod.
Lampas, blase.
Lucernarium, leoht-fæt.
Emunctorium, candel-snytels.
Papirus, weoce.
Horologium, dæg-mæl.
Gnomon, dægmæls-pilu.
Salinare, vel salinum, sealt-fæt.[4]
Gausape, beod-rægl
Mensorium, meose
Legula, vel coclea, vel code, mete-sacca.
Dapes, vel fercula, wista, *vel* sand.
Fercula, bær-disc.
Discifer, vel discoforus, disc-þen.
Satira, hlæd-disc.
Mantile, hand-hrægl.
Mappula, bearm-clað, *vel* rægl.

---

[1] *i. e.*, a wooden shoe—a rather curious interpretation of the Latin *cothurnus*.

[2] A rough shoe, worn by the Scots in the fourteenth century, was called a *riveling*.

[3] This humble enumeration of the parts of a common dwelling-house, posts, rafters, laths, a roof, and a floor, (it is evidently supposed to be built of nothing but timber,) offers a strong contrast with the elaborate details in the later vocabularies, and reminds us of the remarks of William of Malmesbury, on the great development of domestic architecture after the **Norman Conquest**.

[4] We are now supposed to return to the hall, or eating room, and to the dinner table. The list of articles of cookery is not very numerous; nor does it bespeak a very high degree of refinement in gastronomy.

Mappa, wæter-sceat.
Foculare, heorð.
Focarius, fyr-beta.
Carbo, coll.
Pruna, gled.
Titio, vel torris, brand.
Andena, vel tripes, brand-isen.
Fuscinula, vel tridens, awul.
Veru, spitu.
Rotabulum, ofer-raca.
Verriculum, vel scopæ, bysm
Olitor, lec-tun-ward.
Comedia, racu, tunlic spæc.
Pastillus, litel hlaf.
Assura, vel assatura, bræde.
Coctus, gesoden, gebacen.
Elixus cibus, gesoden mæt on wætere.
Offa, vel frustum, sticce.
Offella, vel particula, spicces snæd.
Offarius, vel particularius, twickere.
Gastrimargia, gyfernys, *vel* ofer-fil.
Isicia, mærh-gehæt.
Omenta, vel membrana, fylmena.
Fermentum, ofen-bacen hlaf.
Polentum, wurt-mete mid meluwe.
Spumaticum, mete of meluwe and of bane gesoden.
Minutal, gebeaten fisc.
Martisia, vel baptitura, gebeaten flæsc.
Succidia, eald hryter flæsc.
Obesta, beost.
Colostrum, byst.
Silotrum, pillsape.
Excoriatus, beflæ.
Culliole, hnute-hula.

DE GENERIBUS POTIONUM.[1]

Cervisia, celia, eala.

Vinum, merum, win.
Acetum, eced.
Oleum, ele.
Oleaginus, ele-beamen.
Olea, vel oliva, ele-beam.
Medo, medu, *vel medus*.
Mellicratum, geswet win.
Ydromellum, beor, *vel* ofetes wos.
Oximellum, geswet eced.
Inomellum, must mid hunig gemenged.
Mulsum, beor.
Mustum, niwe win.
Sicera, ælces kynnes gewring butan wine and wætere.
Liquor, wæta.
Sapa, pere wos.
Falernum, þæt seleste win.
Infertum vinum, messe win.
Limpidum vinum, scir win.
Spurcum vinum, ful win.
Crudum vinum, weala win.
Succinacium vinum, geolo win.
Honorarium vinum, hlaforda win.
Compositum vinum, vel conditum, gewyrtod win.
Myrratum vinum, gemenged mid myrran.
Defecatum vinum, gehluttrad win.
Meracum vinum, gehlyttrod win.
Defrutum vinum, gesoden win, *vel passum*.
Fecula, gesoden win-berigen.
Carenum, morað.
Favus, beo-bread.
Liguamen, vel garum, fisc-bryne.
Salsugo, muria, bryne.
Serum, hwæg.
Raptura, syring.
Coagulum, rynning.

[1] From the dishes we are introduced to the drinks of the Anglo-Saxons, which appear to be proportionally more numerous. They are followed by another batch of words relating to ecclesiastical matters, and others of a miscellaneous character; after which we return again to the subject of natural history, in a list of birds.

Coagulatus, gerunnen.
Oxygala, sur meolc, *acidum lac.*
Colustrum, bysting, þicce meolc.
Fusta, hacine.
Sapa, æfter eala.
Lexinum, leh-mealt-wurt.
Acinum, meal-wurt.
Feces, drosna.
Irriguum, stream, *vel* wæto.
Caupo, tabernarius, tæppere, win-brytta.
Divisor, dælere.
Dispensator, dihtnere.
Economus, stiward.
Ephemeris, anes dæges weorc.
Diarium, dægwine.
Bucida, qui boves mactat, hryþer-heawere.

Cantor, sangere.
Trenos, sarlic sang.
Præcentor, fore-singend.
Threnum, wanung.
Succentor, æfter-singend.
Ymeneus, vel epithalamium, bryd-sang.
Concentor, mid-singend.
Monodia, g., latersicinium, quasi solicinium, þæt is anes sones.
Bicinium, twegra sang.
Ymnus, lof-sang.
Chorus, singende heap.
Chorea, hluddra sang.
Matutinum officium, uht-gebed, *vel* þenung
Vespertinum officium, æfen-gebed, *vel* þeowdom.
Responsorium, reps.
Lectio, ræding.
Diaphonia, ungeswege sang.
Canticum, sum swege sang.
Psalmus, proprie, hearp-sang.
Canticum, psalm æfter hærpan sang.
Psalmus, ær hærpan sang.
Armonia, geðwære sang.

Simphonia, answege sang.
Fertura, messe-lac.
Offertorium, lane sang.
Oblatio, ofrung.
Dano, sawl-sceat, *vel* syndrig Godes lac.
Dedicatum, Gode gesylð.
Consecratum, Gode gehalgað.
Officium, þenung.
Immolatio, onsægung.
Sacrificium, offrung.
Mactatio, sniþung.
Holocaustum, eal-offrung.
Libatio, win-tifer.
Omilia, folclic lar.
Ceremoniæ, g. orgia, geld haeal halgung.
Munus, vel zenia, lac.
Eleemosyna, vel agape, ælmesse.
Donum, datum, vel donatum, gifu.
Pretium, wurð.
Depretiatus, wurðleas.
Care valet, pretiosum est, deor hit is.
Vile valet, undeor hit is.
Care vendidit, deore he hit bohte, *vel* scalde.
Vile vendidit, undeore he bohte.
Vilis, waclic.
Carus, leof.
Odiosus, þurhlað.
Vivus, cuce.
Redivivus, geedcuced.
Mortuus, dead.
Defunctus, forðfaren.
Defungitur, forðfærð.
Longævus, lang-life.
Capillamenta, rupe oððe drisne.
Polio, ic smeðie.
Plano, vel levigo, ic gegnide.
Conficio, ic gemenge.
Commolio, ic grinde.
Commolitus, gegrunde.
Deroto, ic wyrge.

Devotatio, wergnes, *vel* gehat.
Compensatio, edleanung.

NOMINA AVIUM.

Cignus, ylfete.
Pavo, pavus, pawe.
Aquila, earn.
Beacita, vel sturnus, stearn.
Herodios, g., swan.
Olor, swan.
Ardea, hragra, *diomedea*.
Ficedula, swertling.
Strix, vel cavanna, vel noctua, vel ulula, ule.
Lucinia, vel philomela, nightegale.
Mergus, scealfr.
Mergulus, fugel-doppe.
Auca, gos.
Aucarius, gos-hafuc.
Anser, ganra.
Anas, ened.
Ciconia, storc.
Rubisca, rudduc.[1]
Auricinctus, goldfinc.
Alauda, laverce.[2]
Bugium, hæfen-blæte.
Alcedo, vel alcion, mæw.[3]
Columba, culfer.[4]
Palumbus, wude-culfre.
Bitorius, vel pintorus, wrenna.
Cicada, vicetula, heges-sugge.[5]
Cicada, hilhama.
Turdus, scric.[6]

Cornix, crawe.
Butio, cyta.
Turtur, turtle.
Corvus, remn.
Nicticorax, niht-remn.
Gracculus, vel monedula, ceo.[7]
Gaia, vel catanus, higere.
Cuculus, geac.
Stronus, stærn.
Turdus, stær[8]
Turdella, se mare stær.
Coturnix, ærschen.
Pica, agu.
Pluvialis, hulfestre.
Bubo, uf.
Picus, fina.
Gracculus, vel garrulus, hroc.
Milvus, glida.[9]
Ibis, geolna.
Fulica, dop-enid.
Vultur, earn-geap.
Aceta, snite, *vel* rude cocc.
Grus, cran.
Florentius, gold-finc.
Luscinus, geole-wearte.
Parrax, wrenna, *vel* hicemase.
Merula, vel plara, þrosle.
Accipiter, vel raptor, spear-hafoc.
Cintus, vel frugellus, gold-finc.
Hirundo, swalewe.
Carduelis, linetwige.
Rapariolus, fiscere.
Tanticus, ærðling.

---

[1] *Ruddock* continued long to be the regular English name for the redbreast, or robin; and I am not sure that it has yet entirely disappeared from our local dialects.

[2] The *laverok* of old English, now softened down into *lark*.

[3] The mew.

[4] The pigeon is still called a *culver* in some of our dialects.

[5] The hedge-sparrow is still called, in Gloucestershire, a *haysuck*.

[6] The shrike.

[7] *Ceo* is the modern word *chough*.

[8] The stare, or starling. One would suppose that in the next line *mare* is an error for *læssa*.

[9] *Glede* continued to be the usual English name for the kite till a comparatively late period, and will be found in our vocabularies of the fifteenth century.

Capo, capun.
Gallus, coc.
Gallinacus, capun.
Pullus, cicen.
Falco, vel capus, a capiendo, wealh-hafoc.
Storicarius, bleripittel.
Bardioriolus, colmase.
Oscines aves, wigole-fugeles.

NOMINA HERBARUM.[1]

Apiago, beo-wyrt.
Lilium, lilie.
Fasida, leomue.
Colochintida, wylde cyrfet.
Rosa, rose.
Brionia, vel ampelos leuce, g., hwit wilde wingeard.
Labrusca, wingerd.
Brabasca, vel amplos male, blac wingeard.
Botanicum, vel viridarium, wyrt-tun.
Cucumerarium, wyrt-tun.
Caluna, mægþa.
Feniculum, fynel.
Nepita, næpte.
Adriatica, vel malum terræ, galluc.
Costus, cost.
Trifolium, geaces-sure,[2] *vel* þri-lefe.
Vaccinium, bran-wyrt.
Abrotonum, superne-wude.
Lubestica, lufestice.
Volvi, sinwealte swammas.
Sinpatus, cneowhole.

Solsequium, vel heliotropium, solsece, *vel* sigel-hwerfe.
Astula regia, wuderofe.
Millefolium, vel myrifilon, g. vel centifolia, gæruwe.
Tanaceta, helde.
Samum, hyl-wurt.
Herba, gærs, vel wyrt.
Butunus, heope.
Apium, merce.
Venenifuga, atterlaðe.
Febrefugia, vel febrifuga, fefer-fuge.
Ruta, rude.
Blitum, vel lappa, clate, *vel* clyf-wyrt.[3]
Simphoniaca, henne-belle.
Gersussa, biscop-wyrt.
Ramusium, ramesan.
Dilla, vel acrocorium, docce.
Anetum, dile.
Cucumer, hwerhwette.
Anadonia, feldwyrd.
Gladiolum, glædene.
Cinoglossa, vel plantago, vel lapatium, wegbræde.
Artemisia, vel matrum herba, mug-wyrt.
Annuosa, æscþrotu.
Amorfolia, clate.
Cepe, ennelec.
Saxifraga, sund-corn.
Philantropium, lawra, clate.
Auris leporis, hals-wyrt.
Ebulum, wal-wyrt.
Allium, garleac.
Herba munda, gið-corn.
Poletis, hwit-leac.

[1] The list of plants is rather copious, and many of their Anglo-Saxon names are still preserved as the popular names of wild plants. The cause of the list being so numerous was no doubt the circumstance of their being so much used for medicinal purposes.

[2] *Geaces-sure,* or *gæces-sure,* literally cuckoo's-sour, was the plant we now know by the name of wood-sorrel, which is still called in some parts of the country *cuckoo-sorrel.*

[3] *Clyf-wyrt* is generally understood as designating the plant now called *foxglove* (the *digitalis purpurea*). The Anglo-Saxon herbal of the Cottonian MS. (Vitel. C. III.) gives three names of this plant—clyf-wyrt sume man hataðð foxes-clifa, sume ea-wyrt.

ARCHBISHOP ALFRIC'S VOCABULARY. 31

Malletina, mede-wyrt.
Porrus, por-leac.
Cameleon, g., wulfes camb.
Cynocephaleon, heort-clæfre.
Electrum, clehtre.
Ficus, fic-wyrt.
Papaver, popig.
Saliunca, wilde-popig.
Apiaster, wude-merce.
Petrosilion, stan-merce.
Menta, minte.
Alumen, vel stiptura, efne.
Viola, hofe.
Gerobotana, vel verbena, vel sagmen, biscop-wyrtil.
Calta, vel trifillon, clæfre.
Crispa, victoriola, smering-wyrt.
Centauria, eorð-gealle.
Strumus, vel uva lupina, niht-scada.
Salvia, fen-fearn.
Colocasia, harewinta.
Filix, fearn.
Herba putida, mægða.
Cresco, kerse.
Vermiculi, mæddre.
Filix aboratica, eferfearn.
Sintea, vel senecion, grundeswelge.[1]
Nap silvatica, spere-wyrt, *vel* wilde næp.
Carex, vel sabium, vel lisca, secg.
Rubia, mæddre.
Juncus, risc.
Scirpus, æ-risc.
Bremium, earic.
Ulva, græde.
Gramen, cwice.
Alga, sæ-waur.[2]
Consolda, dægesege.

Raphanum, vel radix, rædic.
Tursus, cimia, crop.
Centaurea major, curmelle.
Brittannica, cusloppe.
Malva, malwe, *vel* geormen-letic.
Pastinaca, feldmora.
Daucus, wealmora.
Napus, næp.
Citocacia, giþ-corn.
Cariota, waldmora.
Sinapis, senep.
Cucurbita, cyrfæt.
Papirus, duðhumor.
Nasturtium, tun-kerse.
Rapa, næp.
Fungus, vel tuber, mette-swam.
Carduus, þistel.
Coliandrum, celendre.
Cerefolium, cærfille.
Elleborum, vel veratrum, wode-þistle.
Cicuta, hemlic.
Aconita, þung.
Betonica, seo læssa biscop[-wyrt].
Urtica, netle.
Archangelica, blinde netle.
Sisimbrium, balsminte.
Calumus, vel canna, vel harundo, reod.
Quinquefolium, pentafillon, fif-leafe.
Vinca, pervincæ.
Viscarago, mistiltan.
Marrubium, vel prassium, harhune.
Canicula, argentilla.
Fraga, strea-berige.
Framen, streaberie-wisan.
Nimphea, ea-docca.[3]
Eruca, calf-wyrt.
Caballopodia, vel ungula caballi, colt-græig.

[1] Now softened down into *groundsell*, the name of a well-known plant.
[2] Still called *waure* in Kent.
[3] Literally, the water-dock, the beautiful plant we now call the water-lily. One might suppose that the Anglo-Saxons named their plants with more regard to the leaves than to the flowers, to judge by this instance.

Ciminum, cymen.
Agrimonia, stic-wyrt.
Modera, cicena-mete.
Helena, hors-helene.
Diptamnus, vel bibulcos, wilde næp.
Sandix, wad.
Fucus, waad.
Tinctura, teging.
Arboracia, vel lapsana, cal.
Alfa, æðelfyrding-wyrt.
Origanum, warmelle.
Altea, vel eviscus, seo-mint.
Cardamon, cærse.
Pionia, pionia.
Mandragora, corð-æppel.
Oxylapation, g., anes cynnes clate.
Brionia, wild cyrfet, *vel* hwit wingeard.
Satirion, suðerige.
Pollegia, hyl-wyrt.
Hermodactyla, crawan-leac.
Centaurea minor, ban-wyrt.
Hedera nigra, wudebinde.
Pappus, þistles blostm.
Sarrabum, wilde lactuce.
Fromos, vel lucernaris, vel insana, vel lucubros, candel-wyrt.

NOMINA ARBORUM.

Arbor, treow.
Quercus, vel ilex, ac.
Robur, iung ac.
Quernum, ac-leac.
Corilus, hæsel.
Saginus, hwit hæsel.

Juglantis, vel nux, hnutu.
Fraxinus, æsc.
Æsculus, boc
Fagus, boc.
Faginus, becen.
Suberies, mæsten-triow.
Nemus, vel lucus, bearu.
Saltus, holt.
Spartus, þyfel.
Arbustum, iung treow.
Truncus, stoc.
Stipes, stofn.[1]
Surculus, vel virgultum, sprauta.
Daphnis, vel laurus, laur-beam.
Seno, vel tilia, lind.
Malus, apulder.[2]
Malus matranus, surmelst apulder.
Malomellus, swite apulder.
Mespila, open-ærs.[3]
Pirus, pirige.[4]
Persicarius, persoc-treow.
Cariscus, cwic-beam.
Pinus, pin-treow.
Prunus, plum-treow.
Ficus, fic-beam.
Cerasus, cyrs-treow.
Cornus, corn-treow.
Carica, fic-æppel.
Morus, vel rubus, mor-beam.
Palma, palm-twig, *vel* palm.
Abies, vel gallica, gyr-treow.
Ulmus, ulm-treow.
Genista, brom.
Taxus, iw.

[1] This word is still preserved in Leicestershire under the form *stovin*, signifying the stump of a tree.

[2] The Anglo-Saxon name of the apple-tree is preserved in the names of several places, such as Appledurford, or Appledurcomb, in the Isle of Wight, Appledore in Kent, and another Appledore in Devonshire, and perhaps Appledram in Sussex.

[3] It is rather singular that we should find this not very delicate name of the medlar at so early a period. It is found in MSS. of the fifteenth century, and is a word sufficiently familiar to the readers of the popular literature of the sixteenth and seventeenth centuries.

[4] In the fifteenth century the English name for the pear-tree still continued to be *piry*, *piré*, or *perye*.

ARCHBISHOP ALFRIC'S VOCABULARY.

Acer, mapulder;[1] *acernum*, mapuldern.
Populus, byrc.
Marica, vel brogus, hæð.[2]
Alnus, alr.
Castanea, cystel, *vel* cyst-beam.[3]
Glans, æcern.
Granum, cyrnel.
Corimbi, berigen.
Flos, blostm.
Cauliculus, stela.
Radix, wyrtruma.
Vimen, læl.
Viticella, wiðwinde.[4]
Pirorium, læfer-bed.
Pirus, gladiolus, læfer.
Ramus, boga.
Olea, oliva, ele-beam.
Amurca, eles drosna.
Oleaster, unwæstmbære ele-beam.
Betulus, byrc.
Betulentum, byrc-holt.
Rubus, heop-brymel.
Acrifolius, holen.
Gignalia, hagan.
Variculus, hwiting-treow.
Cresis, cwic-treow.
Sicomorus, vel celsa, æps.
Pruniculus, plum-sla.
Flavi, vel mori, blace-berian.
Ligustrum, hunisuge.
Bacido, botrus, clyster.
Accidinetum, gost.

Coquimella, vel prunus, vel nixa, plum-treow.
Amigdala, vel nutida, magdala-treow.
Nux, vel nucarius, hnut-beam.
Buxus, box.
Ornus, eow.
Cedrus, ceder-beam.
Cedria, hissæp.
Abellanæ, hæsl, *vel* hæsel-hnutu.
Sentes, þornas; *senticosus*, þorniht.
Frutex, þyfel.
Ramnus, þife-þorn.
Spina, þorn.
Tribulus, þorn.
Alba spina, hæg-þorn.
Spina, vel sentrix, þyfel.
Vepres, bremlas.
Mastix, vel resina, cuter.
Carpo balsami, balsames blæd.
Opobalsamum, balsames tear.
Vitis, win-treow.
Salix, wiþig.[5]
Mirica, hæþ.
Silva, wudu; *calones*, wudieras.
Lignum, ahæawan treow.
Stirps, styb, *vel* sprauta.
Glans, glandis, pic-bred.
Amenus locus, luffendlic stede.

Clava, styng.[6]
Contus, spreot.
Capsella, scrin.

---

[1] *Mapulder*, the maple. It still occurs in the Anglo-Saxon form in names of places, as in Mappledurwell in Hampshire, and Mapplederham in Oxfordshire.

[2] *Marica* seems to be only an error for *myrica*, under which form it is repeated below. Somner conjectures that *brogus* is a corruption of *brya*.

[3] The modern word *chestnut* is merely *cyst-hnut*, the nut of the cyst-tree.

[4] *Withwind* is still a name for the wild convolvulus; but how it came to find a place among trees, is not clear. The same may be said of the bulrush (*lefer*).

[5] *Withy* is still a common provincial name for the willow.

[6] The compiler of the vocabulary now goes off again into a series of miscellaneous words, which are at first taken, as in several instances before, from an alphabetical dictionary. He first breaks into the regularity of the alphabetical words by introducing one or two on account of their similar meaning, or from contrast, and then he leaves them altogether.

Cardinarius, i. primarius, se yldesta.
Causidicus, advocatus, fore-speca.
Carpentum, currus, hors-wæn.
Caragius, fugel-hwata.
Circinum, mæl-tange.
Emisperia, healf-tryndel.
Clatrum, pearruc.
Tribus, cneores.
Cimiterium, poliandrium, halig leger-[stow].
Coccum, rubicundum, bis tinctum, weolc-read.
Conquilium, weoloces scyll.
Contubernalis, geþofta.
Coclea, gewend.
Conniveo, ic wincige.
Confuto, ic oferstæle.
Conflatilis, gegoten.
Columen, i. culmen, rof.
Commentator, expositor, dihtere.
Conspiratio, geewidrædden.
Crates, i. flecta, hyrdel.
Crisoletus, auricolor, gold-bleoh.
Bida, vel basterna, vel capsus, vel currus, vel esseda, vel quadriga, vel carpentum, cræt.
Capsus, betogan cræt.
Cuba, byden.
Pilentum, vel petorritum, vel rada, crat.
Carracutium, heh-hwiolad wæn.
Crepido, uteweard.
Cassata, forhrered.
Classendis, sweordes scead.
Categia, i. telum, gesceot.
Oppidum, fæsten.
Urbanus, burh-sita, *vel* burh-man.
Civis, ceaster-ware.
Castellum, wic, *vel* lytel port.

Molendinarius, vel molinarius, mylen-wyrd.
Molitura, grist
Cerealis pistor, gristra.
Pistor, bæcere.
Pistrinum, bæc-ern.
Fornax, clibanus, ofn.
Cribrum, sife.
Cribellum, lytel sife.
Vannus, fann.
Ventilabrum, windwig-syfe.
Capisterium, hridder.
Taratantara, hridder.
Sporta, cawl.
Corbes, leap.
Tritorium, þerscel.
Pila, pilstre.
Pilum, pilstampe.
Pilunus, pilere.
Apludis, vel cantalna, hwæte gryttan.
Ergasterium, were-hus.
Officina, smidde.
Incus, anfilte.
Aries, ram to wurce.
Securis, vel secespita, æx.
Dolabrum, brad-æx.
Bipennis, twibille, *vel* stan-æx.
Falcastrum, bill.
Ascia, adesa.
Falciola, vel falcicula, sicol.
Falx, siðe.
Vitrum, vel hialum, glæs.
Electrum, smilting, *vel* glær.
Metallum, ælces kynnes weeg, *vel* ora oððe clyna.
Massa, dad, *vel* bloma.[1]

[1] *Bloma*, the metal taken from the ore. It is the origin of the technical term *bloomery*, for the places where one of the operations of smelting is performed.

NOMINA ARMORUM.[1]

Arma, wæpna.
Armamentarium, wæpna-hus.
Galea, leþer helm.
Cassis, iren helm.
Corona, diadema, cyne-helm.
Lorica, vel torax, vel squama, byrne.[2]
Gladius, vel machera, vel spata, vel framea, vel pugio, sweord.
Spatarius, swyrd-bora.
Armiger, wæpen-bora.
Signifer, vexillifer, tacn-bora.
Lancea, falarica, spere.
Venabulum, bar-spere, vel huntig-spere.
Sica, litel-sweord.
Capulum, hilte.
Mucro, swurdes ord
Intestinum bellum, necheburena gefeoht.
Civile bellum, burware gefeoht.
Asta, quiris, sceaft.
Vagina, sceað.
Manubrium, hæft and helfe.
Rasorium, scear-sex.
Novaculum, nægl-sex.
Faretra, coker.
Telum, sagitta, fla.[3]
Arcus, boga.
Anquina, bogen-streng.
Scutum, vel clipeus, vel parme. scyld.
Pelta, lytel scyld.
Umbo, rand-beh, vel bucula.

Funda, lyðre.
Fundabulum, stæf-liðere.
Classica, blæd-hornas.
Ensis, hilt-leas sweord.
Capulus, hilte.
Mucro, ælces wæpnes ord.
Machera, an-ecge sweord.
Pugio, vel clunabulum, lytel sweord, vel hype-sex.
Spolia, vel manubie, vel prede, herereaf.
Preda, reaflac.
Hasta, getridwet spere.
Hastilia, gafelucas.[4]
Contus, spere-leas sceaft.
Trudes, vel amites, spreotas.
Clava, vel cateia, vel teutona, anes cynnes gesceot.
Pila, gesceot.
Lancea, wigar.
Amentum, wegures gerið-spere.
Falarica, vel fala, wig-spere.
Telum, vel obeliscus, flaa.
Sagitta, vel spiculum, gefyðerad flaa.
Scorpius, gecettrad flaa.
Cuspis, sceaft.
Coriti, boge-fodder.
Theca, fodder.
Dolones, stæf-sweord.
Balista, gelocen boge.
Clipeus, testudo, scyld.
Ancile, win-tryndel, lytel scyld.
Peltæ, vel parmæ, þa læssan scyldas.

[1] In this chapter we have apparently a tolerably good account of the arms, offensive and defensive, of the Anglo-Saxon fighting men. The former are the sword and spear, bows and arrows for the archer, and slings; the latter are principally the shield, the helm, and the byrnie or coat of mail.

[2] The byrnie, or brunie, of early English poetry, where it seems to be used as a general term for the armour of the body—

The knyghtis redy on justers,
Alle y-armed swithe wel,
Bruny, and launce, and sword of stel.
Kyng Alisaundre, l. 1867.

[3] The word flo, for an arrow, was in use in the English language as late as the time of Chaucer.

[4] The *garelok* of the English of a later period. Thus we are told in one of the metrical romances—

Gavelokes also thike flowe
So gnattes, ichil avowe
Arthour and Merlin, p. 338.

Apex, summitas galeæ, helmes top.
Crista, helmes camb.
Conus, helmes byge.
Specula, sceawere.
Bipennis, twybill.
Caduceatores, vel pacifici, gesibbe ærendracan.
Præfeciales, gefeohtes bodan.

NOMINA XII. VENTORUM.[1]

Subsolanus, easten wind.
Auster, vel nothus, suþen wind.
Favonius, vel zephirus, westen wind.
Septentrio, norþan wind.
Vulturnus, eastan suþan wind.
Eurus, euroauster, norðan eastan wind
Euroafricus, suðan easten wind.
Africus, suðan westan wind.
Corus, norðan westan wind.
Circius, norðan easten wind.
Aquilo, vel boreas, norðan westann wind.

Spiracula, unclænra gasta wunungstow.
Baratrum, vorago profunda, ewie-susl, vel helelic deopnes.

Erebum, helle-sceað.
Stix, hele-mere.
Tartara, vel gehenna, helle-wite.
Infernus, helle.
Colonia, i. peregrinorum cultura, elelændra eorð-bigennys.
Municipium, burhscipe.
Vicus, wic.
Castellum, port.
Castrum, heah-fæsten.
Pagi, tun-stede.
Conciliabula, manna gegaderung.
Compita, ceorla samnung vel gemot-stow.
Platea, wid stræt.
Quintane, fifte dæl þære strete.
Murus, weal.
Menia, burh-weall.
Porta, port-geat.
Promurale, fore-burh.
Turris, stypel.
Propugnacula, wig-hus.
Arx, se hihsta wig-hus.
Cocleæ, adul-seaþe.[2]
Forus, vel prorostra, mot-stow on burge.
Curia, dom-hus.
Theatrum, wafung-stede.[3]

---

[1] This list of names of the points of the winds, is substantially the same as the list of Frankish names which Eginhard imagined to have been first given to the winds by Charlemagne. Ventis vero hoc modo nomina imposuit, ut subsolanum vocaret *ostroniwint*, eurum *ostsundroni*, euroaustrum *sundostroni*, austrum *sundroni*, austroafricum *sundwestroni*, africum *westsundroni*, zephyrum *westroni*, corum *west nordroni*, circium *nordwestroni*, septentrionem *nordroni*, aquilonem *nordostroni*, vulturnum *ostnordroni*. *Vit. Caroli Imp.*, p. 92, ed. *Teulet*. The writer of the manuscript of our Anglo-Saxon vocabulary has evidently made some confusion in copying the list, so as to leave one wind entirely out. It probably stood originally thus, which would agree exactly with the list and description given by Isidore, lib. xiii., c. 11·

Subsolanus, eastan wind.
Auster, vel nothus, suþan wind.
Favonius, vel zephirus, westan wind.
Septentrio, norþan wind.
Vulturnus, eastan norðan wind.]
Eurus, eastan suðan wind.
Euroauster, suðan eastan wind.
Austroafricus, suðan westan wind.
Africus, westan suðan wind.
Corus, westan norðan wind.
Circius, norðan westan wind.
Aquilo, norðan eastan wind.

[2] *Adul-seaþe*, or *adel-seaþe*, is a sewer or sink. *Cocleæ* is an evident error for *cloaca*.

[3] Literally, *a place for sights*, explaining the word according to its Greek derivation. This, and the translation of the following word (*syneweald wafung stede*, a circular place for sights),

Amphitheatrum, syneweald wafung-stede.
Farus, here-beac[n].
Coclea, windel-stan.
Circuitus ascensus, gewind.
Termas, vel gymnasium, bæð-stede.
Apodyterium, baðiendra manna hus, *i. domus qua vestimenta balneantium ponuntur,* þær hi hi unscredað inne.
Tabernæ, vel gurgustia, lytle hus of bredan.
Macellum, flæc-stræt, *vel* flæc-cyping.
Mercatum, ceping.
Teloneum, scipmanne myrt se ceping.
Apoditerium, breaw-ern.
Librarius, vel bibliopola, vel antiquarius, vel scriba, vel fenestella, wry-tere.
Festivitas, solempnitas, vel celebritas, vel ceremonia, freols-dæg.
Fasti, weorc-dagas.
Scena, vel tabernaculum, geteld.
Capitilavium, heafod-þweal.
Pedilavium, fot-þweal.
Cenum, miox.¹
Favilla, ysle.
Gleba, turf.
Labina, sliddor.
Volutabrum, sol, *vel* gesyd.
Uligo, moor.
Sabulum, molde.
Argilla, laam.
Samia, clæg.
Sulphur, swefel.
Alumen, efne.

Creta, vel cimola, hwit heard stan.
Creta argentea, spær-stan.
Bitumen, anes cynnes lim.
Arena, sand.
Agger, eorð-byre, *vel* geworht stræt, *strata vel delapidata.*
Vallum, scidwealles eorð-byri.²
Iter, vel itus, eað-fere weg.
Itiner, lang and stearc weg.
Actus, anes wænes gang-weg.
Via, twegra wæna gang-weg.
Publica via, ealles here-weg.
Privata via, tuun weg.
Semita, manna pað.
Callis, deora pað.
Tramites, wæter-weg.
Divortia, diverticula, mistlice woge wegas.
Compita, weg-gelæta.
Ambitus, twicen.
Orbita, wænes weð.
Limus, lutum, fenn.³
Rus, un-ered land.
Satio, seminatio, sædnað.
Fundus, þrop.
Alluvius ager, wæterig æcer.
Novalis ager, brocen land, *vel* geworht land.
Proscissio, land-openung.
Squalidus ager, forlætan æcer.
Uliginosus ager, fennig æcer.
Subcisiva, hryding.
Centuria, twa hund æcera.
Area, breda þiling, *vel* flor on to þerscenne.

show that our Anglo-Saxon forefathers were not acquainted with the uses of theatres and amphitheatres, and had no words in their language to express them.

¹ The Anglo-Saxon *miox,* or *meox,* dung, filth, is the origin of the provincial term *mixen,* a dunghill, and of the modern *muck.*

² Literally, an embankment for a wall of pa-lings; a curious mode of interpreting the Latin, which would seem to intimate that the *valla* which surrounded the Saxon camps or residences were always, or at least usually, crowned with palings, or timber fences.

³ The word *fen* preserved its original meaning of mud, in the English language, till at least the fifteenth century.

Pratum, mæd.
Fines, gemære.
Limites, hafud-land.
Decumanus, tioðe hafud-æcer.
Pertica, met-geard.
Porca, balc.
Miliarium, leouue, mile.
Passus, stæpe.
Stadium, furlang.
Diversorium, to-cir-hus, *vel* cumen-hus.
Hospitium, vel metatum, cumena wicung.
Prandium, undern-gereord.
Cena, æfen-gereord.
Merenda, non-mete.
Tabulatorium, wah-þyling.
Entheca, g., suppellex, in-eddisc, *vel* in-orf.
Canalis, þeote.
Tegulæ, imbrices, lateres, vel laterculi, hrof-tigla.
Silex, flint.
Scopulum, torr.
Spelea, spelunca, scræf.
Cautes, vel murices, scearpeste stanas.
Calculus, sæ-cysul.
Scrupulus, lytel stan.
Cos, hwet-stan.
Pumex, pumic-stan.
Calcisria, gebærdstan.[1]
Gagates, gagat-stan.
Pirites, vel focaris lapis, fyr-stan.
Specularis, þurhscyne stan.
Succinum, vel electrum, sap, smelting.
Flestria, gim þe bið on coches micga.[2]

Aurum obrizum, read gold.
Bractea, gylden læfr.
Pecuarius, feoh-strang man.
Pondus, vel pondo, gewyht, *vel* pund.
Dipondius, twegra pundra gewiht.
Trutina, wæga.
Lanx, scale.
Bilances, twa scale.
Examen, wæge-tunge.
Momentana, vel statam, wytle-wæga.
Campana, wul-wæga.

NOMINA TRITICI SUNT.

Frumentum, corn.
Scandula, twisld corn.
Farrago, grene berc-cræs.[3]
Spica, ear.
Arista, egla.[4]
Culmus, healm.[5]
Folliculus, codd.
Stipulæ, healmes laf.
Palea, ceaf.
Migma, æsceda.
Legumen, ofet.
Vicia, muse pise.

Caudex, vel codex, hrind.
Liber, seo inre hrind.
Spadones, unberende telgan.
Capreoli, vel cincinni, vel uncinuli, wingearda hocas þe hi mid bindað þæt him nehst bið.
Corimbi, wingearda hringa.
Præcoquæ, rædripe win-berige.
Ceraunie, reade win-berige.

---

[1] Somner conjectures that, in this article, the Latin should be *calx riva*, and the Anglo-Saxon *gebærn stan*, or *gebærned stan*.

[2] The precious stone, pretended, according to a legend of great antiquity, to be found in the maw or gizzard of a cock, is called by Pliny *alectoria* (from the Greek ἀλίκτωρ, a cock), and by Isidore *electria*. The latter word seems to have been corrupted by our compiler into *flestria*.

[3] *Cræs* is no doubt an error for *græs*.

[4] The beards of barley are still called *ails* in Essex.

[5] The straw of corn, as well as the stalks of many other plants, are still called *haulm* in many of our provincial dialects.

Aminea vitis, hwit win-geard.
Ablaqueatio, niderwart treowes delfing, bedelfing.
Putatio, screadung.
Cima, crop.
Propaginatio, win-twiga plantung.
Fossio, dicung.
Fossor, dikere.
Arbusta, iung treow, *vel* treow-stede.
Frutecta, plur., þyfelas.
Capreoli, wingearda gewind.
Aviaria, weglæsa beara, *secreta nemora*.
Recidiva, ed-growung.
Plantaria, gesawena plantan.
Plante, treowes sprancan.
Radix, wyrtrume.
Surculus, wæter-boh.
Virgultum, telgan.
Germen, berende boh.
Matura mors, ripe deað.
Immatura, unripe deað.
Fomes, geswælud spoon, *vel* tynder.
Præcoquus fructus, rædripe wæstm.
Ramnus, vel sentix ursina, þyfe-þorn.
Herbitum, orf-gebitt.
Crustumie, vel volemis, vel insana, vel melimendrum, healf reade peran.
Digladior, pugno, ic feohte.
Derogo, ic ofteo.
Derogatio, lehtrung.
Degenero, ic misðeo.
Derivo, ic gelæde.
Discludo, ic todæle.
Discriminatus, geglenged.

Saltus, hlyp.[1]
Luctatio, wraxlung.
Spectacula, vel ludicra, yppe, *vel* weard-steal.

Orcestra, vel pulpitus, gligmanna yppe.
Carceres, horsa steal.
Auriga, scrid-wisa, *vel* wænere.
Tragedi, vel comedi, unweorþe scopes.
Temelici, idel sangere.
Histriones, truþas.
Mimus, jocista, scurra, gligmon.
Pantomimus, gligman.
Saltator, tumbere.
Alea, tæfel.
Aleæ, tæfel-stanas.
Aliator, tæflere.
Pirgus, cynning-stan on tæfle.
Tessere, vel lepusculæ, feðerscite tæfel.
Tessella, lytle feþerscitte flor-stanas.
Pila, vel sfera, ðoþer.
Rogus, aad.
Strues, wude-fine.
Calones, wudigeras.
Mationes, stan-wyrhte.
Fistulæ, þeote.
Constructio, vel instructio, hyrdung.
Instructio, ealdere timbrunga bote.
Constructio, niwe timbrung.
Norma, wæter-pund.
Circinum, mæl-tange.
Centrum, mæl-tanges prica.
Epigri, vel clavi, nægles.
Perpendiculum, wealles rihtung-þred.
Commissura, borda gefeg.
Sectio, cliofung.
Serra, saga.

VESTIUM NOMINA.

Vestitus, hræglung.
Habitus, scruud.
Cultus, reaf.
Tunica, tunicæ.
Bombicinum, scolcen.

[1] After another intercalation from the alphabetical dictionary, the compiler now proceeds to give a rather brief list of games and amusements. Leaping and wrestling appear here as the principal gymnastic sports in use among the Anglo-Saxons.

Bombix, seolc-wyrm
Sericum, seolc.
Olosericum, eal seolcen.
Tramasericum, seolcen ab.[1]
Bissum, g., papagen, swiþe hwit fleax.
Lineum, linen.
Laneum, wyllen.
Linostema, linen wearp, *vel* wyllen ab.
Præsegmina, præcisiones, screadan.
Segmentata vestis, geræwen hrægel.
Pavidensis, þicce gewefen hrægel.
Levidensis, þenne gewefen hrægel.
Clarus, vel purpura, purpuren hrægel.
Polymita, feala-hiwes hrægel.
Ralla, vel rasilis, wogum bewerod hrægel.
Interpola vestis, geedniwod eald hrægel.
Panucla, geclutad hrægel.
Acupicta, vel frigia, gediht *vel* gesiwad hrægel.
Trilicis, þrylen hrægel.
Colobium, slef-leas scrud.
Levitonarium, slef-leas ancra scrud.
Lumbare, vel renale, lenden sid-reaf.
Linna, hnysce hwitel.
Renones, stiðe and ruge breost-rocces.
Birrus, unsmeðe hrægel.
Diplois, twifeld hrægel.
Melotes, vel pera, gæten *vel* broccen roc.
Anaboladium, vel sindo, linen heafodes wrigels.
Circumtectum, twyndyled reaf.
Trabea, cynelic reaf.
Paludamentum, cæseres reaf to gefeohte.
Regillum, vel peplum, vel palla, vel amiculum, ricerœ wife *vel* deorwurðe wæfels.
Timbria, fnado, *vel* læppan.

Stola, vel ricinum, orl.
Sipla, an healf hruh tæppet.
Stuppa, æcumbe.[2]
Tomentum, hnygela.
Platum, seolce hnygele.
Tinctura, deah.
Coccus, read deah.
Ferrugo, blac purpur.
Calathus, wearp-fæt.
Pensum, vel diarium, dægwine.
Infula, biscop-heafod lin.
Cidaris, vel mitra, hufe.
Diadema, bend agimmed and gesmiðed.
Nimbus, mid golde gesiwud bend.
Capitulum, vel capitularium, heafod-clað, *vel* cappa.
Antiæ, ear-loccas.
Monile, vel serpentinum, myne, *vel* sweor-beh.
Antrax, vel clavus, vel strophium, ang seta, *vel* gyrdel, *vel* agimmed gerdel.
Carbunculus, seo blace begne.
Fibula, preon, *vel* oferfeng, *vel* dalc.
Speculea, sceawere.
Periscelides, sceang-bendas.
Tinius, smeðe ringce.
Zona, vel zonarium, vel brachile, vel redimiculum, gyrdel.
Baltheus, swyrdes gyrdel.
Ungulus, agymmed hringe.
Samothracius, geheafdod hringce.
Subfibulum, vel subligaculum, under-hwrædel.
Fasciola, nosle, *vel* sar-claö.
Saccus, vel fiscus, kinges gafoles biger-del.
Saccellus, lytel sæc.
Marsupium, vel marsippa, seod.
Mastruga, crusne.
Clamis, hacele, *vel* fot-sið sticcel.

---

[1] The yarn of a weaver's warp is, I believe, still called an *abb*.

[2] What we now call *oakum*, *i. e.*, the hemp from old ropes.

Sagum, hwitel.
Toga candida, vel cretata, gehwit brægel.
Toga, sid-reaf swilce meteres wyrceð on anlicnysse.
Toga palmata, vel toga picta, sige-reaf.
Cinctus gabinus, twi-læpped scrud on twam healfan gescredde swa meteras metað on anlicnyssan.
Anelus, lytel hring.
Inauris, ear-preon, *vel* ear-ring.
Calamanca, hæt.

Accubitus, hnylung.
Affluentia, oferflowendnys.
Opulentia, metes genihtsumnys.
Epulæ, wist.
Dapes, keninga wist, *vel* estas.
Merendo, meridiendo, to middan dæge ic ete.
Fermentacius panis, gehafen hlaf.
Azimus, ðeorf.
Cibarius, ceorlisc hlaf.
Acrizimus panis, geseorid hlaf.
Siligeneus, vel triticeus, hwæten hlaf.
Subcinericius, vel focarius, heorð-bacen hlaf.
Clibanius, ofen-bacen hlaf.
Amolium, dust of ðæm . . . .
Frixius panis, gehyrst hlaf.
Simila, vel pollis, smedma.
Involucrum, gewynd.
Thorus genialis, bryd-bed.
Pluteus, brederes inneweard.
Sponda, ut-healf þæs beddes.
Lectica, bed-rest.
Storia, vel psiata, meatta.
Cama, sceort bed wið eorþan.
Bajunula, fer-bed.

Scabellum, vel subpedaneum, fot-scamul.
Scansilia, stapas, *vel* stirapas.
Cilindrus, scort sinewealt stan *vel* treow.
Pala, vel rentilabrum, wind-swingla.
Furcilla, litel forca.
Fisclum, ele-seocche.
Mensurnum opus, monðes weorc.
Funalia, rel funes, candel-weoca.
Lampas, candeles leoma.
Lucubrum, leohtes leohting.
Pira, upstandende here-beacn.
Rogus, bustum, forbærned [aad].
Farus, here-beacn.
Fictilia, vel samia, læmene fatu.[1]
Alsierina, readde læmene fatu.
Crisendeta, gyldena, *vel* gegylde fatu.
Celata, adrifene fatu.[2]

Cœlum, heofen.
Angelus, vel nuntius, encgel.
Archangelus, heah encgel.
Stella, steorra.
Sidus, tungel.
Sol, sunne.
Luna, mona.
Firmamentum, roder.
Cursus, ryne.
Mundus, middan-eard.
Tellus, terra, solum, vel arvum, eorþa.
Humus, rus, arvum, molde, *vel* land.
Mare, vel æquor, sæ.
Sinus, sæ-æbbung.
Oceanus, garsecg.
Mare eoum, east sæ
Mare arctoum, norð sæ.
Promuntorium, clif.

Patriarcha, heah-fæder.
Propheta, vel vates, witega.

---

[1] Earthen vessels, for which the Latin *Samia* is here used as a general term. In the next line, *Alsierina* is no doubt an error of the scribe for *Aretina.* See the chapter *de rasis escariis* in Isidori Etymolog., lib. xx., c. 4.

[2] *i. e.,* engraved or embossed vessels.

Apostolus, ærendraca.
Episcopus, biscop.
Archiepiscopus, arcebiscop.
Diœcesis, vel parochia, bisceop-scir, *vel* biscop-ric.
Rex, cyncg.
Regnum, rice.
Sceptrum, cyne-geard, cyne-dom.
Regina, cwen.
Imperator, vel Cæsar, vel Augustus, casere.
Imperatrix, vel Augusta, caseres wif.
Dux, heretoga, *vel* heorl.
Princeps, vel comes, ealdorman.
Fasces, ealdordomas.
Primas, heafodman, *vel* þegn.
Clito, æðeling.
Obses, gifel.
Satrapa, þegn.
Judex, vel censor, vel arbiter, dema.
Monachus, munuc.
Monacha, vel monialis, mynecenu.
Presbiter, mæsse-preost.
Sacellanus, hand-preost.
Sacerdos, sacerd, *vel* cyrc-þingere.
Clericus, preost, *vel* þingere.
Diaconus, vel levita, diacon.
Subdiaconus, under-diacon.
Archidiaconus, arce-diacon.
Eremita, westen-setla.
Anachoreta, ancra.
Nonna, arwurðe wurdewe, *vel* nunne.

Homo, man, *vel microcosmus*, læsse middaneard.[1]
Anima, sawl.
Animus, mod, *vel* geþonc.
Spiritus, gast.

Sensus, gewit.
Intellectus, andgit.
Cogitatio, geðanc.
Corpus, lichama.
Caro, flæc.
Vertex, hnol.[2]
Calvarium, forheafod, *vel* heafod-panne.
Anciput, forheafod.
Occiput, vel postex, æfteweard hæfod.
Sinciput, ofer healf heafod.
Coma, vel cirrus, locc unscoren.
Cerebrum, vel cerebellum, brægen.
Cesaries, fex.
Uncinus, locc.
Crines, wifmannes loccas.
Timpus, þunwang.
Facies, anwlita, *vel* neb.
Vultus, anwlita, *vel* rudu.
Species, hiw.
Visus, gesihð.
Tactus, repung, *vel* æthrin.
Auditus, hlyst.
Odor, odoratus, stenge.
Odor, breð.
Gustus, anbyrignys.
Sapor, swæcc.
Odor, olfactus, stenge.
Pili, hær.
Capilli, heafod-hær.
Comæ, loccas, *vel* uscoren hær.
Compago, gefeg.
Compages, gefcinega.
Frons, for-heafod.
Oculus, eage; *oculi*, eagan.
Supercilia, ofer-brua.
Cilia, brun.
Palpebræ, breawas.
Circulus, ðæs seo hringe.

[1] *Microcosmus*, derived from the two Greek words μικρὸς and κόσμος. *i.e.*, a little world, or the world in miniature, first applied metaphorically to the human frame by one of the Greek philosophers, was a favourite word with the mediæval writers to signify a man.

[2] We still use the word *noll*, in trivial speech, for the top of a man's head.

ARCHBISHOP ALFRIC'S VOCABULARY. 43

Pupilla, vel pupula, seo.
Yrqui, beah-hyrne, *vel* agneras; *volvos dicimus angulos oculorum.*
Præfolium, fel ufan eagan.
Intercilium, betwux oferbruan and bræwum.
Corona, vel circulus, wulder-beah.
Teuco, hring-ban ðæs eagan.
Lacryma, tear.
Luscus, scyl-egede.
Monoftalmus, an-egede.
Cæcus, blind.
Genæ, heoga-swind.
Malæ, hleor.
Maxilla, gewenge.
Mandibula, ceac-ban, *vel* ceacan, *vel* cin-ban.
Pinnula, ear-læppa, *vel* ufwaard earc.
Pinnulæ, flæran, *vel* ear-læppan.
Nasus, nosu.
Columna, eal ufweard nosu.
Nares, nosðyrla.
Internasus, vel interfinium, vel interpinium, nose-grystle, *vel* middel-flere.
Pirula, foreweard nosu.
Pinnulæ, uteweard nosterle.
Auris, eare.
Labium, ufeweard lippa.
Labrum, niðera lippe.
Rostrum, foreweard feng þære lippena togædere.
Lingua, vel plectrum, tunge, *vel* hearp-nægel.
Sublinguium, huf.
Dentes, teð.
Præcisores, fore-teð.
Canini, vel colomelli, mannes tuxas.
Molares, vel genuini, wang-teð.
Gingivæ, toða-flæsc.

Adversi dentes, ða eahta forworden teþ betwux tuxum.
Palatum, vel uranon, goma, *vel* hrof þæs muðes.
Collum, sweora, *vel* swura.
Fauces, brucan.
Arteriæ, wind-æddran.
Guttur, þrotu.
Mentum, cin.
Gurgulio, þrot-bolla.
Chautrum, eal þrot-bolla.
Rumen, wasend, *vel* edroc.[1]
Cervix, vel jugulum, hnecca.
Humerus, eaxla.
Ola, ufeweard exle ðe sæftran dæles.
Brachium, hearm.
Torus, vel musculus, vel lacertus, mus[cl] ðæs earmes.
Torosus, earm-strang.
Cuba, elboga.
Cubitum, fædm betwux elboga and handwyrste.
Palmus, span, *vel* hand-bred.
Ulna, eln, *vel* spanning betwux þuman and scite fingre.
Vola, vel tenar, vel ir, middeweard hand.
Pugillus, se gripe þære hand.
Palma, hand-bred.
Pugnus, fyst.
Artus, þa maran liða.
Ungula, hof.
Unguis, nægel; *ungues,* næglas.
Cartilago, gristle.
Impetigo, eagan wean, *vel* wearh-bræde.
Albugo, eag-flea.
Mentedra, vel oscedo, muð-adl on goman.
Ascella, vel subhircos, oxn, *vel* ruh-oxn.

[1] It must not be supposed that the words *wasend* and *edroc* are synonymous; but the compiler seems to have been doubtful whether the Latin word meant the weasand (*wasend*), or whether it was identical with the rather similar Latin word derived from it, *ruminatio.*

Cada, hrisel; *cadula,* lytel hrisel.
Lacertus, bog.
Digiti, fingras.
Pollex, ðuma.
Index, vel salutaris, scyte-finger.
Medius, vel impudicus, middel finger.
Medicus, vel annularis, gold-finger.
Auricularis, læce-finger.
Præcordia, fore-breost.
Pectus, breost.
Pectusculum, breost-ban.
Torax, foran-bodig, *vel* breost-beden.
Mamilla, tit.
Ubera, meolce-breost.
Papilla, titt-strycel.
Truncus, heafodleas bodig.
Cutis, vel pellis, hyd.
Corium, vel tergus, hyd.
Costa, rib.
Arvina, vel adeps, vel axungia, vel abdomen, hrysel, *vel* gelend, *vel* swind, *vel* swines-smere.
Pulpa, vel viscum, lira.
Os, ban.
Nervi, sinu.
Latus, side.
Pori, i. spiramenta unde sudor emanat, þic-þeotan, *vel* swat-þyrlu.
Ventriculus, mage.
Scapula, sculder.
Pale, gesculdre.
Interscapilium, middel gesculdru.
Dorsum, hrieg.
Tergum, bæc.
Vertigo, hwerfa.
Vertibulum, vel vertebra, hwer-ban.
Spondilia, geloda, *vel* gelyndu.
Sacra spina, lenden-ban neoþeweard.
Renes, vel lumbi, lendenu, *vel* hype-ban.

Catacrina, hype-ban.
Alvus, rif, *vel* seo inre wamb.
Matrix, uterus, wifmannes innoð, *vel* cild-hama.
Folliculus, cild-hama.
Secundæ, cild-hama.
Medulla, vel lecanica, mearh.
Omentum, fylmen.
Intestina, smæl-þearmas, *vel* inneweard.
Ilium, scare.
Ilia, smæle-þearmas.
Tolia, vel porunula, reada.
Extales, snædel, *vel* bæc-þearm.
Exta, midrif.
Umbilicus, navela.
Disseptum, midrif.
Clunes, hypas.
Nates, ears-lyre.
Anus, vel verpus, cars-þerl.
Crementum, weres-sæd, *vel* cið.
Vesica, blæddre.
Meatus, forðgang.
Veretrum, wepen-gecynd.
Genitalia, gecind-limu.
Femen, inneweard þeoh.
Coxa, þeoh.
Femur, utanweard þeoh.
Posteriora, bæce.
Cecum intestinum, æmuþa.
Suffragines, hamma.
Poples, hamm.
Renunculi, lund-lagan.
Crus, sceance; *crura,* sceanca.[1]
Genu, cneow.
Geniculi, cneow-wyrste.
Sura, spær-lira.
Tibia, scina, *vel* scin-ban.
Pes, fot.
Talus, ancleow.[2]

[1] The shank. When his subjects and contemporaries gave our first Edward the title of *Long-shanks,* they meant literally long legged, without supposing they were using any trivial or derogatory term.

[2] The ankle is still called *ankley* in Sussex;

ARCHBISHOP ALFRIC'S VOCABULARY.

Taxillus, lytel ancleow.
Plante, fot-welm.
Planta, foreweard fot.
Subtel, middel fot.
Calx, hoh-spor.
Solum, læst.
Viscera, beflagen flæc, *vel* innoþes innewearde.
Cor, heorte.
Bucleamen, heort-hama.
Jecor, lifre.
Pulmo, vel fecatum, vel pleumon, vel epar, lungen.
Splen, milte.
Rien, crop.
Lien, lund-laga.
Pulsus, clæppetung.
Fibræ, lifre-læppan, *vel* þearmas.
Fel, vel bilis, gealla.
Obligia, nytte.
Stomachus, maga.
Colus, roop.
Venter, seo utre wamb.
Cauliculus, fearh-hama.
Matrix, cwið, *vel* cild-hama.
Mentagra, tan.
Allox, micele tan.
Botrax, yce.
Mentera, bæd-þearm.[1]
Hermafroditus, wæpen-wifestre, *vel* scritta,[2] *vel* bæddel.
Hirniosus, healede.
Scamma in homine, se rude on þam men.
Glyppus, g., grymede.
Varix, cwydele, *vel* hwylca.
Cronculus, angseta.
Capitosus, mycel-heafdode.

Petilus, litel-fota.
Frontalis, vel calidus, steornede.
Ventriculosus, wæmbede.
Tergosus, earsode.
Genosus, cneowede.
Talaricus, cleonede.
Calcaneus, honede.
Surosus, spærlirede.
Mentagricus, tanede.
Mancus, woh-handede.
Peduncus, woh-fotede.
Podagricus, deagwyrmede, *vel* deaggede.
Flegmaticus, mældropiende.
Reumaticus, saftriende, *vel* drefliende.
Molaricus, swediende.
Plegus, earming.
Balbus, stamer.
Catax, heolt.
Blesus, wlisp.
Surdus, vel surdaster, deaf.
Debilis, vel enervatus, lame.
Strabus, scyl-eagede.
Lippus, sur-eagede.
Unimanus, an-hende.
Æger, vel ægrotus, adlig.
Morbus, adl.
Paraclitus, bed-rida.
Clinicus, hof-rede.
Ulcerosus, hreofla.
Leprosus, lic-þrowere.
Lunaticus, monað-seoc.
Demoniacus, deofol-seoc.
Energumenus, gewit-seoc.
Elisa mens, vel dejecta, forscrenct.
Demens, gemendleas.
Rabidus, vel insanus, wod.
Rabies, wodnys.
Freneticus, se þe for sleape awed.

and the word *anclow* continued in use in the English language till the fifteenth century.

[1] *Mentera*, should perhaps be *entera*, or *exentera*; and *bæd* appears to be a mere error of the copyist for *bæc*. The process of forming *t, c*, and *d*, was so similar, that they are often confounded.

[2] The old English word *scrat*, which meant similarly a hermaphrodite.

Lethargus, ungelimplice slapfulnys.
Vigil, vel vigilans, wacul.
Pervigil, þurh-wacul.
Vigilia, wecen.
Incolumis, gesund.
Enervis, mægenleas.
Lotium, þweal.
Urina, micga.
Minctio, miggung.
Exugium, micgern.
Callus, ile.
Viscum, gerunnen blod.
Menstrua, monað-blod.
Fantasma, vel fantasia, gedwimor.
Pituita, i. minuta saliva, horas, *vel* hræcunda, *vel* spatlung.
Pitisso, ic spatlige.
Evomitio, spiwinge.
Oscitatio, ganung.
Singultus, siccitung.
Sternutatio, vel sternutamentum, snytinge, *vel* sneosung.
Spiratio, eðung.
Pedatio, feorting.
Fesciculatio, fisting.
Sibilatio, hwistlung.
Pluvicinatio, stanc.
Pluvicino, ic stancrige.

NOMINA COLORUM.

Color, bleoh.
Albus, hwit.
Amineus, vel albus, hwit.
Subalbus, healf-hwit.
Niger, blac.
Ater, teter, sweart.
Unicolor, anes bleos.
Bicolor, twi-hiwe.
Discolor, mistlic bleo.
Varius, vel discolor, fah.
Viridis, grene.
Busius, fealu.
Dosinus, vel cinereus, asse-dun.
Bruntus, wann.
Balidinus, hryte.
Avidius, grinu.
Natius, dun.
Gilvus, geolu hwit.
Cervinus, dun-falu.
Myrteus, bleo-reod.
Glaucus, greg.
Elbus, deorce græg.
Guttatus, cylu.
Roseus, vel rubeus, vel pheniceus, read.
Perseus, blæwen.
Succinaceus, vel croceus, vel flavus, geolu.
Ceruleus, sweart.
Limpidus, scir.

Doctor, vel imbutor, vel eruditor, lareow.
Discipulus, vel mathites, leorning-cniht.
Disciplina, lar, *vel* steor.
Doctrina, lar.
Dogmatista, lareow.
Pædagogus, cilda-hyrde, *vel* lareow.
Documentum, vel specimen, lar-bysn.
Scolasticus, vel cliens, scol-man.
Curaxatio, gewrit.
Epistola, vel pitacium, ærend-gewrit.
Quaternio, cine.
Planca, spelt.
Diploma, bod on cine.
Membrana, boc-fel.
Scedula, ymle.
Sceda, screade.
Graphium, vel scriptorium, græf.
Pictor, metere.
Pictura, metinge.
Minium, read teafor.[1]

---

[1] This word is still preserved among the peasantry in various parts of England in the form

ARCHBISHOP ALFRIC'S VOCABULARY. 47

Gluten, lim to fugele.[1]
Glara, eg-lim.
Incaustum, vel atramentum, blæc.
Sculptor, vel celator, græfere.
Sculptura, græft.
Agalma, vel iconisma, vel idea, anlicnes.
Scalprum, vel scalpellum, vel cœlum, græf-sex.
Ingenium, orðanc.
Artifex, cræftica.
Opifex, wyrhta.
Architectus, yldest wyrhta.
Aurifex, gold-smið.
Argentarius, seolfer-smið.
Ærarius, mæstlinc-smið.
Nummularius, mynetere.
Palatium, kynelic-botl.
Thesaurus, gold-hord.
Gazophilacium, madm-hus.
Ædificium, getimbrung.
Basis, post.
Postis, vel fulcimentum, sylle.
Forus, vel prorostra, mot-stow.
Logotheta, gemot-man.
Negotium, intinga.
Negotiatio, cypinge.
Sacramentum, vel mysterium, geryna, *vel* digla.
Testimonium, gewitnes, *vel* gecyðnes.
Recompensatio, edlean.
Dispendium, vel damnum, vel detrimentum, hynð, *vel* lyre, *vel* hearm.
Commodum, questus, hyð, *vel* freme.
Commutatio, gehwearf.
Nihil, nanwiht.
Nihili, naht.

Fronimus, wis.
Prudens, snotor.
Sagax, vel gnarus, vel astutus, vel callidus, petig, *vel* abered.
Frugi, vel parcus, uncystig.
Largus, vel dapsilis, cystig.
Famosus, vel opinosus, hlisful.
Sophus, vel sophista, wis.
Sophista, wite.
Insipidus, ungeræd.
Stultus, stunt.
Stultomalus, yfel-dysig.
Impudens, scamleas.
Tenax, fæsthafel.
Falcidicus, vel falsiloquus, unsoð-sagul.
Avarus, vel cupidus, gitsere.
Raptor, vel prædo, vel spoliator, reafere.
Fallax, vel mendax, swicol.
Planus, vel seductor, swica.
Eloquium, vel dictio, sagn.
Empiria, manega embe-smeagunga.
Emunctoria, candel-twist.
Ephemerides, numerus quotidianus, gerim.
Emeritus, provectus, geþungen.
Epithalamium, carmen nubentium, gift-leoð.

NOMINA NAVIUM.

Navis, vel faselus, scip.
Rates, scipu.
Naviscella, vel cimba, vel campolus, vel musculus, sceort scip.
Scapha, vel trieris, litel scip, *vel* sccigð.
Linter, bat.
Pontonium, punt.[2]

---

tiver, applied to a composition of tar and red ochre, which is used to mark sheep, or to colour wood, and protect it against the effects of exposure to weather.

[1] The compiler of the vocabulary has mistaken the Latin word *gluten* to signify here *bird-lime,* instead of glue.

[2] It is hardly necessary to say that the word *punt,* as a name for a sort of boat, is as well known among us in the present day, as it was among the Anglo-Saxons in the tenth century. It will be remarked how many of the Anglo-Saxon words, connected with shipping, have been preserved in our navy.

Carabus, scipincel.
Littoraria, troh-scip.
Carina, scipes botm.
Nauclerus, scipes hlaford.
Proreta, ancor-man.
Gubernator, steor-man.
Gubernio, steora.
Nauta, roþer.
Remex, reþra.
Puppis, steor-setl.
Remus, steor-roþer.[1]
Prora, anfer-setl, *vel* forscip.
Trudes, spreotas.[2]
Transtra, scip-setl.
Trastra, vel juga, þofta.
Palmula, roþres blæd.
Antenna, segel-gyrd.[3]
Cornua, segel-gyrde endas.
Malus, vel artemo, mæst.
Portisculus, vel hortator remigum, scip-hamor.
Anchora, vel saburra, ancra.
Velum, segel.
Dalum, lytel segel.
Rudentes, scip-rapas.
Propes, fot-rap.
Plagæ, net-rapas.
Verriculum, dræg-net.[4]
Nassa, boge-net, *vel* leap.
Cassis, deor-net.
Conopeum, fleoh-net.

[1] The rudder.
[2] Sprits — preserved especially in the term bow-sprit.
[3] The yards.
[4] As the ordinary ships were used especially for fishing, the compiler goes on naturally enough to speak of nets, with which he concludes rather abruptly.

SUPPLEMENT TO ALFRIC'S VOCABULARY,[1]

(TENTH OR ELEVENTH CENTURY.)

Reus, scyldig.
Damnatus, fordemed.
Hosticus, vel hostilis, feondlic.
Osor, feond.
Facinus, maan.
Pejero, ic forswerige.
Gibborosus, vel strumosus, hoferede.
Profanus, manful.
Exosus, perosus, ansæte.
Callidus, geap.
Versutus, hindergeap.
Simulator, hiwere.
Fictor, vel hipocrita, liccetere.
Adulator, vel favisor, liffetere.
Adulatio, liffetung.
Deceptor, bepæcend.
Seductor, læfend.
Proditor, læwend.
Delator, wroht-bora.
Patricida, fæder-slaga.

Parricida, mæg-slaga.
Cicatrix, dolh-swað.
Soma, lichama.
Truncus, heafodleas bodig.
Funus, lic, *vel* hreaw.
Feretrum, bære.[2]
Mausoleum, vel bustum, kyninga byrgen.
Sarcofagum, þruh.[3]
Unguina, vel unguenta, smyrels, *vel* sealfi
Redas, vel deces, vel piger, slaw.
Infidus, ungetreowe.
Injuriosus, teonful.
Contentiosus, geflitful.
Impiger, vel propes, unslæw.
Lentus, vel piger, sleac.
Conciliabulum, gemot-stow.
Consulo tibi, ic ræde þe.
Consulo te, ic frine þe.
Consiliatio, gesib-sumung.

---

[1] This Vocabulary is said to have been found, as a sort of Supplement to the former, following it in the same manuscript, but with some intervening matter of another description It seems, indeed, to have been the design of the compiler to give at more length some classes of words which are given less numerously in the vocabulary of Alfric, such as those belonging to the family and domestic relations, some classes of natural phenomena, naval terms, the names of various classes of buildings in use among the Romans, and a few words connected with the ancient religious belief. Many words found in Alfric's vocabulary are repeated, but sometimes with variations in the interpretation, which are not without interest.

[2] A bier.

[3] This word, which is of common use in Anglo-Saxon, and is evidently connected with the modern *trough*, was preserved in the old English words *throh, thrugh,* and *thuruc,* signifying a coffin. A flat gravestone is still called a *through* in the dialects of the north of England.

Consiliator, ræd-gifa.
Concilio, ic gesibbige.
Concionor, vel meditor, vel precor, ic smeage.
Judex, vel consul, ealdorman.
Censor, vel arbiter, dema.
Mas, hys cild.
Sexus, werhad, *vel* wifhad.[1]
Conjunx, gemæcga.[2]
Conjuges, vel conjugales, gesinhiwan.
Conjugium, vel matrimonium, gesinscipe.
Complex, vel consentiens, gegada.
Complices, conspirantes, gegadan, *vel* geþwærniende.
Incestus, vel impurus, unclæne.
Ancilla, serva, abra, vel dula, g., wyln.
Servus, dulus, g., þeowa.
Emptitius, geboht þeowa.
Verna, vel vernaculus, inberdling, *vel* fostorling.
Alumnus, foster-fæder.
Præpositus, fore-set, *vel* gerefa.
Fatigatus, atered.
Exercitatus, acostnod.
Populus, folc, *vel* byre-treow.
Exercitus, here.
Procinctus, fyrdinge.
Edictum, geban.
Apparatus, gearcung.
Vulgus, vel plebs, ceorlisc folc.
Heros, hlaford.
Congregatio, concio, gegaderung.
Conventus, conventio, gesamnung.
Arrabo, wedlac.
Clitus, vel clientulus, cniht.
Ephebus, vel buteo, beardleas.

Galos, glos, swere swuster.
Sponsalia, brytofta, *vel* brydgifa.
Procus, wogere.
Sponsus, brydiguma.
Pronuba, hadswape.
Sponsa, bryd.
Paranymphus, hadswape.
Infans, vel alogos, g., unsprecende cild.[3]
Paranymphus, brydguma, *vel* dryht-ealdor.
Unicuba, anligere wifman.
Uxoratus, þe wif hæfð.
Nympha, bryt.
Derelicta, laf, *vel* forlæten wif.
Privignus, steop-cild.
Anula, vel vetula, eald wif.
Adolescens, vel investis, vel investiceps, geong man.
Pubetenus, frum-byrdling.
Pecuniosus, feoh-strang.
Locuples, land-spedig.
Gamos, bryd.
Egenus, wædla.
Zeno, wemere, *vel* tihtere.
Telonearius, tolnere, *vel* tollere.
Profugus, flyma.
Erul, utlaga.
Hebes, dwæs, *vel* sott.
Hebetudo, dwæsnys, *vel* sotscipe.
Edax, vel glutto, frettol.
Vorator, grædig.
Ambro, gifere, *vel* frec.
Frocax, vel pervicax, gemah.
Procacitas, vel pervicacia, gemahnys.
Cachinnatio, ceahhetung, *vel* cincung.
Hilaris, glædman.

---

[1] It is curious that the Anglo-Saxon language seems to have had no abstract term for *sex*, which was expressed only severally as manhood or womanhood.

[2] The old English word *make*, applied either to husband or wife.

[3] The compiler of the vocabulary has translated the Greek word *alogos*, rather than the Latin *infans*. The latter, however, is explained by Isidore, lib. xi., c. 2, thus—Infans dicitur homo primæ ætatis, dictus autem infans, quia adhuc fari nescit, id est, loqui non potest; nondum enim bene ordinatis dentibus, minor est sermonis expressio

SUPPLEMENT TO ALFRIC'S VOCABULARY. 51

Tristis, unrot, *vel* gealh.
Mœstus, vel mœrens, dreorig.
Fames, vel popina, hunger.
Derisio, tæl-hlehter.
Tripudium, gefea.
Rancor, anda.
Abstinentia, syfernys.
Abstinens, syfer.
Cura, cara.
Obesus, ofer-fæt.
Pinguedo, smyltnys.
Crassitudo, fætnys.
Corpulentus, ðiccul.
Grossus, græat.
Macer, hlæne.
Macilentus, ðynnul.
Macies, vel tabitudo, hlænnes.
Gracilis, vel exilis, vel subtilis, smæl.
Exiguus, gehwæde.
Irsutus, vel ispidus, ruh.
Validus, vel vegetus, trum.
Invalidus, unstrang.
Inbecillis, wanhal.
Sollicitus, ymb-hedig.
Curiosus, carful.
Securitas, karleasnes.
Studium, bigegnes, *vel* smeagung.
Causa, vel negotium, intinga.
Obstinatus, pertinax, anwilla.
Obstinatio, pertinacia, anwilnes.
Verecundus, vel pudens, scamfæst.
Pudicus, sideful.
Impudicus, unsideful.
Castus, clæne.
Incestus, unclæne.
Exilium, wræc-sið.
Feregrinatio, ælðeodignes.
Prohemium, ðurhlocung.
Præfatio, forespæc.
Reconciliatio, edþingung.
Pacificatio, gesibsumung.
Relegatus, wide asent.

Religatus, vel vinculatus, gewriðen.
Deportatus, to wite asent butan his gode.
Exterminator, ut-dræfere.
Exterminatus, ut-adrifen.
Expers, dælleas.
Exsors, or-hlita.
Pater, fæder.
Mater, moder.
Avus, ealde-fæder.
Patruus, fædera.
Matertera, moddrige.
Avia, ealde-moder.
Proavus, þridde fæder.
Proavia, þridde moder.
Abavus, feowerþe fæder.
Abavia, feowerþe moder.
Tritavus, fifte fæder.
Tritavia, fifte moder.
Familia, hyred.
Propago, cynren.
Generatio, encores.
Soboles, vel proles, bearn, *vel* cnosl, *vel* tudder.
Filius, sunu.
Filia, dochtor, dohter.
Liberi, freobearn, *vel* æðelborene cild.
Soror, suster.
Filiaster, step-dohter.
Frater, broþer.
Nepos, suna sune, *vel* broder sune, *vel* suster sune, þæt is nefa.
Neptis, broðer dochter, *vel* suster dohter, nefene, þridde dohter.
Abnepos, feowerþe sune.
Abneptis, feowerðe dohter.
Adnepos, fifte sune.
Adneptis, fifte dohter.
Trinepos, sixte sune.
Trineptis, sixte dohter.
Agnati, fædern magas.
Cognati, meddern magas.
Propinquus, mæs, *vel* gesibling.

SUPPLEMENT TO ALFRIC'S VOCABULARY.

Patrueles, fæderan sunan.
Matrueles, moddrian sunan.
Fratres, gebroþru, vel gelodan, *vel* siblingas.
Fratres patrueles, fæderon sunan.
Consobrini, gesustrenu.
Sobrini, geswusterenu bearn.
Socer, sweor.
Socrus, sweger.
Gener, aþum.
Nurus, snoru.
Vitricus, vel patraster, steop-fæder.
Privignus, steop-sunu.
Patruus meus, min fædera.
Patruus meus magnus, mines fæderan fæder.
Propatruus meus, mines fæderan eldre fæder.
Abpatruus meus, mines fæderan þridde fæder.
Amita mea, min faðu.
Amita mea magna, minra faða moder.
Proamita mea, minre faþan yldre moder.
Abamita mea, minra faþan þridde moder.
Avunculus meus, min eam.
Avunculus meus magnus, mines eames fæder.
Proavunculus meus, mines eames yldre fæder.
Abavunculus meus, mines eames þridde fæder.
Matertera mea, min moddrige.
Matertera mea magna, minre moddrige moder.
Promatertera mea, minre moddrian eldre moder.
Abmatertera mea, minre moddrian þridde moder.
Pronuba, hadswæpa; *ipsa est et paranimpha*.

Fratrissa, brodor wif.
Levir, tacor, i. frater mariti.
Janitrices, gebroþre wif.
Conjuges, gemæccan.
Nupta, beweddod.
Innuba, unbeweddod.
Conjugium, vel connubium, gesynscipe.
Contubernium, gegadorwist.

Annus, gear.
Tempus, tid.
Cursus, ryne.
Arcus, bigels.
Iris, ren-boga.
Pluvia, ren.
Ninguidus, besniwod.
Tonitruum, vel tonitrus, þunor.
Fulgor, vel fulmen, ligit.
Nix, snaw.
Niveus, snaw-hwit.
Nivalis, snawlic.
Grando, hagol.
Gelu, forst.
Pruina, hrim.
Glacies, is.
Glacialis, forstlic.
Aer, lyft.
Æther, hroder.
Ventus, wind.
Nubes, wolc.[1]
Aura, hwiþa, *vel* reder.
Nimbus, scur.
Nebula, mist, *vel* genip.
Procella, storm.
Imber, færlic ren.
Ros, deaw.
Lux, leoht.
Tenebræ, vel furfuraculum, ðystru.
Seculum, woruld.
Ærum, yld.
Dies, dæg.

[1] The origin of the modern *welkin*.

SUPPLEMENT TO ALFRIC'S VOCABULARY. 53

Caligo, dimnes.
Mane, ær myrgen.
Crepusculum, tweone leoht, *vel* deorcung.
Conticinium, vel gallicinium, hancred.
Intempestum, vel intempesta nox, midniht.
Maligna lux, vel dubia, tweonul-leoht.
Matutinum, uhten-tid.
Diluculum, dægred.
Aurora, dægrima.
Prima, prim.
Tertia, undern.
Sexta, mid-dæg.
Nona, non.
Suprema, ofer-non, oððe geloten dæg.
Vesperum, æfen.
Serum, bed-tid.
Hora, tid.
Horoscopus, tid-sceawere.
Ebdomada, vel septimana, wucu.
Mensis, monað.
Ver, lencten.[1]
Æstas, sumor.
Autumnus, hærfest.
Hyems, winter.
Vernalis dies, lengtenlic dæg.
Ver novum, foreweard lencten, *vel* middewærd lencten.
Ver adultum, æfterwærd lencten. *Eodem modo et œstas et autumnus vocantur,* on þa ylcan wisan sumor and hærfest bioð gecigede.
Æstivus dies, sumorlic dæg.
Autumnalis dies, hærfestlic dæg.
Hiemalis dies, winterlic dæg, *vel nox,* oððe niht.

Pridie, vel esternum, æren-dæg.
Postpridie, to-dæg.
Postperendie, ofer þrige [dæg].
Centurias, getalu, *vel* heapas, *vel* hundredu.
Kalendæ, geheald-dagas, *vel* halige dagas.
Nonæ, ceap-dagas.
Idus, swæsing-dagas, *ab edendo dicuntur.*
Æquinoctium, em-niht.
Frigus, cyle.
Calor, hæte.
Æstus, vel cauma, swoloð.[2]
Fervor, hæte micel.
Siccitas, vel ariditas, drugaþe.
Humor, vel mador, wæte.
Sterilitas, vel infœcunditas, unwestmbærnys.
Fertilitas, westmbærnys.
Ubertas, genyhtsumnys.

Campus, feld.
Planities, smeþnys.
Æquor, brym, sæ.
Pascua, læs.
Pratum, mæd.
Ager, æcer.
Compascuus ager, gemæne læs.
Seges, gesawen æcer *vel* land.
Via, weg.
Bivia, vel bivium, twi-weg.
Trivium, wege-læton.
Iter, siðfæt.
Invium, compitum, weg-gedal.
Invium, ungefere *vel* wegleas pæð.
Desertum, vel heremus, westen.

---

[1] *Lenten,* or *Lent,* remained long in the English language in its original signification of *Spring.* Thus, in a lyric composition of the thirteenth century, (printed in my *Lyric Poetry of the Thirteenth Century,* p. 43,) the approach of Spring is described as follows:

> Lenten ys come with love to toune,
> With blosmen ant with briddes roune,
> That al this blysse bryngeth.

[2] Hence our modern word *swelter.*

SUPPLEMENT TO ALFRIC'S VOCABULARY.

Patria, eard.[1]
Pagus, tun.
Provincia, scir.
Mons, munt.
Tumulus, beorh.
Collis, hyll.
Monticellus, beorh ufeweard.
Vallis, dene.
Diluvium, flod.
Vadum, ford.
Pons, bricg
Aqua, wæter.
Limpha, hluttor wæter.
Gutta, vel stilla, dropa.
Stagnum, mere.
Amnis, ea mid treowum ymbset.
Flumen, flod, *vel* yrnende ea.
Fluvius, singal-flowende ea.
Ripa, stæð.[2]
Rivus, rið.
Latex, burna.
Torrens, broc.
Unde, eð.
Litus, strand.
Crepido, brerd, *vel* ofer.
Alveus, stream, *vel* stream-racu.
Rivulus, lytel rið.
Fluctus, wealcynde ea.
Fons, well.
Latex, wel-spreng.
Lacus, vel lacuna, seað.
Harena, sand-cesel.
Spuma, fam.
Gurges, wæl.
Abyssus, deopnys.
Vortex, edwinde.
Vorago, swelgend.
Vivarium, fiscpol.

Euripus, vel piscina, fiscpol.
Una serra, an gerif fisca.
Saltus, holt
Solum, vel tellus, vel terra, vel arvum, land.

Aporiamur, we synd bereafod.
Bonis nostris, urum godum.
Pessime, luþerlice.
Reprehensibiliter, tallice.
Non mihi est cordi, nis me on geþance, *vel* on mode.
Non animadverto, ic ne understande.
Non mihi occurrit, ne com hit me ongean.
Persuadeo, ic lære.
Collatio, word-mittung, *vel* word-somnung.
Imperito, ic wealdige, *vel* oferbebeode.
Pecuniosus, welig.
Colorare, hiwian.
Affabre, cræftlice, *vel* smicere.
De popularibus, of beorh-leodum.
Venusto, ic cyrtenlæce.
Orno, ic smicere geglengce.
Obumbro, ic ofersceadewige.
Habilis conjunctio, gedafenlic seodnys.
Prærogativa, frum gifu, *vel* synder wurðmynt.
Ruminatio, ciwung, *vel* edroc, *vel* aceocung.
Runia, vel paleare, fræt-læppa.
Singultus, geocsung.
Sarpta vinea, gescreaded wingeard.
Scorteus, leðern.
Porus, vel spiramentum, orðung.
Usus, nyttung, *vel* þearf, *vel* gewuna.
Delinimentum, stracung, *vel* olæcung.

---

[1] In the Latin writers of the close of the Roman empire of the West, the word *patria* had come into use in the mere meaning of a land or province, as it is explained here.

[2] The more modern *stade*, or *staith*, which is still used in some parts of the country in the signification of a bank of a river, or, in some places, of a wharf or quay.

SUPPLEMENT TO ALFRIC'S VOCABULARY.

Lepida, vel facunda, getingce.
Splendida, vel ornata, beorht.
Exagonum, six-ecge.
Sexangulatum, six-hernede.
Insusurrare, i. occulte detrahere, diglice tælan.
Diverticulum, weg-twiflung.
Compitum, wega gemittung.
Ancillantur, hyrsumiað.
Formulantur, þeowiað.
Sinuatio, besining.
Anfractus, abrocen land, *vel* hilces.
Inprovida, vel inconsiderata, unbesceawode.
Summatim, breviter, vel commatice, sceortlice.
Obsurduit, adeafede.
Volubile scema, sinewealt gesceap.
Globositas, sinewealtnes.
Semirotundum, healf-sinewealt.
Fœnerata domino, gode on borgh geseald.
Scema locutionis, spece wise.
Fabulositas, spellung.
Anilis fabula, ealdra cwena spell.
Sermo commentitius, gesmead spræc.
Aquarum alluvio, wætera gewæsc
Defecatio, vel purgatio, hlyttrung.
Omne genus holitorum, i. holerum, æghwylc wyrt-cyn.
Omne genus arbustorum, æghwilc treow-cyn.
Omne genus seminarum, æghwilc sædcyn.
Zizania, laser.
Lolium, boþen. *et cetera adulterina genera,* and oðre lyðre-cynn.
Cophinus, wilige, *vel* leap.
Conversantur, vel commorantur, samod wuniað.
In procinctu, to gefeohte.
Promptus, gearu.

Specula, vel conspicilium, weard-steal.
Præruptum, henge-clif.
Spectaculum, wæfð, *vel* wæfer-syn, *vel* wafung.
Idioma, proprietas linguæ, agen *vel* gecynde spræc.
Idiota, ungelæred.
Imperitus, ungleaw.
Inportunus, gemah.
Petitiosus, bedul.
Eculeus, vel catasta, wæarh-rod, *vel* þrypeluf.
Distractio, ceap.
Venditio, sala.
Contractio, vel contractus, næmingce.

NOMINA PISCIUM.

Balena, vel cete, vel cetus, vel pistrix, hwæl.
Cetarius, hwæl-hunta.
Delphin, vel bocharius, vel simones, mere-swin.
Rombus, styria
Lupus, vel scardo, bærs.
Gobio, blæge.[1]
Murena, vel murina, vel lampreda, mere-næddra.
Murenula, tigle.
Mulus, vel mugilis, heardra.
Platesia, facg.
Esocius, vel salmo, lex.
Sparus, ðunor-bodu.
Lucius, hacod.
Tinca, sliw.
Tructa, truht.
Capito, myne, *vel* ælepute.
Turnus, forn.
Rocca, scylga.
Cancer, crabba.
Foca, seol.

---

[1] The modern *bleak*, called in some parts a *blay*.

SUPPLEMENT TO ALFRIC'S VOCABULARY.

Musculus, hran.[1]
Polypus, loppestre.
Allec, vel jairus, vel taricius, vel sardina, hæring.
Pansor, floc.
Fannus, reohhe.
Sepia, cudele, *vel* wase-scite.
Conchæ, vel cochleæ, scille, *vel* sæ-snæglas.[2]
Murice, vel conchyleum, weluc.[3]
Nassa, æwul, *vel* boga-net.

NOMINA NAVIUM, ET INSTRUMENTA EARUM.

Linter, bat.
Ratis, scip.
Navicula, scippincel.
Trieris, sceið.
Ypogavus, horsa scip.
Nauta, gereðru.
Nauclerus, scip-hlaford.
Gubernator, steora.
Gubernio, steor-man.
Aplustre, gereþru, *vel* scip-getawu.
Archiromacus, swift-scip.
Myoparo, hið-scip.
Barca, flot-scip.
Liburna, hulc.[4]
Dromo, æsc, *vel* barð.
Pontonium, flyte.
Caudex, punt.
Paro, sceaþena scip.
Trabaria, an-byme scip.
Littoraria, vel tonsilla, troh-scip.
Cumba, vel caupolus, þurruc.

Scalpus, scip, *vel* seig.
Cimba, vel carina, scipes botm.
Musculus, sceort scip.
Celox, flot-scip.
Parunculus, pleg-scip.
Fori, scipes flor.
Struppus, strop, *vel* ar-wiððe.
Palmula, ar-blæd.
Antenna, vel temo, segel-gyrd.
Cornua, þa twegen endas þære segl-gyrde.
Transtra, þoftan.
Clavus, helma.
Artemon, vel malus, mæst.
Parastates, mæst-twist.
Proreta, ancer-man.
Gubernaculum, steor-sceofl.[5]
Ponsis, scip-hlædder.
Velum, segl.
Naulum, scip-tol.
Cavernamen, pranga.
Acateon, se mæsta segl.[6]
Epidromas, se medemesta segl.
Dalum, se lesta segl.
Pulvini, slidor.
Puppis, steor-setl.
Anguina, cops.
Prora, ancer-setl.
Funes, vel restes, rapas.
Porticulus, hamor.
Spiræ, linan.
Sipara, anes fotes segl.
Propes, sceac-line.
Safon, stæð.

[1] *Hran*, or *hron*, is usually interpreted as meaning a whale. In the Anglo Saxon writers, the sea was termed poetically *hron mere*, the whale's pool, *hron rad*, the whale's road, *hrones-bað*, the whale's bath, &c.

[2] *Sæ-snægl*, sea-snail, appears to have been the common name for shell-fish. I believe the term is still in use among our American brethren.

[3] *Weluc*, the modern word whelk.

[4] Our modern name *hulk*, for the body of the ship.

[5] Literally, the ship-shovel, the rudder.

[6] Perhaps we may conclude from this, and the two following words, that the ordinary Anglo-Saxon ships had only three sails, as here named —the large sail, the middle sail, and the small sail; but these names may be only an attempt to explain the Latin words, by describing what they meant in the want of equivalent terms.

SUPPLEMENT TO ALFRIC'S VOCABULARY. 57

Rudentes, scip-rapas.
Opisfera, seding-line.
Pronesium, mærels-rap.
Tonsilla, scip-mærls.
Remulcus, toh-line.
Strupiar, midla.
Bolidis, sund-gyrd.
Cataprorates, sund-line.
Æstuaria, fleotes-tonette.
Æstus, recessus et accessus maris, yst.
Ledona, nep-flod, *vel* ebba.
Malina, heah-flod.
Remex, reþra.
Peeris, geara feng.
Uncini, hocas.
Trudes, spreotas.
Accessus, flod.
Recessus, ebbe.
Syrtes, sand-rid.
Reuma, ebbe, *vel* gyte-stream.
Plagæ, net-rapas.
Tragum, vel verriculum, dræge.
Nassa, boge-net.
Conopeum, fleoh-net, *vel* micg-net.
Labrum, margo, vel crepido, stæð, *vel* brerd.
Loramentum, vel tormentum, wiððe.

Lasciva, gagol.
Allugo, fyne.
Alluginatus, fynig.[1]
Numisma, scylling.
Mensularius, pennig-hwyrfere.
Collybista, pennig-mangere.

Trapezita, vel monetarius, mynetere.
Paracaraximus, flas pennig.
Folles, dyneras.
Procuratio, scir.
Procurator, scir-man.
Proconsul, heh-gerefa.
Curator, gerefa.
Augur, vel ariolus, wicca.
Sortilegus, tan-hlytere.
Advocatus, patronus, vel interpellator, forspeca, *vel* mundbora.
Apologia, ladung.
Apologeticus, beladung.

Domus, hus, hywræden.[2]
Proaula, i. domus coram aula, selde.
Zetas æstivales, sumer-selde.
Zetas hyemales, winter-selde.
Salutatorium, greting-hus.
Consistorium, þæt hus þær man ðweað heora handa.
Tricorum, vel triclinium, gereord-hus.
Epicausterium, dom-hus, *vel* mot-hus.
Thermas, bæð-hus, *vel* bæð-stow.
Gymnasium, leorning-hus.
Coquina, vel culina, cicen.
Colimbus, i. aquæductus, wæterscipes hus.
Ypodromum, gold-hord-hus,[3] *vel spondoromum,* digle gang-ern.
Ecclesia, circe.
Ædes, hofa.
Ædicula, lytel hof.
Templum, templ.

---

[1] The Latin of these two words should no doubt be *uligo* and *uliginosus*.

[2] The words which follow are very curious. The compiler is endeavouring to explain, in Anglo-Saxon, the various descriptions of Roman buildings, and parts of a Roman house; and the way in which he does this not only shows that the greater part of them were unknown to the Anglo-Saxons, but he gives us the Anglo-Saxon names for such buildings, and parts of buildings, as were known to our remote forefathers, and helps us to comprehend their meaning.

[3] This word is very curious as a name for a privy, in connection with the words *gold-finder* and *gold-farmer,* which were used in the sixteenth and seventeenth centuries for a cleaner-out of privies. The durability of such popular phrases is extraordinary.

SUPPLEMENT TO ALFRIC'S VOCABULARY.

Basilica, cinges hof, *vel* cyrce.
Porticus, portic.
Peribolum, scire.
Aula, heall.
Triclinium, bur þry-beddod.[1]
Camera, bur.
Caminatum, fyr-hus.
Cubiculum, bed-cofa.
Refectorium, beod-ern.
Dormitorium, slæp-ern.
Auditorium, spræc-hus.
Capitolium, dom-hus.
Curia, vel senatus, uþwitena spræc-hus.
Cella, cete.
Cellarium, hord-ern.
Lardarium, spic-hus.
Carnale, flæsc-hus.
Apotheca, win-hus.
Ærarium, feoh-hus.
Piscinale, fisc-hus.
Popina, snæding-hus.
Lautorium, wæsc-ern.
Officina, smiðþe, *vel* weorc-hus.
Equiale, hors-ern.
Bostar, vel boviale, scipen.
Ovile, i. sepimenta, vel caulæ, sceapa-hus.
Caprile, gata-hus.
Casa, vel casula, insæte hus, *vel* lytel hus.
Gurgustulum, vel gurgustium, neara scræf.
Tugurium, hulc.
Magalia, vel mappalia, vel capanna, byre, *vel* sceap-heorden.
Carcer, vel ergastulum, vel lautumia, cwærtern.
Latrina, vel secessus, gang.

Absida, sinewealt cleofa, *vel* portic.
Asseres, latta, *vel* reafteres.
Abaso, infirmatorium, seoccra manna hus.
Cancelli, lytle porticas.
Brationarium, mealt-hus.
Pistrina, bæc-ern.
Pistrilla, lytel bæc-ern.
Farinale, meale-hus.
Granarium, corn-hus.
Horreum, bern.
Siccatorium, cyln, *vel* ast.
Tornatorium, þryl-hus.
Vestiarium, hrægel-hus.
Bibliotheca, vel armarium, vel ar chirum, booc-hord.
Librarium, boc-hus.
Salinarium, sealt-hus.
Cænaculum, gemæne met-ern.
Zenodochium, gif-hus ælðcodigra manna.
Nosocomium, seocra manna hus.
Lupanar, vel circus, vel theatrum, myltestre-hus.[2]
Balnearium, vel thermarium, bæð-hus.
Pomarium, vel cucumerarium, æppel-hus.
Claustrum, fæsten, *vel* clauster.
Spelunca, vel specus, vel antrum, scræf.
Scriptorium, pislefer-hus.
Aumatium, vel armarium, ælces cynnes cæpe-hus.
Fanile, hig-hus.
Atrium, mycel and rum heall, *vel* cafertun.
Gazophylacium, madm-hus.
Thesaurarium, gold-hord.
Oratorium, vel oraculum, gebed-hus.

[1] A very singular translation of *triclinium*, as if it meant a three-bedded room.

[2] It is rather curious that the Anglo-Saxon scholar should confound a theatre with a brothel; but the mistake arose probably from his forming his judgment of the character of the Roman stage only from the ecclesiastical writers, who decried both the theatrical performances, which had become degraded enough, and the drama in general.

Propitiatorium, vel sanctum sanctorum, vel secretarium, vel pastoforum, gesceot bæftan þæm heah weofode.
Asylum, friðhus, *vel* gener-stede.
Sutrina domus, sutera hus.
Potionarium, ælces cinnes drenc-hus.
Cœnobium, feala muneca wunung.
Ergasterium, vel operatorium, weorc-hus.
Genitium, tow-hus of wulle.[1]
Parietinæ, roflease and monlease ealde weallas.
Ypogæum, vel subterraneum, eorð-hus.

Lustra, wild-deora holl and denn.
Lucus, vel nemus, beora.
Papilio, gang-geteld.
Tenda, tyld-syle.
Clavus tentorii, fiter-sticca.
Circumlutus locus, mid wæter ymbtyrnd stede.
Allurium, wæter-gewæsc.
Netorium, in-spinn.
Pectica, fleþe-camb.
Liciatorium, lorh, *vel* web-beam.
Tela, lang web.
Licium, hefeld.
Lacerna, hacele geflenod *vel* gecorded.
Vertigo, hwyorfa.
Suppar, interula, syrc.
Radiolum, hrisl.
Alibrum, hreol.
Tramarium, meðema wersa.
Ragana, under-hwitel.

Mataxa, vel corductum, vel stramentum, stræl, *vel* bedding.
Peblum, web.
Lectisternia, bed-reaf.
Stamen, wearp.
Fulcra, eal bed-reaf.
Lodix, wæstling.
Globus, clywe.
Glomus, unwunden gearn.
Glomer, globellum, cleowen.
Deponile, wefta, *vel* weft.
Panuli, planus vel panus, colus, dis-stæf.
Ciclas, vel oraria, orlas.
Apidiscus, web-hoc.
Ordior, ic hefaldige.
Insubulæ, web-beamas.
Percussorium, slege.
Tara, web-gereþru.
Pecten, bannuc-camb.
Texo, ic wefe.
Textor, webba.
Textrix, webbestre.
Trama, vel subtemen, oweb, *vel* ab.
Polymita, vel orbiculata, wingfah.
Ependeton, cop, *vel* hoppada, *vel* ufre-scrud.
Fasces, ealdordomas, *vel* þa hehstan wurðscipas.
Flamininus honor, biscoplic wurðscipe.
Flammeolum, vel flammeum, biscopes huf.
Flamen, biscop.
Mancipatio, þeowdom.
Manumissor, freot-gifa.

---

[1] *Genitium* is apparently a corruption of *gineceum (gynecæum)*, the apartment of the women. Under the Franks on the Continent, and the Saxons in Britain, the term *gynecæum* was preserved in the mansions of the great, and was applied to the room in which the maidens attached to the noble lady's household were assembled, in the various employments peculiar to them, such as the various branches of spinning, weaving, sewing, embroidering, &c., of which the lord made a profit. It is probably with this idea that the Anglo-Saxon compiler of the glossary interprets *gynecæum* as "a tow-house of wool." The different words belonging to weaving, and women's domestic employments, follow immediately after.

Manumissio, freot-gife.
Emancipatio, freodom.
Manus impositio, hand-gang.
Manumissus, gefreod.
Liricus, scop.
Poema, leoð.
Poesis, leoð-weorc.
Poeta, vel vates, leoð-wyrhta.
Tragicus, vel comicus, unwurð scop.
Pythonissa, helle-rune, *vel* hægtesse.
Horoscopus, dægmel-sceawere.[1]
Mathematicus, tungel-witega, *vel* gebyrd-witega.
Sortilegus, tan-hlyta.
Oreades, munt-ælfen.
Dryades, wudu-elfen.
Moides, feld-elfen.
Hamadryades, wylde-elfen.
Naiades, sæ-elfen.
Castalides, dun-elfen.
Penates, cof-godas.
Tisiphona, wælcyrre.[2]
Parcæ, hægtesse.
Satyri, vel fauni, unfæle men.
Ficarii, vel invii, wude-wasan.[3]
Abatis, fæt-fellere.
Lictor, vel virgifer, hyldere.
Lanio, vel lanista, vel carnifex, vel macellarius, hyldere, *vel* cwellere, *vel* flæsc-tawere.

Quæstionarius, dema.
Creditor, lænere.
Ariolus, wicca.
Commentariensis, gerefa.
A secretis, vel principis consiliarius, geruna.
A responsis, i. magister responsorum, yldest ærendraca.
A caliculis, magister calicum, yldest byrla.
Assecla, folgere.
Teloneum, tol-setl.
Pincerna, byrle.
Plagiarius, nytena ðeof.
Questor, dema.
Transilio, ic oferhleape.
Transilitor, oferhleapend.
Questus, vel lucrum, gestreon.
Altilis, fedels.
Citharedus, hearpere.
Citharista, hearpestre.
Auledus, reod-pipere.[4]
Salpista, aule, bymere.
Salpica, byme-sangere.
Salpizo, vel buccino, ic byme.[5]
Sponsor, vel præs, vel fidejussor, vel vas, vel vadator, borh-hand.
Emulus, gesaca, *vel* gewinna.
Accidiosus, vel tediosus, asolcen.
Petitor, vel petax, biddere.

[1] The compiler has again followed the derivation of the word, instead of the meaning of the word itself; and, instead of interpreting *horoscopus* as one who tells people's fortunes by calculating their nativities, he took it to mean one who announces the hours of the day. The words which follow are curious illustrations of the fairy mythology of our forefathers.

[2] The Anglo-Saxon of this and the following word appear to be transposed. *Hægtesse* means properly a fury, or, in its modern representative, a hag, and would apply singly to Tysiphone, while *wal-cyrian* was the name of the three fates of the Anglo-Saxon mythology.

[3] The Anglo-Saxon of this and the preceding word seem to have been similarly transposed. It furnishes us with a very curious and instructive example of the long preservation of words connected with popular superstitions; for, in Withal's *Dictionarie*, ed. 1608, p. 62, we have, in the list of four-footed beasts, "a woodwose, *satyrus*."

[4] The compiler perhaps thought the pipe of the Roman minstrel was a pipe of reeds. Somner supposes that *aule*, in the next line, should be *auletes*, or *auledus*.

[5] *Beme* was the common word in old English for a trumpet, and *bemere* for a trumpeter.

SUPPLEMENT TO ALFRIC'S VOCABULARY.

Pigmæus, vel nanus, vel pumilio, dweorg.
Paponius, druncen.
Cancellarius, vel scriniarius, bur-þen.
Sacriscriniarius, cyrc-weard.
Antigrafus, writere.
Æstimator, æhtere.
Æstimatio, æhtunge.
Lana succida, vel sucilenta, unawæscen wull.
Sideratus, vel ictuatus, færunge astorfen.
Dextrochirium, brad earm-beah.
Dissologia, twig-spræc.
Acetabulum, vel garale, eced-fæt.
Exentera, unsceot, *vel* geopena.
Decorticatum, æfelle, *vel* rindleas.
Struma, halsgang.
Nevum, werh-bræde.
Eucharis, swæs, *vel* wynsum.
Facetus, swæs-wyrde.
*Faceti*æ, wynsum gliw.
Delumentum,[1] þweal.
Commonitorium, vel pictacium, ærend-gewrit.
Canalis, vel colimbus, vel aquæductus, wæter-þeote.
Cataclysmus, brym-flod.
Ductilis, astrengd.

Proventus, sped.
Argutiæ, gleawnys.
Academice, snotorlice.
Affectuose, vel devote, holdlice.
Evax, wilcume.
Eatenus, vel eotenus, oð þæt.
Gratiosus, ðoncful.
Officiosus, estful, *vel* gehyrsum.
Inofficiosus, ingratus, unestful.
Votivus, estful.
Lentus, waac.
Familiaris, hiwcuð.
Affabilis, word-wynsum.
Ineptus, ungefege.
Incongruus, ungeþæslic.
Familiaritas, hiwcuðrædnys.
Contubernalis, vel socius, gefera.
Contubernium, gador-wist.
Terribilis, ahwilc, *vel* egeslic, *vel* dryslic.
Siliquastrum, vel cathedra quadrata, fiþerscyte setl.
Corollarium, i. merces, med.
Peripetasma, limb-stefning.
Cementum, grund-stanas.
Basis, syll.
Fultura, fot-stan.

---

[1] No doubt an error for *delutamentum*.

ANGLO-SAXON VOCABULARY,

(OF THE ELEVENTH CENTURY.)[1]

Aquila, earn.
Arpa, earngeap.
Griphus, giow.
Ossigra, gos.
Cignus, elfetu.
Mergulus, dop-fugel.[2]
Fulix, ganot.[3]
Aneta, æned.[4]
Velanax, æned.
Anser, hwit gos.
Ganta, græg gos.
Olor, swann.
Alcedo, mæw.
Accipiter, gos-hafoc.
Erodius, wealh-hafoc.
Hetum, spear-hafoc.
Siricarius, mus-hafoc.[5]
Milvus, glida.
Ciconia, storc.
Grus, cran.
Onocrotalus, rara dumbla, þæt is pur.[6]
Cucurata, hleape-wince.[7]
Accgia, snite.

Fursianus, wor-hana.
Luscinia, nihtegala.
Columba, culfre.
Palumbes, cuscote,[8] wudu-culfre
Corvus, hræfn.
Cornix, crawe.
Cornicula, cyo.
Gralus, hroc.
Beatica, stearn.
Marsopicus, fina.
Picus, higera.
Noctua, ule.
Rubisca, salt-haga, *vel* rudduc.
Fringilla, finc.
Sigatula, fræc-mase.
Parra, col-mase.
Parrula, swic-mase.
Bitorius, wrænna.
Tilaris, lawerce.
Ficitula, sugga.
Scututis, rago-finc.
Merula, þrostle.
Cardella, linete.

---

[1] This vocabulary is taken from a manuscript in the Royal Library at Brussels. It contains fewer classes of words than the other vocabularies, and those words are chiefly on Natural History and Anatomy; but as far as it goes, it is more copious.

[2] Literally, a dipping fowl—the moor-hen; still called in Dutch, *dooprogel*.

[3] The word is interpreted as meaning specially the pen-duck, but it seems to have been used as a general term for a sea-fowl. *Ganotes baðð*, the ganot's bath, was a common poetical term for the sea.

[4] The Dutch *eend*, answering to the Latin *anas*, a wild duck.

[5] The mouse-hawk.

[6] The bittern

[7] The lapwing.

[8] Still called, in different parts of the country, *cushots*, or *cowshots*.

Turdus, scric.
Strutio, þryssce.
Cuculus, geac.
Birbicaliolus, eorðling.
Pullus, cycen.
Sturnus, stær.
Passer, spearewa.
Gallus, coc.
Gallinaceus, capun.
Gallina, hæn.
Hirundo, swealewe.
Nycticorax, niht-hræfn.
Ardea, hragra.
Diomedia, swan.
Turdella, scealfor.
Mergula, scealfor.
Buteo, cyta.
Soricarius, blerea, wyctel.
Bubo, huf.
Pellicanus, stan-gella, *vel* wan-fota.
Ortigometra, secg-scara.
Coturnix, ersc-hæn.
Philomela, nihtegale.
Ciupella, hulfstan.
Ismarus, spear-hafoc.
Viperina, nædder-winde.
Scorellus, clod-hamer, *vel* felde-fare.

[DE NAVE ET PARTIBUS EJUS.]

Nauta, roþra.
Navis, scip.
Archiromachus, swift scip.
Scapha, ærend-scip.
Barca, flot-scip.
Liburna, hulc.
Dromo, æsc.
Pontonium, flyte.
Trabaria, vel caudex, punt.
Puppis, se æften-stemn.
Cumba, þurruc.
Carina, bycme.
Fori, vel tabulata navium, scipes flor.
Columbaria, ar-locu.
Remi, ara.
Transtra, þoftan.
Palmula, ar-bled.
Antenna, segl-gyrd.
Cornua, þa ytemestan endas þare segl-gyrde.
Malus, mest.
Modius, mast-cyst.
Carchesia, hun-þyrlu.
Parastates, mæstwist.
Clavis, helma.
Gubernaculum, steor-roþur.
Pons, scip-hlæder.
Vela, seglu.
Prora, frum-stemn.
Funes, restes, rapas.
Spiræ, linan.
Propes, sceat-line.
Pes veli, sceata.
Safo, stæg.
Opisfera, stedin-line.
Proxnesium, marels.
Anguina, racca.
Remulcum, toh-line.
Strupiar, midlu.
Cataprorates, sund-line.
Bolis, sund-gyrd.
Aplustra, gereðru.
Æstuaria, fleotas.
Glarea, ceosel-stan.
Oneraria, scip-læst.
Syrtis, sand-gewurp.
Juncetum, risc-þyfel.
Ledo, nep-flod.
Proceris, gearu-fang.
Arula, heorð.
Remex, reþra.
Reuma, gyte-stream.
Scalmus, þoll.
Tabula, bord.
Unci, hocas.

Trieris, scægð.
Musculus, sceort-scip.
Carabus, scipincel.
Littoraria, troh-scip.
Puppis, steor-setl.
Prora, ancer-setl.
Trudes, spreotas.
Transtra, scip-setl, þoftan.
Una serca, an gerif fisca, oððe an snæs fisca, oððe oðra þinga.

DE MEMBRIS HOMINUM.

Anima, sawl.
Homo, man.
Anthropus, man.
Microcosmus, læssa middaneard.
Corpus, lichama
Caro, flæsc.
Crementum, cyð.
Sensus, sefa.
Visus, gesyhð.
Odoratus, swæc.
Gustus, byrignes.
Tactus, gehrine.
Caput, heafod.
Vertex, hnol.
Calvaria, heafod-panne.
Cerebrum, brægn.
Obcaput, forweard-heafod
Capilli, loccas.
Tautones, bruwa.
Coma, feax.
Pilus, hær.
Crines, loccas.
Tempus, þunwange.
Supercilium, ofer-bruwa.
Intercilium, betweoh-bruwum.
Cilium, bruwa.
Palpebræ, bræwas.
Oculus, eage.
Lacryma, tear.
Corona, helm.

Pupilla, seo.
Genæ, hago-swind.
Barba, beard.
Mentum, cin.
Malæ, ceocan.
Maxillæ, cin-ban.
Mandibulæ, ceacan.
Auris, eare.
Nasus, nosu.
Cartilago, nosu-grisle.
Internasum, neb.
Phlegma, hrog.
Os, muð.
Labrum, wæler.
Dens, toð.
Ingua, toð-reoma.
Lingua, tunge.
Faus, weo.
Palatum, muðes hrof.
Sublingua, uf.
Toles, grynlas.
Rumen, wasend.
Gurgulio, þrot-bolla.
Arteria, æddre.
Gula, hracu.
Collum, swyra.
Cervix, hnoll.
Humeri, eaxla.
Scapulus, souldur.
Brachium, earm.
Asella, oxn.
Ulna, eln.
Cubitus, fæðm.
Manus, hand, duma.
Pugna, fist.
Pugilla, gripe.
Palma, handbred.
Artus, liþu.
Digiti, fingras.
Pollex, þuma.
Index, bycniend.
Salutaris, hæletend.

Pudicus,[1] unewisc.
Annularis, fingerlic.
Auricularis, ear-scrypel.
Ungula, nægel.
Truncus, bodig,
Thorax, breost.
Mamillæ, tittas.
Pupillæ, seon.
Lac, meoluc.
Cutis, hid.
Pellis, fel.
Pulpa, lira
Viscus, herð-bylig.
Arvina, lind.
Nervi, sena.
Vertuba, hweorfa.
Costa, ribb.
Dorsum, ricg.
Terga, bæc.
Pale, ricg-rible.
Radioli, spacan.
Spondilia, hricg-rib.
Medulla, mearh.
Sacra spina, se haliga . . .
Renes, æddran.
Lumbi, lændenu.
Genitalia, þa cennendan.
Virilia, þa wærlican.
Virilitas, pintel.
Calamus, teors.
Testiculi, herþan.
Viscera, inelfe.
Meatus, utgong.
S . . em,[2] gor.
Anus, bæc-þearm.
Nates, ears-endu,
Femur, þeoh.
Coxa, þeoh-scanca.

Suffragines, hamma.
Genua, cnyowu.
Crura, sconcan.
Tibia, scina.
Sura, sper-lira.
Talus, ancleo.
Pedes, fet.
Planta, fot-welma.
Calx, ile.
Cor, heorte.
Sanguis, blod.
Jecur, lifer.
Pulmon, lungen.
Splena, milte.
Fel, gealla.
Stomachus, maga.
Intestinum, inelfe.
Omentum, mid-hriðre.[3]
Disceptum, nette.
Renunculæ, lund-lagan.

NOMINA PISCIUM.

Cetus, hwæl.
Piscis, fisc.
Bacharus, mere-swin.
Ballena, hran.
Porcupiscis, stiriga.
Phoca, seolh.
Cancer, crabba.
Ysox, leax.
Ostrea, ostre.
Geniscula, mucxle.
Sardina, hæring.
Platissa, floc.
Id, etbubla [4]
Cochlea, weoluc.
Lucius, hacud.
Mugil, *idem*.

---

[1] An evident error for *Impudicus*. See before, p. 44.
[2] It seems evident from the Anglo-Saxon interpretation that this should be *sanguis*.
[3] More correctly spelt *mid-hrife*, the modern English word *midriff*.
[4] The reading of this appears to be doubtful. Mone prints it, *Item et* bubla.

Tincus, sliu.
Lupus, bærs.
Castor, befor.
Cephalus, heardra.
Murænula, æl.
Anguilla, smæl æl.
Sartate, smylt.[1]
Bisarius, fisc-welle.

[DE ARTE TEXTORIA.]

Textrina, web.
Liciatorium, web-sceaft.
Fusum, srlin.
Radius, hrefl.
Cladica, wefl.
Deponile, wefta.
Netorium, inspin.
Verticillum, hweorfa.
Colus, wulmod.
Glomus, cliwen.
Conductum, gearn-winde.
Plumaria, byrdinge.
Stamen, wearp.
Subtegmen, awebb.
Pectica, flæþe-comb.
Apidiscus, web-hoc.
Scapus, uma.
Tara, web-gereþru.
Claus, tæbere.
Filum, ðred.
Lana, wul.
Vellus, flis.

Leno, wif-þegn.
Alibrum, riul.
Insubula, meoduma.[2]
Ansa, hringe.
Cingulum, gyrdels.

Andeda, brond-reda.
Arula, fyr-panne.
Sica, tindre.
Scintilla, spearca.
Titio, brand.
Scindula, scid.
Igniarium, algeweorc.
Finis, ærce.
Favilla, ysle.
Fumus, rec.
Atandilia, weocan.
Alea, tæfel.
Calculus, tæfel-stan.
Aleator, tæflere.
Carpentarius, wæn-wyrhta.
Plaustrum, wæn.
Rota, hweol.
Temo, þistle.
Radii, spacan.
Canthi, felgan.
Navalium, dinege.

NOMINA HERBARUM, GRÆCE ET LATINE.[3]

Scalonia, ynne-leac.
Aubila, leac.
Acinus, hynd-berige.[4]
Ambrosia, hynd-hælepe.
Artemisia, mug-wyrt.
Apollinaris, glof-wyrt.
Cynoglossa, ribbe.
Septiphilos, hymelic.
Astula regia, baso, popig.
Carduus, smœl þistle.
Cliton, clate.
Cardamon, cærse.
Apium, merce.
Batrachium, clufþung.
Anethum, dile.

---

[1] The smelt.
[2] A weaver's beam.
[3] i. e., both Latin and Greek names of plants are here given with the Anglo-Saxon equivalents. This explains why there are so many repetitions of the same plant.
[4] The raspberry is still called a *hind-berry* in the North of England.

ANGLO-SAXON VOCABULARY.

Bobonica, bratele.
Acetula, ramese.
Carex, segg.
Brassica, wudu-cerfille.
Acanton, beǫ-wyrt.
Camedus, heort-clæfre.
Ascoloma, cipe.
Catharticum, libb-corn.
Camellia, wulfes camb.
Arnaglosse, wegbrade.
Cucumeris, hwærhwætte.
Camesete, ellen-wyrt.
Agrimonia, gar-clife.
Centauria, heorð-gealla.
Coxa, þung.
Aconitum, þung.
Aristolochia, smert-wyrt.
Callitriche, wæter-wyrt.
Artemesia, tagantes helde.
Althea, mersc-mealewe.
Coantrum, cellendre.
Britannica, hæwen-hyldele.
Absynthium, weremod.
Buglosse, foxes glofa.[1]
Vaccinia, berige.
Camemelon alba, se brada wulfes camb.
Beneolentem, mageðe.
Canis lingua, hundes tunge.
Batracion, cluf-wyrt.
Cicuta, hymelic.
Anteleuce, smæl þistel.
Bucstalinum, hwit mægeðe.
Appasina, clife.
Cerefolium, enne-leac.
Achillea, collon-croh.
Culmus, healm.
Cicuta, wode-þisele.
Anchorum, mædere.
Apis sylvatica, wudu-merce.
Conixe, lubestica.

Iris Illyrica, hwatend.
Calcesta, hwite clæfre.
Fynuclum, finol.
Innula, colone.
Filix, fearn.
Calcilum, iaces sure.
Lactuca, leahtric.
Cinnamomum, cymen.
Furfur, sifeða.
Leontopodium, leon-fot.
Felix minuta, eofor-fearn.
Laterculum, beolone.
Cyclamen, slite.
Lappacium, docce.
Gladiolum, secgg.
Malva, mealewe.
Gramen, cwice.
Genista, brom.
Mercurialis, cedelc, cyrlic.
Millefolium, gearewe.
Galla, galloc.
Erimigio, hynd-berige.
Mosilicum, ragu.
Ebolum, ellen-wyrt.
Mentha, minte.
Marrubium, hare-hune.
Beriballum, greate-wyrt.
Maliterre, elehtre.
Betonica, byscop-wyrt.
Nasturtium, tun-cærse.
Fraga, streaw-berige.
Caltha, reade clefre.
Lacyride, lib-corn.
Fungus, swamm.
Lappa, clate.
Fœnum græcum, wylle-cyrse.
Lagena, crog.
Lolium, ate.
Colucus, cofor-þrote.
Firula, æsc-þrote.

[1] See before, the note on p. 30. The Anglo Saxons themselves seem to have fallen into some confusion in regard to their equivalents for the Latin and Greek terms of plants.

Felicina, eofor-fearn.
Corymbus, ifig-crop.
Ligustrum, hunisuce.
Delphinion, fugeles wyse.
Heliotropus, sigell-hweorfa.
Malagma, sealf.
Gentiana, feld-wyrt.
Mastix, hwit cwuda.
Heraclea, calcatrippe.
Heptaphyllon, gelod-wyrt.
Hedera nigra, eorð-ifig.
Eripheon, lið-wyrt.
Herba iras, gorst.
Swige, ban-wyrt.
Callitriche, stæl-wyrt.
Eicios, haran-spreccel.
Innule campane, spere-wyrt.
Napis, næp.
Pastinace, wudu-cerfille.
Nymphœa, collon-croh.
Orianthum, eolone.
Rolon, earbe.
Quinquenerbia, ribbe.
Tenedisse, helde.
Urtica, netle.
Toxa, þung.
Quinquefila, hræfnes fot.
Origanum, ælepe.
Sinfitum, gallac.
Radiolum, eofor-fearn.
Prosopes, bete.
Prassion, hune.
Titemallos, singrene.
Rhamnus, þefe-þorn.
Juncus, risce.
Sigsonte, stan-merce.
Ocimum, mistel.
Veneria, mædere.
Nereta, sæ-minte.
Plantago, weg-brade.
Viola aurosa et viola purpurea, ban-wyrt.

Senecio, grund-swylige, syr.
Symphoniaca, beolone.
Pissli, reosan.
Viumum, fugeles leac.
Speragus, wudu-cærfille.
Sarpulum, brade leac.
Tribulus, gorst.
Rosmarinum, feld-mædere.
Obtalmon, mageðe.
Ruscus, cneowholen.[1]
Thiaspis, lambes cerse.
Rodinaps, ompre, docce.
Salsa, sure.
Tytymalosca, lib-corn.
Papaver, popig.
Umbilicum, berwinde.
Scilla, glædene.
Victoriala, cneowholen.
Perdicalis, homor-wyrt.
Pollegia, broðer-wyrt, hæl-wyrt, dweorges drostle.
Unio, ynneleac.
Peucidanum, cammoce.
Sempervivum, sinfulle.
Vermenaca, rædic.
Pilogonus et sanguinaria, ðæt is unfortredde.
Viola, simering-wyrt.
Stena, hæþ-cole.
Pentaphyllon, fif-leafe.
Sandix, wad.
Sinapdones, cærsan.
Sicalia, lyge.
Hierobotanum, hrætel-wyrt.
Brassica sylvatica, wudu-cerefille.
Gramis birecta, cwice.
Solsequia, golde.
Rosmarinus, sun-деaw.
Gagantes, mug-wyrt.
Althea, sæ-minte.
Heliotropus, sigell-ihweorfa.

[1] The plant still called *knee-holly* in the South of England.

Ruta, rude.
Iva, ive.
Sisymbrium, broc-minte.
Colatidis, singrene.
Scilla et gladiola, glædene.
Scolonia, cipe.
Samsuhthon, cyninges wyrt.
Vulnetrum, mold-corn.
Scirpio, læfer.
Viticella, weodu-binde.
Poloten, crawan-leac.
Scolimbos, se umbrada þistel.
Pastinace, moran.
Lapadium, eloþre.
Malva herratice, geormen-leaf.
Canafel sylvatica, hænep.

Ebulus, ellen-wyrt.
Mentarium, feld-minte.
Cerefolium, cerfelle.
Sinapis, senap.
Abrotonum, sæþrene-wuda.
Peonia, peonia.
Lubestica, lufestice.
Rosa, rosa.
Spimon, vel reverion, brun-wyrt.
Ostriago, liþ-wyrt.
Muronis, cicena mete.
Humblonis, hege-hymele.
Hulsida, camedris.
Arciotidas, fyrses berian.
Actis, vel sambucus, ellen.
Elimos, vel lini semen, lin-sæd.

ANGLO-SAXON VOCABULARY,[1]

(OF THE ELEVENTH CENTURY.)

Deus omnipotens, þæt is God ælmihtig, se wæs æfre unbegunnen and æfre byð ungeendod.
Celum, heofen.
Angelus, engel.
Archangelus, heah-engel.
Stella, steorra.
Sol, sunna.
Luna, mona.
Firmamentum, roder.
Cursus, ryne.
Mundus, vel cosmus, middan-eard.
Tellus, vel terra, corþe.
Humus, molde.
Mare, vel equor, sæ.
Pelagus, wid sæ.
Occanum, garsecge.
Homo, man.
Mas, vel masculus, werhades man.
Femina, wifhades man.
Sexus, werhad oððe wifhad.
Membrum, an lim.
Membra, ma lima.
Capud, heafod.
Capita, ma.
Vertex, hnol.
Cerebrum, bragen.
Cervix, hnecca.

Collum, swyre.
Frons, forewearde heafod.
Nasus, vel naris, nosu.
Capillus, hær.
Capilli, ma.
Cesaries, fex.
Coma, loc.
Auris, eare.
Aures, ma.
Timpus, þun-wenege.
Timpora, ma.
Maxilla, hleor.
Facies, ansyn.
Supercilium, ofer-bruwa.
Palpebre, bræwas.
Oculus, eaga.
Oculi, ma.
Papilla, seo.
Os, muð.
Os, ban.
Medulla, mærh.
Labium, weler.
Labia, ma.
Dens, toð.
Dentes, ma.
Lingua, tunge.
Palatum, goma.
Guttur, þrota.

[1] Although there seems to be little room for doubt that the first of the Vocabularies printed in the present volume is rightly ascribed to Alfric, yet in the known MSS. Alfric's Grammar is followed by a vocabulary which is differently arranged, and more condensed. This vocabulary is here printed from a copy in MS. Cotton., Julius A. II., in the British Museum. Another occurs in the MS. in St. John's College, Oxford, already alluded to.

Mentum, cin.
Barba, beard.
Pectus, breost.
Cor, heorte.
Pulmones, lungena.
Jecur, lifer.
Fel, gealla.
Stomachus, maga.
Splen, milte.
Adeps, rysel.
Arvina, ungel.
Viscus, innoð.
Viscera, ma.
Ixta, ðearmas.
Sanguis, blod.
Caro, flæsc.
Cutis, hyd.
Pellis, fell.
Scapula, sculdra.
Dorsum, hryc.
Venter, wamb.
Brachium, earm.
Brachia, ma.
Ulna, eleboga.
Manus, hand.
Digitus, finger.
Digiti, ma.
Unguis, nægl.
Ungues, ma.
Pollex, þuma.
Index, scytel-finger.
Medius, middel-finger.
Medicus, læce-finger.
Auricularius, eare-finger
Palma, hand-bred.
Artus, lið.
Latus, side.
Latera, ma.
Costa, rib.
Coste, vel costas, ma.
Renes, lendena.

Nervus, sinu.
Nervi, ma.
Vena, æddre.
Vene, ma.
Femur, þeoh.
Femora, ma.
Coxa, þeoh.
Clunis, hype.
Poples, ham.
Poplites, ma.
Genu, cneow.
Genua, ma.
Pulpa, lira.
Sura, spær-lira.
Crus, sceanca.
Crura, ma.
Tibia, scyne, oððe scin-ban.
Talus, ancleow.
Pes, fot.
Pedes, ma.
Planta, fot-wylm.
Plante, vel plantas, ma.
Allox, ta.
Alloces, ma.
Ungula, hof, oððe clawu.
Patriarcha, heah-fæder.
Propheta, witega.
Apostolus, apostol.
Archiepiscopus, erce-bisceop.
Episcopus, leod-bisceop.
Diocessis, vel parochia, bisceop-rice.
Regnum, rice.
Abbas, abbod, oððe fæder.
Presbiter, mæsse-preost.
Sacerdos, sacerd.
Clericus, preost, oððe cleric.
Diaconus, vel levita, diacon.
Subdiaconus, under-diacon.
Archidiaconus, erce-diacon.
Monachus, munuc, oððe anstandende.
Monacha, vel monialis, mycenu.[1]

---

[1] No doubt an error of the scribe for *mynecen*.

Anachorita, ancra.
Eremita, westen-setla
Nonna, arwurþe wydewe, oððe nunna.
Cantor, sangere.
Cantrix, sangystre.
Lector, rædere.
Lectrix, rædistre.
Laicus, læwede man.
Conjunx, gemecca.
Conjuges, vel conjugales, gesinhiwan.
Conjungium, vel matrimonium, sincipe.
Castus, clæne.
Incestus, unclæne.
Pulcher homo, fæger man.
Formosus, wel gewlitegod.
Deformis, hiwleas.
Speciosus, vel decorus, wlitig.
Pater, fæder.
Mater, moder.
Avus, ealda fæder.
Abavus, þridde fæder.
Proavus, feorþa fæder.
Atavus, fifta fæder.
Filius, sunu.
Filia, dohter.
Soboles, bearn.
Liberi, ma bearn.
Familia, hiwræden, oððe hired.
Frater, broðer.
Soror, swuster.
Vitricus, steop-fæder.
Noverca, steop-moder.
Privignus, steop-sunu.
Filiaster, steop-dohter.
Nepos, neva.
Neptis, bewimmen.
Altor, vel nutritor, foster-fæder.
Altrix, vel nutrix, foster-moder.
Alumpnus, foster-cild.
Patruus, fædera.
Matertera, moddrige.
Avunculus, eam.

Amita, faþu.
Osculum, cos.
Propinquus, mæg.
Affinis, vel consanguineos, sibling.
Amicus, freond.
Progenies, vel tribus, mægþ.
Generatio, cynren.
Gener, aðum.
Socer, sweor.
Socrus, sweger.
Nurus, snoru.
Rex, cyning.
Sceptrum, cyne-gyrd.
Regina, cwen.
Imperator, vel cesar, vel augustus, casere.
Imperatrix, vel augusta, þes caseres cwen.
Princeps, eoldorman.
Dux, heoretoga, oððe lateow.
Comes, ealdorman, oððe gerefa.
Clito, æþelinge.
Obses, gysel.
Primas, heafod-man.
Satrapa, þegn.
Judex, dema.
Prepositus, gerefa, oððe prafost.
Miles, vel adleta, cempa.
Exercitus, here.
Populus, folc.
Procinctus, fyrdinge.
Edictum, geban.
Vulgus, ceorl-folc.
Congregatio, vel contio, gegaderung.
Conventus, vel conventio, gemetinge.
Sinodus, sinoð.
Dominus, vel herus, hlaford.
Matrona, forð-wif.
Domina, hlæfdige.
Cliens, vel clientulus, in-cniht.
Empticius, geboht þeowa.
Vernaculus, inbyrdlinge.

Servus, þeowa.
Ancilla, vel serva, vel abra, wyln.
Custos, vel pastor, hyrde.
Puer, cnapa.
Puella, mæden, oððe geong wif-man.
Virgo, mæden-man.
Procus, wogere.
Sponsus, bryd-guma.
Sponsa, bryd
Infans, unsprecende cild.
Vir, wer, oððe wæp-man.
Mulier, wif.
Maritus, ceorl þe wif hæfð.
Uxor, wif þe wer hæfð.
Vidua, widewe.
Senex, eald-man.
Anus, eald-wif.
Adolescens, iung man.
Juvenis, iunglingc.
Paterfamilias, hyredes hlaford.
Materfamilias, hiredes moder oððe hlæfdige.
Consiliarius, rædbora.
Consilium, ræd.
Contionator, gemot-man.
Operarius, wyrhta.
Faber, vel cudo, smið.
Officina, smiððe.
Ferrarius, isen-wyrhta.
Lignarius, treow-wyrhta.
Aurifex, gold-smið.
Argentarius, seolfor-smið.
Erarius, mæslingc-smið.
Rusticus, æcer-ceorl.
Arator, yrðlingc.
Ars, cræf[t].
Artifex, cræftca.
Opus, weorc.
Opifex, cræftca.
Architectus, yldest wyrhta.
Piscator, fiscere.
Rete, nyt.

Amus, angel.
Venator, hunta.
Venabulum, bar-spere.
Auceps, fugelere.
Laqueus, gryn.
Trapezeta, vel nummularius, mynetere.
Nummisma, mynet.
Sollers, mænig-tiwe.
Iners, cræftleas.
Potens, mihtig
Gigas, ent.
Nanus, dweorh.
Fidis, streng.
Citharista, hearpere.
Cithara, hearpe.
Tubicen, bymere.
Tuba, byma.
Tibicen, pipere.
Musa, pipe, oððe hwistle.
Fidicen, fiðelere.
Fidicina, fiþelestre.
Cornicen, horn-blawere.
Cornu, horn.
Fistula, hwistle.
Liticen, truð.
Lituus, truð-horn, oððe sarga.
Poeta, sceop, oððe leoð-wyrhta.
Mimus, vel scurra, glig-man.
Saltator, hleapere.
Saltatrix, hleapestre.
Mercator, vel negotiator, mangere.
Merx, waru.
Pirata, wicing, oððe flot-man.
Classis, scip-here.
Navis, scip.
Remus, roðer.
Remex, vel nauta, reðra.
Gubernator, vel nauclerus, steor-man.
Proreta, ancer-man.
Prora, þær se ancer-man sit.
Puppis, steor-setl.
Anchora, ancer.

Antempna, segel-gyrd.
Velum, segl, oððe wah-reft.[1]
Clavus, steor-sceofol, oðþe nægl.
Medicus, læce.
Medicina, læce-dom.
Arsura, vel ustulatio, bærnet.[2]
Potio, drenc.
Unguentum, smyrels, oððe sealfe.
Malagma, cliðu.
Salinator, scaltere.
Sutor, sutere.
Sartor, seamere.
Sartrix, seamestre.
Dispensator, dihtnere.
Divisor, dælere.
Pincerna, byrle.
Caupo, tæppere.
Dives, welig.
Locuples, land-spedig.
Inops, hafenleas.
Pauper, ðearfa.
Egenus, wædla.
Fur, þeof.
Latro, sceaþa.
Profugus, flyma.
Exul, utlaga.
Fidelis, getreowe, oððe geleafful.
Infidelis, ungetreowe.
Felix, gesælig.
Infelix, ungesælig.
Contentiosus, geflitful.
Injuriosus, teonful.
Piger, sleac.
Inpiger, unsleaw.
Hebes, dwæs.
Parasitus, leas-olecere.
Augur, wiglere.

Incantator, galere.
Veneficus, unlyb-wyrhta.
Maleficus, yfel-dæda.
Magus, dry.
Phytonyssa, wycce.
Centurio, hundredes ealdor.
Persecutor, ehtere.
Theolenarius, tollere.
Bonus homo, god man.
Malus, yfel.
Bonum, god.
Malum, yfel.
Dispendium, vel dampnum, hynð.
Jactura, lyre.
Commodum, hyð.
Res, þinge.
Anulus, hringe.
Armilla, beah.
Diadema, cyne-healm.
Capitium, hæt.
Monile, myne, oððe swur-beah.
Spinther, dolc, oððe preon.
Fibula, ofer-fenge.
Vitta, snod.
Inauris, ear-preon.
Indigena, vel incolo, inlendisc.
Advena, utan-cuman.
Peregrinus, ælþeodig.
Colonus, tilia.[3]
Agricola, æcer-man.
Messor, riptere.
Messis, gerip.
Acervus, hreac, oððe hype.[4]
Aratrum, sulh.
Vomer, scear.
Cultor, culter.
Jugum, geoc.

[1] *Wah reft,* or *wah rif,* means properly tapestry, or hangings for walls.

[2] Burning, or cauterising, was one of the great processes of the healing art in the middle ages; and full directions for it are given in the old treatises on leech-craft.

[3] The compiler of this vocabulary has given a correct interpretation of the word *colonus,* as signifying a husbandman. See before, p. 18.

[4] These two Anglo-Saxon words are the originals of our modern words rick (applied to hay, &c.) and heap.

ANGLO-SAXON VOCABULARY.

Stimulus, gad.
Aculeus, sticels.
Circus, vel circulus, wiðða.
Funis, vel funiculus, rap.
Doctor, lareow.
Magister, mægister.
Scriptor, writere.
Scriptura, gewrit.
Euvangelium, id est, bonum nuntium, god-spel.
Quaternio, cine.[1]
Planta, spelt.
Diploma, boga.
Enula, wærl.
Pergamentum, vel membranum, boc-fel.
Sceda, vel scedula, ymele.
Penna, feþer.
Graffium, græf.[2]
Pictor, metere.
Pictura, metinge.
Minium, teafor.
Gluten, lim.
Cementum, lim to wealle.
Sculptor, grafere.
Sculpture, græft.
Imaga, vel agalma, anlycnyss.
Scalprum, vel scalpellum, græf-sex.
Scola, scol.
Scolasticus, scol-man.
Pedagogus, cildre-hyrda.
Discipulus, leorning-cniht.
Disciplina, lar, oððe steor.
Doctrina, lar.
Miser, earminge.
Caecus, blind.
Claudus, healt.
Mutus, dumb.

Balbus, stamur.
Blessus, wlips.
Surdus, deaf.
Debilis, lama.
Luscus, vel monoptalmus, an-egede.
Strabo, scelg-egede.
Lippus, sur-egede.
Mancus, an-hende.
Infirmus, untrum.
Eger, vel egrotus, adlig.
Paraclytus, frofer-gast.
Paraliticus, beddreda, oððe se þe hæfð paralisin.
Leprosus, hreoflig, oððe lic-ðrowere.
Lunaticus, monað-seoc.
Demoniacus, deofol-seoc.
Energuminus, gewit-seoc.
Morbus, adl.
Pestis, cwild.
Amens, vel demens, gemyndleas.
Rabidus, vel insanus, wod.
Sanus, hal.
Rabies, wodnys.
Incolomis, gesund.
Freneticus, se þe þurh sleapleaste awet.
Frenesis, seo untrumnys.
Lethargus, vel letargicus, ungelimplice slapol.
Lethargia, ungelimplic slapolnys.
Vigil, wacol.
Vigila, wæcce.
Perrigil, þurh-wacol.
Pius, arfæst.
Impius, arleas.
Justus, rihtwis.
Injustus, unrihtwis.
Famosus, hlisful.

---

[1] The word *cine* does not appear in the Anglo-Saxon dictionaries. It means, here, the four leaves of parchment which were folded together, and answered to our modern sheet, in the binding of a book. From the mediæval use of the Latin word *quaternio* we derive our modern word quire, applied to paper.

[2] The *græf* was the instrument used for writing on the table-book, answering to the Roman *stylus*.

Fama, hlisa.
Infamis, unhlisful.
Infamia, unhlisa.
Largus, cystig.
Tenax, fæst-hafod, oððe uncystig.
Frugi, vel parcus, spær-hende.
Avarus, gytsere.
Raptor, reafere.
Sagax, vel gnarus, gleaw.
Sapiens, wis.
Insipiens, unwis.
Prudens, snoter.
Inprudens, unsnoter.
Astutus, pætig.
Stultus, stunt.
Sottus, sot.
Verax, soðfæst.
Veridicus, soð-sagol.
Fallax, vel mendax, leas.
Falsidicus, unsoð-sagol.
Testis, gewita.
Testimonium, gewitnys, oððe gecyðnys.
Sermo, vel locutio, spræc.
Cursor, rynel.
Superbus, modig.
Superbia, modignys.
Humilis, eadmod.
Humilitas, eadmodnys.
Vita, lif.
Anima, sawul.
Spiritus, gast.
Mors deað.
Yris, vel arcus, ren-boga.
Tonitruum, þunor.
Fulgor, leget.
Pluvia, ren.
Nix, snaw.
Grando, hagol.
Gelu, forst.
Glacies, is.
Aer, lyft.
Ventus, wind.

Aura, hwiða, oððe weder.
Nimbus, scur.
Procella, storm.
Nubes, wolcn.
Lux, leoht.
Tenebre, þeostru.
Flamma, lig.
Seculum, weorld.
Dies, dæg.
Nox, niht.
Mane, merien.
Vesperum, æfen.
Hora, tid.
Ebdomada, wucu.
Mensis, monað.
Ver, lengcten.
Estas, sumor.
Autumnus, herfest.
Hyemps, winter.
Vernum tempus, lencten-tid.
Vernalis dies, lenctenlic deg.
Hiemalis nox, winterlic niht.
Annus, year.
Tempus, tima.
Hodie, to dæg.
Cras, to merigen.
Heri, gystan-dæg.
Nunc, vel modo, nu.
Sursum, up.
Deorsum, nyðer.
Calor, hæte.
Frigus, cyle.
Ferfor, mycel hæte.
Cauma, swaloð.
Siccitas, drugað, oððe hæð.
Humor, wæta.
Sterelitas, unwæstmbærnigs.
Fertilitas, wæstbernys.
Color, bleoh.
Albus, hwit.
Niger, blac.
Rubor, read.

ANGLO-SAXON VOCABULARY.

Fulvus, vel flavus, geolu.
Viridis, grene.
Varius, fah.
Unius coloris, anes bleos.
Discolor, mistlices bleos.
Forma, hiw.
Fantasma, gedwimor.
Umbra, sceadu.
Creator, scyppend.
Creatura, ges[c]eaft.
Avis, vel volatilis, fugel.
Aquila, earn.
Corvus, hræm.
Milvus, glida.
Accipiter, heafuc.
Grus, cran.
Ardea, hragra.
Ciconia, storc.
Merula, þrostle.
Columbe, culfre.
Palumba, wudu-culfre.
Anetia, ened.
Alcedo, mæw.
Pavo, pawa.
Olor, vel cingnus, ylfette.
Rostrum, bile.
Mergus, vel mergulus, scealfra.
Hyrundo, swalewe.
Passer, spearwa, oððe lytel fugel.
Turduh, stær.
Ficus, fina.
Auca, gos.
Anser, ganra.
Gallus, coc.
Gallina, hen.
Conturnix, ersc-hen.
Pullus, cicen, oððe brid, oððe fola.
Ovum, æg.
Nidus, nest.
Vespertilio, hrere-mus.[1]

Noctua, vel strinx, ule.
Fulco, vel capum, hweal-hafoc.
Turtur, turtle.
Graculus, hroc.
Alauda, laverce.
Parrax, wrenne.
Apis, beo.
Fucus, dræn.
Vespa, weaps.
Bruchus, ceafor.
Scabro, hyrnete.
Scarabeus, scærn-wibba.
Musca, fleoge.
Cinomia, hundes lus.
Culex, stut.
Scinifes, gnæt.
Piscis, fisc.
Cetus, hwæl.
Delfinus, merc-swin.
Ysicius, vel salmo, lex.
Mugilis, vel mugil, mæce-fisc.
Taricus, vel allec, hærinc.
Mullus, heardra.
Tructa, truht.
Anguilla, æl.
Fannus, reohche.
Rocea, scealga.
Canger, crabba.
Polipos, loppestre.
Ostrea, vel ostreum, ostre.
Muscula, muxle.
Murena, vel murenula, myre-næddra.
Luceus, hacod.
Belua, egeslic nyten on sæ, oððe on lande.
Conchra, scyl.
Fera, wildeor.
Lupus, wulf.
Leo, leo.
Linx, gemencged hund and wulf.

[1] *Rere-mouse*, or *rear-mouse*, was the common name in English for a bat till a late period; and I believe it is still in use in some parts of the country.

Unicornis, an-hyrned deor; þæt deor hæfþ ænne horn bufan þam twam eagum, swa strangne and swa scearpne þæt he fiht wið þone mycłan ylp, and hine oft gewundað on ðære wambe of deað. He hatte eac *rinoceron* and *monoceron*.

Griffus, fiðer-fote fugel, leone gelic on wæstme, and earne gelic on heafde and on fiðerum; se is swa mycel þæt he gewylt hors and men.

Vulpis, fox.
Taxo, vel melus, broc.
Equus, hors.
Equa, myre.
Asinus, vel asina, assa.
Camelus, olfend.
Onager, wilde assa.
Mulus, mul.
Elefans, ylp.
Ursus, bera.
Ursa, heo.[1]
Simia, apa.
Lutrius, oter.
Fiber, beofer.
Feruncus, mærð.
Mustela, wesle.
Talpa, wande-wurpe.
Cattus, vel murilegutus, aut muriceps, cat.
Yricius, vel equinacius, il.
Glis, sise-mus.
Mus, vel sorex, mus.
Vermis, wyrm.
Lubricus, angel-twicca.
Cervus, heort.
Cerva, hynd.
Damma, vel dammula, da.
Hinnulus, hind-cealf.
Capreolus, rah-deor.
Caprea, ræge.

Caper, vel hircus, bucca.
Capra, vel capella, gat.
Hedus, ticcen.
Lepus, hara.
Porcus, vel sus, swin.
Scroffa, suga.
Aper, vel verres, bar.
Magalis, bearh.
Porcellus, fearh.
Bos, oxa.
Vacca, vel bucula, cu.
Vitulus, cealf.
Juvencus, styrc.
Ovis, sceap.
Aries, ram.
Vervex, weþer.
Agnus, lamb.
Pecus, vel jumentum, nyten.
Animal, ælc þinge þe cucu byð.
Canis, hund.
Molosus, ryðða.
Catulus, hwylp.
Dracus, draca.
Vipera, vel serpens, vel anguis, næddre.
Coluber, snaca.
Rubeta, tadie.
Rana, frogga.
Lacerta, efeta.
Stellio, sla-wyrm.
Locusta, gærs-stapa.
Sanguissuga, vel hyrundo, læce.
Limax, snegel.
Testudo, se þe hæfð hus.
Formica, æmette.
Eruca, mæl-sceafa.
Peduculus, lus.
Pulex, flea.
Cimex, maðu.
Tinea, moððe.
Herba, gærs, oððe wyrt.
Allium, leac.

---

[1] *Heo*, she, i. e., the female of the bear.

Dilla, docca.
Libestica, lufestice.
Febrefugia, feferfugia.
Simphoniaca, henne-belle.
Aradonia, felt-wyrt.
Aprotanum, suðerne-wudu.
Sinitia, grunde-swelige.
Feniculum, fenol.
Anetum, dyle.
Electrum, electre.
Malfa, hoc-leaf.
Malva crispa, symeringc-wyrt.
Polipedium, hremmes-fot.
Consolda, dæges-eage.
Solsequium, solsæce.
Sclaregia, slarege.
Adriaca, galluc.
Ruta, rude.
Betonica, seo læsse biscoep-wyrt.
Petrocilium, petersilium.
Costa, cost
Epicurium, half-wyrt.
Millefolium, gearwe.
Tanicetum, helde.
Saxifraga, sund-corn.
Citsana, fana.
Calamus, vel canna, vel arundo, hreod.
Papaver, popig.
Absintium, wermod.
Urtica, netel.
Archangelica, blind-netel.
Plantago, wegbræde.
Quinquefolium, fif-leafe.
Vinca, pervince.
Marubium, harhune.
Camiculo, argentille.
Fraga, streaw-berian wisan.
Ciminum, cimen.
Modera, cicena mete.
Appium, merce.

Lappa, clate, oððe clyf-wyrt.
Helena, hors-elene
Sandix, wad.
Caula, vel magudaris, caul.
Cresco, cærse.
Menta, minte.
Serpillum, fille.
Artemessia, mug-wyrt.
Salvia, salvige.
Felterre, vel centauria, eorð-gealle.
Ambrosia, hind-heolað.
Pionia,[1]
Mandragora, agene nama.[2]
Pollegia, hyl-wyrt, oððe dwyrge dwysle.
Organe, agene naman.
Cardus, ðystel.
Hermodoctula, vel tidolosa, crawan-leac.
Pastinaca, weal-mora.
Lilium, lilige.
Rosa, rose.
Viola, clæfre.
Agrimonia, car-clife.
Rafanu, rædic.
Filex, fearn.
Carex, sege.
Juncus, vel scyrpus, resce.
Arbor, treow.
Cortex, rinde.
Flos, blosan.
Folium, leaf.
Buxus, box.
Fraxinus, æsc.
Quercus, vel ilex, ac.
Taxus, iw.
Corilus, hæscl.
Fagus, boc-treow.
Alnus, alr.
Laurus, lauwer-beam.
Malus, æpeltre.
Pinus, pin-treow.

[1] The Anglo-Saxon equivalent is omitted in the manuscript.

[2] "Its own name," *i. e.*, it has no Anglo-Saxon equivalent.

Fructus, wæstm.
Baculus, stæf.
Virga, gyrd.
Virgultum, telgra.
Ramus, boh.
Glans, æcern.
Granum, cyrnel.
Radix, wyrtruma.
Pirus, pirige.
Prunus, plum-treow.
Ficus, fic-treow.
Ulcia, holen.
Populus, byrc.
Palma, twaltiga.
Sabina, savine.
Genesta, brom.
Cedrus, ceder-beam.
Cypressus, næfð nænne Englisce naman.
Sentes, þornas.
Frutex, ðyfel.
Ramnus, fyrs.
Spina, þorn.
Vepres, bremclas.
Abies, æps.
Olea, vel oliva, cle-beam.
Murus, mor-beam.
Vitis, win-treow.
Salix, wiðig.
Silva, wudu.
Lignum, aheawen treow.
Ligna, drige wudu.
Truncus, stoc.
Styrps, styb.
Nemus, vel saltus, holt.
Desertum, vel heremus, wæsten.
Via, weg.
Semita, pæð.
Invium, butan wege.
Iter, siðfæt.
Patria, æþel.

Provincia, vel pagus, scir.
Mons, dun.
Collis, hyl, oððe beorh.
Vallis, dene.
Foenum, hig, oððe gærs.
Ayer, æcer.
Seges, asawen æcer.
Campus, feld.
Pascua, læswe.[1]
Pons, brygc.
Vadum, ford.
Pratum, mæd.
Aqua, wæter.
Gutta, vel stilla, dropa.
Stagnum, mere.
Amnis, ea.
Flumen, vel fluvius, flod.
Ripa, stæð.
Litus, sæ-strand.
Alveus, stream.
Torrens, burna.
Rivus, rið.
Fons, wyl.
Arena, sand-ceosel.
Gurges, wæl.[2]
Vivarium, fisc-pol.
Puteus, pyt.
Lacus, seað.
Latex, burna, oððe broc.
*D*omus, hus.
Templum, tempel.
Aecclesia, cyrce, oððe geleafful gaderung.
Angulus, hyrne, oððe heal.
Altera, weofod.
Liber, vel codex, vel volumen, boc.
Littera, stæf.
Folium, leaf.
Pagina, tramet.
Arca, scrin.
Loculus, cyst, oððe mederce.

---

[1] This is the modern *leasow*—a word still in use, in some parts of England, in the signification of a pasture land.

[2] A whirlpool, called in Lancashire a *weele*.

ANGLO-SAXON VOCABULARY.

Calix, calic.
Patina, husel-disc.
Crux, vel staurus, rod.
Candelabrum, candel-stæf.
Cathedra, bisceop-stæf.
Fundamentum, grund-weal.[1]
Parimentum, vel solum, flor.
Paries, wah.[2]
Tectum, þæcen, oððe rof.
Fenestra, eh-ðyrl.[3]
Hostium, duru.
Hostiarius, dure-weard.
Janua, vel valva, geat.
Arcus, vel fornix, bigels.
Columpna, swer.
Januarius, geat-weard.
Clausura, loc.
Clavis, cæg.
Clavus, nægel.
Sera, hæpse.
Chorus, chor.
Gradus, stæpe.
Indicatorium, æstel.
Scabellum, sceamul.
Thus, stor.
Odor, bræþ.
Turibulum, stor-cyl.
Legula, sticca.
Regola, reogol-sticca.
Lampas, vel lucerna, vel laterna, leoht-fæt.
Lichinus, blacern.
Cereus, tapor.
Cera, weax.
Candela, candel.
Munctorium, isen-tanga.
Clocca, belle.

Cloccarium, vel lucar, bel-hus.
Tintinnabulum, litel belle.
Compana, mycel belle.
Vestis, vel vestimentum, vel indumentum, reaf.
Alba, albe.
Casula, mæsse-hacele.
Stola, stole.
Superhumerale, sculdor-hrægl.
Planeta, cæppe.
Manualis, hand-lin, oððe hand-boc.
Cingulum, vel zona, vel cinctorium, gyrdel.
Caliga, vel ocrea, hosa.
Fico, sceo.
Calciamentum, gescy.
Suptalaris, swyftlere.
Tractorium, tigl.
Flagrum, vel flagellum, scypu.
Virga, gyrd.
Dormitorium, slæp-ern.
Lectum, vet lectulum, bed.
Stramentum, beddinge.
Stragula, wæstlinge.
Sagum, hwytel.
Pulvinar, pyle.
Syndo, scyte.
Fulcra, eal bed-reaf.
Femoralia, bræc.
Perizomata, vel campestria, wæd-brec.
Filum, þræd.
Fimbrium, fnæd.
Cappa, cæppe.
Pellicie, pylece
Colobium, vel interula, syric.
Manica, slyf.
Cuculla, cugle.

---

[1] Literally, the ground wall. The Anglo-Saxons perhaps understood by a foundation the low wall of stone on which the wooden walls of the house were raised.

[2] *Wah*, or *wag*, was applied especially to the walls of a house, and was preserved in the later English *wawe*, or *waghe*.

[3] *Eh-þyrl*, or *eag þyrl*, means literally an eye hole. A window was also called in Anglo-Saxon *eag-duru*, an eye-door

Pedulos, meon.
Commissura, clut.
Toral, roc.
Mastruga, cruscne, oððe deor-fellen roc.
Tela, vel peplum, web.
Linum, fleax.
Lana, wul.
Glomus, cliwen.
Colus, distæf.
Fusus, spinl.
Textrinum opus, towlic weorc.
Latrina, gang
Trabes, beam.
Tignum, ræfter.
Laquear, fyrst.
Cleata, hyrdel.
Cymbalum, cimbal.
Refectorium, beoddern, oððe gercord-ung-hus.
Tapeta, set-rægl.
Matta, meatte.
Mensa, beod, oððe myse.
Discus, disc.
Discifer, disc-þegn.
Minister, þen.
Lardum, spic.
Caseus, cyse.
Butyrum, butere.
Ovum, æg.
Sal, sealt.
Panis, hlaf.
Olera, wyrta.
Cervisa, vel celea, eale.
Medo, meodu.
Ydromellum, vel mulsum, beor.
Lac, meolc.
Mustum, must.

Sicera, ælces cynnes gewrinc buton wine anum.
Manuterium, vel mantele, sceat.
Cultellus, sex.
Artavus, cnif.
Vas, fæt.
Poculum, drenc-cuppe.
Anaphus, hnæp.[1]
Patera, bledu.
Cibus, vel esca, mete.
Potus, drenc.
Liquor, wæta[2]
Claustrum, claustre.
Coquina, cycene.
Cocus, coc.
Ignis, vel focus, fyr.
Flamma, lig.
Pruna, gled.
An, (sic) brand-isen.
Litio, brand.
Olla, crocca.
Caccabus, cytel.
Lebes, hwyr.
Caro, flæsc.
Jus, broð.
Jutilis canis, broð-hund.
Fascinula, awel.
Comedia, racu.
Daps, sand.
Ferculum, bærdisc.
Veru, spitu.
Assura, bræde.
Sartano, isen-panna.
Frixorium, hyrstynge.
Coctio, gesod.
Coctus, gesoden, oððe gebacen.
Frustrum, stycce.
Offa, snæd.

[1] It is hardly necessary to remark that this word, which has occurred before, (see p. 24,) was the original of the later mediæval word *hanap*, also applied to a cup for the table.

[2] This is probably the origin of the modern use of the word *wet*, in such phrases as *heavy wet, i. e.*, strong liquor or drink, in tavern language.

ANGLO-SAXON VOCABULARY. 83

Mica, cruma.
Vestiarium, rægel-hus.
Testamentum, cwyde.
Sigillum, insegl.
Cellarium, hyddern.
Cellerarius, hordere.
Molendenum, myln.
Mola, cwyrn-stan.[1]
Mel, hunig.
Victus, bigleofa.
Pecunia, vel nummus, feoh.
Marsupium, seod.[2]
Pistrinum, bæcern.
Fornax, vel clibanus, ofen.
Pistor, bæcestre.
Granum, corn.
Farina, melu.
Bratium, mealt.
Acus, sifeþa.
Cribra, vel cribellum, sife.
Furfures, gretta.
Fex, drosna.
Anfora, sester.
Languena, buc.[3]
Dolium, cyfe.
Cupa, tunne.
Utensilia, andluman.
Supplex, yddisce.
Aula, heal.
Triclinium, bur.
Solarium, up-flor.
Turris, stypel.
Cardo, hearre.
Strigil, vel strigilis, hors-camb.
Risus, hleahter.
Letus, bliþe.

Tristis, unrot.
Mestus, dreorig.
Famis, hunger.
Abundantia, vel copia, genihtsumnys.
Letitia, blys.
Tristitia, unrotnys.
Jejunium, fæsten.
Jejunius, fæstende.
Pinguis, fæt.
Pinguedo, fætnys.
Corpulentus, þiccol.
Macer, vel macilentus, hlæne.
Macies, lænnys.
Grossus, great.
Gracilis, smæl.
Longus, lang.
Brevis, sceort.
Magnus, mycel.
Parvus, lytel.
Fortis, strang.
Invalidus, unstrang.
Sollitus, carful.
Securus, orsorh.
Cura, caru.
Securitas, orsorhnys.
Causa, intinga.
Accusator, wregere.
Excusator, beladigend.
Accusatio, wregine.
Excusatio, beladung.
Magnum, vel multum, mycel.
Nichil, naht.
Aliquid, sumþinge.
Sella, sadol, oððe setl.
Mento, felt.
Ulcea, garan.

---

[1] The *quern*, or stones turned with the hand to grind corn (the domestic mill), appears to have remained in constant use since the time of the Romans, and has fallen into disuse only very recently in some parts of the country.

[2] The bag, or purse, carried at the girdle, called at a later period of the middle ages a *gypsere* (in French *gibbecière*.) The remains of this article are found not uncommonly in the Anglo-Saxon graves of the Pagan period.

[3] What we now call a *bucket*. A pail is still called a *bouk* in Cheshire.

Scansile, stig-rap.[1]
Corrigia, ðwange.
Calcar, spura.
Antela, forð-gyrd.
Postela, æfter-rap.
Falere, geræðu.
Frenum, bridel.
Capistrum, hælftre.
Arma, wæpnu.
Galea, helm.
Lorica, byrne.
Gladius, vel machera, vel spata, vel framea, [swurd].
Spatarius, swurd-bora.
Armiger, wæpn-bora.
Bellum, vel pugna, gefeoht.
Signifer, tacn-bora.
Lancea, vel falarica, spere.
Victor, sigefæst.
Victoria, sige.
Acies, egc.
Cupulum, hiltan.
Mucro, swurdes ord, oððe oðres wæpnes.
Sica, lytel swurd, oððe hand-sex.
Asta, vel quiris, sceaft.
Vagina, sceað.
Manubrium, hæft.
Sagitta, vel telum, fla.
Fustis, sagol.
Vectis, stenge.
Arcus, boga.
Faretra, cocer.
Scutum, vel clipeus, scyld.
Umbro, rand-beah.
Funda, liþere.

Atrium, cavertun, oððe inburh.
Fundibalum, stæf-liðere.
Civitas, ceaster.
Porta, port-geat.
Civis, ceaster-gewara, oððe port-man.
Preco, bydel.
Oppidum, fæsten.
Castellum, wic, oððe lytel port.
Urbs, burh.
Urbanus, burh-wita.
Suburbanus, se þe sit buton ðære berig.
Carcer, cweartrn.
Oppidanus, se þe on fæstene sit.
Villa, tun.
Villanus, tun-man.
Villicus, tun-gerefa.
Ortus, orcyrd.
Ortulanus, orcerd-weard.
Pomerium, æppel-tun.
Viridiarium, wyrtun.
Horreum, bern.
Sepes, hege.
Fossa, dic.
Puteus, pyt.
Predium, worþig.[2]
Ferramentum, tol.
Securis, ex.
Ascia, adesa.
Terebrum, navegar.
Terebro, ic borige.
Foramen, ðyrl.
Vanga, vel fossorium, spædu.
Ligo, becca.
Bipennis, stan-ex.[3]
Palus, pal.

---

[1] The origin of our word *stirrup*. It might be supposed, from the form of the Anglo-Saxon word, that the Teutons originally used ropes for stirrups.

[2] The origin of so many names of localities in England ending in -*worth* or -*worthy*, as Wandsworth, Rickmansworth, Holdsworthy, &c.

[3] A stone-axe. The use of this expression, in the explanation of the Latin *bipennis*, is curious, as showing, apparently, either that the Anglo-Saxons did use axes made of stone, or that they believed that the axes of stone, so often found in different parts of England, and usually ascribed to the Celtic population of the island, were really the Roman weapon designated by that name.

Serra, snid.
Falx, sicol.
Falcastrum, siþe.
Acus, nædl.
Subula, æl.
Aurum, gold.
Argentum, seolfer.
Auricalcum, gold-mæslinc.
Es, bræs.
Stagnum, tin.
Plumbum, lead.
Vitrum, glæs.
Ferrum, isen.
Electrum, smyltinc.
Metallum, ælces cynnes wegc.
Massa, bloma, oððe dah.
Lapis, vel petra, stan.
Rima, vel fissura, cinu.
Marmor, marm-stan.
Saxum, weorc-stan.
Silex, flint.
Gipsum, spær-stan.
Gemma, gim-stan.
Margarita, meregrota.
Calx, cealc-stan.
Aries, ram.
Cimentum, andweorc to wealle.
Cimentarius, weal-wyrhta.
Rogus, ad.
Jocus, plega.
Locus, stow.
Omnis, ælc.
Omne, æl.
Totum, eal.
Prophanus, manful.
Exosus, vel perosus, andsæte.
Callidus, geap.
Simulator, hiwere.
Ypochrita, liccetere.
Adulator, lyffetere.
Adulatio, lyffetung.
Deceptor, vel seductor, bewæcend.

Proditor, vel traditor, læwa.
Homicida, man-slaga.
Patricida, fæder-slaga.
Matricida, modor-slaga.
Fratricida, broðor-slaga.
Parricida, mæg-slaga.
Vulnus, wund.
Cicatrix, dolh-swaþu.
Corpus, lic ægþer ge cuces ge deaðes.
Truncus, heafodleas bodig.
Fumus, lic, oððe hreaw.
Cadaver, lic, oððe hold.
Feretrum, bær.
Vivus, cucu.
Mortuus, dead.
Defunctus, forðfaren.
Longevus, lang-lif.
Nobilis, æþel-boren.
Presiosius, deorwurþe.
Vilis, waclice.
Carus, leof.
Odiosus, lað.
Limen, oferslæge, oððe þrexwold.
Sciffus, læfel.
Usceus, ceac.
Pulvis, wæter-mæle.
Plaustrum, vel carrum, wæn.
Rota, hweol.
Currus, vel basterna, vel hesseda, cræt.
Stabulum, fald, oððe hus be wege.
Caula, loc.
Tugurium, hulc.
Cella, cyte.
Mausoleum, ðruh, oððe ofer-geweorc.
Monumentum, vel sepulchrum, byrigen.
Sarcofagum, ðurh.
Elemosina, ælmesse.
Donum, vel datum, gyfu.
Munus, lac.
Uter, byt.
Flasco, butruc.
Tentorium, vel tabernaculum, geteld.

Pretium, wurð.
Corbis, vel cofinus, wylige, oððe meox-bearwe.
Sportella, tænel.
Cartallum, windel.
Calathus, wearp-fæt.
Pila, pil-stoc, oððe þoðer.
Loquela, spræc.
Vox, stemn.
Sonus, swæg.
Verbum, word.
Pecten, camb.
Sopo, sape.
Perna, flicce.
Sagene, sæ-net.
Follis, bylig.
Malleus, slegc.
Lima, feole.
Scorium, synder.
Forceps, tange.
Carbo, col.
Forfex, sceara.
Novacula, nægl-sex.
Cos, hwet-stan.
Apricus locus, hleow-stede.
Apricitas, hleowð.
Edificium, getimbrung.
Palatium, cyne-botl.
Basis, syl.
Postis, post.
Catena, racenteah.
Compes, vel cippus, fot-cops.
Bogia, iuc, oððe swur-cops.
Manice, hand-cops.
Complex, gegada.
Poena, vel supplicium, wite.
Vincula, vel ligamen, bend.
Pellis, fel.

Cutis, vel corium, hyd.
Nebris, næsc, oððe heorþa.
Mercennarius, hyr-man.
Horologium, dæg-mæl.
Gnomon, dægmæles pil.
Hospes, cuma.
Hospitium, gæst-hus.
Hostis, vel osor, feond.
Mansio, wunung.
Thesaurus, hord.
Gazaphilacium, maðm-hus.
Edax, vel glutto, ofer-eotol.
Ambro, frec.
Gulosus, gifre.
Procax, gemah.
Procacitas, gemahnes.
Obstinatus, anwille.
Abstinantia, anwilnys.
Verecundus, sceamfæst.
Impudens, unsceamfæst.
Pudicus, sydeful.
Inpudicus, unsydeful.
Interpres, wealhstod.
Reus, scyldig.
Damnatus, vel condempnatus, fordemed.
Peccator, synful.
Peccatum, syn.
Sceleratus, vel facinorosus, forscyldegod.
Scelus, scyld.
Facinus, vel culpa, gylt.
Adulter, forligr.
Perjurus, forsworen.
Gybberosus, vel strumosus, hoferede.
Gibbus, vel struma, hofer.
Meretrix, vel scorta, myltestre.
Pelex, cyfes.
We ne magon swa þeah ealle naman awritan ne furþor geþencan.

SEMI-SAXON VOCABULARY.[1]

(OF THE TWELFTH CENTURY.)

Verte,r, nol.
Cer[*vix*], necca.
Timpus, þunwænge.
Timpora, mo.[2]
Maxilla, leor.
Facies, onsene.
Palpebre, bre . . .
Pupilla, seo.
Labium, weler.
Labia, mo.
Adeps, rusel.
Arvina, ungel.
Viscus, ...
Viscera, mo.
Exta, þermes.
Ulna, elbowe.
Femur, vel coxa, þih.
Clunis, hupe.
Pulpa, ...
Sura, sperlire.
Crus, sceonke.
Tibia, scine.
Talus, oncleou.

Planta, fot-welm.
Al . . . , toa.
Ungula, hof, *vel* clau.
Diocesis, vel parochia, biscopriche.
Heremita, westense . . .
Conjunx, imæcca.
Conjuges, vel conjugales, isinheowen.
Conjugium, vel matrimonium, sins . . . .
Castus, clæne.
Formosus, wel iwlitegod.
Deformis, heowleas.
Decorus, wliti.
Sobole[*s, vel*] *liberi*, bearn.
Victricius, stepfeder.
Privivignus, stepsune.
Fileaster, stepd . . ter.
Nepos, neva.
Altor, vel nutritor, foster-fæder.
Altrix, vel nutrix, foster-moder.
Alumnus, foster-cild.
Propinquus, mæi.
Affinis, vel consanguineus, sibling.
. . *mes, vel tribus*, mæiþ.

[1] The vocabulary given above, which appears from the decadence of the grammatical forms, and from the orthography, to belong to about the middle of the twelfth century, is an abridgment of the foregoing Vocabulary from the Cottonian MS. It was discovered, in the fragmentary form in which it is here printed, on some leaves of vellum used as the cover or binding of one of the old registers of Worcester Cathedral, by Sir Thomas Phillipps, who printed a few copies privately. It there followed a copy of Alfric's Grammar, written in the same language, and is an extremely curious monument of this latter in its state of transition. It has been carefully corrected in the present edition.

[2] *Mo*, i. e. more, (*ma* in the purer Anglo-Saxon text,) is merely the mode of indicating the plural number.

Generatio, cunrun.
Gener, oþam.
Socer, sweor.
So . . , sweʒer.
Nurus, snore.
Princeps, aldermon.
Dux, heretowa, *vel* lætteow.
Comes, aldermon, *vel* ireva.
Clito, æþeling.
Obses, ʒysel.
Primas, heaved-mon.
Satrapa, þein.
Judex, dema.
Miles, vel athleta . . . , kempe.
Procinctus, furding.
Edictum, iban.
Vulgus, cheorl.
. . . . , folc.
Congregatio, vel contio, igæderung.
Conventus, vel conventio, imeting.
Sinodus, sinoþ, *vel* . . . . .
. . . , imot.
Dominus, vel herus, loverd.
Materna, ...
. . . . . , wif.
Cliens, vel clientulus, inkuiht.[1]

. . . . ln, *vel* þiuen.
Cu . . . .
. . . . de child.
Paterfamilias, hiredes loverd.
Consiliarius, rædbora.
Con[cio]nator, imot-mon.
Operarius, wurhta.
Faber, vel cudo, smiþ.
Officina, smiþ . . . .
Ærarius, mæstling-smiþ.

Arator, urþling.
Artifex, cræftca.
Opus, werc.
Opi[fex], cræftca.
Architectus, eldest wurhtena.
Amus, angel.
Venator, hunta.
Vena . . . *um*, bor-sper.
Auceps, fuwelare.
Trapezeta, vel nummularius, munetare.
Num[i]sma, munet.
Sollers, menituwe.
Iners, creftleas.
Nanus, dwæruh.
Fidis, ... eng.
Tubicen, bemare.
Tibicen, pipare.
Musa, pipe, *vel* hwistle.
Fidicen, fiþela.
Fistula, hwistle.
Liticen, truþ.
Lituus, truþhorn.
Poeta, scop, *vel* leoþ-wurhta.
. . . *nus, vel scurra,* gleomon.
Mercator, vel negociator, mangare.
Classis, scip . . . e.
Remus, roþer.
Remex, vel nauta, reþra.
Gubernator, vel nauclerus, steor[mo]n.
Proreta, ankermon.
Prora, þer þe ankermon sit.
Puppis, steor . . . . .
Antenna, seil-ʒerd.
Velum, seil, *vel* wahreft.
Clavus, steor-scofle, *vel* næil.
. . . *gma,* cliwa.
Sartor, seamære.
Sartrix, heo.
Dispensator, dihtnare.

[1] The leaves of the MS. had been cut at the top and bottom, when they were used to form the cover of a book, which caused the lacunæ indicated by these breaks. The lesser deficiencies are the result of mutilations of the edges of the leaves.

SEMI-SAXON VOCABULARY.

Di . . . r, delare.
Pincerna, birle.
Caupo, tæppare.
Dives, weli.
Locuples, lond . . . di.
Inops, havenleas.
Pauper, þærfa.
Egenus, wædla.
Fur, þeof.
Latro, ... aþa.
Merx, waræ.
Concors, iþwære.
Profugus, flemæ.
Exul, utlawe.
Conten[tios]us, iflitful.
Injuriosus, teonful.
Piger, slac.
Hebes, dwæs.
Parasitus, . . . olæcere.
Augur, wielare.
Incantator, galere.
Veneficus, unlib-wurhta.
[Ma]leficus, ufel-dede.
Magus, dri.
Phitonissa, wicche.
Centurio, hundredes . . . . or.
Persecutor, ehtere.
Dispendium, vel damnum, hinþ.
Jactura, lure.
Commodum, hinþ.
. . *milla*, beah.
Diadema, kine-helm.
Capicium, hæt.
Monile, mune, *vel* sweor-beah.
. . *nter*, dalc, *vel* preon.
Fibula, oferfeng.
Vitta, snod.
Inauris, ear-preon.
Indigena, vel incola, inlendisc.
Advena, utan-cumen.
Peregrinus, alþeodi.
Messor, riftere.

Messis, irip.
Acervus, hreac, *vel* hupel.
Stimulus, gode.
Aculeus, sticels.
Circus, vel circulus, wiþþe.
Epistola, ærind-iwrit.
Quaternio, cine.
Planta, spelt.
Diploma, bowa.
Scedla, vel scedula, ymele.
Pictor, metere.
Pictura, meting.
Minium, teapor.
Gluten, lim.
Sculptor, grafere.
Grafium, græf.
Sculptura, græf.
Agalma, onlicnesse.
Scalprum, vel scalpellum, græf-[sex].

. . . *oleum*, w . . . .
. . . . . *vel monoptalmus*, on-ei3e . . .
. . . . . scul-ei3ede.
Lippus, sur-ei3ede.
Mancus, onhende.
Infirmus, untrum.
Eg . . . , *vel languidus*, adli3.
Paraclitus, frofergost.
Paraliticus, bedreda.
Leprosus, ... þroware.
Lunaticus, monnþ-sic.
Demoniacus, deofel-sic.
Energuminus, ...
. . *bus*, adl.
Pestis, cwuld.
Amens, vel demens, imundleas.
Rabidus, vel insanus, ...
. . . . , wodnesse.
Incolumis, isund.
Frenetus, þe þet þuruh slopleaste awet . . .

Letargicus, unilimpliche slapel.
Pervigil, þuruh-wacol.
Pius, orfest.
. . . . leas.
Famosus, hlisful.
Fama, hlisa.
Infamis, unhlisful.
Infamia, unhli . . . .
. . . . . , custi.
Tenax, fest-hafol.
Parcus, uncusti.
Frugi, vel parcus, sparhende.
S . . . . *rus*, gleaw.
Prudens, snoter.
Imprudens, unsnoter.
Astutus, pæti.
Stultu . . . . . .
. . *rax*, soþfest.
Veridicus, soþ-sawel.
Fallax, vel mendax, leas.
Falsidicus, un.
[*Testis*], iwita.
Testimonium, iwitnesse, *vel* icuþnesse.
Cursor, runel.
Superbus, modi.
[*Superbia*, mo]dinesse.
Humilis, edmod.
Humilitas, edmodnesse.
Aer, luft.
Auro, hwiþa.
N . . . , scur.
Procella, storm.
Nubes, weolcne.
Ver, leinten.
Autumnus, herfest.
Vernum temp . . . . .
Vernalis dies, leintenlic dæi.
Cauma, sweoli.
Humor, wæte.
Sterilitas, un . . . . . . se.
Fertilitas, wæstmbernesse.
Color, bleo.

Ruber, read.
Fulvus, vel flavus, ...
. . . . fouh.
Discolor, mislicbes bleos.
Forma, heow.
Fantasma, idwimor.
Merul . . . meaw.
Turdus, ster.
Coternix, ediscine.
Pullus, chiken, *vel* brid, *vel* fole.
Vespertilio, re . . . . .
. . . . *vel strix, vel bubo*, ule.
Graculus, roc.
Parrax, wrænna.
Apis, beo.
Fucus, dro . . . .
. . . . . nette.
Scarabæus, scearnbudoa, *vel* budda.
Cinomia, hundes-fliæ.
Culex, stut.
Cetus, ...
. . . . . . , mære-swin.
Ysicius, vel salmo, lex.
Taricus, vel illec, hæring.
Fannus, ro . . . .
. . . . , crabba.
Polipes, loppestre.
Murena, vel murenula, mere-neddre.
. . . .
Belua, eislic nuten on sæ oþer on londe.
Concha, scel.
Fera, wilde d . . . .
. . . . . . d hund and wulf.
Unicornis, vel rinoceron, vel monoceron, onhurne deo . . .
. . . *lus*, broc.
Camelus, olfend.
Onager, wilde assa.
Elefans, ylp.
Lutrius, ...
. . . . , beofer.
Lubricus, ongel-twæcche.

SEMI-SAXON VOCABULARY.

Capreolus, roa-deor.
Caprea, roa.
. . . . . . , bucca.
Caprea, vel capella, got.
Damma, vel dammula, do.
Cervus, heort.
C . . . . . , kælf.
Hinnulus, hind.
Hedus, ticchen.
Scroffa, suwa.
Aper, vel verres, b . . .
. . . , bæruth.
Vacca, vel bucula, ku.
Juvenencus, steor.
Canis, hund.
Molo . . . . .
. . *beta*, tadde.
Lacerta, evete.
Stellio, slo-wurm.
Locusta, greshoppe.
Li . . . .
. . . . *do*, þe þe haveþ hus.
Eruca, mæsle-sceafe.
Cimex, maþe.
Tine . . . .

. . . . wurt.
Abrotanum, suþerwude.
Malva, hoc.
Malva crispa, ... rt.
Simitia, grundeswulie.
Anetum, dile.
Polipodium, rifnes-fot.
. . . . eies-eien.
Solsequium, ...
. . . . . . , rude.
Betonica, þeo lesse biscop-wurt.
Ta . . . . . . de.
Saxifragia, sundcorn.
Gitsana, fæarn.
Calamus, vel canna, vel . . . . . od.

Papaver, popi.
Absinthium, wermot.
Urtica, netle.
Archan . . . . . de-netle.
Plantago, weibreode.
Vinca, pervenke.
Marrubium, hor . . . .
. . . . . . , stræberie-wise.
Modera, chicne-mete.
Apium, merc.
Lappa, clote, *vel* clif . . . .
. . . . , horselne.
Sandix, wod.
Caula, vel magudaris, caul.
Cresco, carse.
. . . . e.
Artemisia, mugwurt.
Felterræ, vel centaurea, eorþ-galla.
Ambrosia . . . . .
Hermodactula tidolosa, crowe-lec.
Pastinaca, walmore.
Viola, ...
. . . *imonia*, gor-clifu.
Rafanum, redic.
Filex, fearn.
Carex, seg.
Arbor, ...
. . *us, vel ylex*, oc.
Taxus, iw.
Fagus, boc-treow.
Alnus, olr.
Malus, æp . . . .
. . . *ga*, ʒerd.
Virgultum, telʒra.
Granum, kurnel.
Ulcia, holi.
Populus, ...
. . . . palm-twig.
Genesta, brom.
Sentes, þornes.
Frutex, þifel.
Ramnus, ...

. . . . . bremelas.
Abies, æps.
Morus, mor-beam.
Vitis, win-treow.
Salix, wiþi.
. . . .
Lignum, iheawen treow.
Ligna, driȝe wude.
Truncus, stoc.
Stirps, ...
. . . . , *vel saltus,* holt.
Desertum, vel heremus, westen.
Via, wei.
Semita, peþ.
. . . . . . n weie.
Iter, siþfæt.
Patria, eþel.
Provincia, vel pagus, scyr.
Mons, ...
. . . . . . hul, *vel* beoruh.
Vallis, dene.
Fenum, hei, *vel* græs.
Ager, aker.
Se . . . . . . æker.
Campus, feld.
Vadum, ford.
Litus, sæ-strond.
Alveus, stream.
. . . . a.
Rivus, riþ.
Aqua, water.
Gutta, vel stilla, drope.
Stangnum, ...
. . . . . s, enn.
Flumen, flod, *vel fluvius.*
Ripa, steþ.
Gurges, wæl.
Lacus, ...
. . . . . oc, *vel* burna.
Unda, uþæ.
Domus, hus.
Eclesia, chirche, *vel* ileafful . . .

. . . . *vel* ilaþung.
Pagina, tramet.
Archa, scrin.
Loculus, cheste, *vel* . . . .
. . . *ix,* calic.
Patena, husel-disc.
Crux, vel staurus, rod.
Cathedra, ...
Fundamentum, grund-wal.
Pavimentum, vel solum, flor.
Tectum, þecen.
. . . . , *vel fornix,* biȝels.
Columna, sweor.
Clausura, loc.
Clavis, kcie.
. . . . *vel sera,* hespe.
Chorus, chor.
Gradus, stæpe.
Indicatorium, ...
. . . *a,* sticke.
Regula, reȝol-sticke.
Lampas, vel lucerna, vel later, ...
. . . . ab.
Lichinus, blacern.
Munctorium, irene tonge.
Clo . . . .

. . . *lum, vel cinctorium, vel zona,*
  gurdel . . .
Caliga, vel ocrea, hosa.
. . . *tum,* isco.
Suptalaris, swiftlere.
Tractorium, tiȝel.
Flagrum, vel flag . . . . .
Dormitorium, slepern.
Stramentum, bedding.
Stragula, wæls . . . .
. . . . . . hwitel.
Pulvinar, pule.
Sindo, scete.
Fulcra, al bed-reaf.

F . . . .
Perizomata, vel campestria, wæd-brec.
Fimbria, fnæd.
Colobi . . . . suric.
Pedula, meo.
Commissura, clut.
Toral, roc.
Tela, vel pep . . . . .
. . . . cleowen.
Colus, distæf.
Fusus, spindle.
Textrinum opus, teowli . . . .
. . . . . gong.
Trabes, beam.
Tignum, refter.
Laquear, first.
Cleta, hu . . . . .
. . . . *rium,* beoddern, *vel* ireordung-hus.
Tapeta, set-ræiȝel.
Mensa, ...
Discifer, disc-þein.
Minister, þein.
Lardum, spic.
Puls, bri.
A . . . .
. . . . *do,* meodu.
Idromellum, vel mulsum, beor.
Cicera, ilches cunnes iw . . . win one.
Manuterium, vel mantele, scet.
Cultellus, sex.
Artavus, h . . . .
. . . . . drunc cuppe.
Anaphus, nep.
Patera, bledu.
Andena, bron . . .
. . . . . . brond.
Olla, crocke.
Cacabus, chetel.
Lebes, hwer.
Caro, flæsc.
. . . .

. . *tilis canis,* broþ-hund.
Fuscinula, owul.
Uncinus, huc.
Comm . . . . . .
Daps, sonde.
Ferculum, bær-disc.
Veru, spite.
Assura, bræd.
. . . . . , irene ponne.
Frixorium, hursting.
Coctio, isod.
Coctus, isod . . . . .
Frustum, stucche.
Offa, snode.
Vestiarium, ræil-hus.
Sigillum, ...
. . . *larium,* heddern.
Celerarius, hordare.
Mola, cweorn-stan.
Vi . . . . . . ve.
Pecunia, feoh.
Marsupium, seod.
Pistrinum, bakern.
For . . . . *nus,* oven.
Pistor, bakestre.
Bracium, malt.
Acus, sifeþe.
Crib . . . . , sife.
Furfures, gruta.
Fex, drosne.
Anfora, sester.
Lagena, b . . . . .
. . . . . cuf.
Cupa, tunna.
Utensilia, andloman.
Suppellex, yddi . . . .
. . *um,* bur.
Solarium, up-flor.
Cardo, heorre.
Strigil, vel strigilis, ...
Risus, leihter.
Tristis, unrot.

Mestus, dreori.
Abundantia, . . . inihtsumnesse.
Corpulentus, þiccol.
Invalidus, unstrong.
Solli . . . . . .
Amurca, i. fex olei, dersten.
Securus, orseoruh.
Tutus, siker.
C . . sa, intinga.
Occasio, inca.
Excusator, beladiend.
Mento, feh . . . . . .

. . . . . *t*, tocnebora.
Lancea, vel talarica, spere.
Victor, siȝefeit
Victoria, ...
Capulum, hilta.
Mucro, swerdes ord, *vel* oþres wæpnes.
Sica, lutel . . . . . d sex.
Asta, vel quiris, scæft.
Telum, flo.
Fustis, sowel.
Vectis, steng.
Faretra, ...
Clipeus, sceld.
Umbo, rand-beah.
Atrium, cafertun, *vel* inburh.
. . *undibalum*, stef-liþere.
Civitas, chestre.
Civis, cheasteriwara, *vel* . . . .
. . . . *o*, budel.
Oppidum, fæsten.
Castellum, wic, *vel* lutel-port.
Urbs, bu . . . . . .
. . . . . . , buruh-wita.
Suburbanus, þe þe sit buton þære buri.
Car . . . .
Oppidanus, þe þe on fæstene sit.
Villanus, tun-mon.
Villicus, ...

. . . . *tus*, orchard.
Ortolanus, orchard-weard.
Pomerium, æpel-tun.
. . . . . . , wurtun.
Predium, worþiȝ.
Ferramentum, tol.
Securis, æx.
Ascia, ade . .
. . . . . . vegar.
Terebro, ic bore.
Vanga, vel fossorium, spade.
Ligo, becca.
. . . . . . , æx.
Palus, pal.
Serra, snid.
Falx, sicol.
Falcastrum, . . .
Acus, nelde.
. . *uricalcum*, gold-mestling.
Æs, bres.
Electrum, smulting.
Metallum, ... ecg.
Massa, bloma, *vel* dah.
Lapis, vel petra, ston.
Fissura, heone.
Marmor, ...
Saxum, werc-ston.
Silex, flint.
Gipsum, spær-ston.
Gemma, ȝim-ston.
. . . . . regrota.
Calcx, chalc-ston.
Aries, rom.
Cimentum, andweorc to walle.
Cemen . . . . . . hta.
Rogus, od.
Jocus, pleiȝa.
Prophanus, monful.
Exosus, vel perosus, and . . . .
. . . . gleaw (? geap.)
Simulator, heoware.
Hipocrita, licettere.

SEMI-SAXON VOCABULARY.

Adulator, lufe . . . .
. . . *cio,* luffetung.
Deceptor, vel seductor, bewechend.
Proditor, ...
. *omicida,* monsleia.
Patricida, matricida, fratricida, parracida.
. . . *icatrix,* dolh-swaþe.
Truncus, heafedleas bodi.
Corpus, lic.
Funis, ...
. . . *aver,* lic, *vel* hold.
Feretrum, bære.
Defunctus, forþfaren.
Longevus, ...
. . . *lis,* æþelboren.
Ignobilis, unæþelboren.
Vilis, woclic.
Carus, leof . . . . .
Limen, ofersleie, *vel* þreoxwold.
Sciffus, læfel.
Urceus, ceac.
Pelvis, ...
. . *laustrum, vel carrum,* wein.
Currus, vel basterna, vel heseda, kert.
Stabu, ... s bi wei3e.
Caula, loc.
Tugurium, hulc.
Cella, cot.
Mausoleum, þruh . . .
Monumentum, vel sepulcrum, buriles.
Sarcofagum, þruh.
Donum, vel . . . . .
Munus, loc.
Uter, butte.
Flasco, buttruc.
Tentorium, vel taberna, ...

———

. . . . *lum,* næil-sex.
Cos, hweston.
Apricus locus, leow-stude.

Apricitas, leowþ.
Edific . . . , itimbrung.
Palatium, kinelic-botl.
Bassis, sulle.
Postis, post.
Compes, vel cippus, f . . . . .
Boia, ioc, *vel* sweor-cops.
Manica, hond-cops.
Complex, igada.
Pœna, vel sup . . . . , wite.
Nebris, næst.
Mercennarius, hur-mon.
Horologium, dæimæl.
Goomon, (sic) . . . . les pil.
Hospes, cuma.
Hospitium, gest-hus.
Hostis, vel osor, feond.
Thesaurus, hor . . .
. . . *filacium,* madm-hus.
Edax, vel gluto, ofer-etel.
Ambro, fræc.
Gulosus, 3ifre.
P . . . , imouh.
Procacitas, imouhnesse.
Obstinatus, onwille.
Obstinantia, onwilln . . . .
Verecundus, sceomefest.
Inpudens, unsceomefest.
Pudicus, sideful.
Inpud . . . . , unsideful.
Interpres, wealhstod.
Reus, sculdi.
Damnatus, vel condemnatus, for . . .
Sceleratus, vel facinorosus, forsculdegod.
Scelus, sculd.
Facinus, vel culpa, gi . . . .
Adulter, furli3er, *vel* æwbræche.
Gibberosus, vel strumosus, hoferede.
Gibb . . . . *struma,* hofer.
Meretrix, vel scorta, multestre.
Pelex, cyfes, *et cetera.*

THE TREATISE DE UTENSILIBUS

OF

ALEXANDER NECKAM.[1]

(OF THE TWELFTH CENTURY.)

Hic incipit summa magistri Alexandri Nequam de nominibus utensilium.

Qui bene vult disponere familie sue et domui sue et rebus suis, primo provideat sibi in utensilibus et in suppellectilibus.
          quisine   table   cholet   mincé   lentils
In coquina sit mensula, super quam olus apte minuatur, ut lenticule,
peys   grueus   feve frisés   feves en coys   sanc coys   mil
pise, et pultes, et fabe frese, et fabe silique, et fabe esilique, et milium,
uniun   potages   trenchez
cepe, et hujusmodi legumina que resecari possint.

---

[1] Alexander Neckam (whose name is also spelt in the MSS. *Necham* and *Nequam*), one of the most distinguished scholars of the latter end of the twelfth century, was born at St. Albans in 1157, and made such rapid progress in learning that he was entrusted at a very early age with the direction of the celebrated school of Dunstable, and as early as the year 1180 had attained to celebrity as a professor in the University of Paris. He returned to England in 1187, and is said to have resumed his former position in the school of Dunstable. He died in 1217, leaving a considerable number of works as monuments of his talents and learning. That which is here printed was in all probability composed while he directed the school of Dunstable, and may with tolerable safety be ascribed to the twelfth century. It is here printed from a manuscript of the latter end of the thirteenth century, MS. Cotton. Titus D. xx, which is the best copy I have met with, and was evidently written in England, both from the character of the writing, and from the occurrence of several English words in the interlinear gloss. It appears to have been once a popular school-book, and several other manuscripts are known. M. Leopold Delille has kindly furnished me with a copy of one preserved in the Imperial Library in Paris, MS. Latin, No. 7679, written on paper in the fifteenth century, collated with another copy of later date in the same library, No. 217, from which I have extracted a few various readings. In the copy in the Cottonian MS., the text of this treatise is accompanied with an interlinear gloss, and with a grammatical commentary. The former is here printed with the text, and is written chiefly in the Anglo-Norman dialect of the French language of that period, with a few English words intermixed, and here and there grammatical, that it has not been thought necessary to print it, but whenever it contains anything worthy of notice it will be used in my notes. The comment on the first paragraph contains the following remarks on the title and

THE TREATISE OF ALEXANDER NECKAM.

In coquina sint olle, tripodes, securis, mortarium, pilus, contus, uncus, [glosses: poz treves [brales] conie — morter pestel movur croc]
creagra, cacabus, aenum, patella, sartago, craticula, urciolus, discus, scutella, [glosses: caudrun idem paele idem graunt paele gridilie pocenet quele idem]
perabsis,[1] salsarium, artavi, quibus pisces possunt exenterari. [glosses: dubler sauser cnives[2] i. aperiri]

Sit ibi coclear magnum, quo spume et ebuliciones possint castigari. [glosses: in coquina luche espumet]

Gurgustio, vel funda, vel fuscina,[3] vel jaculo, vel amitte levi,[4] vel [glosses: retis [un rei] virga hamata idem [alge] reiz hamus [heym]]
nassa in vivario depressi.[6] Item habeat archimacherus capanam [glosses: idem [fis-lep][5] viver capti magister cocus parvam cameram]
in coquina, vel culina, ubi species aromaticas et amolum, vel saltem [glosses: quisine idem especes virtuosas [odurantes] flur de furment]
panem cribro scinceratum et contritum ad pisciculos consolidandos in [glosses: cribre ecclersy [defuli] triblé afrinceres]
abditorio reponat. Sint etiam ibi alucia, ubi volatilium et anserum [glosses: forcer[7] met. lavurs [guteres] (owegars)]
et avium domesticarum entera et extremitates crebro a lixa [glosses: bueus (de le quistrun, i. protia)]
proiciantur et purgentur. Item habeat lixa aquam calidam qua pulli [glosses: (quistrun)]
possint excaturizari. [glosses: estre escaudet]

Mola assit piperalis, et mola manualis. Pisciculi coquendi in salsamento [glosses: mole [le meyn] parvi pisces saus]
sive in muria, quod est aqua sali mixta, ponantur; et dicitur muria [glosses: idem]
quasi maria, quia maris saporem sapit vel exprimit.

Assit etiam micatorium, et ruder, ad quod sordes coquine defluere [glosses: miur guter decure]
possint. Salsamentum superius enumeratum omnibus piscibus non dicitur [glosses: sauz omnimodi piscibus]
competere. Nam diversi sunt, utpote mugiles, amphinia,[8] congrus, et [glosses: competens esse pisces pro sicut saumuns soles cunger]
murena, musculus, et epimera, gobio, melanurus, et capito, ypotamus, [glosses: lampré baleyne[9] etpirlinge gujun bar de mer caborche equs marinus]

---

design of the book itself:—" Materia hujus libri sunt nomina utensilium. Intencio autoris est colligere sub compendio nomina utensilium. Causa suscepti operis est puerilis instructio. Artifex est magister Alexander Nequam. Titulus talis est: Hic incipit summa magistri Alexandri Nequam de nominibus utensilium. Utilitas est partium expositio. Sed quia expositio quandoque fit per compositionem, quandoque per etthimologiam, quandoque per interpretationem, istarum prescienda est differentia," etc.

[1] *Parapsis*, in the Parisian MS. No. 7679.

[2] *Cnives* is perhaps an English gloss, though the word is found in a nearly similar form in old French, *canif, canivet*, or *knivet*.

[3] An eel-spear.

[4] *Hamite levi*, Paris MS.

[5] Fis-lep, in old English, meant a fish-basket, or basket for taking fish. We have already seen (p. 9) that the Anglo-Saxons fished with baskets. The Parisian MS. has *lassa*, for *nassa*.

[6] The Parisian MS. reads *in vivario sive in stanno deprensi.*

[7] This is further glossed *in secreto loco* by a rather later hand.

[8] MS. Paris, No. 7679, reads *amphiria;* MS. Paris, 217, *amphiviera*.

[9] Our taste in the article of fish has certainly

<small>moru   plays   mulet   raye   canis marinus makerel   turbut   arangue</small>
morus, pelamides, mulus, uranoscopus, dentrix, megarus, turtur, et alecia,
<small>pinosche. stanstikel¹   frié   hoysters   barse de mer</small>
gamarus, dimidio ovo confrictus,² hostria, et bocca marina.
<small>   idem   mapes   tualeys   tuayles</small>
In dispensa, sive in dispensatorio, sint gausape, mantile, manutergium;
<small>la perche   suriz</small>
et a pertica propter insidias murium vestes apte dependeant. Sint ibi
<small>culteus   sauser   idem   peynt   hec [casi hord]</small>
cultelli, salsarium vel salinum sculptum, et theca caseorum, candelabrum,
<small>baskes</small>
absconsa, laterna, calathi ad portandum.
<small>   celer   idem   idem   barils coutereus³ tunneus</small>
In promptuario, sive in celario, sive in penu, sint cadi, utres, dolea,
<small>anaps   anapers   culiers   dusyis   bacyns corbayls vins   idem scisere</small>
ciphi, cophini, coclearia, clepsedre, pelves, corbes, mera, vina, scicera,
<small>cerveyse   idem   must   idem   claré⁴   piment⁵   idem</small>
cervicia, sive celia, mustum, mulsum, claretum, nectar, sive pigmentum,
<small>mede   idem   idem   piré   vin</small>
medo, sive secundum Ysodorum medus, sive ydromellum, piretum, vinum
<small>rosé   feré   de Auverne⁶   gelofré à lecchurs</small>
rosetum, vinum feratum, vinum falernum, vinum gariofilatum, lambris et
<small>à glutuns   insedabilis</small>
ambubagis, quorum sitis est incompleta, appetibile, quorum summum
<small>   i. deam latrocinii onorare   genium dicitur</small>
studium est lavernam colere et genium deum nature.
<small>li asnjurner   furé   cote   manches</small>
Perhendinaturus jupam habeat penulatam,⁷ et tunicam manubiis et
<small>geruns   panos   brays</small>
birris munitam,⁸ et laciniis. Femoralibus etiam opus est, ubi pudibunda

been much refined since the middle ages, for there can be no doubt that even whale was then eaten. It is enumerated, in a manuscript of the thirteenth century, given by Roquefort, in his histoire de la Vie privée des François, tom. ii, p. 83, among the fish then imported into France for the table. In the curious fabliau of the Bataille de Karesme et de Charnage, Karesme (Lent) reckons the whale as well as the chien-de-mer (dog fish) among his dependents.

    Del harenc a fet messagier,
    Si l en envoie sans targier
    As chiens de-mer, et as balaines,
    Conter les noveles certaines,
    Et as saumons, et as craspois, etc.
                      Barbazan, vol. iv., p. 85.

Directions for cooking the chien-de-mer are given in the Menagier de Paris, ii., 195.

[1] This is another English gloss. It is hardly necessary to remark that the *stanstucle* is the small fish we more commonly call a *stickleback*.

[2] *Constrictus*, MS. Paris, No. 7679.

[3] *Outres*, or leathern vessels for containing wine, had not gone out of use in the fourteenth century. See Roquefort, Vie pr. des Fr. ii., 420.

[4] The *claré* of the middle ages was a mixture of white wine with honey, sugar, and certain spices.

[5] Piment was a mixture of wine, honey, and spices, and was held in great esteem in the middle ages. It appears to have been distinguished from *claré* by being made of red wine.

[6] The wine of Auverne was celebrated at an early period, and is often mentioned by the old writers. The schoolmen seem to have considered it as equivalent to the Falerne wine of the ancients.

[7] *Manubriatam et penulatam*, MS. Paris, No. 7679.

[8] *Manibus et birris laticiis munitum*, MS. Paris, 7679.

lateant nature; et opus est lumbaribus, caligis tibie muniantur, pedes
estivalibus, vel calceis laquealis vel consutilibus.

Camisia sindonis, vel serici, vel bissi¹ materiam sorciatur, vel saltem
lini. Penula mantelli sit ex scisimis,² vel experiolis, sive scurellis, vel
ex cuniculis, vel ex laeronibus; cujus urla sit ex sabelino et matrice, vel
bivere, sive fibro, vel vulpecula, roserella.

Equitaturus³ capam habeat manuleatam sive manubeatam. Cujus capucium aeris minas non exhorreat vel sudum non formidet. Ocreas habeat
et calcarea, sive stimulos hortatorios, quibus equo insideat, neque succu-
santi, neque cespitanti, neque recalcitranti, neque recursanti, neque reculanti,
neque stimulos neganti, neque repedanti, neque antepedanti, sed bene
ambulanti, et ad mittendum habili. Ferri clavis bene sint firmati.

Carentivillo tergum sit coopertum, postmodum sudario, vel suario, vel
panello, super quem sella apte collocetur, tenuis sudarii apte super
clunes equi pendentibus. Strepe, sive scansilia, a sella apte dependeant.

---

¹ *Sendal, soye* (silk), and *cheysil*, or, as it is more usually called, *bis*, are given as the three finest stuffs then in use. They appear all to have had silk in their composition. *Sendal*, or *Cendal*, was an inferior description of silk, supposed to have been nearly identical with what we now call taffeta; it was commonly used for making banners, or flags. A poet of the thirteenth century (Guillaume Guyart) tells us that the oriflamme was of this material.

L'oriflame est une banniere,
Aucun poi plus forte que guimple.
De cendal roujoyans, et simple
Sans pouretraiture d'autre affaire.

The word *cheysil* seems to be more frequently used by English than by French writers. Thus, in a poem of the fourteenth century,—

Of v. thinges he bitaught hem werke,
As to hem wald bifalle,
Of flex, of silk, of *cheisel*.

Legend of Joachim and Anne.

It is identified with *bis* in our text by the Latin equivalent, *byssus*, which evidently was not taken in the middle ages, as some lexicographers have supposed, in its classical sense of *linen*, from which it is clearly distinguished in our text. *Bis* is often spoken of in old poetry as being of a purple colour, and as the material of the dresses of ladies of rank.

² *Ex cicivis*, MS. Paris, No. 7679. *Gris*, usually Latinised into *griseus*, was one of the richest furs used in the middle ages, but it seems to be uncertain from what animal it was obtained. The word *cisimus*, for a sort of fur, and for the animal which furnished it, occurs in several Latin writers of the twelfth century: it is perhaps synonymous with *vair*, supposed to be some kind of weasel.

³ The minute account of the caparison of the horse is very curious, and will be found of considerable interest to the antiquary.

    arsuns   arsun devant et derere   peytereus
Arculi duo, scilicet antella et postella, suas habeat antellas et postellas,
     en pleyt   trusse   peyterel
ut vestes sub involucro posite bene disponantur in mantica. Pectorale
    arneys   lescez   bernac
autem et cetere falere usui equitantis necessarie non obmittantur. Camum,
   chevestre   chaufreyn   idem   frenum dico
vel capistrum, frenum, vel lupatum, sive salivare, spumis sanguineis infectum,
 reyns   cengle   ardylyun bucle   bache
habenas, et cingulum, et lingulam, pusculam, et pulvillum, et trussulam
     nomen fictum   lestrilie
sponte pretereo. Garcio[1] autem, sive pedes, strigilem ferat.
   en la chaumbre   idem   envirunet curtine   vesture
 In camera, sive in talamo, parietes ambiat cortina, sive canopeum
 i. teatrale
scenicum, ad muscarum evitacionem et aranearum. Altilis, sive epistilis,
 del piler   chalun   idem
columpne, tapetum sive tapete dependeant.
       chaere   idem lecto i. scannum
Juxta lectum cathedra locetur, ad pedes sive ad bases cui scabellum
     chaere   lit quilte
subjungatur, cui lectica associetur.[2] Supra thorum culcitra ponatur plumalis,
  orler   quilte poynté   rayé
cui cervical maritetur. Hanc cooperiat culcitra punctata, vel vestis stragulata,
     quissine
super quam pulvinar parti capitis supponende desuper ponatur.
      linceus   de sendel   cheysil   lin
Dehinc autem lintheamina ex syndone vel ex bisso, vel saltem ex lino,
   launges   vert say pane de teysun
vel lodices supponantur. Deinde coopertorium de viridi sagio, penula taxea,
 chat   bevere   sabelin   purpre
vel catina, vel beverina, vel sabelina, muniatur, si forte desit purpura
 curtine
vel catumvolatile.
             muscher etperver idem aloues
Assit et pertica[3] cui insidere possit capus, nisus, et alietus, circi
i. veloci odiosus gerfauc   tercel faucun peleryn   auteyn
perpeti infestus, erodius et tercellus, falco peregrinus, et falco ascensorius,
 laner   gruer   oustur
tardearius,[4] et gruarius, et ancipiter.

---

 [1] *Garcio*, the stable-boy; *strigile*, the horse-comb.

 [2] This is exactly the arrangement of the bed in the numerous pictures of interiors of chambers in the illuminations of manuscripts; the chair is invariably placed beside the head of the bed, and a bench at the bed foot.

 [3] The chamber was furnished with a horizontal rod, called a perche, for the purpose of hanging articles of dress, &c. It would appear from the statement made here that it was customary for people also to keep their hawks on a perche in the bed-room. I have seen confirmation of this practice in illuminations of manuscripts.

 [4] The Paris MS. adds here, *et ardearius*.

                                         chemisis cuverchefs petiz cuverchefs brays
    Ab alia autem pertica dependeant supera, flamea,   flameola, peryzoma,
chape   manttel   cuvele   cote   froge¹   surcote
capa, pallium, toga, tunica, collobium, et epitogium. Preter hec autem
   roket   curtepye   idem   vardecors²   idem
instita matronalis, lumbarie, sive lunbatorium, renale, sive ventrale; non
       vesture suyle lunge chimises (bone vestures)   curte veste
autem   limata,   sed aspergines, sparta, et sirmata,
       de purpre   laungea   roket   rive
et longa girophea, et lodice trabeales,³ et collobium, et teristrum.
                mechine   enclersith
Assit etiam nimphula,⁴ cujus facies talamum serenet et amenet, que
                       sarence   orfrey   lasures   plies
quandoque fallat diem; cum mataxa autem aurifrigii nexus et tricaturas
                                                     cuscet
complicet et explicet; aut vestes laneas, vel pannos lineos, apte consuat
   dubet   gauns   coupez
et sarciat. Cirotecas habeat primis digitorum porcionibus amputatis.
     del   de quir   aguyl   encuntraunt   communiter
Tecam habeat corigialem⁵ acus insidiis obviantem, que vulgariter
   del   force   boyzte
polliceum dicitur. Forficem habeat, et philarium, non dico philatorium,
                                   jussel
quod ad ecclesiam pertinet; et glomos fili extricet, et varias acus habeat,
                                      tripharye⁶
parvas et subtiles ad opus anaglafarium, minus subtiles ad opus plumale,
                       custre   gerun   ply-
parum subtiles ad consuendum opus vulgare, grossas ad byrritricas poli-
ez   introducendos   enveysursis
endas, grossiores ad laqueos inducendos, grossissimas cum amoris illecebris
             vimple⁷   exponat   [retpyne]
indulgeat. Nunc peplo intemperiem aeris excipiat, nunc corolla, nunc
   kalle   bende   kalle   de chevus   conjungat
corocalla, nunc crinali vel reticulo libertatem comarum discurrencium refrenet.
   nucle   quasi spina tenax   fustanie   colers
Monile habeat,   spinter,   quo tunice fuscotincti vel camisie⁸ colaria con-
                    beve de or   ornamenta aurium
jungat; habeat etiam torques et   inaures.
               [une bacese]   ofs   i. pullos faciencia   agars
Assit etiam androgia, que gallinis ova supponat pullificancia, et anseribus
curayles agraventet   ayneus   parvos unius anni
acera substernat, que agnellos morbidos, non dico anniculos in sua teneri-

---

¹ A frock.
² *Gardecorps*, a sort of vest.
³ The Paris MS. No. 7679, reads *cerophea et indices teatrales*.
⁴ The same Paris MS. has *menfula* for *nimphula*.
⁵ A leather thimble — of cuirbouilli, probably,
which seems to have been the ordinary material of thimbles.
⁶ *Opus anaglapherium* and *tripharye* appear to be here used for embroidery.
⁷ A wimple.
⁸ The Paris MS. No. 7679, reads *camisie ex lino vel bisso*.

^{nutriat} ^{feblement dentez deseverez}
tate lacte foveat alieno; vitulos autem et subruinos ablactatos inclusos
^{parroc¹} ^{fenerye}
teneat in pargulo juxta fenile. Cujus indumenta in festivis diebus sint
^{à dames pelysenns sineroket idem}
matronales serapelline, recinium, teristrum.

^{androgie} ^{porchers mege à bovers à vachers}
Hujus autem usus est subulcis colustrum et bubulcis et armentariis,
^{supers sur leyt idem, vel crem}
domino autem et suis collateralibus in obsoniis oxigallum sive quactum
^{in magnis discis duner in secreto loco [gras]}
in cimbiis ministrare, et catulis in abditorio repositis pingue serum
^{[o pain] de bren [donner]}
cum pane furfureo porrigere.

^{asce de porc suvenerment}
Assa carnis suille, diligenti tractu assata, vel versata crebro super
^{gridil breces fume}
craticulam, prunis carbonum ardentibus suppositis, fumo et flamma cessan-
^{dedeynet sel}
tibus, condimentum dedignatur aliud quam purum salem vel simplicem
^{alyè chapun en cunscis de peyvere}
aliatam. Altilis in consciso parata piperis non renuit aspersionem.

^{domesche brosche}
Auca domestica, dummodo sit tenera, veru longo circumvoluta, aliatam
^{de reysins pinnes de boys}
fortem desiderat, vino vel viridi succo racemorum sive pomorum silvestrium
^{compositam octaude cimim}
distemperatam. Gallina ex quo sit scaturizata, membratim divisa, cimino
^{quist rostye gutementz lard}
condiatur, si elixa fuerit. Si assata sit, crebris gutticulis lardi refficiatur;
^{alié simple sause}
nec condimentum renuit aliate, sapidissima tamen erit cum simplici salsa.

^{i. facta}
Pisces autem exenterati cum salsa coquantur composita ex vino et aqua;
^{capiantur verde sause sauge persil}
postmodum sumantur cum viridi sapore, cujus materia sit salgea, petrosillium,
^{ditayne petre avle}
costus, ditanum, serpillum, et alia, cum pipere; non omittatur salis bene-
^{saciat a tali loco}
ficium.² Sed hoc sumentem precipue exillarat et reficit vinum passum et
^{saulé vino i. admirando videre}
defructum, in quo admirari possit quis usque ad fundum ciphi perspicui-
^{¹vinum hominis penitentis}
tate; quod quidem lacrimarum penitenciam agentis claritati conformetur.

^{vini major bove vinum}
Cujus color³ bubali cornu virorem representet. Sumptum descendat

---

¹ The Anglo-Saxon *parruc*, a park.

² These four words, which are not found in the Cottonian MS., are added from the MS in the National Library of Paris.

³ Neckam evidently had in his mind, in what follows, a popular declaration of the virtues of good wine which is found in Anglo-Norman in more than one manuscript of a later date, and

   cito   fudre   noyz de l'almaunde rapaunt
impetuose ad modum fulminis, sapidum ut nux Philidis, repens ad modum
     saliaunt   vinum
esperioli, gesticulans ad modum caprioli, forte sicut edificii grisorum mona-
   i. rutilans   i. claritati
chorum,[1] emicans ad modum scintille; subtilitati Parvipontane[2] veritatis
        cheysil   cristal pasez
equiparetur; delicatum ut bissus; frigiditatem cristalli excedat.
    chastel   estre aparayle
  Si castrum[3] decenter construi debeat, duplici fossa cingatur; situm loci
      mote
muniatur natura, ut mota sibi super nativam rupem sedem debitam sorciatur,
         ausilium det   la pesentime
vel nature defectui artis succurrat beneficium, ut moles muralis, ex
 ciment   altum vel exurgat
cemento et lapidibus constructa, in arduum opus excrescat.
     molem   haye   peuz   runchis
  Super hanc erigatur sepes horrida, palis quadrangulatis et vepribus pun-
           bayl larges   espaces
gentibus bene sit armata. Postmodum vallum amplis gaudeat intersticiis.
       veyns   aparisauns
Fundamentum muri venis terre maritetur. Muri etiam supereminentes

of which the following is the best and most complete copy I have met with. It is printed from MS. Lansdowne, No. 397, fol. 9, v°., of the fourteenth century.

De vino. Savez-vous coment homme deit le vyn prisir, quant homm le trove freit et de bon boysoun? xx. lettres y ad, bien les sai, ore les escotez et jeo les vous nomerai. iij. B, iij. C, iij. N, iij. S, et viij. F. Les iij. B dient q'il est bons, bens, et bevale; les iij. C dient q'il est court, clers, et crespe; les iij. N q'il est net, neays, et naturels; les iij. S dient q'il est sec, sayn, et sade; les viij. F dient q'il est freit, fresche, fryant, fremissaunt, furmentel, feire, fyn, e Fraunceys. Et où crust-il? Il crust sur le croupel de la mountaigne en coundos d'un lary en agayt du soleil où li un grayn regard lui autres sicom confel fait poucin en arrys du vilayn, où onkes grayn de feus n'i entra, si le douz russinolle ne le portast en son duz bek volaunt, et ret cum rasoure de gyngaunt qe ret mil moignes à un afilée, estencele cum carboun de chenvert, rampaunt cum esquirel du boys, beaux cum chevaler, pleisaunt cum dame, fort cum toure, descendant cum foudre, ciliaunt cum fuge de charrete, poignant cum aloyn de cordewaner, cler cum lerme de senge qe plort par force de vent de bise quant set sur croup de somer, poy-soun au vilayn, treacle à dame. E coment fait à boivre? un tenum, od un tendre flemyschele ellise cognule ryolle, un soffle, et descreve cum emfs qui ad la verole. Eye, vin, bons es-tu, douz es-tu, mult des melles fais-tu; mès quant tu les ad fait, tu les peeses; ore tere ta bouche, si ma beses.

[1] The *grisei monachi* were the Cistercians, who became celebrated for their wealth and for the grandeur of their monastic buildings. The Paris MS. 7679 reads, *forte ad modum grossiorum monachorum.*

[2] A celebrated school was established at the Petit-Pont in Paris towards the middle of the twelfth century, by one of the English men of learning who then frequented the Parisian University, and who derived from it his name of Adam du Petit-Pont. He was remarkable for a refined subtlety of reasoning, which seems to have been preserved in the school which he founded. A satirical poet of the thirteenth century, in a piece entitled *La Bataille des vii. ars,* speaks of "Petit-Pont et lor vanité."

[3] The account of building, fortifying, and storing a medieval castle, as here given, is extremely curious, and adds something to our knowledge of feudal manners, and of the military architecture of our forefathers.

THE TREATISE DE UTENSILIBUS

columpnis[1] exterius apodientur (*apoyés*). Superficies autem muri trulle (*plane*) equalitatem et cementarii (*maszun*) operam representet (*karneus*). Cancelli debitis distignantur proporcionibus (*brestasches* ... *karneus* ... *positam*). Propugnacula et pinne turrim in eminenti loco sitam muniant, nec desint crates (*cleyes*) sustinentes (*peres*) molares eiciendos.

Si forte castrum obsideatur (*seyt asegé*), ne defensores nostri opidi ad dedicionem (*del chastel abaundunement*) cogantur, muniantur farre (*blé*), et blado (*idem*), vino, pernis (*pernes*), baconibus (*bacuns*), carne (*en*) in succiduo (*suce*) posita, hyllis (*aundulyes*), salsuciis (*saucistres*), tucetis (*pudingis*), carne suilla (*poro*), carne arietina (*mutun*), carne bovina (*de bof*), carne ovina (*potages*), et leguminibus diversis; fonte jugiter scaturiente (*i. perhenne surdaunt*), posticis (*posternes*) subtilibus (*viis subterraneis*), cateractibus subterraneis (*aye succurs aporters*), quibus opem et succursum alaturi latenter incedant.

Assint et lancee (*launces*), catapulte (*setes*), antillia (*barbelez*), pelte (*talevaz*), baliste (*idem*), fustibula (*arblaz*), funde (*manygeneuz lenges*), baleares (*a loco*), sudes ferri (*peus*), clave nodose (*maces*), fustes (*bastuns*), torres (*tisuns*) ignem sapientes (*sentientes*), quibus assultus (*s. castrum*) assidencium (*seyent blecés*) elidantur et enerventur (*i. debilitantur*), ne propositum assequantur.

Assint et arietes, vinee (*machine belli*) vites (*berfreys*), crates (*cleyes*), baleare (*perers*), et cetere machine.[2]

Assint etiam manni (*palefreys*), gradarii (*chacurs*), palefridi (*palefreys*), dextrarii (*deyteres*) usibus militum apti; quibus exeuntibus (*militibus*) ut melius animenter (*seyent enardiez*) consonent tibie, tube (*estives busins*), litui (*ruez*), buxus (*flegoles*), cornu (*societates*), et acies (*idem*), et cunei (*idem*), legiones (*idem*), et cohortes (*idem*), turma (*oste*), et excercitus (*conestables*) tribunis milicie ordinabuntur. Cum autem prosilient ad trojanum agmen (*à turneyment*), vel ad troinapium,[3] (*idem*) vel ad tornamentum (*idem*), vel ad hastiludium (*burdis*), vel ad hastiledium (*justes*), vel ad tirocinium (*idem*).

Assint etiam runcini (*runcins*), sive succursorii (*chazurs*), vernis (*à sergauns*) et vespilionibus (*robeurs*) apti, et scoterellis (*ribauz*).[4] Sint etiam in castro viri prudentes (*virorum*), quorum prudencia medi-

---

[1] *i. e.*, by buttresses.

[2] The Cottonian MS. reads *baleare machine;* the words *et cetere* are inserted from the Parisian MS. 7679, as being evidently necessary to the sense.

[3] The Parisian MS. has *trojanopium*. I have not before met with either this name or that of *trojanum agmen* applied to a tournament.

[4] The Paris MS. reads *coterellis*. The name *coterelli*, said by some to be derived from their being armed with formidable knives, was given to the fierce independent soldiery who, in the twelfth century, overrun western Europe in the same manner as the *compagnies* in the fourteenth century. In time of war they served any party for pay, and in peace they plundered and

OF ALEXANDER NECKAM.

<small>i. pacis   i. sine consilio</small>
ante in tempore toge vel in tempore belli nichil agatur inconsulte; penes
<small>milites la paraliment   militum   i. ordinacione</small>
quos moles regni et summa consilii constat; quorum dispensacione
<small>plus deboneyrement   i. judicii   redur   lever-</small>
micius agatur cum supplicibus; quorum censure rigore degras-
<small>reyurs   frangentes legem destatuz de pople male usores   i. mali expositores</small>
satores, legisrumpi, plebicitorum abusores, sive prevaricatores plebis statu-
<small>laruns   latrones pecorum faus pelrims[1]   murdisurs   ocsur de gens   homicide</small>
torum, clepi, abactores, sicarii, multatores, enectores, antropocedi,
<small>verberentur fustibus   cumperunt   i. ablacione capitis   damnez</small>
fustigentur, et puniantur, vel capitali sentencia condempnantur;
<small>militum   charzeté   mensura   i.</small>
quorum vita sapiat frugalitatem. Est autem frugalitas parcitas in habun-
<small>copia   militum</small>
dancia. Quorum sentencia est ad simile hortans, vel ad simile deortans,[2]
<small>i. sine opinione   i. sumpta quidaunce</small>
sine conjectura, nam conjectura est ex signo sensibili orta opinio. Sint
<small>strepitum facientes quam facientes pacem</small>
etiam tam clangatores quam caduciatores.

<small>fortes milites ostes sternentes   militibus   locum refugii</small>
'Assint 'etiam stratillates, quibus decertantibus scatesum[3] mancat
<small>i. invictum   stratillatibus</small>
inconcussum; quibus victoriam et belli finem consequentibus, victoriarum
<small>pro sicut colaria pugilum omnibus pictoribus   immo cum laude   traduntur</small>
scripta, utpote nichiteria,[4] punctis pupplicis non illaudabiliter committuntur.
Cum autem triplex sit ordo militum, assint etiam milites evocati,[5] milites
<small>i. facientes tumultum   ecclesiastici[6]   enardiez busine</small>
tumultuarii, milites sacramentales, quos animet tuba ducis decertantis
<small>i. in spissitudine   dubitacionem   ducis dico   milites   i. mutua</small>
in nube telorum et aleam belli optinentis; quos moneant ducis dona-
<small>munera donata   soud   dicitur   i. oboli donacio</small>
tiva, et stipendia, unde stipendium quasi stipis pendio.

<small>prisuns   divisi   carcerum</small>
Assint etiam carceres debitis mansionibus distingti, in quorum fundum
<small>liez   en manicles   de fer   ceps</small>
detrudantur compediti in manicis ferreis positi. Assint et cippi, et

---

ravaged the country on their own account. *Scuterellis* is evidently a mere corruption.

[1] *Sicarii* means simply assassins. One does not easily perceive why this Anglo-Norman translation was given to it.

[2] The MS. gives the following rather long interlinear gloss on this and the six words preceding : *quod faciant quod facere debent, ut dimittant quod dimittere debent.*

[3] The Paris MSS. read severally *scatillum* and *stantillum*, neither of which words occur in Ducange, any more than that given in our text.

[4] The Paris MS. 7079 reads *nicheteria*. Both words represent the Greek νικητήρια, i. e., rewards of victory, which were worn round the necks of those who had obtained them, explained by some as torques.

[5] Glossed in the MS. by the words, *s. ab alia regione vocati ad debellandum.*

[6] *i. milites pugnantes contra incredulos,* is added to the interlinear gloss in the MS. The allusion is of course to the templars and hospitallers.

THE TREATISE DE UTENSILIBUS

  pilories   veytes[1] veliables   noyse
columbaria. Assint etiam excubie vigiles, cornibus suis strepitum et
noyse   sun
clangorem et sonitum facientes.

      grener   idem   estrie cumb[3] mesure van buscel
In granario, sive in penu, sit historium,[2] corus, modius, vannus, batus,
 posiciuns de furment   blé batu orge segle aveyne   nel
diverse teche frumenti sive tritici, ordei, siliginis,[4] vel avene, vel lollii.
         nomen fictum payles coses   nel   havernu
Assint etiam usui avium cortis palee, silique, lollium, avena sterilis.
       la curt   pucins gocs gelines chapuns cokereuns
Aves autem cortis sunt hee : pulli, galli, galline, gallinarii, gallinacii, altiles
   chapunz gars adnes [heydes] sygonie eyruns illius fluvii fesauns
sive altilia, anceres, anates, cigonie, ardee, aves Phasidos sive phasiani,
illius terre oyseus   grues mavices   plunguns
Libie volucres sive grues, fulice,[5] alunbes, mergites sive mergiaciones,
 coc de bosco pouns   idem
galli palustres, povones sive junonius ales.

    estabe   creeche boveric porcherie anges   parvi alvei estrilie bernac
In stabulo sit presepe, boscar, are, alvei, sive alveoli, strigilis, camus,
chaufreyn cuier   carette chevestre harneys
salivare, cenovectorium sive epirodium, capistrum, et phalere cetere equorum
        numbri
superius sunt enumerate.

   tiscur chivaler à tere   estrus   i. apodians
Textor, terestris eques, qui duarum streparum adnitens apodiamento
 alaschet   parva jurné estrus
equum admittit assidue, contentum exili dieta. Scansilia autem ejus fortune
i. modum   entrechaungable feze
condicionem representancia,[6] mutua gaudent vicissitudine, ut dum unum
et susleve scansile   envie abatu vindeyse   environ-
evehitur, reliquum sine nota livoris deprimatur. Trocleam habeat circum-
turnable troclee drap   apte adjungi
volubilem, cui pannus evolvendus ydonee maritari possit.
  lates   ad modum trabe pertux   divisas   parte
Cindulas habeat trabales, columbaribus distingtas, et e diversa regione
         kyvilis   croce   treus
sese respicientes, cavillis ad modum pedorum curvatis, trabibus tenorem
la teyle   de frenges   idem
tele abientibus, linthia etiam tam tenuis quam fimbriis apte socientur,
  in superficie tele   esteym   de-
virgis in capucio debitis insignitis intersticiis stamen deducat tam sup-

---

[1] More correctly written in old French *gaite*, or *geyte*; in old English *waytes* (watchmen). The word is only preserved in the English language for the waits who at Christmas patrol the streets at night with music.

[2] The Paris MS. 7679 reads *astorium*.

[3] *Cumb*, the name of a measure of liquid, is not an Anglo-Norman word, but Anglo-Saxon.

[4] The Paris MS. 7679 reads *siliginis vel sigalli*.

[5] *Philices*, in the Paris MS.

[6] The movement of the weaver's machinery is compared to the well known mediæval emblem of the wheel of fortune, in which, as the object on one side rose, that on the other descended. The whole description of the weaving apparatus is extremely interesting.

suz (ponendum) desur (quam) la trome (Trama) navette (naviclere)
ponendum quam superponendum. Trama autem beneficio naviclere trans-
afermet (transmissa) broche (pano) fust (ligneo)
euntis transmissa opus consolidet; que pano ferreo vel saltem ligneo
brosche (infra) navette (spola)
muniatur infra fenestrellas. Panus autem spola vestiatur; spola autem
de fil (penso) luscel (glomeris) trome (trame)
penso ad modum glomeris cooperiatur. Ex hoc penso materia trame
del tistur (textoris) launcet (jaculetur)
sumetur, ut manus altera textoris jaculetur naviculam usque in sociam
arere enveer (remissuram)
manum, idem beneficium priori manui remissuram.

in vanum urderat (ordietur) teyle (telam) peynies de fer (pectines ferrei) loco capillorum (pro capillis)
Sed frustra ordietur aliquis telam, nisi pectines ferrei, lanam pro capillis
lanam dico (lanam) rehete (reciproco) estrif (certamine)
gerentes, virtute ignis molliendam longo et reciproco certamine sese prius
detrexerint (depilaverint) orsmené (educta)
depilaverint. Ut magis scincera pars et habilior lane educta ad opus
flokuns (floccis) erdes. estupes (stuparum) remenauns (superstitibus)
staminis reservetur, laneis floccis ad modum stuparum superstitibus.

varence (sandicis) vedh¹ (sindicis)
Postmodum lana sandicis vel sindicis ad modum populi Belvacensis²
ausilium capiat (opem sorciatur) teynture suvenere (tinctura crebro condimento) brasyl (granee)
opem sorciatur, ut tinctura crebro condimento granee inebrietur; postmodum,
del tyztur chalaunget (textoris vendicet)
textoris vendicet artificium; sed antequam in formam vestium prorumpat,
fullun (fullonis) entente (indulgentie) susjezt (subiciat) demaundaunt (exposcens)
fullonis indulgentie sese subiciat, frequentem ablucionem exposcens.

pardurable (eternam)
Sic antequam vestem eternam suscipiamus, inter motus rationis et
batalye (perduellio) avent (decet) tiztre (contexere)
sensus longa precedet perduellio; postea decet opus caritatis contexere, et
tezthes (maculas) outer (abluere) l'em dit (dicitur)
maculas sordium abluere, ut adimpleatur quod dicitur ad litteram: Lava-
nez (mini) nos (estote) celestem (supernam) onsemble (convo-)
mini, et mundi estote, et mundati deinde ad supernam patriam convo-
volrum (labimur) i. pugna anime (sycomachia) curiusté (solicitudo)
labimus, ubi non erit sycomachia neque solicitudo, sed locus graciosus
i. superna gracia (epicaris) i. bona gratia (eucaris)
et epicaris et dilectionis et eucaris.

caretter (Veredus) equum trahentem bigam (veredarium ducturus) cuvele (cucullam)
Veredus, veredarium ducturus, cucullam habeat, capucio armatam
frogge (collobium) maunche (manubeatum) avera plu isent (libuerit exeant)
grisio,⁴ et collobium habeat manubeatum, ut manus, cum libuerit, exeant;

---

¹ The plant called in English woad (A.-S. *wod*), and still known in French by the name of *guède*.

² Beauvais was celebrated in the middle ages for the manufacture of cloth, which was dis- tinguished by the richness of its dyes.

⁴ This description of the costume of the carter answers perfectly to the figures which are met with in the illuminations of manuscripts of differ-

vel, si agasonis vel mulionis officium explere velit, aculeo fruatur, aut
flagello, aut scorpione equos cedat, vel lenta virga aurem regat, unde
auriga nomen debito modo sortitur, vel eo quod aurem equi regat.

Habeat autem ocreas, ne tesqua vel lutosas vel cenosas plateas expavescat.
Cum autem radicem montis, vel latus, vel jugum ascendunt equi, aptetur honus
carri, vel carrus, vel bige, vel quadrige, anteriori parti conjunctum. Cum
autem declives vias descendendo legere oportet, dissocientur equi sinjugi,
et unus currum trahat, alter capistro posteriori parti quadrige ligatus se
sua virtute impetum motus quadrige retardare, sinuato poplite laborante,
attestetur; et cavillam temonis juxta restim anteriorem erectam manu
forti veredus teneat.

Habeat et epiphia equus tam supra dorsum quam in collo centone multi-
plici sociata, jugum, phaleras, suarium[1] vel subcellium, et carentivillum
omitto, cum alias enumeraverim quando scutarium vel armigerum sive
quemcumque equitem munivi, circumstantiis necessariis non operis execu-
cione, sed verborum imposicione, in quibus tenacissimi avari sive prodigi
reperiuntur.

Sed ipsam quadrigam de cetero armemus rota, rote beneficio axis inter-
positi societur e diversa regione sita. Axis autem circumvolvetur in
timpano, sive in modio vel in modiolo. Cavilla axis firmiter sit intrusa.
In modiolo aptari habent[2] radii, in cantos transmittendi, quorum extremitates stelliones dicuntur, videlicet orbite. Vestigia profundius inscribunt.
Circumferencia rote ferro clavis munito vestiatur, ne scrupulorum
insidias vel offendicula sive inequalitatem non pavescat. Asseres sub

---

ent periods, and it probably underwent scarcely
any change during many successive ages.

[1] *Sudarium*, in the Paris MS.

[2] The Paris MS. has the perhaps more correct reading, *debent*.

   cleyes   seynt mis   bastuns   pertuz   lates
cratibus in aera quadrige collocentur, limonibus per columbaria cindularum
                     adrezces
ex transverso ductarum erectis, qui limones baculi sunt quadrige, vel a limo
          knuls   timun
vel a ligando dicti.   Cavillas temonis prius enumeravi.   Currus noster sit
       suslevaund   prophete
armatus, elevando nos in ethera currum Elye imitetur.
           cors   la sale   porch   ordiné
Corpus aule[1] vestibulo muniatur, juxta quod porticus honeste sit disposita.
   curt   de ço   rues
Atrium etiam habeat, quod ab atro dicitur, eo quod coquine juxta plateas
                       trespassauns i. odorem
fieri solebant, ut transeuntes nidorem coquine sentirent.   In aula sint
    posz   divisi   cloues   es   lates   necesse
postes[2] debitis intersticiis distincti.   Clavis, asseribus, cidulis, et latis opus
     trefs   cheverans   i. ad summitatem domus
est, et trabibus, et tignis, usque ad doma edificii attingentibus.
   parvis tignis   cheveruns
Tigillis etiam opus est usque ad domus commissuram porrectis. Pari-
     diversa parte   positi   plus aut
etes e diversa regione siti, quanto remocius a fundamento surgunt tanto
              i. si non distant   enginiment
magis distant;[3] alioquin ruinam minabitur tota machina domus et ita
  periculum   luvers[5]   ordiné
discrimen erit.[4] Specularia autem competenter sint disposita in domo
                                hoistes   hoystes   sub aere humido
orientales partes respiciencia, ubi suctina vel pixides tortiles   sub divo
ponantur.
              pixidibus illius electuarie i. bona gutta   illius electuarie lie   illius fecis
In quibus   storacis   calamita, non autem   storacis sigia nec sigie,
  baselie   arbore consectum   mulcens imfirmitatem
corimbrum contineatur sed serapinum, amomatum,[6] opanaclum, abdel-

---

[1] The compiler now proceeds to describe the hall, as the principal part of the baronial mansion.

[2] The Norman hall had generally two rows of columns down the middle. Examples will be found in Hudson Turner's "Domestic Architecture in England."

[3] This seems to have been a favourite theory with Alexander Neckam, who imagined that, because heavy bodies tend to the centre of the earth, the walls of a house ought to be built not exactly perpendicular, but leaning from each other, forgetting that the smallness of the angle would make the two perpendiculars as nearly as possible parallel. He argues the question in the following manner, which seems to intimate a glimpse of the Newtonian system of gravitation, in his treatise *De naturis rerum*, (MS. Reg. 12, G. xi., fol. 79, v°, in the British Museum):— Oportet namque necessario ut quanto amplius parietes a terra surgunt, tanto major distantia inter ipsos reperiatur. Cum enim omne ponderosum naturaliter tendat ad centrum, intellige parietes angulariter sibi sociari. Videsne igitur quonammodo radii ex modiolo bigæ procedentes majori et minori distantia se jungantur usque dum rotæ ipsi maritentur? Sic et parietes elevantur, cœli convexa respicientes.

[4] The word *erit*, omitted in the Cottonian MS., is supplied from that of Paris.

[5] The term *louvre* appears here not to be used in its usual sense, but to be applied to the side window of the hall.

[6] This word is explained by the interlinear gloss, *i. electuarium factum ex pluribus confectionibus*.

           unguentum   idem   factum a mastice arbore gummi populi arboris olie   de lorer
lum, euforbium, sarcotalla,   masticum,   popileon,   oleum, laurinum,
factum de uvis factum de pinguedine castoris factum de succo   unguenta facta de timis floribus
vinfacileon,   castrorium,   anatileon, et   epithimata.

       cleyes domo   chaume   ros i. crescenti in palustrile
    Crates tecto supponantur, que culmo supposito aut calamo   palustri
       ros   seynt cuverz   cengles   teules   idem
aut arundine cooperiantur, aut cidulis suppositis lateres sive tegule suppo-
              las   i. fundamentum
nantur. Laquearia insidias aeris expellant; projectum sive pes parietis
baztuns
stipitibus muniatur.

          us   loc   loc pendaunt¹   idem   barres   guns   bars
       Ostium seram habeat, pensulam vel pensulum, vectes, gumphos, repagula.
    portes   duble portes   verteveles
Valve vel bifores juxta porticum ponantur vel collocentur, et cardinibus
              ordinez
debito modo dispositis muniantur.

           vileyn   chaump vivens   veliesce   cunsiler
       Rusticus rure degens, inopi senecte consulere volens, domum habeat
        corbeus   ruches   de oseres   paners   anaps
munitam corbibus, cumeris vimineis, calathis, cophinis, et sportis. Habeat
            sunie, Anglice belger   croké   implere
etiam   fuscinam   hamatam, ut se piscibus reficere possit.

           fescel. chesbat   idem   ficella   buket
       Nec fiscina   nec fiscella careat, in qua lac a multra diligentur sus-
                 pressé   suvenere   furmage
ceptum et sepius expressum crebra coagulacione in formam casei transeat,
  meg   mag. vel crem   potandis
sero tamen eliquato. Colustrum etiam reservetur teneris pueris propinandis.
                                                    junc   idem
Postea caseus in sua teneritate in techa ex papiro, vel ex cirpis, vel ex
  idem   de mareys   caseus   suriz
junccis palustribus composita lateat coopertus foliis, propter insidias murium,
   musches   vibez   muches   idem
muscarum, cinifum, locustarum, brucorum.

           palies   cutalies   bren   gelins i. alimenta   anês
       Palcas habeat et acera, et fulfurem, que sunt gallinis pabula, anatibus,
  ouues   oysuns   gars   la curt
aucis, et auculis, et anseribus, et hujusmodi cortis avibus. Habeat etiam
bulter. biltepoke   sarz   taratantaro flur
polentrudium, et taratantarum, ut illo polen cliquatur, illo etiam crebro
 cerveyse   cule   purgé
cervisia coletur vel specificetur vel purificetur.

                    espeye   bezche. spade   idem   gisarme   flaele
       Habeat etiam gladium latum, spatam sive vangam, frameam, tribulam,

---

¹ *i. e.*, a padlock.

      truble. soule   runces semeser. sadlep   semeysun
et tribulum, non dico tribulos, saticulum ad tempus sacionis conservatum,
    civere   panier   basket   ratnere
cenevectorium, qualum, quaxillum,[1] muscipulam contra murium insidias.
             calketrap   idem   pedica
Habeat pedicam sive descipulam, qua lupi capiantur.
           bastuns   peuz   endurziz   idem
Habeat etiam fustes et palos sepius in igne probatos vel exploratos.
             bisagu   enveyeracer runces   idem   espines   idem
Habeat etiam bisacutam ad radicandum[2] vepres, tribulos, et sentes, spinas,
verges bastarz baztarz   ruz. hulver   ays   à renuvelirs
et vitulamina spuria, et ruscum, ad sepes firmandas et renovandas, ne
  nentchalur   privé   fures pecorum bovers   porchers
per incuriam sub tempore furtive noctis abactores, bubulcis et subulcis
dormientibus   la curt   greges pecorum enveye menunt
sopitis, subintrent curiam, et armenta abducant.
            magnum cultellum   entes   trenchet
Habeat etiam artavum quo surculos exsecet,[3] et eosdem arboribus
à enters   afermet   picoyses   bastuns
oculandis, inseret, si opus fuerit. Habeat etiam ligones, quibus tirsos[4]
enracet   herbes beneyte urtie. nettle   neus   haverun   averun
extirpet, et incubas, urticas, vel crvos, lollia, carduos, avenas steriles.
      herbe   avenaument   croc   picoyse
Quedam tamen hujusmodi habilius extirpantur unco quam ligone.
           bover   bercher
Habeat et bubulcum et opilionem propter insidias luporum.[5] Habeat
     faude   idem   ualies   iloc   plus gras
etiam caulam, sive ovile, ut oves ibidem posite terram pinguiorem et
  lé   comporture   plenté   hulet
leciorem reddant stercorum opulencia. Assit etiam tugurium pastoris, sive
idem   idem   tugurio   gardein moram per noctem faciat
mapale, vel magale, in quo canis fidelis custos secum pernoctet. Trans-

---

[1] *Scacillum*, Paris MS.

[2] *Eradicandum*, Paris MS.

[3] *Excedet*, Paris MS.

[4] *Tirpos*, Paris MS.

[5] We have here, and just above, two allusions to the ravages committed by wolves in England in the time of Alexander Neckam, for we can hardly doubt that this treatise was written in England. Wolves appear to have been tolerably abundant in this island not only during the eleventh and twelfth centuries, but even late in the thirteenth, when they are still spoken of as very troublesome. The following order for the destruction of these animals in the counties of Gloucester, Worcester, Hereford, Salop, and Stafford, is found in the Patent Rolls of 9 Ed. I. (A.D. 1281): "Rex omnibus ballivis, etc. Sciatis quod injunximus dilecto et fideli nostro Petro Corbet, quod in omnibus forestis et parcis et aliis locis infra comitatus nostros Gloucestrie, Wigornie, Herefordie, Salopie, et Staffordie, in quibus lupi poterunt inveniri, lupos cum hominibus, canibus, et ingeniis suis capiat et destruat modis omnibus quibus viderit expedire. Et ideo vobis mandamus quod eidem Petro in omnibus quæ ad captionem luporum in comitatibus prædictis pertinet intendentes sitis et auxiliantes, quotiens opus fuerit et prædictus Petrus vobis scire faciet ex parte nostra. In cujus, etc., duratur quandiu nobis placuerit. Teste rege apud Westmonasterium, decimo quarto die Maii." Wolves are also mentioned in various records relating to tenures of land, &c., during the fourteenth century. They seem not to have become quite extinct till late in the fifteenth century.

     faude   place   pisure
feratur sepius ovile, ut tota campi area tam beneficium mincture quam
fenerie beztes
stercoracionis pecorum senciat.
         crezche buverie presepe   bostar bous
  Habeat etiam rusticus noster presepe, bostar, hoc equis, illud, bobus,
factum   i. secundum aliquam quantitatem floreat vel crescat
aptandum ; et si etiam aliquantulum arrideat prosperitas
rustico   faventis   aner   muler araz
ei fortune blandientis, habeat agasonem et mulionem, et in equicio
           chevers   bous vaches jenices
emissarium equum. Habeat etiam oves, capras, et boves, vaccas, juvencas,
tors   parvos boves anes savages   bugles   muttuns
tauros, juvencos buculos, onagros, buculas, bubalos, asinos, arietes et
idem   idem
verveces, et multones, ciciros, et burdones.
     reys   idem   idem   laz ettenduz envirun-
  Habeat etiam casses, et recia, et reticula, et laqueos extensos ad circum-
turners   deym cheverez cervs   founs brazches
volvendos lepores, damas, capriolas, cervos, cervas, hinulos, hodorinsecos,
   leveres
et leporarios.
     armes   estrumenz   rusticus
  Hec sunt arma vel instrumenta rusticorum. Habeat autem aratrum
         i. valde   aratri   capiat
usibus humane vite admodum necessarium ; cujus medium sorciatur grave
  robur   tref   timun   robur
robur, quod usualiter trabem vel temonem dicimus ; quod quasi bifurcando
         teim. furz idem plulé fiat
in binas aures procedat, ut lira, vel sulcus, lecior efficiatur. Quoddam tamen
        i. aure apahé
aratrum unica aure vel ansa contentum est.
       bem curvaund [tunura] [auba]
  Procedat etiam robur curvando in burim, que cauda bovis vel aratri
interpretatur. Buris autem dicitur, quasi bos uros ; uros[1] enim idem est
          serpens
quod cauda vel bos, unde coluros, quasi colens nuros, quod idem est
           seit levé estive en etclenkaunt stiva
quod membrum bovis silvestris. Elevetur stiva obliquando, qua regatur
       seit fichi
aratrum, cui capulus infigatur.
        de gref guvernement i. dura terra
  Est autem aratrum difficilis regiminis cum antimonia vel in terra
i. calida i. lutosa   aratrum. enprent i. equorum et boum trahencium jus
gipsea vel alumpniosa sit inpressum, ubi subjugalium juga et
trayz. dractes sunt depescez de sauz   hefd   sock
retinabula[2] franguntur salingna.[3] Supponatur dentile vel dentale, cui vomer,

---

[1] οὐρὰ, in Greek, signifies a tail, and οὖρος, a wild ox, or buffalo.
[2] *Retinacula*, Paris MS.
[3] *Salina*, id.

     idem   fichi   haye   cleye   cloues   knules   outre
vel vomis, infigatur. Sepem, cratem, clavos, et cavillas, restim, cultrum,
   pase
sponte pretereo.
     i. quomodo   compoter chaumps   fens[1]   reclarcler
Quonammodo oporteat stercorare agros, vel fimo pascere, aut resarcire,
varez. faleues   varez   marl   marler
aut novalia iterando rebinare, aut veracta renovare, aut creta letificare, aut
in illo signo   idem   mesuns   estoks
sub cane, aut sub anticane, vel sub edis cadentibus, aut igne stipulis
ardauns   erce   purger   lapide quadrato equam facere   erces
incensis trahe beneficio purgare, aut chilindro   equare, aut dentibus cratis
       etpines   garnir   ble   baylye   erce
factis de spinis agros munire, et cererem terre commissam trahe beneficio
couverir   baylier
cooperire, aut granum terre commendare, ut granum in terra mortifi-
       herbé   sursaliet   chalemel
catum vel fissum in herbam prorumpat, postmodum herba in calamum
seit fermé   coses   etpics   greyns   chargé
solidetur, calamus in techis et spicis granorum muniatur et honeretur.
    i. quomodo   syer   place   batre
Quonammodo agros oporteat metere, aut in area triturare, aut ab area
gaveles   garbes   ensemble cuyliet graunges   rastel
manipulos sive gelimas submotas et collectas horreis commendare, rastro
 netter   van   ennettir   mola estre depescé
mundare, vanno mundificare, postmodum granum a mola confringi et
         cribré[1]   pertuz cribre   art   peztrir
disolvi, et scinceratum[1] foraminibus cribri eliquare, aut arte piscendi in
     furmer   ayent cunuz à demustrer   idem
usum panis transformare, hiis qui talia noverint enuclienda vel edisserenda
relinqquo.
 aguylun   erce   viscre idem est   ortorum   nentsa-
Aculeum et traham, larvam, larvatam ymaginem priapi, non ex ignoran-
chaunt   à memorie   jo lesse
cia, sed quia memorie non occurrunt, ad presens omitto. Multa etiam
   purpos. vel ad opus presens   ensuy
talia ad   propositum   pertinencia in aliis meis litteris consecutus
       autorem   magistros   delitit nuvelerye
sum, ut non me sicut quamplurimos juvat polinodia.
 de nefs   differencie   sequentibus   i. nominantur
Navium diversitates hiis versibus comprehenduntur :

      Navis, navicula, linterque, cheloxque, chelindra,
      Et ratis, et lembus, scapha, cimba, liburna, phaselus;
        Rostrum curvando nomina navis habet.
      Prora prior navis pars dicitur, ultima puppis ;
      Hiis interposita pars est dicenda carina ;
        Sed summam partem dicimus esse ratem.
      Queque ratis navis, navium collectio classis.

---

[1] The commentary in the Cottonian MS. gives the following explanation of this word: "Hic fimus, *fens*, et hic limus, *ray* (?), et a fimo fimidus, -da, -dum, unde ager fimidus, *chaump compoté*."

[2] The Paris MS. No. 7679 reads *cinceratum*, instead of *scinceratum*.

THE TREATISE DE UTENSILIBUS

       ille   *une pere*   *faut naute*
Qui ergo munitam vult habere navem, albestum habeat, ne desit ei
fu   *aguyl*   *mis*   *turne*
beneficium ignis.[1] Habeat etiam acum[2] jaculo suppositam, rotabitur enim
e enurun   *aguyl*   *poynt*   *agardet*   *est*   *tali modo*
et circumvolvetur acus donec cuspis acus respiciat orientem, sicque com-
       i. ubi   *mariners*   *atapist*   *de l'eyr*
prehendunt quo tendere debeant naute cum cinossura[3] latet in aeris
tempeste   *cinossura* *achecement*   *circle*   *petit*
turbacione, quamvis ad occasum nunquam tendat propter circuli brevitatem.
blé   *viaunde*   *vin*   *idem necesse*   *armes*   *asours*
Farre, et cibo, et vino, mero, opus est; armis muniti sint, scilicet, securi,
mast   *et hic dico*   *cessante*   *i. que abscissio mali*
ut malus abscindi possit tempestate emergente, quod ultimus malorum
           robeur de mer   *es*   *cordes clouues*
cumulus, ut piratarum possint elidi insidie. Asseres fidis, clavis conjun-
      marteus i. utraque parte   *pic*   *cire commixta cum pice*
gantur, malliolis utrinque concurrentibus, et pice; cera picata interius
oynt   *oyntez*   *idem*   *grand*
vel unguine lineantur, et exterius levigentur, nimie unctionis haustum
asseres dico.   *trefs*   *cleyes necesse*   *astif*
gliscentes. Cratibus et craticulis opus est, ut pulsacio crebra alipedum
la senibe   *deliet*   *es*   *depart-*
compaginem navis dissociat vel dissolvat. Asseribus opus est proporcion-
ablement   *notiners*   *i. divisis*   *illum magnum lignum*
aliter associatis, ut, mansionibus nautarum distingtis, super modium
malus erigatur.

    hoc nomen   *scilicet*   *mesure*
Modius est nomen equivocum ad mensuram et ad illud instrumentum

---

[1] It was believed that the asbestus, when once lighted, could never be extinguished, and hence Neckam recommends it to be carried on shipboard, that the sailors may never be without fire.

[2] This rather obscure description of the mariner's compass, belonging certainly to the twelfth century, is the earliest allusion to the use of that important instrument in the middle ages. Alexander Neckam has, however, given a rather fuller description of it in another of his books, the treatise *de Naturis Rerum*, lib. ii., c. 89 (MS. Reg. 12 G. xi, fol. 53, v°.) "Nautæ etiam mare legentes, cum beneficium claritatis solis in tempore nubilo non sentiunt, aut etiam cum caligine nocturnarum tenebrarum mundus obvolvitur, et ignorant in quem mundi cardinem prora tendat, acum super magnetem ponunt, quæ circulariter circumvolvitur usque dum, ejus motu cessante, cuspis ipsius septentrionalem plagam respiciat." The earliest account of the mariner's compass, before known, was contained in the following lines of a satirical poem, entitled the *Bible Guiot de Provins*, composed in the thirteenth century. (Barbazan, Fabl., tom. ii., p. 328.)

Un art font qui mentir ne puet
Par la vertu de la maniete,
Une pierre laide et brunete,
Où li fers volentiers se joint,
Ont; si esgardent li droit point,
Puis c'une aguile i ont touchié,
Et en un festu l'ont couchié,
En l'eve le metent sanz plus,
Et li festuz la tient desus;
Puis se torne la pointe toute
Contre l'estoile, si sanz doute,
Que jà nus hom n'en doutera,
Ne jà por rien ne fausera.
Qant la mers est obscure et brune,
C'on ne voit estoile ne lune,
Dont font à l'aguille alumer,
Puis n'ont-il garde d'esgarer;
Contre l'estoile va la pointe,
Por ce sont li marinier cointe
De la droite voie tenir.
C'est uns ars qui ne puet faillir.

[3] The cynosure (κυνοσουρά), or constellation popularly called Charles's wain.

super quod erigitur navis malus. Malus autem dicitur a malo, quod
<small>instrumentum</small> <small>mast</small>
<small>pume per similitudinem rund</small> <small>postea</small>
est pomum, eo quod rotundum est. Dehinc enim velum malo
<small>ajunt kables. cordes envirun seynt ettenduz</small>
maritetur. Rudentes circumquaque parte protendantur, a rudendo dicti,
<small>rudentum veil. seyl mast plus bas</small>
quorum extremitalibus velum malo maritetur. Inferior autem pars veli
<small>enflure seyn</small>
trabibus ex transverso ductis societur. Tumor veli sinus dicitur vel appel-
<small>cordes</small>
latur. Antempnis etiam opus est. Antempne autem sunt corde quasi
<small>eve. i. aquam cordarum verge</small>
ante amnem posite, quarum superiores extremitates cornua dicuntur. Virga
<small>mast</small>
mali carchesium dicitur. Est autem carchesium vas sacrificio aptum, et
<small>mali verge in alio sensu veder-coc</small>
eadem verga cheruca vocatur. Cheruca tamen proprie dicitur ventilogium,
<small>pertuz pertuz</small>
quod in Gallico dicitur *cochet*.[1] Fiant autem fori vel columbaria, non
<small>tereres columbaria enviruns</small>
dico foratoria, per que remi exeunt, vel exire possunt, si opus sit
<small>envirunement hoc nomen</small>
navigio cum se neget aura. Columbar in alia significacione dicitur
<small>cordes. kables cordes tregrosses pualyes</small>
pillori. Parastes autem protendantur, funes, scilicet, grossissimi et stipites
<small>supuauns cordes</small>
malum suppodiantes. Sic autem dicuntur parastes quasi pariter stantes.
<small>turuns les enviruns remus dicitur tonsus dicitur</small>
Remus autem dicitur tonsus, nunc a regendo, nunc a tondendo. Clavum
<small>a palma</small>
habeat et podium, extremitates remi; palmula dicitur, quia plana est ad
<small>magister vel clericus navis i. sedem</small>
modum palme. Habeat etiam nauclerus transtrum, quod est sedes nau-
<small>transtrum sedem windeyse</small>
tarum, a transverso ductum. Juxta transtrum assit troclea, et dicitur a
<small>Grece lant ro</small>
troclos, quod est rotundum, vel a rota dictum instrumentum, eo quod
<small>kables. cordes veil</small>
circumvolvitur troclea ut rudentes circumligati firmiores sint, et ut velum
<small>diversete venti susleve avale vindoyse</small>
per variacionem aure nunc superioretur, nunc inferioretur. Dicitur troclea
<small>necesse aunkre de ço ventum</small>
rotunda moles. Opus etiam est anchora, sic dicta eo quod contra chorum,
<small>quoddam signum</small>
ut ponatur species pro genere. Vel porticulum habe. Navis ergo nostra
<small>ordiné havene</small>
sic ordinetur, ut ad portum salutis sic applicetur.

---

[1] An early Latin-French vocabulary, cited by Ducange (sub v. *ventilogium*), has "*Ventilogium*, le coichet, qui est sur le mostier." *Cochet* was the old French name for a weathercock.

Scriptor[1] habeat rasorium (*escrivur*), sive novaculam (*rasur*), ad abradendum (*idem*) sordes (*à enveyerere*) pergameni (*parchemin*) sive membrane (*idem*); et pumicem (*pumice*) habeat mordacem (*mordable*), et planulam (*plane*) ad purgandum (*purger*) et equandum (*idem*) superficiem (*la superfice*) pergameni; plumbum (*plum*) habeat et linulam (*reulur*), sive regulam (*idem*), quibus linietur (*linié*) pagina (*pagine*),[2] margine circumquaque (*utraque parte*) tam ex parte carnis (*del dos*) quam ex parte tergi (*et hic dico*) existente libera.

Assit ei quaternus (*quaer*),[3] non dico quaternio, qui aliquantam partem exercitus (*ductor militum*)[4] designat (*agnice*). Cedula sive apendice tam superiori parte quam inferiori folia (*foyz*) habeat conjuncta (*ensemble*). Habeat etiam registrum (*cordula libri*)[5] et punctorium (*poyntur*) a quo possit dicere: "punxi (*poyntay*) quaternum (*quaer*) meum, et non pupigi (*puniay*)." (*haestrifere*) Scripturus autem in cathedra (*chaere*) sedeat, ansis (*braces*) utrinque (*i. utraque parte*) elevatis, pluteum (*carole*) sive asserem (*es*) sustinentibus, scabello (*chamel*) apte supposito (*mis*) pedibus, ut firmius sedeat.[6]

Scriptor habeat epicausterium (*talem asserem*) centone (*feutre*) coopertum (*cnivet*). Habeat artavum, quo pennam (*furmet*) informet ut sit habilis et ydonea ad scribendum (*penna*), ylo (*i. medulla penne*) a penna extracto (*mutun sengler illius alitis pla-*). Habeat et dentem verris, sive apri, sive leofe,[7] ad poliendum (*nier*) pergamenum (*parchemin*), ut non liquescat (*decuret*) littera, non dico elementum (*element*), sive litura facta sit, sive litteras ascriptas vel ascriptis cancelaverit (*i. removerit*).

Cavillam (*i. speculum*) habeat, vel spectaculum, ne ob errorem (*errur*) moram (*demure*) faciat dispendiosam (*i. dampnificam*). Habeat etiam prunas (*breses*) in epicausterio (*chiminé*), ut cicius in tempore nubiloso (*yemali*) vel aquoso (*ensicchir*) desiccari (*enke*) possit incaustum super pergamenum (*parchemin*) exaratum (*scriptum*). Habeat

---

[1] The description of the writer, or scribe, seated at his desk with his various materials and implements, answers exactly to the numerous pictures which we find in illuminated manuscripts of all periods.

[2] Before writing, the parchment was always ruled with parallel lines, marked with lead or with a hard point of some kind, on which the letters were to be placed.

[3] The parchment was folded in divisions of four leaves, each of which was termed a quaternio, or, in French, and the old English word derived from that language, a *quaer* or *quair*. After the writing of the manuscript had been completed, the different *quaers* were bound together in a volume. From this word, and the practice it designated, we derive our modern word *quire*, applied to paper, in modern French *cahier*.

[4] The Cottonian MS. reads *exterius*.

[5] The cord attached to the book for the purpose of placing between the leaves, to mark a place to which one wishes to return.

[6] These four words are inserted from the Paris MS.

[7] Hec leoffa, -fe, est ales habens longos dentes, et est nomen Grecum. *Comment. in MS. Cotton.*

et lodium, cujus beneficio lux intrare possit si forte fenestrellam inpugnet (viket / fenestral)
insultus venti aquilonaris; fenestrella panniculo lineo vel membrana viridi (les asauz / del norz / fenestral / petit drap / parchemin / de verd)
colore vel nigro distingta muniatur. Color enim viridis et niger radiis (culur / neyr / garni / luminibus)
oculorum prebent solacium. Albedo autem incensa visum digressat, et (blaunchure / ardaunt)
maxime nimium obtinctum obtenebrat. Habeat etiam minium, ad formandas (obscuret / vermilliun)
litteras rubeas, vel puniceas, vel feniceas, sive capitales. Habeat et (ruges / idem / idem / capitaus)
fuscum pulverem, vel azuram, a Salamone repertam. (nigrum / azure)

Sciat etiam notarius vel librarius ubi scribere debeat sylen, ubi (notur / i. librorum reparator / i. siccitas)
diasyan, ubi otomegam, ubi otomicron, ubi delta, ubi eta, ubi hee, ubi (magnus sonus / i. o. longam / i. o. brevem / e. longam / e. brevem)
digama, ubi vau, ubi iota, ubi sima, ubi antisima, ne loquendo barbara- (i. f. / i. u. / i. i. / i. s. / i. x.)
lixim vel scribendo barbarismum incurrat, quasi grafficus falsus. Barba- (illam figuram / vicium gramatice / scriptor)
rismus appellatur, qui mos barbarorum. (asi usus / barbarims)

Sciat autem ubi yrmos designari debeat, ubi yperbaton, ubi apostrofus (illa figura / quædam figura / alia figura)
suscribi debeat, vel dici, ubi virgula representans diptongum.[1] (una figura / longum)

Alium etiam modum sorciatur scribendi in signatis et in cirographis, (enseus / cirografs)
cartis et in transactionibus, alium in texum et alium in glosis.[2] Glosa (chartres / tist / glose)
enim per subbrevitatem et compendiosam per apices scribi debet. (brefté / brevem et utilem / titles)

Aurifaber habeat caminum in summo perforatum, ut possit fumus per (orfefvre / cheminé / percé / fume)
cuntos meatus evaporare. Manus altera levi pulsu folles regat summa (par tutes les alures / exire / suflement sufles)

---

[1] To explain this, it must be stated that, during the earlier period of the middle ages, the two letters of the diphthongs were written distinctly, sometimes separately and sometimes joined together. It became afterwards the custom to represent the first letter of the diphthong by a mere loop or mark *(virgula)* under the e, and this was used indiscriminately with the full diphthong until the end of the twelfth century, when both were abandoned, and a simple letter *e* used for both diphthongs. The diphthong was not resumed in writing until the period of the revival of learning. As this treatise by Neckam was written in the twelfth century, we have directions for writing the diphthong which would have been thrown away a few years later, and which indeed were apparently not understood by the glossator.

[2] Those who are much acquainted with medieval manuscripts will understand at once all these distinctions. The glosses or commentaries are usually written in very small characters, and are loaded with abbreviations, and hence they are more difficult to read than the text.

THE TREATISE DE UTENSILIBUS

<small>extente   ventus   freyceles breses illuminet</small>
diligencia, ita ut spiritus exiens[1] intus per fistulas prunas accendat, aque
<small>esperpliement   nurisement   clume</small>
etiam crebra aspersione igni prebeat alimentum. Assit etiam incus duricie
<small>indeficientis   enmoli</small>
inexhauste, vel exararate, super quam ferrum positum vel aurum emoliatur,
<small>   de tanalye   furmé</small>
et debitam formam suscipiat.[2] Hinc usu forcipis teneatur formatum, ut
<small>martel</small>
usu mallei produci possit et extendi.
<small>   petit martel   plates   de or   plates</small>
Habeat etiam malleolum ad britteas criseas formandas, quandoque laminas
<small>de argent   de fer   de esteim   quivere</small>
argenteas, quandoque ferreas, quandoque stagneas, quandoque cupreas,
<small>   orpetres   chisel   agu   i. tali gummi</small>
quandoque auricalcas. Habeat etiam celtem preacutam, qua in electro, vel
<small>ademaunt   tes   lapide   ulem   precioso lapide</small>
adamante, vel offelte, vel marmore, vel jacinto, vel smaragdo, vel sma-
<small>idem   charbunche   quidam lapis   idem</small>
ragdine, vel carbunculo, vel jaspide, vel saphiro, vel margarita, figuras
<small>   talier   enfurmer</small>
multiplices sculpere et informare possit.
<small>   vestun[3]   idem   i. probet   mule mola</small>
Habeat etiam cotem vel cotim, qua metallum exploret, et molam qua
<small>agnosce dat   pé de levere   pede planer</small>
ferro aciem conferat. Habeat et pedem leporinum, quo levigare et pollire
<small>tarder</small>
et tergere possit superficiem auri et argenti, et granula metallorum ne
<small>granula   gerun de quir   quoddem vas   ampulyes</small>
percant colligantur in gremio coriali. Habeat autem acerras et ampullas
<small>parva vasa   poter officium   une sye. syze   denté</small>
et vasa minuta, que figuli opus representent, et serram dentatam et
<small>   de orfrey   fil   de argent   filo anaps depescez   cusé</small>
lineam et aurifrigium, filum argenteum quo ciphi fracti apte consui vel
<small>ensemble treyt   penné</small>
contrahi possint. Peritus esse debet tam in opere plumali quam in
<small>amenable   fundable   trifarie</small>
opere ductili, tam in opere fusili quam in opere anaglafario.[4]
<small>   disciple   novice   parvam tabulam ciré   a cera</small>
Habeat etiam discipulus ejus rudis tabellam ceratam, vel ceromate
<small>arida terra oynte   flurs   purtreres   depeynz</small>
unctam, vel argilla oblitam, ad flosculos protrahendos et depingendos variis
<small>maneres   lie de argent   lapidem argenteum</small>
modis, ne in offensione procedat, cadimam congnoscat, litargium, et aurum,

---

[1] The Paris MS. reads *existens*, which is perhaps the more correct.

[2] These four words, not found in the Cottonian MS., are supplied from the Paris MS. 7679.

[3] *i. e.*, a whetstone—*vestun* evidently represents the English word.

[4] *Anaglapharium*, or more properly *anaglypharium*, *opus* (Gr. ἀνάγλυφον), called also *trifarium*, or *trifariatum*, was embossing, or sculpturing in relief.

    i. purum   quivere   purgato
et obrisum discernat ab auricalco et a cupro, ne pro auro elito emat auricalcum.

     greve chose mercatoris   perfidiam locus ubi
  Nam grave est institoris fallacis effugere tergiversacionem fabra-
 fabri habitant   aurifabri   seyt garni
teriam subintrantis, nisi perfectis animi motibus muniatur. Nam tres
   i. pertinentes ad animum de hiis que transacta sunt que nunc sunt   que
sunt animi motus, memoria preteritorum, sciencia presentium, prudentia
erunt
futurorum.

  Instauramenta ecclesie sunt hec: lavacrum sive fons, mariolum, crusi-
fixum, et alie ymagines, pulpitum sive anologium, urceus, urceolus, pelves,
sartago, cathedra, tronus, curile, tribunal sive curile, scamnum, absconsa,
sacrarium, vestibulum, sive vestiarium, altare, altarium, manutergium, facitergium, ymaginarium, fiole, et pixides. Sunt etiam ibi loculus, feretrum.
Juxta altare sit finaculum, examitam, vel amicum. Sint ibi crisiles,
columpne aurate vel deaurate, cum basibus argenteis vel marmoreis. Sint
ibi in ecclesia libri, codices, missale, breviarium, antiphonarium, gradale vel
gradarium. Sint ibi etiam manuale et processionale, ymnarium, psalterum,
troparium, ordinale sive consuetudinarium. Vestes sacerdotis sint ibi,
casula, superpellicium, et caphicesium, infula, alba, dalmatica, stola, cingulum, sive tropheum, sive zona, sive balteum, fanum. Sint ibi trabes acerne
sive quercine. Sint ibi etiam tingna vel tigilla per succendines. Sint
etiam clavi ut lingnum hujus pagine forti aderat tegminibus, sive cidulis,
sive plumbo, sive tegula, sive culmo, sive calamo, sive arundine. Opus est
clavis ferreis et ligneis, aut opus est quibus tegule lateres suspendant,
unde nole, et immense campane et tintinabula in turre debent collocari.
Colus, sive [1] pinaculus, sive camparium turris, pro eadem sunt. Possint
si greve ventilogium desuper arduissimo collocetur. Sint etiam ibi cheruca,
vectes, gunphi, repagula, pessule, sere; sint etiam limen, cardines, et hec
aditum templi, quod idem sunt basilica, id est ecclessia, oratorium, can-
cellum, ecclesia, monasterium, apterium, capella; sed diversa consequntur
nomen vocabullum, ne inter supradicta defficiat filitorium, in quo conser-
vetur dignissime eucaristia, salus anime fidelium, quam nisi quisque fideliter
firmiterque crediderit, salvus esse non poterit.

---

[1] The Cottonian MS. ends here abruptly, in consequence of the loss of the concluding leaf; I have added the rest from the transcript of the Paris MS., furnished by M. Delille. The names of the ecclesiastical service-books, and other church furniture, may be compared with the lists given further on by John de Garlande, and in the later English vocabularies.

THE DICTIONARIUS OF
JOHN DE GARLANDE.[1]
(FIRST HALF OF THE THIRTEENTH CENTURY.)

Magistri Johannis de Gallandia Dictionarius.

Dictionarius dicitur libellus iste a dictionibus magis necessariis, quas tenetur quilibet scolaris, non tantum in scrinio de lingnis facto, sed in cordis armariolo firmiter retinere, ut ad faciliorem oracionis constructionem perveniat. Primo igitur sciat vulgaria nominare. Placet igitur a menbris humani corporis incoare, rerum promtuarium evolvendo.

---

[1] John de Garlande was an Englishman, born probably about the middle of the second half of the twelfth century, and studied at Oxford. He established himself in the University of Paris in the first years of the thirteenth century, and was long celebrated there for his scholastic learning. He appears to have been employed at Toulouse against the heretical Albigeois, and we learn from a paragraph in the following treatise that he was there in 1218, when Simon de Montfort was slain. At a later period, on the foundation of the University of Toulouse in 1229, John de Garlande was chosen as one of the professors, and remained there three years, after which he resumed his position in Paris, where he probably died soon after the middle of the thirteenth century. See, for further information, the introduction to my edition of his poem *De Triumphis Ecclesiæ*, printed for the Roxburgh Club in 1856. The French bibliographers have fallen into a very strange blunder with regard to this writer, whom they place in the eleventh century instead of the thirteenth.

All we know of the date at which the *Dictionarius* was composed is, that it must have been subsequently to the year 1218; and as the events of that year seem to have been fresh in the author's memory, it was perhaps compiled soon after his return, between that date and 1229.

It was edited in Paris, in one of the volumes of the government historical commission, by M. H. Géraud, entitled *Paris sous Philippe-le-Bel, d'après des documents originaux* (4to, 1837). M. Géraud shared in the error on the date of the writer, which is the more to be regretted as it has had an influence upon other parts of his work. The manuscripts of the *Dictionarius* are not uncommon, either in England or on the continent. M. Géraud edited it from three copies in the National Library in Paris, one of the thirteenth century, and the other two of the fifteenth. I have taken my text from a MS. of the end of the thirteenth century in the British Museum (MS. Cotton. Titus D. xx), and collated it with another of the fifteenth century in the same library (MS. Harl. No. 1002, fol. 176, v°.) The commentary is taken almost entirely from the Parisian MS. of the thirteenth century, with some additions, within parentheses ( ), from one of the Paris MSS. of the fifteenth, and within brackets [ ], from the Cottonian MS. The Harleian MS. contains a few interlineary glosses in English, of the fifteenth century, which I have here printed in their places. It must be kept in mind that the commentary here printed consists only of such passages of the original commentary as contain useful explanations or French equivalents for the Latin words.

Inter partes humani corporis, scilicet, pes est inferior, cujus pars est planta callosa, talus rotundus, articuli quinque divisi cum unguibus totidem; colateralis est sophena caville, cui vicina est tibia, quasi columpna, totum subportans corporis edificium. Os tibie concavum rotunde medulla debet repleri. Tibie vero partes sunt musculus, et cartilago. Musculum subsequitur poples, et genu, et internodium; et ei crus vicinum sive femur pubi maritetur.

    Pes dicitur a *pos* Grece, quod *pes* Latinus, unde antipodes dicuntur habitatores alterius regionis vel emisperii, si verum est illos esse.[1] Planta callosa, id est callus, qui est cutis mortificata in pedibus et in manibus per longum laborem. (Musculus, Gallice *molet.*) Sophena dicitur quasi sophie vena, quia, si grossa est in dextro pede, significat bonum ingenium. Pubes, nomen equivoquum est, scilicet ad juvenem et ad pubem, qui Gallice dicitur *penil.*[2] Internodium apud Ovidium[3] dicitur tota dispositio ipsius genu cum sua concavitate.

Si velim reserare secreta humane nature causa doctrine, non debet ascribi rusticitati sed rationi, cum pudor sit ignorare cujus causam assignare natura tria dedit homini genitalia, quæ sunt virga virilis et duo fratres pendiculi, qui sunt testiculi, prope peritoneon; in muliere valva, quæ dicitur vulva, quam subsequitur matrix, in qua concipitur infans voluptate viri et mulieris, cujus virtus est in umbiculo et in renibus ejus, cujus nates desplicent viro religioso.

Tergum, et spondilia, cum ventre, causa doctrine, inter has partes corporis numquid nominabo? que rusticus derisorie nominabit, tentiginem, cullum, menpirium, podicem, non nominabo, sed subintelligam, sed ista: latera, lacertos, cubitos, palmas, digitos, juncturas, ungues; nec preterire volo policem, indicem, medium, medicum, auricularem, humeros, et acellas. Pars humeri est homoplata. Pars pectoris est torax et mamilla, quod munimentum ventris dicitur. Collum candidum, cum gutture candido, in muliere placet, et nigra supercilia, et frons libera. Retro in capite sunt fontinella, et duo cornua, quibus vicine sunt aures, per quas colera expurgatur.

Partes nasi sunt iste: pirula naris, interfinium. Partes oris sunt iste: uvula, lingua, palatum, guttur, dentes, gingiva, labra vel labia, ysofagus, et ephiglotum. Partes oculi sunt palpebra, cilia, pupilla, et tunica sclirotica. Frons supercilio proxima est. In fronte nitent capilli, qui dependent undique circa discrimen. In corona clericali ostenditur sanctuarium Dei.

    Medicus dicitur digitus eo quod illo medici imponunt medicinam. Torax est ferreum munimen ventris quod habent milites, et idem est quod tunica ferrea. Mamilla dicitur per onomathopeon, id est per nomen fictum a sono in ore pueri lactentis. Fontinnella

---

[1] The existence of antipodes was a question on which the Church affected to throw discredit, and which even scholars of the highest credit did not venture to assert positively. In the eighth century, Virgil, afterwards bishop of Salzburg, was excommunicated for having believed in the antipodes.

[2] The Paris MS. of the thirteenth century reads *pervilg*, which is perhaps a mere error of the copyist.

[3] The passage of Ovid referred to will be found in the Metamorphoses, lib. vi., l. 255.
    Ictus erat, qua crus esse incipit, et qua
    Mollia nervosus facit internodia poples.

122   THE DICTIONARIUS OF

est concavitas colli inter duos tumores qui dicentur cornua.   Interfinium dicitur ab inter
et finis, quod est paries inter duas nares.   (Ysophagus, *gisier* Gallice).

In cerebro sub craneo sunt tres celule; prima est ymaginaria, secunda rationalis, tertia memorialis.[1] Pulmo est flabellum quo calor cordis refrigeratur. Cibus in stomaco dequoquitur, a quo, per venas miseraicas, liquor eliquatur ad epar, ubi generantur quatuor humores, scilicet colera, sanguis, fleuma, et melancolia. Si vero superfluant, fleobotomator indigenti minuat cum fleobotomo.[2] Vene originem habent ab epate, que deveunt quatuor humores predictos per totum corpus. Cistis fellis recipit coleram; et splen purgat melancoliam. Per zirbum et longaonem[3] feces decendunt ad anum in decessum.

   Miseraice sunt vene a stomacho usque ad epar.   Cistis, id est cista, receptaculum.
Splen, receptaculum est melancolie.   Zirbum est intestinum longum, a longitudine scilicet
dictum, quia per illud feces exeunt.

Inter hæc membra, tria sunt que terminant in n. litteram, scilicet splen, ren, lien, et unum nomen Grecum quod est neutri generis, scilicet diafragma, quod dividit spiritualia a vitalibus. Istis ita nominatis, nominanda sunt instrumenta urbana et rusticana; sed prius nominabuntur res quas, eundo per civitatem Parisius,[4] denotavi.

   Ren, -nis, in singulari nota, Gallice *rognon*;   rênes, in plurali, Gallice *rains*.   A lien
dicitur lienteria, genus fluxus ventris.

                                                                                perche
Unus vicinorum nostrorum tulit hodie ad vendendum in pertica una sotu-
         ylasyd   typpys   bogyllis
lares ad laqueos, cum liripipiis,[5] et ad laqueos, et ad nodulos, et ad plusculas,
legharneys   botys
tibialia et cruralia,[6] et crepitas femineas et monacales.

   Pluscula dicitur Gallice *boucle* [*bucle*] (*bouglettes*).   Tybialia dicuntur Gallice *estivaus*.
Cruralia, Gallice *hueses*.   Crepite, Gallice *botes à creperon*, quod est dubium, quia dubium est
utrum pes fuerit intus vel foris, sicut videmus in monachis; vel dicitur hæc crepita a
crepo, quia crepat, id est sonat in incessu.[7]

---

[1] The division of the brain into three cells, as here described, was an established doctrine of physiological science in the middle ages, and is often treated of in the manuscripts, sometimes with an illustrative diagram. It seems to have been a foreshadowing of the modern doctrines of phrenology. The other physiological theories here given are no less curious.

[2] Phlebotomy, from the Greek φλεβοτομία, *i. e.*, the cutting a vein, was the old name for bloodletting, which was very largely practised by the medieval physicians. It was customary for people to be bled regularly at different periods of the year, although in perfect health.

[3] Zirbus, the omentum. *Longaon*, or *lagaon*, according to the reading of the Paris MSS., appears to be intended for the Greek word λαγών, and to mean the ilium.

[4] Parisius, the Latin form of the name of the metropolis of France in the middle ages, was an indeclinable word.

[5] *Liripipium*, a long tail or tippet, suspended to different parts of the dress, but especially to the hood, called in old English a *liripippe*, or *leripoop*.

[6] These two words I give from the Paris MS.

[7] John de Garlande is rather given to casting satirical reflections upon the customs and manners of his contemporaries, and these are sometimes very amusing. This commentator seems to have been seized at times with the same spirit, as in his remark on the names of the boots worn by monks.

gurdelersystodyd
Corigiarii habent ante se zonas albas, nigras, rubeas, bene membratas
coper   kosis   ybarryd
ferro vel cupro, texta stipata argento.[1]

Corrigiarii dicuntur a corrigiis quas faciunt. Zona tres habet significationes; in una accipitur pro cingulo. Texta, a textum, -ti, cingulum factum de serico (*tissus*); stipata, id est fulta vel appodiata, Gallice *ceint* [Gallice *barré*].

sadelerspylnys   canvassys
Sellarii vendunt sellas nudas et pictas, et panellos, pulvillos,[2] carentivillas,[3]
styropys
et trusulas,[4] et strepas.

Pulvillos, Gallice *bas*. Trusullas, Gallice *estrisles*. Strepas, *estrieulz*.

schylmakers
Scutarii prosunt civitatibus totius Anglie,[5] qui vendunt militibus scuta
latyn
tecta tela, corio, et auricalco, leonibus et foliis liliorum depicta.[6]

bogelersbogyls
Pluscularii sunt divites per plusculas suas, et lingulas, et mordacula, per
brydels
limas, et loralia equina.

Pluscularii dicuntur Gallice *boucliers* [*buclers*]. Plusculas, Gallice *boucles*. Lingula, de lingua, dicitur Gallice *hardilon* [*hardeliun*]. Mordaculum, id est *mordaunt*. Loralia dicuntur Gallice *lorains*, id est *poitraus*. [Gallice *loreins*, Anglice *peytereles*.]

nedyls
Willelmus, vicinus noster, habet in foro ista vendenda ante se, acus, et
nedylcasys   sope   myrrys   rasors wetstonys   vyrehyryns
acuaria, smigma sive saponem, et specula, et rasoria, cotes, et piricudia, et
spyndels
fusillos.

Acuaria dicuntur instrumenta illa ubi servantur acus. (Saponem, Gallice *savelon*.) (Fusillos, Gallice *fouesil*.)

Lorimarii quam plurimum diliguntur a nobilibus militibus Francie, propter calcaria argentata et aurata, et propter pectoralia resonancia et frena bene fabricata.

Lorimarii dicuntur a loris (seu loralibus) quæ faciunt.

huestertrencher-knyvys
Vidi hodie institorem habentem ante se cultellos ad mensam, mensaculos,[7] et artavos, vaginas parvas et magnas, stilos, et stilaria.

Artavus dicitur Gallice *keniret*, scilicet cultellus qui tendit in altum; vel dicitur ab arte, quia eo artifices utuntur. (Stilos, Gallice *greffe*.)[8]

---

[1] The manufacture of belts or girdles, which were made of leather and ornamented with buckles and studs, was a very important one in the middle ages.

[2] The old commentator explains *pulvillos* by *bâts*, or packsaddles.

[3] The French editor has made a singular error in regard to this word, and has thought it necessary to correct it to *carenti villosas*. *Carentivilla* was the common medieval word for canvas; see before, in the treatise of Alexander Neckam, de Utensilibus, pp. 99, 108.

[4] A curry-comb; perhaps the word is a corruption of the Latin *strigilis*.

[5] The French text has *Gallie* instead of *Anglie*, which has been substituted for it in the English manuscript.

[6] This word is inserted from the Paris MS.

[7] Carving knives, or, as the English gloss interprets the word, trencher-knives (in old French *trenchouers*).

[8] The Anglo-Saxon *græf*. See before, p. 75.

124   THE DICTIONARIUS OF

   furbyars
 Euruginatores gladiorum cumulant denarios vendendo gladios euruginatos,
     pomels hyltys
qui habent tolos[1] et capulos rotillantes et novas vaginas.

   Eruginatores dicuntur ab eruginare, Gallice *fourbir* [*furber*]. Tolos dicuntur *pomeaux à tolon*, quod est ornamentum, [Gallice *pumel*]. Scapulus dicitur Gallice *hancere* [*hente*]. Item, dicitur scapulus pro pharetra.

 Mercatores habitantes super Magnum Pontem,[2] vendunt capistrum, lum-
     powchys
baria, ligulas, marsupia sive bursas, de coreo cervino, ovino, bovino, et porcino.

   Capistrum dicitur a capite, Gallice *chevestre*. Ligulas, Gallice *lasnieres*.

                   glovys
 Cirotecarii Parisius decipiunt scolares vendendo eis cirotecas simplices,
  yfurryd   lomys skynys konyngys scynnys foxys skynnys myttyns
et furratas pellibus agninis, cuniculinis, vulpinis, et mitas de coreo factas.

   Cirothecarii dicuntur a cirotheca, et illud a *ciros*, quod est manus, et *tecon*, quod est tributum, quia attribuitur manui.[3] Mitas, Gallice *mitheines* [*miteynes*]. Fiebant etiam de panno lineo.

     hattys feltte   cappys
 Capellarii faciunt capella de fultro sive centone, et de pennis pavonis,
   of kotyn
et pillea de bumbace, et quedam pilleola de lana et pilis.[4]

   Fultro, dicitur Gallice *fautre (feultre)* [*feutre*]. Pillea, nomen etheroclitum a pilis dictum, Gallice *chapel de cotun*. Bumbace dicitur ab hoc nomine bombix, quod est vermis qui egerit sericum. Ab hoc nomine, quod est bumbace, quod est *cotun* Gallice, dicitur bombacinum, quod est Gallice *pourpoins* [*purpoynt*].

 Ad portam Sancti Lazarii[5] manent architenentes, qui faciunt balistas, arcus de acere, viburno, taxo,[6] sagittas et hastas, et tela, et petilia, de fraxino.

   Architenentes dicuntur Gallice *archiers*[7] [*archers*]. (Balistas, Gallice *arbalestre*.) Acer, arbor, Gallice *arable*; unde derivatur acerra, vas in quo thus ponitur super altare. [Viburnus est arbor, scilicet *auburn*, unde fit nardus.] Taxus est arbor que Gallice dicitur *hous*[8] [*hif*]; taxus aliter Gallice *taisons* [*teysun*], et taxum, Gallice *lardun*. [Fraxinus, Gallice *frene*.]

---

[1] The Greek θόλις, signifying a dome, or cupola. It appears in medieval Latin to have been applied to anything which terminated in a dome or sphere. *Pommels*, in French *pommeaux*, because the hilt of the sword in the Anglo-Norman period terminated in a ball or apple *(pomme)*.

[2] The Grand-Pont in Paris was the bridge known at a later period as the Pont-au-Change, opposite the Châtelet and the Rue St. Denis.

[3] The correct derivation of the word is of course from the Greek χειρ, a hand, and θήκη, a case.

[4] This is a curious description of the sorts of hats and caps worn in the thirteenth century. The felt hat with the peacock's feather is seen, I think, in illuminated manuscripts, but I am not sure if any are of this period.

[5] The priory of St. Lazare stood outside the Porte St. Denis.

[6] Of the three woods here stated to be used for making bows, two, maple *(acer)* and yew *(taxus)*, are well known, but it is not so clear what wood is meant by *viburnum*. In one of the Paris MSS., and in the Cottonian MS., it is glossed by a French word, *aubourne*, which also is obscure.

[7] It would appear that the name *archers*, and its Latin equivalent *architenentes*, were given to the makers of bows as well as to those who used them.

[8] The commentator seems to have mistaken the meaning of *taxus*, when he translated it by *hous*, or holly. The comment of the Cottonian MS. is more correct.

Firmacularii habent ante se firmacula[1] parva et magna, de plumbo facta et de stangno, ferro, cupro, et calibe; habent etiam herea, pulcra monilia, et nolas resonantes.

(Plumbum, Gallice *pellon*.)

Artifices illi subtiles sunt qui fundunt campanas de here sonoro, per quas in ecclesiis hore diei denunciantur, motu batillorum[2] et cordarum atractarum.

Campane dicuntur a rusticis qui habitant in campo, qui nesciunt judicare horas nisi per campanas. Ecclesiæ clocorium, Gallice dicitur *clochier*.

Pictaciarii viles sunt, qui consuunt sotulares veteres, renovando pictacia, et intercucia, et soleas, et inpedeas. *(clowtars ... clowtys ... waltys)*

Pictaciarii dicuntur *savetiers*. Pictacia dicuntur *tacons*. Intercucia dicuntur Gallice *rives*.[3] Soleas dicuntur Gallice *semelles* [*semeus*]. Impedias dicuntur Gallice *empiegnes* [*enpenyes*].

Allutarii sunt qui faciunt calciamenta de alluta, et prosunt civitati Parisius; qui conservant sibi forumpedias, equitibialia, et spatulas. Qui alutarii secant cum rasorio vel ansorio corium atramentario denigratum, et consuunt calciamenta cum subula et licino et seta porcina. *(cordueners)*

Alutarii dicuntur [*cordewaners*] qui operantur in alluta quod est Gallice *corduan* [*cordewan*], alio modo dicitur cordubunum, a Corduba, civitate Hispaniæ, ubi fiebat primo.[4] Formipedias dicuntur *formes* [*furmes*], quia pedes informant. Equitibialia dicuntur *estivax*, ab equus, -a, -um, quia adequantur tibie. Spatulas, Gallice *esclices*. Ansarium est cultrum ipsius sutoris. Licinium dicitur a licio, quod est *fil*. [Atramentario, Gallice *arnement*. Licinio, Gallice *linolles*.]

Pelliparii ditantur per sua pelicia, et per penulas, furraturas factas partim de pellibus agninis, partim catinis, partim vulpinis, partim leporinis.

Pelliparii dicuntur a pellis et paro, -as, qui parant vel consuunt pelles; et alio modo dicuntur pellifices *(peletiers)*. Catinis dicuntur ab hoc nomine catus, -ti, qui alio nomine vocatur murilegus, quasi legens mures.

Peliparii pelles deliciosas vendunt cuniculorum, et cirogrillorum, et lutriciorum, et mustelarum, et esperiolorum, qui minores sunt cirogrillis secundum Ysidorum, sed carius vendunt cicinum,[5] et urlas de sabelino et laerone.[6]

[Cuniculus, Gallice *cunin*.] Cirogrilli Gallice dicuntur *escureus*, qui tamen secundum alios dicuntur esperioli, ab Esperia regione ubi habitant. Lutricius dicitur Gallice *loutre* [*lutres*]. Mustele dicitur a mure et *telon*, quod est longum, quasi longus mus. Cisimus est idem aliter quod defert *vair et gris*. [Cicinus, aliter est quod dicitur *veyr et gris*. Sabelinus, Gallice *sabelin*. Laerone, *lerun*.]

---

[1] Fermails, or clasps for the dress, which were worn under the neck. They were sometimes made of richer materials than those here enumerated.

[2] *Batillum*, the clapper of the bell.

[3] The pieces of leather inserted between the soles.

[4] The leather of Cordova was famous in the middle ages. It was called in England *cordewayne*, whence the name *cordwainers*, for shoemakers.

[5] By the explanation of the commentator this would seem to be synonymous with vair, the skin or fur of a species of weasel.

[6] The skin of the lérot, an animal of the dormouse kind.

Quidam clamatores[1] peliciorum reparandorum discurrunt per plateas civitatis, et reparant furraturas epitogiorum eorum et palliorum, partim furando.
<small>i. togarum   of mantels</small>

<small>Epythogium Gallice dicitur *surcot*. (Pallium, *mantel* Gallice.)</small>

Reparatores ciphorum exclamant ciphos reparandos cum filo ereo et
argenteo. Ciphos autem reparant de murinis, et planis, et brucis, de acere,
et tremulo.
<small>masers   of warrys   mapyl   haspe</small>

<small>Murrinis dicuntur *madre* [Gallice *mazer*].[2] Quidam tamen dicunt quod murra, -e, dicatur arbor illa unde Lucanus,[3]</small>

<small>In auro murrave bibunt.</small>

<small>Brucis, Gallice dicitur *bruis*[4] [*bruces*]. Acer, -eris, *arable*. Tremulo Gallice dicitur *tremble*.</small>

Precones vini clamant gula yante vinum ataminatum[5] in tabernis, ad
quatuor denarios, et ad sex, et ad octo, et ad duodecim, portando vinum
temptando fusum in craterem a lagena.
<small>cryers   galpyng   atamyd   tavernys   the pyse   galun</small>

<small>Lagena, Gallice dicitur *quarte*[6] [Gallice *galun*].</small>

Precones nebularum et gafrarum[7] pronunciant de nocte gafras et nebulas et
artocreas vendendas in calatis velatis albo manutergio; et calati suspendentur
frequenter ad fenestras clericorum, senione perditi.[8]
<small>wafurs   idem est   schewyt   wafurs   idem est</small>

<small>Arthocreas dicuntur *roissoles* [*russel*], ab *artos*, quod est panis, et *creas* quod est caro, quia fiunt de carne minuta et pane. Senio, -onis, dicitur numerus senarius, Gallice *hasard*.</small>

Auxionarii mittunt servos et servas per vicos ad decipiendum clericos,
quibus vendunt nimis care cerasa, pruna alba et nigra, et poma inmatura,
et pira, et lactucas, et nasturcia.[9]

<small>Aucionarii dicuntur Gallice *regratiers* [*regrateres*]. Prunum, fructus; prunus est arbor; pruina Gallice dicitur *brese*; pruina dicitur *gelée*. Nasturcium dicitur Gallice *creson*.</small>

Placente, flamicie, et ingnacie jacent ad fenestras augxionariorum, et casei

---

[1] *i. e.*, street-criers.

[2] It seems very doubtful what was the wood which was at this time known by the name of *madre*, or *mazer*. At a considerably later period the maple appears to have usurped the name, but they are here distinctly enumerated apart. The medieval Latin scholars, by a confusion of the word murra applied to the mazer in their Latin, imagined the myrrhine vases of antiquity to have been mazer, and hence the mistake of our commentator with respect to the line of Lucan.

[3] Lucan, Pharsal. lib. iv., l. 380. Our commentator has not quoted correctly—the line stands in the original,—

Non auro murrhaque bibunt.

[4] Another name for box-wood.

[5] Diluted, or corrupted. They passed upon people wine which had been diluted in the tavern.

[6] The French "quarte" was a measure which held about five pints of wine. It is curious that the English commentator should substitute *gallon*.

[7] These two articles are represented by the modern French words *oublies* and *gauffres*, which are not quite identical, as the English gloss would seem to indicate.

[8] *i. e.*, the clerks, or scholars, hung at their windows the baskets of cakes they had gained at hazard. Perhaps the allusion is to the practice of games for cakes, like those still in use in our country fairs.

[9] *Narstucas*, MS. Cotton.

molles et duri, cum candelis sulfuratis, ut melius ardeant, habentes lichinos vel lichnos grossos.

<small>Placente dicuntur Gallice *simeniaus* [*simeneus*].[1] Flamicie, Gallice *flamiche*. Ignacia, Gallice *fouace* [*fuaces*].[2] Lichinus dicitur Gallice *meche* [*mecches*].</small>

Pistores Parisius pinsunt pastam et formant panes, numero, pondere, et mensura, quos quocunt in furno mundato cum tersorio.[3] Vendunt autem panes de frumento, de siligine, de ordeo, de avena, de acere,[4] et frequenter de furfure.

<small>[Pistores, Gallice *baxtres*.][5] Acer Gallice dicitur *ravane*, vel id quod ejicitur de vanno. (Siligo dicitur Gallice *segle*.) Furfur, Gallice *son*; furfura dicuntur etiam resolutiones urine.</small>

Pistores habent servos qui politruduant farinam grossam cum polentrudio delicato, et immittunt pastefermentum ut elevent panem in alveo. Arcas etiam radunt aliquando cum costa pastali et polenta.

<small>Pollitrudiant, id est *buletent*, et dicitur a pollem, quod est farina, et trudo. Pollitrudium Gallice dicitur *buletel* [*bultel*].</small>

pye-makyers   pasteys
Pastillarii quam plurimum lucrantur, vendendo clericis pastillos de car-
            chykyns   helys   tarlatys
nibus porcinis, et pullinis, et de anguillis, cum pipere, exponendo tartas, et
flathen ystuffyd   nessche
flaones fartos caseis molibus et ovis sanis et frequenter inmundis.

<small>Fartos, id est repletos, a farcio, -cis, -si, fartum; Gallico *farcir* [*farsir*], unde fartores dicuntur pastillarii [Gallice *farsures*].</small>

         kokys
Coquinarii quocunt et vertunt in verubus colurnis[6] anseres, et columbas,
                                              rawe   to sympyl
et altilia; sed frequenter vendunt carnes crudas simplicibus mancipiis scola-
         sawse   ytemperd   bowchers
rium cum salsamentis[7] et aleatis[8] male disteperatis. Quibus invident carnifices
in bocherewys   oxe flessche   schepys flessche   hogges flessche
in macillis,[9] vendentes carnes grossas bovinas, et   ovinas,   et porcinas,
         with lepur   ysemyte
aliquando lepra percussas; maceras et mensaculas scolaribus incucientes. Sed mactatores a scolarisis animosis mactantur, propter hillias immundas, et salsucias, tuceta,[10] et scruta,[11] que popello conveniunt tunicato.[12]

---

[1] The cakes called *simnels*, made of fine flour cooked in a particular manner. In Shropshire the name is still retained, and applied to a large plumcake with a raised and very hard crust. They are not unfrequently mentioned in old English writers.

[2] A sort of cake, apparently resembling our pancake, well known to the readers of Rabelais. The *flamiche*, or *flamusse*, is considered by Roquefort to be identical with the *flan*, a sort of custard cake.

[3] In one of the Paris MSS. this word is explained in an interlinear gloss by *escovelon*.

[4] The same glossator has explained this word by *mestelon*. It was, in fact, what was called in English *mastlin*, or *meslin*, a mixture of wheat and rye.

[5] It is singular that the commentator in the English MS. should have supposed *baxter* to be a French word.

[6] *De coudre*—French interlinear gloss.

[7] *Sausses*—Idem.

[8] *Aillies*—Idem.

[9] *Macatres*—Idem.

[10] *Trunteta*, in the Paris MS. which is glossed in one MS. by *banel*.

[11] *Tripes*—French interlinear gloss.

[12] *Popello tunicato* means, no doubt, the scho-

128   THE DICTIONARIUS OF

[Colurnus, Gallice *coudre*.] Matheca, Gallice *haschette*. Hilla, Gallice *andouille*. Salcice, Gallice *sauchises*. Trunteta, Gallice *boudin*.

Trapezete numerant trapezetum super trapetam unam monetam parisiensem, parum sterliugos, [a sto stas, et lingo, -is, quasi lingens statum hominis,[1]] cum talentis, et alias monetas rutilantes, super Mangnum Pontem;[2] et hoc faciunt intentione lucrandi, dum incurrunt usure crimen.

Trapezete dicuntur Gallice *chongeors* [*chaunjurs*], a trapeta, Gallice *planche*, que est mensa super quam ponuntur denarii.

Numularii, qui fabricant monetam, videntur divites esse, sed non sunt; licet denarios monetant, sui non sunt denarii, sed mittuntur ad cambium, ut a cambitoribus, vel casoribus, sub spe lucrandi cambiantur.

Aurifabri sedent ante fornaces suas et tabellas super Mangnum Pontem, et fabricant pateras de auro et argento, firmacula, monilia, et spintera, et nodulos, religunt ad anulos granula, et jaspides, saphiros, et smaracdos.

Pateras dicuntur cuppas, *hanaps*. Spincter dicitur *espingle* [*aficayl*]. Jaspis Gallice dicitur *jaspe*. Saphirus dicitur *saphirs*. Smaraudus dicitur *esmeraude*.

the bysynys
Aurifabrorum industria intendit super incudem ferream, cum maleolis sub-
goldyn
tilibus, laminas criseas et argenteas, et includit gemmas preciosas infra ancas[3] anulorum quibus utuntur barones et femine generose.

Lamina Gallice dicuntur *platines*. Criseas dicuntur a *crisis*,[4] quod est aurum. Barones dicuntur a *barim*,[5] quod est grave, quasi grave persone. Ancas, id est fossas in quibus sunt gemmæ.

Artifices dicuntur cipharii qui incrustant vasa crustis aureis,et a rgenteis,[6] et pedes subponunt crateribus, quos circulis coronant, ut ipsi sint pulcriores et durabiliores.

Pannarii, nimia cupiditate ducti, fallaces vendunt pannos, albos, nigros, camelinos, et blodios, burneticos, virides, scarleticos, et radiatos, et stamfordiatos;[7] sed ipsi defraudant emtores, ulnando cum ulna curta et cum pollice fallaci.

Pannarii, qui vendunt pannos. Camelinos dicuntur a camelo, qui habent colorem similem camelo.

---

lars of the University, and there is no need for the emendation of the French editor, *tunicata*, or of his elaborate explanation of this reading. The allusion to the quarrels between the scholars and the cooks and butchers is a curious picture of university manners.

[1] This odd derivation of the word *sterling*, which is omitted in the Cottonian MS., has, at all events, the merit of originality.

[2] It was because the changers inhabited the Grand-Pont that it took afterwards its name of Pont-aux-Changeoirs. See before, p. 124.

[3] The word *anca*, *ancha*, or sometimes *ancu*, in old French *anche*, was given to the hollow in the ring in which the gems were set.

[4] The Greek χρυσὸς, gold.

[5] The Greek βαρὺς, heavy, grave. It is hardly necessary to say that this derivation of the word *baron* is a very erroneous and absurd one.

[6] *i. e.*, They mounted cups of mazer, &c., in gold and silver.

[7] The town of Stamford, in Lincolnshire, was celebrated in the middle ages for the manufacture of cloth.

Quidam homines usurpant sibi oficia mulierum, qui vendunt mappas et manutergia, linteamina, et camisias, et braccas, teristra, supara, staminas, et telas, et pepla, et flameola.

> Teristra dicuntur Gallice *chainse* [*cimise*], quedam vestis mulieris de lino. Supara, Gallice *rochet;* et nota quod supara sunt plice veli in navi. Staminias, ab hoc nomine stamen, Gallice *estamine* [*stamieus*]. Telas, a *telon*, . . unde protelare, Gallico *estendre*. Pepla, *wimples*.] Flammeola dicuntur Gallice *cuevrechief*, et dicuntur a flamma, quia solebant pendere ante flammeos vultus.

Apotecarii, causa lucri, concumulant confectiones et electuaria, radices cum erbis, zedoarium cum zinzibero, piper cum cimino, gariofilos cum cinamomo, anisum cum maratro, ceram cum cereis ecclesiasticis, zucuram cum licuricia.[1]

> Zinziberum, Gallice *gengibre*. Gariophilus, Gallice dicitur *cleu de girofle* [*clou de gelofre*. Cinamomum, Gallice *canel*.] Maratrum dicitur semen feniculi. Liquiricia dicitur Gallice *syrop rigolice*.

Apotecarii in apoteca habent hec, que sunt zinziberum conditum et alexandrinum, que conveniunt frigidis complexionibus; diapendion, quod gratum est consumis; diaprunis, diadragantum, que infrigidant, eleborum operantur ad egestionem.

> Apothecarii Gallice dicuntur *espiciers* [*espicere*]. Nomina electuariorum sunt multa; quedam sunt quorum hic nomina ponuntur. Diapendion . . . . valet ad restaurationem humanitatis perdite.[2] Dyadragantum dicitur quod fit de diadragento, quod est genus gummi.[3] Elleborus herba, Gallice *masaire*, qua acuuntur medecine laxative.

Carpentarii diversis instrumentis fabricant diversa, que videmus in cupariis, qui fabricant cupas, et dolia ferata, cados, onofora que ligantur circulis tenacibus, et cavillis, et cuneis cuparedum.

> Notandum quod carpentum idem est quod biga, et inde potest dici carpentarius. Cuppas dicuntur Gallico *cuves* [*cuvers*). Dolea, *tuneus*. Cados, Gallice *baril*. Colum, *tunne*.] Onofora Gallice dicuntur *bouceax* [*buceus*], de corio facta,[4] et dicuntur ab *onos*, quod est vinum, et *foros*, quod est ferre,[5] quia intus vinum defertur. Colum, Gallice *entounceor*, et prelum, proprie videlicet torcularis.

Rotarii cumulant denarios fabricando vel vendendo bigas, et quadrigas, et plaustra, quorum partes canti rotarum, et radii, et modii, vel timphana, axes, cavillae, limones, et timones, juga, cum arquillis.

> Rotarii dicuntur illi qui faciunt rotas. Canti dicuntur Gallice *charetes*.[6] Modii dicuntur Gallice *moieus*. Arquillis, id est circulis qui circumdant colla boum vel pecorum ne intrent sepes, id est *haies*.

Carucarii reparant diversa instrumenta aratri, stivam, trabem, et dentem sive dentalea, juga in quibus boves trahunt, corbes, et flagella, et vannos,

---

[1] *i. e.*, sugar and liquorice.

[2] Diapenidion was the term for a medicine which was to cure all diseases, and even to restore life.

[3] Gum tragacanth.

[4] This is another proof that the leathern vessels for wine *(utres)* continued in use during the middle ages. See before, p. 98. It is remarked by the French editor that *boucel*, the singular of *bouceax*, was probably the original of the modern French *bocal*.

[5] The word is of course derived from *οἶνος*, wine, and φέρω, to carry.

[6] This is an error of the old commentator. The *canti*, or more correctly *canthi*, were the fellies of the wheels. See before, pp. 16, 108.

et sarcula, uncos, et cultros, tribulas, vangas, sarpas, et ligones, et ephifia equina. Et in orreis scobe sunt, rastra,[1] furce. Flagellorum partes sunt manutentum, virga, et cappa.

Stiva (aratri) anterior pars, quam rusticus tenet in manu, et dicitur Gallice *manchon* [Gallice *handle*].[2] Tribulum, scilicet flabellum; tribula, Gallice dicitur *palai*; tribulus, Gallice *rinse* [*runce*]. Vangas dicuntur *beches* [*besches*], palas ferratas. (Sarpas, *serpes*.) Epiphia dicuntur collaria equorum [Gallice *horeus*, scilicet *hame de cheval*].

Molendinarii fabricant faricapsias, et rotas versatiles et aquaticas, et fusos, anaglocitana, et scarioballa,[3] et apte collocant molares, qui molunt de faricapsia
              clapere
farinam, que batillo molendini descendit in alveum farinosum.[4]

Molendinarii dicuntur *mouniers*. Farricapsie sunt in quibus ponuntur frumenta molendini, et dicuntur a far et capio. Scanoballa sunt quidam nodi in interiori rota qui movent fusum molendini [*les nous de la roe*]. Molares (spectat) ad magnum lapidem molendini.
                        gryte noyse   barbycons
In civitate Tholose,[5] nondum sedato tumultu belli, vidi antemuralia,[6] licias,
                    brytegys   schafftys
super fossata profunda, turres, propungnacula, tabula,[7] et craticula ex trabibus erecta, cestus, clipeos, targia, brachiola, et perareas sive tormenta, quarum una
                                 grete gunnys staf-slyngys
pessumdedit Simonem comitem Montisfortis;[8] mangonalia, fustibula, et trebu-
             baryls   turnyng
cheta, arietes, sues, vineas, et cados versatilles, que omnia sunt machine bellice; secures, bipennes, dacas, jesa Gallicorum, sparos Yspaniorum, catieas et pugiones in dolonibus Teutonicorum; anelacias[9] Anglicorum, pila Romanorum, hasta, sarissas Macedonum,[10] peltas Amazonum, Tholosoniarum arcus, Trojanorum palos, et malleos fereos et ligones, clavas ferreas, et jacula, et catapultas, galeros et conos, toraces, et bombicinia, galeas, loricas, ocreas et femoralia, genualea ferrea, lanceas, et hastas, contos, et uncos, cathenas, cippos, et barream, et ingnem pelasgum, et vitrum liquefactum, fundas et glandes, balistas trocleatas, cum telis et materaciis, que omnia fiunt ut per ea corpus miseri hominis destruatur. Cetera arma militaria in alio capitulo[11] continentur.

---

[1] The words *sunt*, *rastra*, are added from the Paris MS.

[2] It is curious that the commentator in the English MS. should give an English word as French, in this and in another instance, p. 127.

[3] Instead of these three words, the Paris MS. reads, *fusos de ferro, et scanoballa, cavillas, et cinociglontorium.*

[4] I have adopted this reading of the Paris MS., in place of that of the Cottonian MS., *formosum.*

[5] Jean de Garlande, as I have already stated, was at Toulouse at the time of the siege by Simon de Montfort, in 1218. See a former note, p. 120.

[6] *Antemuralia*, the barbacans, or timber defences in advance of the gates and walls. One of the later MSS. in Paris, which reads corruptly *mutalia*, has the gloss *eschauffoulz*.

[7] The *bretasches*, or timber constructions erected on the top of the walls in time of siege.

[8] Simon de Montfort was slain, on the 25th of June, 1218, by a stone thrown from one of the engines of war called in old French a *perriere.*

[9] The Paris MS. reads *avalancias.*

[10] The author had evidently in his eye the passage of the comment of Servius on Virgil, Æn. lib. vii., l. 664—"Pilum Romanorum, geus Gallorum, sarissa Macedonum est."

[11] The chapter here announced is not found in any of the examples of John de Garlande's book.

JOHN DE GARLANDE. 131

(Propugnacula, Gallice *barbaquenne.*) [Antemuralia, *barbechant.* Licia, Gallice *lices.* Propugnacula, *breteche.* Tabula, Gallice *placeus.* Craticula, Gallice *engins.*] Cestus est scutum pugilis. Targie [Gallice *targes*] sunt quedam magna scuta que componuntur telis. Brachiola, parva scuta adherentia brachiis. Perraria [Gallice *pereres*] (peralia) est tormentum minus. Fustibula, quedam machina cum funda et baculo. Trabuceta sunt etiam tormenta murorum [Gallice *trebuches*]. [Jesa, *gisarm.*] Spares, genus cultelli quorum vagine sunt dolones. [Anelacias, Gallice *anelaz*]. Avalancias, cultellus quadratus. Catapultas, pili ferrei. Galerus est coopertorium capitis cujuscumque modi; galea est tegumen capitis militis; conus est in summitate galee. Toraces sunt munimenta corporis. [Bombicinia, Gallice *aketun*, a bombex, -icis, Gallice *cotun.* Mangonalia, Gallice *mangeneus.* Ocreas, Gallice *chausces de fer.* Femoralia, Gallice *quissers*]. Genualia dicuntur a genu, Gallice *genouilliers* [*genuliers*]. Contos, Gallice *perche* [*perches.* Uncos, Gallice *crokes*, .. inde uncus, -ci, Gallice, *petit croket*]. Cippus est quilibet truncus, et specialiter truncus ille quo crura latronum coarctantur, Gallice *cep.* Barrarias dicuntur a barris, que sunt vectes; Gallice dicuntur *barres.* Ignem pelasgum dicitur *feu grejois* [*fu gregcys*]. Fundas [Gallice *fuydes*] dicuntur a fundo, quia fundunt lapidem, qui transumptive dicitur glans, unde subjungitur glandes. Balistas dicuntur *arbaleste.* Trocleatas, ab hoc nomine troclea, que Gallice dicitur *vis,* est quedam rota artificiosa.

Fullones, nudi fullantes, fullant pannos laneos et pilosos in alveo concavo, in quo est argilla et aqua calida. Post hoc, desiccant pannos lotos contra solem, in aere sereno, quos ipsi radunt cum carduis[1] multis, ut sint, vendibiliores.

Fullones vulgale est. Dum fullant pannos, laboriose et turpiter se gerunt; unde dicuntur fullantes vel sufflantes.[2] Satirica est reprehentio, sicut contingit in multis locis in isto libello.

                                        mader   wode   mader
Tinctores pannorum tingunt pannos in rubea majore, gaudone, et sandice; qua de causa ungues habent pictos, quorum autem quidam rubei, quidam nigri, quidam blodii, et ideo contempnuntur a mulieribus formosis, nisi gratia numismatis accipiantur.

Sandice, omnimode tincture, et commune nomen. Sandis dicitur Gallice *saide,* vel *waide.* Sequitur, more solito, satirica reprehensio.

                   hydys   stockys
Serdones student frunire corea equina et taurina in truncis concavis, et rudunt illa cum cultro qui dicitur scalprum; coria vero vertunt in frunio, ut cruditas fetida coriorum discedat.

Cerdones dicuntur Gallice *taneeurs;* et nota quod cerdo potest dici quilibet qui operatur in corio. Frunire dicitur *taner,* unde frunium, Gallice *tan.* Notandum quod in allumia est omne vas solubile indigens frunio. Est vero frunium unum eorum que consolidant vitrum fractum.

Fabri fabricant super incudem, cum malleolis et forcipibus et vertilacione follium, cultros, et vomeres, ferros equinos, ferrum ad vangam, ad tribulam,
                     wedyng-hokys
ad ligones, ad sarcula, non pretereundo falces ad prata et falcillos ad messes.

Incus Gallice dicitur *enclume.* Vangam, Gallice *beche,* vel ferratam palam. Tribulam

---

[1] i. e., with teasels, which were formerly used for this purpose.

[2] The Paris MS. reads *nudi et sufflantes,* for *nudi fullantes,* in the text.

dicitur *pele;* tribulus dicitur *ronce* et *pestel* et *cardon*.¹ Sarcula dicitur *sarcel;* ab hoc verbo sarcire, quod est reparare ; a quo sartores, id est reparatores pannorum.

In hospitio probi hominis debent esse ista : mensa decens, mappa candida,
manutergium fimbriatum, tripodes alti, trestelli² fortes, torres, cremalia,³
     yhemmyd   schydys
focalia, stipes, cippi, vectes, sedilia, scanna, chathedra, sponde et fercula
    stockys to bren   stolys   formys   cheyre
facta de lingnis levigatis, culcitre, cervicalia, et pulvinaria, cribrum, haustum,
                           quyltes   bolsterrys   a syve   a boket
taratantarum, multra, caseorum, muscipula.
  here-syvys   melkyng pele chyse fate a musse stocke

Torres dicuntur a torreo, magnus truncus in capite ignis ; idem truncus dicitur tetropofocinium, vel ligni fulcium ; dicitur Gallice *treffouel.* Cremale, Gallice *cremaul.* Stipes, Gallice dicuntur *conches.* Cippi, Gallice *cep.* Vectes Gallice dicuntur *barres ;* barri sunt genus ludi, Gallice *barres.*⁴ Sedilia dicuntur a sedeo, Gallice *bans.*⁵ Scannum dicitur *forme* Gallice. Sponde dicitur Gallice *chalit.* Ferculum genus est cathedre que potest claudi et aperi.⁶ Levigatis, id est planis. Cervicalia dicuntur *oriliere.* Pulvinaria dicuntur Gallice *coussin.* Pultra, Gallice *scoille.* Muscipula, Gallice *retoire.*⁷

Coci mundant in aqua calida cacabos, et urceas, patellas, et sartagines, pelves, ydrias, ollas, mortaria, scutellas, et rotundalia, acetabula, coclearia, et
amelys
scafas, craticulas, et micatoria,⁸ creagras, distant autem⁹ clibanos, epicausteria, fornaces.

Cacabos, Gallice dicuntur *chauderons.* Patella ponitur pro magna scutella. Sartagines sunt patelle in quibus aguntur et vertuntur carnes super ignem.¹⁰ Pelves dicuntur Gallice *bacin.* Ydrias, dicuntur ab *ydros,* quod est aqua ; Gallice *pot-eau.* Rotundalia, Gallice *taillieurs (trencheurs) ;* et dicuntur a rotunditate. Acetabula, dicuntur lances ubi ponuntur salsa, et dicuntur ab hoc nomine acetum. Scaphas, dicuntur Gallice *auges,* ubi puer balneatur, vel pedes lavantur. Craticulas, dicuntur Gallice *greil.* Creagras, dicuntur Gallice *crochet.* Clibanos, genus fornacis est. Epycauteria, quia desuper imponitur ignis. Fornaces, dicitur ab hoc nomine furnus, Gallice *four (fournaise.)*

Hec sunt instrumenta clericis necessaria : libri, pulpita, crucibolum,¹¹ cum sepo, et absconsa,¹² et laterna ; cornu cum incausto, penna, plumbum, et regula ; tabula, ferule, cathedra, asser, pumex, cum plana, et creta.¹³

Pulpitum, Gallice *letrum,*¹⁴ et nota quod pulpitum est assensus graduum ad locum ubi legitur, quia *letrum,* sive analogium, est id super quod ponitur liber. (Plana proprie dicitur instrumentum ferreum cum quo pergameniste preparant pergamenum.)

In spera sunt paralelli, et coluri, orizon, axis, et galaxias. Organicos imitata modos, mulcet Jovis aures giga, qui es cleri nescia ferre rudes.

---

¹ *i. e.,* these are the different senses in which the Latin word *tribulus* may be taken.

² The trestles, on which the board was placed to form the table.

³ Glossed by the word *cremaus,* in one of the Paris MSS.

⁴ Possibly the game still called bars, or prison bars, well known to school-boys.

⁵ *i. e.,* benches, which were the usual seats.

⁶ These chairs, which open and shut, are not uncommon in the pictures in illuminated MSS.

⁷ *i. e., ratière,* a trap for rats and mice.

⁸ A grater, or instrument for making crumbs.

⁹ The French MS. reads *dum sunt ante,* for *distant autem.*

¹⁰ Frying-pans.

¹¹ A lamp.

¹² A sort of candlestick.

¹³ Glossed by *craie,* in one of the Paris MSS.

¹⁴ The lectern, or reading desk.

Spera sic describitur: spera est quedam figura rotunda, ex circulis composita, mundi similitudinem representans. Cujus partes sunt; paralelli qui sunt quinque, articus, artaticus,[1] solsticialis hiemalis, estivalis, paralellus equinoxialis, qui est in medio, in quo sol facit equinoxium bis in anno, scilicet in ariete et in libra. Coluri duo sunt, unus est verticalis, alius est terre collateralis. Orizon, interpretatur finitor visus. Axis sic describitur: linea ydealis que dirigitur a polo artico ad polum artaticum, per meditullium terre, quod est centrum spere mentalis. Galaxias est circulus qui dirigitur a septentrionali plaga ad australem regionem, per aliud emisperium rediens ad punctum a quo incepit. Giga est instrumentum musicum, et dicitur Gallice *gigue*, et docet clericos ne videantur mimi, quod denotatur dum dicitur organicos.

Supra[2] perticam magistri Johannis de Gallandia diversa indumenta pendent, tunice, supertunicalia, pallia, scapularia,[3] capa, coopertorium, lintheamina, renones, sarabarre, stragule, camisie, bracce, bumbicinia, et tapeta, cuculli, et collobia cum lacernis, et trabee cum paludamentis.

Pertica, Gallice *perche*,[4] unde versus:—

Pertica diversos pannos retinere solebat.

Quedam nomina plana sunt; pallia est equivocum ad mantellum et ad sericum auratum. Renones dicuntur a renibus, Gallice *tabar*,[5] mantellus rotundus lumbardi. Sarrabare sunt indumenta Sarracenorum, Gallice *esclarines*, et dicuntur sarabarre quia gravis vestis est. Stragula est quelibet vestis cum sinu deaurato sine capucio. Cuculli dicuntur Gallice *cole*. Colobia capucia sunt bubulcorum. Lacernis, sic dicuntur quia lacerna est pallium tam tenue et leve, quod homines possunt videri per medium, et dicitur Gallice *bife*. Trabea est regalis infula. Paludimentum, propter aurum et gemmas quas habet, est specialiter ornamentum imperatorum.

Presbiteri libros habent necessarios in ecclesiis suis, missale, gradale sive graduale, troparium, antiphonarium, breviarium, martirologium, psalterium, letaniam, passionarium, bibliothecam, hymnuarium, kalendarium, sine quibus vespere, nec matutine, nec missa possunt celebrari.[6]

Presbiter habeat libros quibus predicet catholice, id est fideliter; doceat typice, id est figurative; loquatur pragmatice, id est causative; proponat quedam ypotetice, id est personaliter vel supponitive, quedam paranetice, id est interponitive, quedam prophonetice, id est exclamatorie, quedam proseutice, id est deprecative; aliquando procedat herotice, quod est amatorie; aliquando diastolice, id est separatorie; aliquando antisiastice, id est contra substantiam, id est contra se ipsum; sepe simboletice, id est reconciliatorie vel collective; sepe prosagoreutice, id est precienter; sepe sillogistice, id est conclusive; interdum loquatur larcheretice, id est gratificative; gemat trenetice, id est lamentorie; canat palinodice, id est recantatorie; canat antipodotice, id est responsorie; canat apostolice, id est suasorie; metricet tropice, id est

---

[1] For antarticus.

[2] The Cottonian MS. unfortunately ends with the first words of this paragraph, apparently through the loss of the subsequent leaves. I have followed, for the rest, the Paris MS. of the thirteenth century, in preference to the Harl. MS. of the fifteenth.

[3] A small mantle, which covered only the shoulders.

[4] Compare the parallel paragraph of Alexander Neckam, p. 101.

[5] The *tabard* of a rather later period.

[6] Compare the parallel paragraph of Alexander Neckam, p. 119.

conversive; dictet ethice, id est moraliter; rideat saterice, id est reprehensorie; mordeat aliquando cinice, id est canine; loquatur de presenti per presens tempus, de imperfectis per parachimenon, de perfectis per loriston, de plusquamperfectis per ypersinteticon; consideret ad tres modos loquendi, scilicet didascalon, id est doctrinale; dragmaticon, id est interrogativum; hermenoticon, id est interpretativum; sancte vivat et sancte doceat, et hec ei sufficiant.

<small>Herotice dicitur ab heros, -ois; Gallice *baron*. Simbolum, -li; Gallice dicitur *escot de taverne*.</small>

His ornatur presbyter ornamentis, scilicet superlicio, alba, talari, et tyara, manipula vel phanula, stola, infula, et cinctorio candidissimo. Sed episcopus celebrat cum mitra et anulo, poderi, rationali, humerali,[1] qui sepissime gerit pedum deauratum.

<small>Alba dicitur Gallice *aube*. Talari, id est longa usque ad talos. Tyara, Gallice dicitur *mitre*. Phanula est id quod sacerdos gerit in brachio.[2] Poderis est vestis similis albe, Gallice *aube*. Rationale est ornamentum episcopale, alio modo dicitur *logion*; illud scilicet quod deferebatur in pectore episcopi ad modum lamine auree, in qua erant duodecim lapides, et in illis duodecim nomina prophetarum; adhuc erant in illa lamina aurea veritas et judicium. Pedum dicitur Gallice *croce*.</small>

In ecclesiis debent esse crux magna et parva, fons sacra, aspersorium, aqua benedicta, vexilla in lancea, campana in campanario, thuribulum, phiala una cum vino et alia cum aqua, et pixis hostiarum.

<small>Vexilla dicitur Gallice *baniere*, vel *confenum*.</small>

In stabulo equino garcifer cum strigilibus asperis et dentatis strigilat equos, et in batis profert avenam ad presepia, et fimos transfert in cenovectorio, ad agros impinguendos.

<small>Batus, -i, proprium nomen est, Gallice dicitur *provendier*. Cenovectorium, Gallice dicitur *civiere*, de cenum, quod est lutum, et veho.</small>

Hec sunt instrumenta mulieribus convenientia: forcipes, et acus, fusus, et theca, vertebrum, et colus, mataxa, trahale, girgillum, excudia, et rupa, ferritorium, linipulus, et culpatorium, cum lexiva et lexivatorio, calotricatorium, licinitorium, quod monachi dicunt lucibruciunculum.

<small>Hec sunt instrumenta, etc. Quedam sunt communia utrique sexui. Theca dicitur Gallice *deel*.[3] Fusus Gallice dicitur *fusel*.[4] Vertebrum dicitur *vertel*, scilicet illud quod pendet in fuso.[5] Mataxa dicitur a manu et teneo; Gallice *tozes*. Trahale dicitur a traho, Gallice *traail*. Girgillus, Gallice *desvuideor*, et dicitur a girus. Excudia dicitur ab excutio, et est illud instrumentum cum quo linum texitur, Gallice *paissel*. Rupa dicitur a rumpo, quoddam instrumentum cum quo rumpitur linum. Ferritorium, Gallice *batoer*. Calotricatorium, Gallice *ridoir*; scilicet illud instrumentum super quod tricant et terent supara. Licinitorium, Gallice dicitur *liche*.[6]</small>

Textrices, que texunt serica texta, projiciunt fila aurata officio cavillarum,

---

[1] A small mantle of silk, buttoned before, which bishops and canons usually wore over the rochet.

[2] A maniple.

[3] A thimble.

[4] The spindle.

[5] A round piece of wood which was fixed to the end of the spindle, to make it turn better.

[6] The piece of wood upon which the clew is wound.

et percuciunt subtemina cum linea spata; de textis vero fiunt cingula et crinalia divitum mulierum et stole sacerdotum.

<small>Cavillarum, dicuntur Gallice *esclices* vel *cavilles;* vulgale est. Subtemen idem est quod trama. Spata instrumentum est mulieris, et ejus diminutivum est spatula. Crinalia dicuntur a crinibus; Gallice *capel.* Stola dicitur a *stolon*,[1] quod est ornamentum, et inde dicitur tolos illud pomellum quod ponitur supra domum in ultimo, quum perfecta est.</small>

Textrices ducunt pectines cum trama, que trahitur a spola et pano. Ipsa textrix percutit tramam cum lama, et volvit spolam in troclea, et telam ductione filorum et globorum ordinatur.

<small>Pectines dicuntur Gallice *pignes.* Spola dicitur a spolio, Gallice *espoulet,* quia sepe spoliatur a filo, hoc est Gallice *chanon,* a filo. Panus est illa virgula in navicula (*narette*), que tenet spolam. Troclea est rota textricis, et dicitur Gallice *trameor.* Lama dicitur Gallice *lamme,* scilicet id instrumentum quo percutit fila.</small>

Pextrices juxta focum sedent, prope cloacam et prope monperia, in pellicibus veteribus et in velaminibus fedatis, dum carpunt lanam villosam, quam pectinibus cum dentibus ferreis depilant.

Devacuatrices sunt que devacuant fila, vel mulieres aurisece; devacuant et secant tota corpora frequenti coitu; devacuant et secant aliquando marsupia scolarium Parisiensium.

<small>Devacuatrices dicuntur Gallice *desvuideresses.* Aurisece Gallice *trencheresses de or,* et dicuntur ab auro et seco; inde sequitur reprehensio saterica.</small>

In platea nova ante paravisum Domine nostre,[2] aves inveniuntur vendende, anseres, galli et galline, capones, anates, perdices, phasiani, alaude, passeres, pluvinarii, ardee, grues, et cigni, pavones, et turtures.

<small>Paravisus est locus ubi libri scolarium venduntur. Phasiani dicuntur Gallice *faisans.* Alaude dicuntur Gallice *aloes.* Pluvinaria dicuntur Gallice *plouviers.* Ardee dicuntur Gallice *hairon.*</small>

Auceps insidiatur avibus in nemore, a quo capiuntur fenix,[3] aquila, herodius, et ancipiter, falco, et capus, merulus et merula, sturnus, et sitacus, philomela, et lucinia; quia milvum, et cornicem, et corvum, et bubonem, vespertilionem, et nicticoracem, et pellicanum capere dedignantur.

<small>Cornix dicitur a cornicor, -aris; Gallice *gengler.*</small>

Piscatores vendunt salmones, et trutas, lampridas, murenas, morium,[4] pectines, anguillas, quibus associantur lucii, stinci,[5] ragedie, allectia, mulli. Ipsi vero piscatores capiunt cum hamis et rethibus percas, gobiones, et gamaros; et canes marini ab equore devehuntur.

---

[1] The Greek στόλος, dress, or attire. The derivation of the word *tolos (tholos),* which follows, is certainly wrong.

[2] The name *paradisus, paravisus,* or *parvisus,* in French *parvis,* was applied in the middle ages to the open place before the portico of a church. The parvis of Nôtre Dame in Paris, like that of St. Paul's in London, was very celebrated. The former was the great market of books. In one part of it, called the Place Neuve of the parvis, there appears also by our text to have been a market of poultry.

[3] Our compiler was so anxious to get the important names of birds into his list, that he overlooked the absurdity of the notion of the fowler going to the woods in the expectation of catching a phœnix!

[4] A species of shell-fish *(morio).*

[5] Translated, in a gloss in one of the Paris MSS., by *espinonge.*

(Ragedie, Gallice *raye*.)

Transitum feci hodie per campum, in quo vidi animalia ista: boves, oves, et tauros, et vaccas, capreos, et capras, et edos, vitulos, et pullos, cum equis et equabus, cum mulis, burdones, et asinos, et asinas, camelos, et dromedarios, per pascua spaciantes, porcos et porcas cum porcellis.

In nemore regis Francie sunt multa animalia silvestria, scilicet cervi et cerve, dammi et damme, hinnuli, capreus, taxus, linces, apri, leones, pardi, tigrides, ursi et urse, lepores, cuniculi, esperioli, simii et simie, lutricii in stangnis, et vulpes astute, et petoides[1] gallinarum hostes.

Hinnulus, fetus cerve ; inula Gallice dicitur *eschaloigne*, unde versus—
Hinnulus in silvis, inule queruntur in hortis.

Tigris est quoddam animal quod, nisi consequatur predam, moritur pre dolore, et cum non habet masculum aperit gulam contra ventum flantem et concipit. Esperioli, Gallice *escuruel*.

In horto magistri Johannis sunt herbe scilicet iste: salvia, petrosilinum, dictamnus, ysopus, celidonia, feniculus, piretum, columbina, rosa, lilium, et viola; et a latere crescit urtica, carduus, et saliunca. Sed medicinales herbe sunt ibi, mercurialis scilicet et malva, agrimonia, cum solatro et solsequio.

Celidonia dicitur a *chelin*,[2] quod est irundo, quia silvis prosilit a terra cum irundine. Saliunca Gallice dicitur *cauchetrepe*; calcaneus dicitur ab illa, quia fit de ferro.[3] Mercurialis est herba medicinalis quæ dicitur a Mercurio, vel quasi merdam creans, quia purgat ventrem. Solatrum dicitur morella, quæ quasi lignum in quodam specie erigitur.

Ortolanus magistri Johannis colit in orto suo olus, quod dicitur caulus; ubi crescit borago vel bleta, porum, et allia, sinapis, unde fit sinapium, poreta, et civolli sive cepule, et inule, quia in nemore suo crescit pimpinella, pilosella, sanica, buglosa, lancea, et cetere herbe que corporibus valent humanis.

Inula Gallice dicitur *eschaloigne*.

In virgulto magistri Johannis cerasus fert cerasa, pirus pira, pomus poma, prunus pruna, coctanus coctana, mespilus mespila, pessicus pessica,[4] castanea castaneas, nux nuces, avellana avellanas, ficus ficus, vitis uvas et pampinos, palmites et antes et phalangas,[5] sine quibus mensa divitis mendicavit.

Hec sunt nomina silvestrium arborum qui sunt in luco magistri Johannis: quercus cum fago, pinus cum lauro, celsus gerens celsa,[6] cum corno qui fert corna, cinus[7] gerens cina, cum buxo, rannus et bedegar, cum rumice, populus, cum salice, et pepulus[8] gerens pepulas, que vulgus manducat, et telia,[9] cum tremulo.

Bedagar dicitur Gallice *aiglentier*.

---

[1] The editor of the French edition conjectures this to be an error for *ictides*, polecats.

[2] For *chelidon*, the Greek χελιδὼν, a swallow.

[3] The *caltrop* (in French *chaussetrape*) was an implement composed of spikes, arranged so that, however it was thrown on the ground, one spike must point upwards, and it was used especially to lame the enemy's horses in war. The name *chaussetrape* was also given in French to a plant, the star-thistle (*centaurea calcitrapa*).

[4] *i. e., mala persica*, or peaches.

[5] The *antes* and *phalangæ* were the lines of vine plants in the vineyard, the *antes* being the first row.

[6] Mulberries.

[7] Holly.

[8] The buckthorn.

[9] The linden.

JOHN DE GARLANDE. 137

In aula mea hec architectari feci : trapetas,¹ [trapytys] solivas, [furstys] lacunaria, tigna, lodia, trabes, latas,² [lasys] laquearia, [pylers] columnas, cujus partes sunt basis, [the fote the schefte] stilus et epistilium. [the hede of the pyler] Hec fabricantur cum securi, [hachet] dolabra, [brode axe] rosticucio, [twybyl] vel bisacuta, [idem est] acucia, terebre, et cum cuneis [wedgys] et cavillis, et celte, et plana,³ et cum calce lathomi, [reule] cum lathomega, [a squyre] amussi, et cum perpendiculo [plomet] ponderoso. [hevy]

Lodia, dicitur a lucem do, quia per lodium intrat lux domum.

Peregre proficiscens vidi per mare has naves : dromones, galeas, cum galeis militaribus, lembos, privas, liburnas, et triremes.

Lembus dicitur quasi leviter per aquam mordens, et est parva navicula. Privas, parve naves sunt. Liburna navis est negociatorum.

Inter naufragia consideravi martirum supplicia, scilicet carceres, patibulum, calofurcium,⁴ eculeos, carastas,⁵ quadragenas, ypodromia, fustes, lacininas, serras, ungulos, scorpiones, et rotas ex contrario versatiles beate Katerine.

Patibulum dicitur a patior, et est idem quod crux, et dicitur locus in quo homines patiuntur; Gallice *gibet* vel *pilori*. Eculeus dicitur quasi equus ligneus; trabs est erecta, acuta, ad modum equi, in quo extendebantur sancti martires. Catasta, carcer ferreus et strictus valde, aculeis repletus, in quo sancti martires extendebantur. Quadragena erat scutica circumdata quadraginta corrigiis, qua verberabatur beatus Paulus, et in unaquaque verberatione deponebatur una corrigia. Ypodromium erat spacium in quo beatus Ypolitus dilaceratus fuit, in quo equi trahebant. Fustes baculi sunt in quibus homines fustigabantur. Serras, dicuntur a seco, Gallice *see*. Ungule, parvi unci quibus caro sanctorum carpebatur. Scorpiones ad scorpionum similitudinem erant quidam unci parvi quibus carpebantur sancti martires. Rotus, dictum est de beata Katerina, que ligabatur inter rotas in diversam partem discurrentes.

Sed in dominibus divitum vidi liricines, tybicines, cornicines, vidulatores cum vidulis, alios cum sistro, cum giga, cum simphonia, cum psalterio, cum choro, cum citola, cum timpano, cum cimbalis. Sed alia parte⁶ vidi meretrices et tripudiatrices, quas torquebant serpentes, scilicet aspis, basiliscus, prester, sive alpiga, chelindri, vipere sive vepe, et dispas, et tabificus ceps.

In hoc loco agit actor⁷ de instrumentis lecatorum,⁸ quorum quidam sunt liricines, etc. Vidulatores dicuntur a vidula, -e; Gallice *riele*. Giga est instrumentum musicum de quo dicitur,ʻʻOrganicos imitata modos:" etc.⁹ Choro, instrumentum musicum est in hoc loco. Citola, Gallice *Citole*. Tympanum dicitur nomen fictum per onomatopeion, Gallice *tabour:* a quo derivatur tympanifes, quod est species ydropisis, quando venter sonat sicut tympanum.

---

¹ Boards; the English interlinear gloss is a word I have not met with before.
² Laths.
³ A carpenter's plane.
⁴ A gibbet.
⁵ For *catasta*, as the word is given more correctly in the commentary.
⁶ We are to understand that the author, reflecting on the wickedness of this class of people (the minstrels, etc.), supposes now that he sees them punished in the infernal regions, which affords him an opportunity of giving a list of serpents, which entered largely into the medieval notions of the future state.
⁷ For *auctor*, the author.
⁸ i. e., of the jougleurs and minstrels, who were included in the class of ribalds or lechers.
⁹ See before, p. 132.

Tripudiatrices dicuntur a tripudiare, quod est facere tripudium, Gallice *treche*. Prester, genus serpentis qui prius (quam) puncturas (faciat) veneno suo distendit corpus ex nimio colore veneni, unde Lucanus,

    Percussit prester; illi rubor igneus omne[1]
    Succendit, tenditque cutem pereunte figura.[2]

Alpiga serpens est qui statim pungendo interficit, unde Lucanus,

    Qui calcare tuas metuat salpiga latebras?[3]

Chelindri sunt serpentes habitantes modo in terra, modo in aqua, et tanti caloris sunt quod faciunt herbas fumare ubi serpunt; unde Lucanus,

    Tractique viam fumare chelindri.[4]

Vepa etiam dicitur vipera, et a vepa dicitur vepos, id est lecator, quia detrahendo mordet sicut vepa. Dispas est serpens, alio modo dicitur situla; de qua Lucanus,

    Exivias positura suas et torrida dispas.[5]

Tabificus ceps; tanti caloris est ille serpens, quod omnia ossa detegit, unde Lucanus,

    Ossaque dissolvens cum corpore tabificus ceps.[6]

In loco delicioso[7] vidi virgines, cum nuptis et viduis castis, coream divine laudis celebrantes cum modulis et hymnis, que beatam virginem Mariam et matrem Dei suis invocabant tripudiis, que fons est misericordie, que sperantes in se non derelinquit, sed illum nobis emollit judicem, qui verbo creavit celestia, terrestria, cui parent quatuor elementa, ignis, aer, aqua, terra, sol et luna, cum aliis planetis et stellis, quam laudant angeli, quam timent demones, cui secreta patent abissi, scilicet dracones, et trachones, et catharacte celi, et cathaduple terre. Et ipse qui venturus est judicare vivos et mortuos dignetur in fine nostri misereri per suam summam misericordiam. Amen.

  Choream, Gallice *charole*, ab hoc nomine chorus. Cathadupla, aquarum fluentium ductus, Gallice *conduit*.

Explicit Dictionarius magistri Johannis de Gallandia.[8]

---

[1] In the original it is *igneus ora*.

[2] Lucan, Pharsal. lib. ix., l. 791. John de Garlande seems to have taken his list of serpents entirely from this poet.

[3] Lucan, Pharsal. lib. ix., l. 837.

[4] Lucan, Pharsal. lib. ix., l. 711.

[5] Lucan, Pharsal. lib. ix., v. 717. The line in the original is accompanied by another, which should have accompanied it, inasmuch as it shows that the two serpents here stated to be the same were different,—

  Et scytale sparsis etiam nunc sola pruinis.
  Exuvias positura suas; et torrida dipsas.

[6] Lucan, Pharsal. lib. ix., v. 722. The word is, of course, properly *seps*.

[7] *i. e.*, in paradise, to which the author now turns.

[8] In MS. Harl. 1002, the Dictionarius ends with the colophon, *Explicit Diccionarius cujus compositor erat Johannes de Garlandea.*

VOCABULARY OF THE NAMES OF PLANTS.[1]

(OF THE MIDDLE OF THE THIRTEENTH CENTURY.)

CHAUDES HERBES.

Artimisie, mug-wrt, merherbarum.
Marubium, maruil, horehune.
Ruta, rue.
Apium, ache.
Buglosa, bugle, wude-brune.
Saniculum, sanicle, wude-merch.
Sinapium, senevel, senei.
Zizania, neele, cockel.
Absinthium, aloigne, wermod.
Elna enula, ialne, gret-wurt.
Bethonica, beteine.
Abrotanum, averoine, suþe-wurt.
Pulegium, puliol, hul-wurt.
Agrimonia, agremoine, garclive.
Consolida, consoude, daiseie.
Cumfiria, cumfirie, galloc.
Mentastrum, mentastre, hors-minte.
Avencia, avence, hare-fot.
Porius, poret, lek.
Regina, reine, med-wurt.
Millefolium, milfoil.
Ebulum, eble, wal-wurt.
Levisticum, luvesche, luvestiche.
Cepa, oingnun, kuc-lek.
Salvia, sauge, fenvern.
Centauria, centoire, hurdreve.
Arcangelica, mort ortie, blinde netle.
Pollipodium, poliol, reven-fot.
Felix arboratica, pollipode, ververn.
Saliunca, gauntelée, foxes-glove.
Butunus, butuns, hoepe.
Nasturtium, kersuns, cressen.
Coliandrum, coriandre, chele priem.
Petrosillum, peresil, stoan-suke.
Closera, alisaundre, wilde pereil.
Farida, favede, leomeke.
Sandix, waisde, wod.
Gladiolum, flamine, gladene.
Febrefugia, fewerfue, adrel-wurt.
Tanesetum, tuneseie, helde.

[1] This vocabulary of names of plants, evidently intended for the use of a medical practitioner, is preserved in a manuscript in a British Museum (MS. Harl. No. 978, fol. 24, v°), which appears to have been written in the period intervening between the battles of Lewes and Evesham, that is, in 1264 or 1265. The explanations of the Latin names are given in Anglo-Norman and in English; and in a few instances either the Anglo-Norman or English is omitted, and even in one or two cases the Latin. It is given here as illustrating the lists of plants in the other vocabularies in the present volume. The history of the popular nomenclature of plants is a very curious and interesting subject; and the manuscripts of all periods are very rich in materials for it. There is another list of names of plants in the three languages, resembling the one here printed, but arranged in alphabetical order, and rather more full, in a manuscript of the fourteenth century in the British Museum, MS. Sloane, No. 5.

Pilosella, peluselle, mus-ere.
Vermiculum, warance, wrotte.
Ruffarium, raiz, redich.
Silimbrium, balsamitis, broc-minten.
Ambrosia, ambrose, hindehele.
Althea, ymalue, holihoc.
Saxifragium, saxifrage, wai-wurt.
Bidella, samsuns, lechis.
Bursa pastoris, sanguinarie, blod-wurt.
Feniculum, fanuil, fenecel.
Quinquefolium, quintfoil, fiflef.
Tapsus barbatus, moleine, softe.
Fabaria, faverole.
Trifolium, trifoil, wite clovere.
Diptannum, ditaundere.
Cotula fetida, ameruche, miwe.
Persicaria, saucheneie, cronesanke.
Lanceolata, launceleie, ribbe.
Mater silva, chevefoil, wudebinde.
Sambucus, suev, ellarne.
Vervena, verveine, iren-harde.
Arundo, rosel, reod.
Osmunda, osmunde, bon-wurt.
Olibanus, encens, stor.
Fungus, wulves-fist.
Cerfolium, cerfoil, villen.
Camomilla, camemille, maiwe.
Nepta, nepte, kattes-minte.
Argentea, argentine, lilie.
Enula, alne, hors-elne.
Ysopus, ysope.
Spurgia, spurge, guweorn.
Lavendula, lavendre.
Fion, camglata, foxes-glove.
Euscute, doder.
Satureia, satureie, timbre.
Borago, burage.
Tribulus marinus, calketrappe, sea-þistel.
Fumus terre, fumetere, cuntehoare.
Calamentum, calemente.
Ypis, herbe Johan, velde-rude.

Organum, organe.
Origanum, puliol real, wde-minte.
Menta, mente, minten.
Anetum, anete, dile.
Elitropium, solsegle, gloden.
Eptaphilos, salerne, vare-wurt.
Elleborum album, alebre blonc.
Eleborum, ellebre, lung-wurt.
Pionia, pioine.
Ortica, ortie, nettle.
Valeriane, stich-wurt.
Celsi, murer, mur-berien.
Avellane, petite noiz, litel nute.
Frisgonem, fresgun, cue-hole.
Sponsa solis, grinnil.
Pinpernele, pinpre, briddes-tunge.
Lingua canis, chen-lange, hundes-tunge.
Dormentille, ortie griesche, doc-nettle.
Lappa, bardane, clote.
Burneta, sprung-wurt.
Epitime, epithimum, fordboh.
Turmentine, nutehede.
Widebalme, halue-wude.
Malva cripia, screpe-malue.
Consolida media, þundre-clovere.
Herba benedicta, herbe beneit, hemeluc.
Hedera nigra, iere, oerþ-ivi.
Herba Roberti, herbe Robert, chareville.
Hinnula campana, spere-wurt.
Hastula regia, muge de bois, wuderove.
Intiba, muruns, chikne-mete.
Iregerontis, cenesuns, grundeswilie.
Juniperii, geneivre, gorst.
Ligustrum, triffoil, hunisuccles.
Labrusca, hundes-berien.
Alleum, ail, garlec.
Murum, blakeberie.
Genesta, genest, brom.
Omfacium, winberi stones.
Ostragium, herbyve, liþe-wurt.
Plantago, planteine, weibrode.

FREIDES HERBES.
Morella, morele, atteɪloþe.
Jovis barba, jubarbe, singrene.
Lactuca, letue, slep-wurt.
Fraga, fraser, streberi-lef.
Ramni, grosiler, þefe-þorn.
Astula regia, popi.
Atriplex, arasches.
Mercurialis, evenlesten, mercurial.
Malva, malue, hoc.
Caulus, cholet, kaul.
Andivia, letrun, þuge-þistel.
Psilliun, luse-sed.
Virga pastoris, wilde tesel.
Ypoquistidos, hundes-rose.

Jusquiamus, chenille, hennebone.
Viola, violé, appel-leaf.
Alimonis, wilde popi.
Aizon, sinfulle.
Tucia, tutie.
Litargirum, escume de or.

INTER FRIGIDUM ET CALIDUM.
Lapis lazuli, pere.
Manna.

INTER FRIGIDUM ET CALIDUM TEMPERATUM.
Mirtus, gaʒel.
Bedagrage, spina alba, wit-þorn.
Arnoglosa, plauntein.

THE TREATISE OF
WALTER DE BIBLESWORTH.[1]

(OF THE CLOSE OF THE THIRTEENTH CENTURY.)

Le treytyz ke moun sire Gauter de Bibelesworthe fist à ma dame Dyonisie de Mounchensy, pur aprise de langwage, ço est à saver, du primer temps ke homme nestra, oweeke trestut le langgage pur saver nurture en sa jurente: pur trestut le Frauncçys de sa neyssaunce, et de membres du cors, oweekt kauntke il apent dedens et deores; pus to le Fraunçoys com il en court en age de husbonderie, cum pur arer, rebiner, waretter, semer, sarcher, syer, faucher, carier, batre, moudre, pestrer, breser, bracer, haute feste arayer; pus tot le Fraunsoys kaunt à espleyt de chas, cum de renerie, pescherie en river ou en estang, checune en sa nature; pus tot le Fraunçoys des bestes et des oyseus, checune assembe par sa naturele aprise; pus tot le Fraunsoys de boys, prés, pasture, vergeyer, gardyn, curtilage, oweeke tot le Fraunsoys de flures et des

---

[1] The name of Walter de Biblesworth is only known by this "treatise" and by a short piece in Anglo-Norman verse (printed from a manuscript in the Bodleian Library, at Oxford, in the "Reliquiæ Antiquæ," vol. i., p. 134), in which Biblesworth is introduced discussing the question of the crusade with the celebrated statesman of the reign of Edward I., Henry de Lacy, earl of Lincoln and Salisbury, who would appear to have been his friend. From that, and from the exordium to the tract now printed, Walter de Biblesworth was evidently a knight, but I have not been able to trace even the locality from which he took his name. The lady Dionysia de Monchensi, at whose desire this tract was composed, was a Kentish heiress, the daughter of William de Monchensi, baron of Swanescombe, and related, apparently, to the Valences, earls of Pembroke. She married Hugh de Vere, the second son of Robert fifth earl of Oxford. Henry de Lacy died in 1312, and Dionysia de Monchensi in 1313; so that we may fairly suppose that Walter de Biblesworth wrote towards the end of the thirteenth century. It is curious that the lady who requested him to write a book for the instruction of children is said to have died *sine prole.*

Several manuscripts of the "treatise," or, as it is also called, "the doctrine (*i. e.* teaching)," of Walter de Biblesworth are known. It is here printed from one in the British Museum (MS. Arundel, No. 220), written in a hand of the reign of Edward II., collated with another copy of the larger portion of it in MS. Sloane, No. 809. The latter, which is of nearly the same date, is written on a small roll of vellum, evidently as a convenient form for the teacher. I have added, between parentheses, or in the notes, some of the English glosses from a good MS. in the public library of the University of Cambridge, as I had formerly printed them in the "Reliquiæ Antiquæ," vol. ii. p. 78.

frus ke il i sount. E tut issi troveret-vus tot le ordre en parler e respoundre ke checun gentyshomme covent saver ; dount touzdis troverez-vus primes le Fraunsoys et pus le Engleys suaunt ; e ke les enfauns pussunt saver les propretez des choses ke veyunt, et kaunt devunt dire moun et ma, soun et sa, le et la, moy et jo.

 Femme, ke approche soun tens
  (belitter)
 Enfaunter, moustre sens,
      a midewif
 Ke ele se purveyt de une ventrere,
 Ke seyt avisé counseylere.
 Kaunt le emfès sera nées,
    yswathid
 Lors deyt estre maylolez.[1]
  a cradel
 En soun berz l'enfaunt chochet,
  a norice
 De une bercere[2] vus purvoyet,
     lulled
 Où par sa norice seyt bercé.
     for to crepen
  Le enfaunt comence[3] de chatouner,
 Avaunt ke sache à pées aler.
  slaveryt of kynde
 L'enfaunt bave de nature ;
     from slavere[4]
 Pur sauver ses dras de baavure,
   norice
 Vus diret à sa bercere,
     a brestclout[5]
 "Festes l'enfaunt une bavere."
  Si tot cum l'emfès set aler,
    befilin hym
 De tay se veut enpaluer.[6]
    hurting
 Pur meynte peril de blessure,
 Garce ou garsoun, ly deyt sure,
  stumble ne falle
 Ke il ne ceste ne ne chece
   ne missitte
 En la bowe ne messece.
   a god quyle
 Ensi covent bone peyce.

---

[1] The Camb. MS. glosses *maylolez* by *sweath-clut ou maylosés* Marg. MS. Arund.

[2] *Berceir*, glossed *a rockeir*, MS. Cam.; *berce*, MS. Sl.

[3] The Sl. MS. reads *covent*.

[4] *Fro slavering*, MS. Cam.

[5] *A slavering-clout*, MS. Cam.

[6] *Espaluer*, glossed *bilagge him*, MS. Cam.

THE TREATISE OF

Quaunt le emfès ad tel age
Ke il seet entendre langage,
Primes en Fraunceys ly devez dire
Coment soun cors deyt descrivere,
Pur' le ordre aver de moun et ma,
Toun et ta, soun et sa,
     betre lered
Ke en parole seyt meut apris,
   scornid
E de nul autre escharnys.
 Ma teste ou moun cheef,
  the schod of my eved
La greve de moun cheef;
Fetes la greve au lever,
   the feldefare
Et mangez la grive au diner.
   (lockes) crispe
Jo ay les cheveuz recelcelez,
 evese my cop
Moun top vus pri estancez;
     a top of heer
En vostre chef vus avet toup,
  Wyn the ram atte wrestli ...[2]
A la lute dereynetz le toup;
    a top of tre
En la rue juvetz à toup,
  hekele a top of flax
E serencez du lyn le toup.
      hernepane
Vus devet dire moun hanapel,
 my forred ant my brayn
Moun frount, e moun cervel,[3]
  my nape ant thonewon ...
Moun haterel ouweke les temples;
E les mousters sunt dist temples.
     lovelik
Vostre regardz est gracious,[4]
    gundy
Mès vos oeyz sunt jaciouz,[5]

---

[1] This and the three following lines are omitted in the Sloane MS.

[2] For some reason or other, a ram was during many ages the usual prize in wrestling matches. An instance occurs in Mathew Paris, under the year 1222. Chaucer, describing the miller, says—
 That prevede wel, for over al ther he cam,
 At wrastlynge he wolde bere away *the ram.*
      Cant. T., l. 549.
So in the Tale of Gamelyn, l. 171—
Ther was ther bysiden cryed a wrastlyng,
And therefor ther was sette up *a ram* and *a ryng.*

[3] The Sloane MS. reads less correctly, as shown by the rhyme, *ma cervele.*

[4] The Sloane MS. reads *sount graciouses,* which is also a various reading given in the margin of the Arundel MS.

[5] *Chaciouse,* glossed *goundi,* in MS. Camb., and in the next line *chacie* and *the gounde.*

     the gunde
Des oiez outez la jacye,
    the maldrope
E de nees la rupye.
    a preciouse ston
Meuz vaut rubye par ·b·,
Ke ne feet rupie par ·p·.
       stones
Si bourse eust taunt de rubies
Cum le nees ad de rupies,
Riche screyt de perye
Ke taunt oust de la rubye.
     the appel of the eye
De le oyl est sauve la pruncle
  the eye-lides
Par les paupeyrs, ke est la pel;
Si la paupere seyt bon e bel,
      the hers of the eye-lide
En les paupyrs sunt les cyz;
      the browes
Amount les oys sunt les surcyz.
E ausy avet-vous par resoun
 nase-thirlis a gristel
Deus narys e un tendroun.
     a co-brid²
Mès war ke la chouwe
   thi cheke
Ne touche vostre jowe.
    a lippe and an hare
Vus avet la levere, et le levere,
 a pound a book
E la livere, et le livere;
La levere si enclost les dens;
Le levere en boys se tent dedens;
La livere sert en marchaundye;
Le livere sert en seynt eglise,
E le livere nous aprent clergye.³
    the roof of the mout
En la bouche amount en palet
  foul or clene
Tastret-vus chose orde ou nette:
Vus dira si vyn seyt bon e net.
    bysie
Les dames sunt ententiwes
    gomes
Pur ben laver lur gyngives;

---

¹ *Heres*, MS. Camb.; *breyes*, MS. Sl.
² *The co*, MS. Camb.

⁴ The Sloane MS. reads here, *aprent enfaunt clergy*.

Kar l'enchesoun est ben¹ certeyne
       god onde
Ke eles le fount pur bon aleyne.
        chin
Le cool, la gorge, le mentoun,
Langage est assez comoun.
        kanel-bon
Desout la gorge est la fourcele,
Un os fourché Frаunceys apele.

N'e pas mester à descrivere
Chose ke checoun seet l'en dire,
(wombe) (bac) (bac-bon)
Ventre, e dos, et l'etchine,
 (schuldir) (arme) (breste)
Les espaules, les bras, et la peytrine;
Mès jo vus fray monstreysoun
Det choses ke ne sount pas comoun.
      the molde²
Le chef devaunt ad la founteyne,
 the overe lippe ant the nethere
La bas levere et la levere suseyne.
     wange-teȝ³
En bouche sunt les messeleres,
   the for-teeȝ
E dens foreyns, si tu les queres.
     a dalk in the nekke
Au cool troveret la fosset;
  the chal⁴ under the tunge
Desout la lange le filet;
      (hole)
E checun orayl si ad mulet,
  herespon (of hernes)
Par cakenole e cervele net.

E pur tut certifier la parole,
Conoustre covent la kakenole.
     the heer abowen⁵
Les temples ount les gernons,
     chuldel-bones⁶
E les espaules ount blasouns.
     arm-hole
Desout les braz le hissel,⁷
     the aviltre
Parmy le char sist le essel.

---

¹ This word is inserted from MS. Sl.
² i. e., the suture of the skull.
³ *Wangeteth*, MS. Camb.
⁴ *The skale*, MS. Camb.
⁵ *Crocud*, MS. Sl.; *thonewonges*, MS. Camb.
⁶ *The soldre-bon*, MS. Sl.; *scholder-bon*, MS. Camb.
⁷ *Ascel*, MS. Camb.

Desutz la mountanye[1] sourt le bruyl, *miist*
En basse tere ad bon soyl. *god hirthe*
Entre pledoures sourd le toyl; *strif*
Le vent de bise mout greve le oyl. *noor-est*[2]
Après le haust chet le foyl, *hervest [the leve]*[3]
Après gelé vent remoyl; *thowyng*
Par deray chet sovent doyl. *sorwe*
Cestes paroles cy recoyl, *gadere*
La reysoun[4] pur quey dire voyl,
Pur l'acord en parlaunce,
E la descord en variaunce.

Des espaules issunt les bras,
Les coudes, les meyns ne lerom pas, *helbowes*
Mès pur estre tot certeyn
Est trové le cou[6] de la meyn; *the hand wriste*[5]
La paume dedens, la claye dehoris. *the bac of the hand*
Le poynt e dist kaunt mayn e clos, *thi fist*
E une poygnée quaunt la meyn *an handful*
Des menus choses[7] est trové plein.
Deus meyns ensemble, vodes ou pleyns,[8]
Sount apelés les galeyns; *the thepsene*[9]
Kar meut vaudroyt une poygné
De gengevere ben tryé,
Ke ne feroye cent galeynes *(thespen)*
De filaundre totes pleynes. *gosesomer*

[1] *Sur la mounteyne*, MS. Sl.
[2] *North hest*, MS. Camb.
[3] This gloss is from MS. Sl.
[4] *L'enoheson*, MS. Sl.
[5] *The virste*, MS. Camb.
[6] The Sloane MS. reads *toice*.
[7] *De menues greyne*, MS. Sl.
[8] The Sloane MS. gives this and the following line thus:—
Ausedouts les mayns, voides ou pleyns
Eu Fraunz apellom les galeyns. *gospes*
[9] *Thespone*, MS. Camb.

THE TREATISE OF

   (a ribbe) (of a side)
  Une coste de une costé
     Ewe
  La primere femme me ad oustée.
  Kaunt dame Eve primis fist,
  Ne porte charge pur quey il sist,[1]
  Ne pur quey ço moot vint en place,
  Mès bon est ke homme le Frauncçys sace
    the ryb
  De la cousté ke signifie;
  Kar totes gens ne l' le sewnt mye.
   a wyne-westere
  Par ventresse en ventre
  Payn de furment entre.[2]
      the nowele
  En my le ventre est umbil,
     the schore
  E par desouz est le penul;[3]
  bottokes theys the clif[4]
  Les nages, et les quissys, e la furchure
      (riding)
  Funt graunt eyse pur chivachure.
   hammes[5] (knes)
  Les jaumbes saun jenuoils e garez
      stiffe[6]
  De genuler serroynt trop redz.
  (hammes) garterys
  Au garez unt ore garteres
  Nos valés et nos esquieres,
     carteres
  Ne mye pur estre charetteres,
  Mè pur sauver lur banneres.
   the caalf le brahun[7]
  En la jambe est la sure,
  E taunt cum braoun i est ensure,
      trestut hm
  De melior force homme se asure;
    the chine-bon
  Mès war le chanel[8] de blessure.
  ancle on joynt a pyn
  Le kyvil du pée, le kyvil de fust,
  Voudreye le checun homme conceust.

---

[1] *Gist*, MS. Sl.
[2] These two lines are inserted from the margin of the Arundel MS.
[3] *Le penule*, glossed *shzare*, MS. Camb.
[4] *Clift*, MS. Camb.
[5] *Legges*, MS. Camb.
[6] *Starke*, MS. Camb.
[7] *Sperlire*, MS. Sl.
[8] *Le kanel*, glossed *shzin-bon*, MS. Camb. The scribe of the Arundel MS. has written *musteus* above *chanel*, as though for a various reading.

    sole the toon the hile
La plaunte, les urtiles, le taloun,
Langage est asset comoun.
  Dedens le cors en checun homme
    (herte) livere ant lunge
Est trové quer, foye, e pomoun;
the milte[1] neres[2] (kidenei)
L'etplen, boueles, et reinoun;
 mawe   senewes
Estomak, veynes, nerfs, environ.
   (fleyx) a karte. a wayn
Vus avet la char e le char,
    of schoren
Mè gardet vus ben det etchar.
Jo vy la char seer en char,
    (scorn)
Et de le char fere eschar.
Eschar per folur homme revylist;
       quaket
La char par hydour en homme fremist;
Ses oos per dolur en secchist,
     starken[3]
Les nerfs de bewor engurdisst.
      hyd. the chyn[4]
Homme et femme unt la peel,
   lether
De morte beste quyr jo apel.
   (laste knel)
Le clerk soune le dreyne apel,
Le prestre fet à Roume apel.
Ore avet ço ke pent à cors,
Dedens ausy et deors.
  Vestet vos dras,[5] me chers enfauns,
Chaucez vos brays, soulers, e gauns;
Mettet le chaperoun, coverz le chef,
unbotone
Tachet vos botouns, e pus derechef
   girte
De une coreye vus ceynet.
   makethe vit childe
Ne dy pas vus enceyntez;
Femme par homme est enceynte,
E de une ceynture est ceynte.

---

[1] *Galle*, MS. Sl.
[2] *Tharme*, MS. Camb.
[3] *Swellin*, MS. Camb.
[4] *A skine*, MS. Camb.

[5] The human body having been described, the teacher now proceeds to clothe it, and afterwards to feed it, and to describe the processes and products which supply food.

    the girdilis ende tipping
De la ceynture le pendaunt
    thout the bokel
Passe par my le mordaunt;
    the tungge
Einsy doyt le hardiloun
  a bore of an alsene[1]
Passer par tru de subiloun.

La mayn lavez de l'enfaunt;
Vers payn se estent demeyntenaunt;
Ore li baylet en sa meyn
  a lumpe
Une bribe de blanc payn.
      eyree
Au dyner le donez de oefs,
E les atyret à soun oues.
   chelle   ore soupe
Outest l'eschale avaunt ke il hume,
  the rime and the qwyte
L'encruyt ausy et le aubume;
    the yelke
Si le donet le mouwel,
Ke à humme seyn est bon morssel.
     the strene
Més remuet le kerminoun[2]
Mal à desire pur checun hom.

De bon droyt enfauns cleymunt
De manger poumes, pur ço ke les cymunt;
   the stalke and the paring
Outez l'estiche et la parure,
    the body of the appel
E lour donez la morsure.
  the scoree
La pipinette[3] engettez,
 the kyrneles
Les pepynes dehors plauntez.

Cher enfaunt, ore entendet,
Après dyner ke cy orrez,
    gadering
De checune assemblé diversement
Vus covent parler proprement.[4]

---

[1] *Of a nalkin*, MS. Camb.
[2] *Germinoun*, with the gloss *sterene*, MS. Camb.
[3] *Pepyner*, glossed *coyke*, MS. Sl.; *pepanere*, and gloss *kore*, MS. Camb.
[4] It was an important point of etiquette and good breeding, in feudal times, to know and apply properly the special term for a company of different animals, and lists of these terms are found not unfrequently in manuscripts. It was a part of the science of hunting, which formed so prominent an occupation of life in the middle ages.

     hertes
Primes ou cerfs sunt ensemblez,
Une herde est appellez;
  cranys
De grues une herde;
  feldefaris
E de gryves saunz ·h· erde.
       (partriz)
Nyec[1] de fesaunz, cové de pertrys,
Une damé des allouues,[2] trippe de berbiz,
       sterlinges
Soundre de porks et d'estourneus,
      (smale briddes)
Bevée des heyrouns, pipée des oyseuz,
 (coltes)   (cherles)
Haras des poleyns, une foule de vileyns,
Route de boufs, moute de chennes,
    mochil (mork)
Masse de argent, femyr de feus,
       teles
Grelée de gelyns, turbe de cercels,
Eschele de batayle, lure de pucels,[3]
    huting
Kar pucele seet saun juper
Les gentifs faucouns alurer.
De dames direct la companye,[4]
Des ouues ausi la companye.[5]
Ceuz deus sunt asociez,
Quele est la resoun ore eliset,
E mettet pus vostre cure
De oyer cy la nature
De noyse[6] ke funt diversement,
Cechun soulum ço ke apent.

---

[1] *Nihe*, MS. Sl.; *nyue*, a marginal reading in the Arundel MS.

[2] *Damoye des alowes*, MS. Sl.; *alouues*, with gloss *larkes*, MS. Camb.

[3] The Arundel MS. gives as a reading, or explanation, in the margin, *lure de faucouns*.

[4] The Sloane MS. inserts before this line one which has no corresponding rhyme—
 Fuyson dist homme de vif anmaile.
The Arundel MS. also gives the words, *fuyson de rif aumayle*, in the margin.

[5] The Arundel MS. gives in the margin *une jangle*, perhaps as another term for a company of ladies.

[6] We also find not unfrequently in old MSS. lists of the particular terms applied to the voices of the different animals, in English and French. The following rather curious memorial verses on this subject are preserved in a MS. of the fifteenth century (MS. Harl., No. 1002, fol. 72, r°):—

At my howse I have a jaye,
He can make mony diverse leye;
He can barkyng as a foxe,
He can lowe as a noxe,
He can crowun as a gus,
He can romy as a masse in his cracche,
He can croden as a trove,
He can barkun as a dogge,
He can cheteron as a wrenne,
He can cakelyn as a henne,
He canne neye as a stede,
Suche a byrde were wode to fede.

THE TREATISE OF

        cryet
Homme parle, homme braye,
         overdoot
Saun resoun sovent se deraye;
   (lowes) (crane) lounet²
Le bouf¹ mugist, la grwe growle;
   (rounes) the hasel quaket
Le leoun rugist, la coudre crowle;
   neyet (larke)
Le chival hinnist, alowe chaunte;
Le coloumbe gemit, le cok chaunte;
   meutet   scisset³
Chat mynowe, serpent ciphele;
 asse criet⁴ an roret
Ane recane, cynge reciphele;⁵
 (wolfe) goulet berket
Le low hule,⁶ le chen baye;
E homme e beste sovent abaye;
        kacclit
Le pork grundile, gelyne patyle,
leyet an hey
Pount en gardyn, pount en vile.
En Fraunce est trové tel estyl,⁷
   coppid leyet kacclit
Ke gelyne hupé pount e patyle.
Ke ço avaunce saun resoun,
A la gelyne est compaynoun,
  kacclit
Ke plus patile pur un ooef,
Ke pur sa arure feet un bouf.
 bletet   hoppes
Berbit baleye, dame balce,
       chaffare
Espicer prent ses mers⁸ de bale.
        gonys⁹
Par trop veyler homme baayle,
A soun serjaunt sa chose bayle.¹⁰
       raskyt hym
Après dormer il ço espreche;
Si prechur scyt, a mouster preche;

---

¹ *Vache*, with the gloss *cowe*, MS. Sl. The Camb. MS., and a variant in the margin of the Arundel MS., also agree in this reading, which is perhaps the best.
² *Crekes*, MS. Camb.
³ *Cisses*, MS. Camb.
⁴ *Roreth*, MS. Camb.
⁵ *Cine recifle*, glossed *suan cissez*, MS. Camb.
⁶ *Oule*, glossed *yolles*, MS. Camb.
⁷ *En Fraunceis i ad tel estile*, MS. Sl.
⁸ *Merces*, MS. Sl.
⁹ *Ganes*, MS. Sl.
¹⁰ To judge by the glosses printed in the Reliquiæ Antiquæ, there follow here some lines in the MS. Camb. which are not in either of the London MSS.

Si pechur seyt, en rivere pecche,
<small>of is neet   and hok</small>
Ore de sa rey, ore de la heche.
<small>   leylond</small>
Le ffally lest sa tere freche,
<small>   fres fles</small>
Pur achater la char freche.
<small>   the ring</small>
Sa femme va mener la treche;
<small>   a spade</small>
Plus vaudroyt en mayn la becche;
<small>   dot on wey the hunger</small>
Kar ele ne ad dount se alecche[1]
De payn de furment une lecche;
<small>   licket</small>
De sa pael soun chael lesche.
<small>   to lapyn</small>
Ore donez le chael à flater,
<small>   licket the deu</small>
Qy lecche la rosée de le herber.
<small>   losenjour</small>
Eschuvet flatour ke seet flater,
<small>   piken[2]</small>
Trop seet ben espeluker;
En toun chaperoun ne voyt lesser
<small>   a mote</small>
Une poyçoun, taunt ad cher,
<small>   thi good</small>
Noun pas vus, mès toun aver,[3]
<small>   (have)</small>
Ke il de toy desire aver.

Pur la diverseté de Fraunsoys,
Ke sonne tout une Engleys,
Veyet sy vent devaunt vus
<small>   a reed knyt</small>
Un beu chivaler rous,
<small> a reed stede</small>
Un destrer soor est mounté,
<small> a reed cheeld</small>
L'eskou de gules ad porté,
<small>   a reed spere</small>
Une launce rouge en l'une mayn,
<small> reed wyn</small>
E vyn vermayl en l'autre mayn.
[Ki ne mangust poynt de peisoun,
Si del haraung sore noun].[4]

---

[1] *Alesche*, with gloss *zivere*, MS. Camb.
[2] *Glounden*, MS. Camb.
[3] *Aveir*, with gloss *catel*, MS. Camb.
[4] These two lines are inserted from the Sl. MS.

     a queen
Jo vy une reyne saun rey
    a frogge
Pur une reyne asser rey;[1]
En my le reaume le rey
   in afforoir[2]
En un reyoun par sey.
      an heved-lond[3]
Un maveys vint en ma forere,
      gonge
Où par despit fist foreyn hier,[4]
Dount jo ly fesoy forveyer
 (thef)   seken forage
Li leres ke vint forreyer.
  Aloum[5] après en chauns,
De aprende Frauneeys à vos enfauns.
 a ssythe (mowe) a swathe (a swethe of mede)
De faux fauchet une audeyne de prée;
 a sikel (rep) a repe of korn
De faucyl syet une javele de blée;
 (repes) (szeves)
Les javeles en garbes lieet,
  in schekes
En tresseus les garbes mettet.
    a pese rys
Un warrok de peys enrascet,
  bene cheves[6]
Les favas des feves de ce lyet.
Kaunt tens est de karier,
Vos chars fetez lors charger;
Ses chivaus deyt le charetter
  a quippe (haling-wippe)
De sa fowette ou de sa ryote gyer.
    golne thi corn
En la graunge vos blées muez,
      stacke thi corn
Dehors la graunge vos blez tassez;
 a mowe[7]
Une moye est dite en graunge,
 (stake)
E taas hors de la graunge;
 (reke)
Moyloun appellez ço ke est de feyn,
E taas ço ke est de greyn.

---

[1] *Fere desrei*, MS. Sl.
[2] *Forwe*, MS. Camb.
[3] *In myn hevede londe*, MS. Camb.
[4] *Foreynere*, MS. Sl.; *foreiner*, MS. Camb. The latter glosses it by *don out of tune*.
[5] We are now introduced to country occupations, in doors as well as out of doors, and the various occupations of farming, brewing, &c., are described, with the various implements which were used in them.
[6] *Ben schaf*, MS. Sl.
[7] *A reke*, MS. Camb.

       fro agunes
En graunge vus gardet des arestes;
En chaumps vos blées sawet de bestes;
      forbroden hefdes
A mouster veiret desgisés testes;
En sale orret estraunge gestes.[1]
Jo loo qe priet à vos festes
Gent ke sount sur enquestes,
Pur les malices ke sunt si prestes
De fere grewaunces et molestes;
Mès si divisée poynt n'estes,
      resty flees
Ke à ceuz donez chars restez.

      thouthen
 Kaunt vostre bléc est batu,
 (windewith) grounden
E venté, e pus molu,
 mille stoon
Par movele[2] devent faryne,
Ke greyn estoyt au matyn;
    (mele)
E de fine farine vent la flour,
    bulting-clot
Par la bolenge le pestour.
 bultingge
Per bolenger est ceveré
  of bren
La flur e le furfre demoré.
A vos chivaus le furfre donez.
E à ewe tenue oue flur medlet
     kned thi douw
Vostre pasté dount pestrez,
 a douw-ribbe a trow
De un rastuer le auge moundez.
 a rake
Le rastel e le raster
Sunt diverses en lour mester.
[Le pestour en mayn tent le rastel,
 (ribbe) (trhow)
Le rastuer fet l'auge biel.][3]
Taunt come feyves sunt en prés,
Est li rastels maynés;

---

[1] This and the following lines are given thus in the Sloane MS.:

 En sale chauntez-vous les gestes;
 Mès si vous cuylez gentz à festes,
 Priez ceux que sount en enquestes,
 Pur lour malices que sount si prestes.

[2] The Sloane MS. reads *moudre*, and glosses it. *wit gryndyng comes mel.*

[3] These two lines are inserted from the Sloane MS. The two English glosses are from the Camb. MS.

Kaunt le past à l'auge ahert,
Le rastuer dounke sert.
           _{a brake.} _{feryn}
Chaufet le fourn de feugere,
Pur defaute de litere.
Litere et liter unt diverse mester
  _(the mower)   _{mowet}
Le fauchour litere fauche,
Chivachur en liter chivache.
La litere saun fayle
          _{stree}
En Fraunce e dite payle;
  _{chaff and stre}
Payl et payle sunt nomez
Kaunt du greyn sunt severez;
E si payle ne seyt pas,
         _{pese stree}
Pernet dount de pessas.
Du peyl mettet payn en fourn,
E tank cum fet la sojorun.
     _{house-wyf}
Alet, dame mesounere,
Seet bone curtelere,
         _{linseed}
Semet cy vostre lynoys,
      _{hempseed}
E la semez vostre canoys.
      _{hoppen}
Du lyn averet le boceaus,[1]
De canbre averez les cordeus.
      _{wed thi flax}
Vostre lyn en tens sarchet,
      _{pik thi flax}
E autre foyze le lyn eslysez.
         _{reet}
Kaunt vostre lyn est rocz,
Pur ensecher au solayl le mettet.
E jo vus pri, dame Muriel,
     _{a swinglestok}
Le donez à vostre pessel.
    _{the swingle}
Ne ublet pas le pesselin,
    _{to swingle thi flax}
De escucher ou estonger vostre lyn.
  _{the hechele}
La serence dont pernet,
    _{hechelet}
E vostre lyn serencet.

---

[1] *Bocheus*, MS. Sl.; *buchraus*, MS. Camb., with gloss *flaxlolles*.

    a distaf. a rocke
De un conul vus purveyet,
   spindel quartel
Le fusil ou le verdoyl ne lessez.
De troys services sert fusil;
F'il est filee par fusil,
    (flint) a fer-hyren [1]
E fu de kayloun fert fusil,
       a mille-spindele [2]
E blée e molu par fusil,
a yar-wyndel
A wudres ore alez;
    wynde thi yarn
E vostre filoe là wudez.
Ke feet ore dame Hude?
  a klewe of yarn (windes)
Un lussel de wudres wude,
E dist "Ore jo voyl,
  do my yaarn on the reel
Ma filee moustre en travayl.
 the spoles
Les tremes fray aparaler
   a webe to wewen
A la tisterere pur tister.
E pur estre saunz blame,
     a slay
Jo ay purvu de unc lame."
Autre chose si apent,
Mè plus ne say verement.[3]

 Seyoms ore entour cerveyse,
Pur fere gens ben à eyse.
     the kex
Alumet, amy, cele lefrenole,[4]
      a spiced kake
E kaunt averas mangés de brakole,[5]
 a mikel fat
En une cuwe large e leez
  oferyet the bere
Cel orge là enfoundrez;
E kaunt sera enfoundré,
    leten out [6]
E le ewe seyt escouloé,
Mountez cel haut soler,
    suepet klene
Si le festes nette baler,

---

[1] *Vir-hirne*, MS. Camb.
[2] *Mulne spinel*, MS. Camb.
[3] The Sloane MS. omits all that follows, till near the close of the treatise.
[4] *Une frenole*, with gloss *keiex*, MS. Camb.
[5] *Brakenole*, glossed *a cake of spices*, MS. Camb.
[6] *Laden outh*, MS. Camb.

E là cochet vostre blée,
       wel atome¹
Taunke seyt ben germée.
De cele houre appelleras
(malt)
Brès, ke blée avant nomas.
Le brès de vostre mayn muez
      on hepe other on rowe
En mounceus ou en rengés;
         a litel basket
Pus le portez en un corbel,²
     (kulne)
Pur ensechier au toral.
Le corbel e le corbiloun
Vus servirunt au fusoyn.
         (grounden)
Kaunt vostre brez est molu,
E de ewe chaude ben enbeu,
    fro wort to ale
De bertiz ver cervoyse
Par art contrové teise.
Ky fet miracles e merveyles,
De une chaundelie deus chandelis,
De homme lay fet bon clerc,
A homme desconu doune merk,
      crepen
Homme fort fet chatoner,
        houten
E homme à roye haut juper.
       barly seym
Taunt de vertu de la grees
      malt
De servoyse fet de brès,
Ke la coyfe de un bricoun
Teyndre seet saunz vermilloun.
Ceste matyre cy repose,
Parlom ore de autre chose.
    (fische)
Ore volums pescher
 a neet
De la rey en un viver.
Vivere est appelé,
En ewe vive est trové,

---

¹ *Spired*, MS. Camb.   ² *Une corbail*, glossed *lepe*, MS. Camb.

         ladit
Le servour espuchet,[1]
De peyssoun là ne faudret.
       (pole)
Ore aloms à cel estang,
Où le ewe est à deturant,[2]
               lake (gret pol)
Si nous espleytoums alum à lay.
           in mire
Cele ewe esteaunt en betumay,
       wit a seyne
Là covent pecher de nase,[3]
   (neth)
Ou petite rey ne troverez grace.
   (the bothem) torne thi boke. (dornhep)
Le gurget   de nase reversez,
 (fulthe)
Le ordure ke leyns est en gettet;
 tode and evete
A crepaud e lesard la mort donez,
neddere ant snake
Serpent et colure ne esparniet;
 gret and flint
Gravele e calyoun regettez,
  a snayl
De un lymassoun force ne facez.
Nous volums partyr le pessoun
    by the giles
Par les wemberges à mesoun.
E coment ore retournerom
    a gap of a theed
Par my cele creveysoun,
            a grene balke
Tankes ke veynoum à vert choral[4]
      the bestes
Où est le pastour ladiual;
        in the sadwe (szadewe)
E pus au boys   en umbrail,
      under the wode-side (wode-hevese)
Passerom   desouz l'overayl;
E pur estre ment à eyse
           lit-gate
Nous passerom par cele heese,
Dount serunt taunt de peres,
     seping-stones
Mès sunt appellés passueres.

---

[1] *Espuchez*, with the gloss *laden hout*, MS. Camb.

[2] *Destoraunt*, glossed *arwei*, MS. Camb.

[3] *Nace*, glossed *seyne*, MS. Camb.

[4] *Cerail*, MS. Camb., and a various reading the margin of the Arundel MS.

      welle-stemes
Pur passer seck les russeaus,
Ke cy sunt et cleres et beus.

  reynet freset
Ore plut, ore gele;
 thouet freset ayen
Ore remet, ore regele.
        yes
Pur le gelé nous awomus glas,
        sliding
E pluvye e gelé fount vereglas.
N'e my bon de trop haster
     slide and falle
Sur vereglas, pur verglacer.
Gelé et pluvye degotaunt
    slidery (sclidinde)
Funt le chimyn trop lidaunt.
 snou   sletez
Ore negge, ore cemoie;
the sletz
Le cem empeyre nostre veye.
       a flay of snow[1]
La bouche me entra la aunf de neyf
Jà quidout ke ousse grant feyf.
        haylet
Nous awom grisil pur ço ke il grele,
      smal
Asset gros, noun pas grele.
 (thonner) thondret
Jo oy tonere, ou tonne,[2]
       a toune
Par taunt enpire cerveyse en tonne.
     towne
Ore suffret moun pée toune,
Nul de vus mot ne sonne.

 the eye of winter weder
Freyt est de yver l'orrée,
 a redels
Un devinal vus est moustré.
En le yver, kaunt l'orrée chaunge,
Une verge crest estraunge,
Verge saun verdour,
Saun foyl et saun flur;
Kaunt vendra le estés,
Cele verge ne ert trové.

---

[1] *A flake of snowe*, MS. Camb.   [2] *Oil i tonne*, marg. MS. Arund.

Red that redeles, red qwat it may beo.

    an ychele
Ce est un esclarcyl[1] en Engeleys.
 Kaunt les deys ne poet pas
Ensemble joyndre, donc dyras,
    so acomeled (wineled)
"Jo ay la mayn si estomye
Ke pur freyt ne puse myc
   the honde-moule
Par moy fere la copinole."[2]
      a softe quarele
Donc meuz voudrey sur plume mole
Seer prè de fu, ke mener karole
  (garlond) bloued (bloweth)
Desouz chapeau de blaverole,
Ou de coyler primerole,
   ydel wordes (keith)
Ky par bost de frivole,
E par knyvet, ou vyrole;
Donc ceus ke sunt de tel escole,
Vendreyunt[3] plus en la jaiole,
Ke ou femme en oriole.
     softe
Amour de femme est si mole,
     (becippe hur)
Kaunt esquyer ou clerk l'acole,
Meyntenaunt à une parole
Cele fole le recole.
Plut à Deux ke teles foles
    pockes
Oussent faces pleyn de viroles,
    maseles (maselinges)
E les fouz les rugeroles;
Les fous lerreyunt les braceroles,
E les foles les caroles.
 Le jour devent beuz e cler,
   pleyen
Aloums dedure, esbanoier;
En ço verger troveroums les flurs
     swote smel
Des queus issunt les douz odours,
Les herbes ausi pur medicine.
Les nouns des uns cy vus devyne.

---

[1] An icicle. The riddle is not a very difficult one to find out.
[2] *Capinole*, MS. Camb.
[3] The Arundel MS. gives in the margin as a various reading, *vendrunt*.

       (lilie)
La flur de rose, la flur de liz ;
Liz vaut pur royne, rose pur piz.
      golde-flurs (solicle)
Cy crest la flur de   surcye,
Qui er les surcyls n'ad nul envye ;
Ly oyl ke est près des surcyls
De ver la surcye ad graunt delitz.
    heyhowe
Eyre de boys e eyre terestre
En ço verger dewnt crestre.
    cousloppe
Primerole et primeveyre
Sur tere aperunt en tens de veyre.
     weybrede
Cy est asset de plaunteyne,
 oxe-tunge
E bucle ausy, une herbe seyne ;
hertis-tounge
Cerflange¹ crest en crevetz ;
     stepes
Cy troveret plenté de navetz ;
dayses (dayseie)
Consoude de blanche flur,
 smerowot (smerdocke)
E mercurial de graunt valur.
    sour-dokke
Pur sauce vaut la surele ;
     the rede dokke (roddok)
Pur roynons homme vaut la parele.
Sy vus trovet en toun verger
 mathen (maythe) and cloten
Ameroke   e gletoner,
    twybel
Les aracez de un besagu,
 gold plantes
E choletz plauntez en lour lu.
 En ço verger les arbres crescent,
     bowet adoun
Par charge de frut les uns abessent ;
(appil-tre) (pere-tre) (chiri-tre)
Pomere, perere, e cerecer ;²
asch brom   plum-tre
Frene, genet, e pruner ;
awe-tre (hawethen)   awes
Ceneler,   ke la cenele porte ;
   bolaces
Le creker, que crekes porte ;

---

¹ *Cerlaunge*, glossed *herte-tong*, MS. Camb.   ² *Cereiser*, MS. Camb.

   (slo-thorne)   slon
Le fourder que la fourdine porte;
  (brere)   hepen (hepes)
Eglenter, qe le piperounges porte;
  (cirne-tre)   cernes
Une allier, qe porte les allyes,
Dount Alienore en amyciennes
Le noun recoyt pur un roy,
    cernes in gold
Ke aveyt allies en oor devant sey.
Issi troverez en ce verger
    a coyn-tre (quince-tre)
Estang un sek   coigner;
        stokken
E pur ço ke seygnur fet coingner
   (stockes)
Soun neif en ceps pur chastier,
   the belte
Pernet le coing, abbatez le coigner,
     (a wegge)
E coupez du coyn une coygner;
E de coigner *of that tre*,
Enveyetz au coigner ke feet monée.
(box) (palm-tre)   mapel
Buz, paume, e arable,
Ne suffret pas en tere arable.
      holyn
Mès en verger crest la hous,
      covertur
Ke de nout ne vaut pur huce;
      holin-leves [holin-tre]
E achar nwe desout la   houce,
Vaudroyt plus giser en succ.
   hilder-tre (helren)
De   suhen[1]   font les souheaus,
Un manger bon e beus;
   wytie[2] (wilwe)   hok   ew (w
De   sauz   e chene e de l'if
En langage n'ad nul estrif.

 Du verger vers le boys
Sanz tonure me voys,
Où la russinole, *the nittegale*,
      an hule
Meut chaunte ke vayre en sale;[3]

---

[1] *Sucan*, MS. Camb.
[2] The name *withy*, for the willow, is still preserved in several of our provincial dialects.
[3] The following short metrical list of singing

     a throstel-kok (bosc)
E meut chaunte maviz en boysoun,
  a balke
Ke chaufe-soriz en mesoun.
      an hosel-brit (osel)
En braunche scet la merle ;
      the selddrake (sheldedrake)
En mareys demurt la herle ;
Regardet cy, Alissaundre,
Une herbe appelé alisauntre.
     gosesomer (stare)
Regardet cy la filaundre,
       wode-larke
Escotet come chaunte la calaundre ;
      a criket
Du fourn troverez la salamaundre ;
       (scheden him frome)
Soffret le peysoun en ewe espaundre.
     a wode-koc
Veyet où tapist un arscye ;
Fraunceyt voyt ke ensi dye.
Plus avaunt ore venet,
E ço ke verret entendet.
  a roddoc
Par cy vole le verder ;
  the wode-ward
Par là chivache le verder.[1]
     a wrenne
Cy vent volaunt une roytel,
     ascht of corn
E se tret vers le tressel ;
Kar meuz voyt le roytel
     (stone)
Envyrrouner le tressel,
    (fithele)
Ke un tret de vyole,
     (floute)
Ou la note de frestele.
Levere is the wrenne
Abouten the scholke renne,

birds is given in a MS. of the fifteenth century, in the British Museum (MS. Harl., No. 1002, fol. 72, r°) :

 To day in the dawnyng,
 I hyrde the fowles syng,
 The names of hem it likyt me to myng :
 The parterygge, the fesant, and the sterlyng,
 The quayle, and the goldefyng. and the lapwyng.

 The thrusche, the maveys, and the wodewale,
 The jaye, the popynjaye, and the nyghtyngale,
 The nottbache, the swalow, and the sernow,
 The chawȝe, the cucko,
 The rooke, the revyn, and the crow.
 Among alle the fowles that maden gle,
 The reremowse and the owle cowde I not see.

[1] *Forester*, glossed *forester* in English, MS. Camb.

*Than the fithel draut,
Other the floute craf.*[1]

   a titemose
Esgardet la musenge,
     seket abouten (thoursekes)
Ke les hayes   renge;
  thi swerd-girdel
Delacez ta renge,
E parnez la musenge.
   a litel bote fleyen to wode [the rede fleye]
Veyet cy   la palenole;
   a goldfinch (golfinges)
Veyet cy la   cardenerole;
     boterfleus
Cy ad plenté de papiliouns,
     thestles
Ky arutent ausi les cardouns,
     a greshoppe
Sy ne fet pas le grisilloun,
Ke en curtilage prent soysoun.
  an hirchoun
Le yrizoun vent le plus,
Ke prent la poume ke chet sous.
  a tele   a doke (doukere)
La cercele et ly plounjoun
En rivere prenunt lur sojourn;
  a wype and   wasthere
La vanele e le pounzot;
En mores sunt lur riot.
     wypes
En mores sunt les vaneles,
     lanes
En viles sunt les vencles;
   a foan (faune)
En graunge e trové van,
    hatrede
En quer de envyous haan.
     a wilde-gos
Jo voy là une owe rossée
  a balled cote
Une blarye à luy associer;
Meuz seray de une blarette pou,
     of a rook
Ke ne seroy de char de fru.
     a swalwe
Plus est ignele une arunde
  a stork
Ke nul cygoyne eń ço munde;

---

[1] This appears to be an old English popular rhyme relating to the wren — a bird which was the object of much superstition and fable in the middle ages.

       a serundel at the   eveses
E severunder à la severunde [1]
                       al abouten
Prent les mussuns à la rounde.
                 a snype (snyte)
Un oysel ke est dist   becaz
                   (streing)
Près du rivere est pris en laz.
               a kocken
I me semble que le cuknel [2]
Tent soun chaunt ben e bel.
              holdende on
A peyne seroyt-il si riotous,
Si soun chaunt fu gracious.
              de la chambre
Plus est delit en le oriol
              a wodewale
Escoter la note de l' oriol.
 Plus avaunt uncore voys
Pur dedure en ço boys.
      a brok
Jo vey cy un teissoun,
Ke ad gerpi sa mesoun,
      fox file
Pur la fiente de goupil,
      flemet hym
Ke l'ad mis en exil.
         a fulmarde
Jo vey cy le putoys; [3]
Seyt en vile, seyt en boys,
Force ne fet més ke il eyt
            to is gladhinge (glading)
Gelyne ou poucyn à soun reheet.
       a wesele
Jo voudrey meut ceste belette,
        (ratonz)
Defera ma graunge de raz nette,
    moldewarpes
Ke touz les taupes [4] ke sount trovez
En tere fowauntez par my les prés.
    a brere-busk
Jo vy cy desut la dume
           the fetheren
Un oysel plumé, cy gist la plume;
Mè cyl ke le oysel ad plumé,
            pullet notes
Meuz voudrey ke il eust noys perluchée.

---

[1] *Cheverounde*, glossed *heresing*, MS. Camb.   [3] *Mauputois*, glossed *fulthmard*, MS. Camb.
[2] *Kokel*, glossed *kochon*, MS. Camb.   [4] *Taupaines*, MS. Camb.

Jo vey ester un pety neym, ^{a dwarw (dweruf)}
Pescher voyt, ne pout pur ceym. ^{sleet (sleth)}
Jo vey cy vener une charette; ^(kart)
Bon est ke m'entremette
En Frounceys la charette descrivere;
E pur enfaunz mettre en livere.
Primer voyl nomer les roes; ^{the queles}
Pus les bendes de les roes, ^{the carte-bondes}
Desout le qi sount de feer, ^{the felues}
Sount les jauntes cachés de fer. ^{the spokes}
En les jauntes entrunt les rays; ^{the sonne-bemes}
E du solayl issunt les rays; ^{rowes}
E de la mer venunt les rays; ^{borer-clot}
E ver la foyre vount les rays. ^(szlakes)
Mès les rays de la charette ^(bureles)
En les moyaus untreceyte. ^{in the nawes}
Dit le moyal de la roef, ^{(xaxes) (wel)}
E le moiel de un oef ^{a yelke (hei)}
Je fu fort à fesse porter,
E jo fu bon, fet l'autre, à manger.
En les meus est mys le essel, ^{the axil-tre (axe-tre)}
E par deuz hietes se tenent owel. ^{the ax-tre pinnes}
Les esseus unt lour joigneres, ^{the axe-tre cloutes}
Ke les eydunt cum bons freres.
Sus les esseuz gist le chartil; ^{the carte body}
E pur sauver du peril,
Le chartil est de braeus, ^{the warwythes}
Ferm lyée as asseuz.

Entre le chartil e les meaus
Sount hurtuers trovez deuz.
Checune charette ke meyne blés
Deyt aver redeles au coustés; *rayes (ronges)*
En les reideles vount les rolous[1] *ronge-stafs*
Par les faiz, sanz nul clous. *(nayles)*
Entre les les meaus sount sauneres, *lether-cloutes (letherin-clout)*
Si unt le charettes lour escheles. *carte-ladderis*
En lymouns va ly limounere, *(thilles) the thillo-hors*
Ke porte à dos une dossere, *rige-leyther*
E au ventre un venter, *a wombe-rop*
E à la koue un analuer.[2] *a tayl-rop*
Les trays si unt braceroles,[3] *henekes of trays*
Ke enbrasunt les lymouns e acolunt. *the thilles (bicluppes)*
Devaunt les braceroles sount biletz, *(pinnes)*
Ke de coteus sunt round deletz. *thiwilet*
Les cous de chivaus portunt esteles, *hames*
Coleres de quyr et bourle boceles. *beru-hames*
En charette est le somer,
Là où seet le charetter,
Ke teynt en mayn la ryoite, *the quyppe (haling-wippe)*
Par unt le chival à chimyn resorte.
De la charette à la charue
Pur descrivere me remonue.
En la charue vus troverez
Diverse nounz assignez.
Le chef e le penoun, *the plou-heved and the foot*
Le manuel, e le tenoun; *the handele and the sterte*

---

[1] *Roilouns*, glossed *staves*, MS. Camb.
[2] *Vauner*, glossed *taylrop*, MS. Camb.
[3] *Bracerole* is glossed by *eyhe* in the Camb. MS.

     the plou-reste
Par desout est l'oriloun,
      the cheld-brede
Plus amound est l'eschuchoun;
   culter and schar
La soke e le vomer
Deyt la carue aver;
Mès war ke ne thoche
   the fore-stobel
La soke la souche.
      the plou-beem
En long la carue est la hay,
 form wode or hegge
Ke vent en boys ou de hay.
     the plou-betel
La charue si ad un maylet,[1]
  the plou-stare
O le moundiloun pur fere net.
Devaunt la haye sount le clavons,
Où sount atachez les tenouns.
    the yokkes
Les boufs portunt les juges,
Pur crestiens et pur Geus.
  oxe-bowes
E par les arsons en jugs formés
      ysstreynned (streingned)
Sunt les boufs si fort artés,
Ke lour covent maugré lour
Par l'agulloun eschure arrour.
De la charue asset awoms,
Redressoms ore nos mesouns.
 Si vus avet en curage
Une chaumbre lever estage,[2]
Primes devez comencer
Le foundement de geter,
   (the wowen hele-woth)
E pus levez la mesere,
    hosewyf
Dount femme e dist mesnere,
 (haiward)
C'est le mour ke environne la court;
   the beret the hous
E mesere est ke acoumble ahurt.

---

[1] The Arundel MS. gives in the margin the various reading, *ou martelet.*

[2] We have now a description of the mode of building and arranging a house, followed by some curious and very interesting notices of domestic life.

Sus la mesere en **travers** outret
                the wiver-tre
Amont heceler mettez la poutre;
  a file
De chenestre liet la poutre,
En vostre soler sus le poutre.
    the gistes
Les solives mettet outre;
          the floor
Amont les solines la plauncie,
De bord ou plaistre ben paveye.
         the balkes
Sus la mesere les trayes[1] mettet,
    raftres
De deuz cheverouns un couple facez.
Le ferm estera sur la mesere,
    pyn and   wymble (nauger)
Par kyvyl et par terere.
De tote la mesoun est combele apert,
  hiling of hous
E cele e tecte dount est covert.
En la chaumbre deyt ben estre
Li annuere à la fenestre.
           the therswald
A l'entré del hus est la lyme;
         the over-slay (hover-dorne)
E entre la teste la suslyme.
        the dor-nothes
De cousté sunt les simeus,[2]
        the ryngges
Où sunt fichez les aneuz.
         hokes
En l'un symel sount les gouns,
  the bondes of hokes (hengles)
E verteveles sunt mys as gouns.
  lacche and hok
Par cliket à cerrure
Ert la mesoun le plus sure.
  Fetes ore apparayler,
Ke nus pussum tot manger.
Un valet de vus katre
        the hert-ston
Va tot munder cele hastre.
        the mochil[3]
Portez les cendres au femyer,
  the chides (szhides)
Les hasteles fetez alumer

---

[1] *Trefs* is added, as a various reading, in the Arundel MS.

[2] *Gyrneaus*, with gloss *dorstodes*, MS. Camb.

[3] *i. e.*, the muck-hill, or dunghill.

    a brond brennende
Par un tysoun de fu enpris,
Ke de la cusyne serra pris.
   schides
Les hastels mettet en travers,
    aundyrnes
Les chenes forgé sunt de fers.
   hors-hames
Si des hesteles du chival
   schides to brennen
Sacet, hasteles vus fret mal.
    of hook
Mettet au fu hastele de chene,
  of allerne of asse
Coupet de aunne ou de frene,
    the bely
E va donk quere le foufou,
    of bech
Quyr enclowé à foust de fou.
Si tu esparnyes del fou le fou,
Tu verras tenuz de ceste fou.
  (grenhed) schides
Mès pur la verdoure des hasteles,
   sparken
Jo ne vey isser estenceles.
 (imbrers) a pot-schoord (szherd)
Va quere breses en une teske,
Attiret le fou, cy vent le eweke.
Ore agardet, beu frere
  fayr feer (glading)
N'avera cy bele chere.
   from hiseles (huysseles)
Gardez vos draas de falemetches;
Mettet en breses peyres et petches;
 mak klene and russet
Mundez la mesoun e la junchet;[1]
Asseet la table, e la coveret.
  hendes and sydes
Les boutes de la table et les eurs
Coveret des napes devant seygnurs.
    dwy
E si la nape seyt trop soyle,[2]
    halle
Ne suffret pas ke vyngne en sale.

[1] It was the usual custom at this time, when carpets had not yet come into use, to strew the floors of the rooms with rushes. There is an allusion to this custom in the Towneley Mysteries, p. 180—

 With alle my harte and alle my wille
 Is he welcom me untylle.

Lo here a chambre fast by,
Therin to make youre maugery,
I shal warande fare stroked;
It shuld not els to you be shewed.

From this common use of rushes arose the modern meaning of the French word *joncher*, to strew.

[2] *Sale*, glossed only, MS. Camb.

Blaunche nape mout usée
E plus honeste ke novele enbrowé.
Lavet les hanapes, mundez l'esqueles,
                          the wortewale (nailes)
Coupet des cisours des ungles   les eles.
              a fles-hook
Va tey, quistroun, ou toun havet,
Estrere le hagiz du pocenet;
            and hyve (huive)
E mettet la veylle   rusche
                   a ladel
Desout le pees, noun pas la lusche
              slike (szhike)
E dy à sonette ke ele lusche,
      a slikestone
De une lechefneyre[1] sur la husche.

Recoylet la gent au manger,
Par poet meymes alloser.
Tayllet le payn ke est parée,[2]
the paringges
Les biscaus à l'amoyne soyt doné.
        brek bred
Fruschet ço payn ke vent de fourn;
      brek the bon
E broset les oos ke awom par venour;
      brek the streng
Rumpet la corde ke fet nusaunce;
      brek forwarde
E freynet le covenaunt de deteynance.
                the schirtes
Prenet valet en vos eschours
De ço frael harang rous,
E donez à cel pelryn
Ke porte escrippe de ermyn.
               the schirte beforn
Par devaunt avet escours,
             gores
E de costé sunt gerouns.

---

[1] *Lucchier*, glossed *szhikinston*, MS. Camb.

[2] It was the custom to pare the crust from the loaf of bread, before it was cut into pieces for the guests at table. This practice is alluded to in the romance of Sir Tristrem, fytte i. st. l.—

    The kyng no seyd no more,
      Bot wesche and yede to mete;
    Bred thai *pard* and schare,
      Ynough thai hadde at ete.

The parings, as stated in the text, were thrown into the alms-basket, or dish, to be given to the poor. Thus, in the Boke of Curtasye, p. 30—

    The aumenere by this hathe sayde grace,
    And the almes-dysshe base sett in place;
    Therin the karver a lofe schalle sette,
    To serve God fyrst, withouten lette;
    These othere lofes *he parys aboute*,
    Lays hit myd dysshe, withouten doute.
    . . . .
    Alle the broken met he kepys ywate,
    To dele to pore men at the gate.

      bilagged wit swirting
 Cy vent un garsoun esclaté;[1]
La resoun coment vus ert moustré.
     of swirtingges
Asset avera de esclautez[2]
     horses steppes
Ky des chivaus fut esclos.
 Jo vy cy vener mester Hughe,
     bote he stote
Ke reyn ne parle s'yl ne bue.[3]
    roble bestes
Ce deuz garsouns chasont preeye,
     wlaffes
A checun mot l'un balbeye;
E ly autre ne pout parler
     snevelet (snyvele)
Une parole sanz nasyer.[4]
N'est pas force s'yl nasye,
     a charbote
A peyne vaut-il un escharrie;[5]
   slaveret
E ke pys est baave;
     an hol roche
Esclos fust-il en une cave.
Unkes ne priast à sa mere,
    a brest-clut
Cele luy fest une bavere.
 Un valet de la novellerie
Vint her de une mangerye,
E de la feste nus ad counté
Coment lou servise fust arrayé.
Saunz payn e vyn e cerveyse
Ne seroyt nule feste à eyse,
     ichesen
Mès touz troys mutz elitz
Il aveyent nos as ditz.
Au primer fust apporté
   a boris heved
La teste de un sengler tot armé,[6]
  (the snout) wit baneres of flurs
E au groyn le coler en banere;
E pus veneysoun, ou la fourmenté;

---

[1] The Camb. MS. as well as the marginal note in the Arundel MS. read *esclavoté*, and the former glosses it *bispirnet*.

[2] *Esclavoz*, margin of Arundel MS.

[3] *Lowe*, margin of Arundel MS.

[4] *Naser* is the reading of other MSS.

[5] *Un aillie*, glossed *a pile of garlec*, MS. Camb.

[6] This brief description of the laying out of a feast is very interesting. The custom of bringing in the boar's head at the beginning of the feast is well known, and several of the songs used in the ceremony are preserved.

Assez par my la mesoun
   taken of gres tyme
De treste du fermeyson.
Pus avyent diversetez en rost,
Eit checun autre de cost,
cranes pokokes swannes
Grues, pounes, e cygnes,
wilde-ges gryses (porceaus) (hennes)
Owes, rosées,[1] porceus, gelyns.
Au tercez cours avient conyns en gravé,
E viaunde de Cypre enfundré,
De maces, e quibibes, e clous de orré,
Vyn blanc e vermayl à graunt plenté.
      wodekok
Pus avoyunt fesauns, assez,[2] et perdriz,
feldefares larkes
Grives, alowes, e pluviers ben rostez;
E braoun, e crispes, e fritune;
Ke soucre roset poudra la temprune.
Après manger avyunt à graunt plenté,
Blaunche poudre, ou la grosse dragé.[3]
E d'autre nobleie à fusoun,
Ensi vous fynys ceo sermoun;
Kar de Fraunceis i ad assez,
De meynte manere dyversetez,
Dount le vous fynys, seynurs, ataunt,
A fitz Dieu vous comaund.

Ici finist la Doctrine monsire Gauter de Byblesworde.

---

[1] For these two words, the Sl. MS. reads *chevrels*, glossed *kydes*, and the Camb. MS. *chevereaus*, with the gloss *kides*.

[2] *Ascies*, glossed *wudkokes*, MS. Sl., and the MS. Camb. has nearly the same reading.

[3] The Arundel MS. ends with this word rather abruptly; the subsequent lines and the colophon at the end are given from the Sloane MS.

METRICAL VOCABULARY.[1]

(PERHAPS OF THE FOURTEENTH CENTURY)

---

  stumlyth yn harneys   i. purpura i. superbus
 Cespitat in phaleris yppus, blattaque suppinus;
i. lingua   i. vino   i. sermo i. stulto
 Glossa velud themato labat emus infatuato,
s. ille i. bonus i. in operacione   i. fidelis i. sermone
 Qui calus in praxi simul est, et pisticus emo,
    i. laus   i. loquitur vel predicat
 Illius[2] oda placet, hic recte theologizat,
       tresory   i. divitus
 Qui cupide servas ypogeum gazophilacis.
     i. celestis   i. altas sedes
 Cerdus ad uranici scandes algalmata regni.
falsos homines i. devoratores qui stant in falsis causis i. depredantes
 Pseustes, ambrones, sicophantes, vispiliones,
             i. circuibunt
 Stix et Cochitus, Lethe, Flagitonque rotabunt.
 the hanches i. cervi i. capre   i. quoquine
  Terga laphi dorceque latus delata popine,
    i. aqua cocta rosste   a payge of the keschyn
 An sint elixa, sint assave, scit bene   lixa.
a stode[3] i. generosi   everey i. sponsas
 Bulla velud proceres, stola sic eburnea nuptas;
   i. lectum i. coopertorium i. ornat borde-clothe
 Utque cubile thoral decusat, gausape mensam,
  a kervere   a surgyon or a chamerleyne
 Cironomon mensis, lectis assistit aleptes.
    fowlere   a murtherer of men derke hernys
 Dumetis auceps latet, et sicarius   antris,
gracilis puer bysnevyllyd colte i. villosus i. hirsutus
 Puseo reumaticus, pullus lappatus et hirtus,

---

[1] This curious vocabulary is printed from a manuscript of the fifteenth century (MS. Harl. 1002, fol. 113, r°), but the text is in all probability of an earlier date. The name of Spencer is subscribed to the end of it, but names signed in this way are those more usually of the copyist than of the author. From the occurrence in the interlinear gloss of several words, such as *sullow* and *bannut*, peculiar to the dialects of the West of England and the Welsh border, we may perhaps conclude that the MS. was written in that part of the island. The Latin contains a rather large number of words adopted from the Greek.

[2] A Latin commentator states in the margin that this word has "Media corrupta causa metri."

[3] i. nodus in cingulo, Latin gloss.

METRICAL VOCABULARY.

               i. nobili
.... nunquam spernantur herili.
        a byttore
.... barrit,¹ onocrotulus hiccine bombit,
      a lytulle frogge   crowkyt
...., ranunculus inde coaxat.
       glasse   i. dominam
.... ..eneus speculum sese speculatur et heram;
     .... i. domino
... ...curus hero, sicque sibi preparat escas.
.... a ...ndyre
.... .t andena sustentus deperit ardens,
     i. falsi servuli   lordlyche
.... sepe spenduli res tabet herilis.
... . dulium promittit heris placitura,
...... tatus alterius fiat et non assecla verus.
.... i. nomen   acuto accentu proferri
.. .. onoma tamen debeat   oxitonari,
.. ...ctus gramaticus   i. illiteratus
... ... ortographus, sed agramatus esse probatur.
     tavenere i. estus aeris
.... acinum caupo canina repellit,
    vermes, Anglice myntys²   drastus
.. .. musti bibiones arcet amurca.
    i. sanctus   i. vana gloria
... ... hic agnus quem sinodoxia tangit,
   i. gravat malus mos   bonum opus orationis dicte
Qu..que premit cathesis non potest diasinaxis.
.. ...ines cubitales   qui obliquo videt
..... pigmeos nanus regnat, strabo luscos,
...... extales, monotalmus quoque cecos.
    whey   whey potte
..t plena cero mea seria, theca leeo,
.... bakere vel panttere
.... et arthocopus acerna popina ferinis.
... .d   a wowere   pame of the honde³
.. .... prava proco spurcum genus, et vola cassa,
... . a crabbe⁴ nostrelle
.... et rini glauconia sit tibi talmi.
    a botelere buschel avener
.... maphos pincerna bathos, abatis quoque orcam,
  a costrelle   cofer
.. .. onophorum, capsa, caper, armiger, arpen.
.. .. watur   barel
..... dat latices, oleum cadus, anphora vinum;

... .ad, Barri, -orum,   west of England.
... . Anglice bace, sed hic   ³ A Latin commentator adds the words, con-
   ..   caritas palmi.
... . in the signification of a   ⁴ The Latin glossator adds, *sed hic est fetor*
   .... the dialects of the   *naris*.

METRICAL VOCABULARY.

       a narow-case bow-case   bow
Et telum pharatra, corito conditur archus.
                        i. pius
Archimandrita sit celebs, eusebiusque.
    horse   palfray   kolte   stede   mare
Equus, caballus, pullus, dextrarius, equina ;
   bole   oxe   cowe   bulloke   calfe   hayfare
Taurus, bos, vacca, buculus, vitulusque, juvenca ;
    wether schepe lombe   lombe a ram
Est vervex, ovis, agnellus, simul agnus, aries ;
   goote buk kede goote idem est doo herte
Hircus, capriolus, caper, capra, damaque, cervus ;
   bore   pygge   swyne sow   ʒelte sow-pyg
Aper, porcellus, porcus, sus, scropha, suilla.
   hond whelpe greyhownd   blodehownde
Canis, caniculus, leporarius, atque molosus.
  catte idem est chytte whesılle rotte mowse
Murelegus, catus, catulus, mustela, rato, mus.
   kocke henne chekynge capone pokoc swanne
Gallus, gallina, pullus, capo, pavoque, signis.
  gandur   goslyng mallard doke   gose
Ancer, et ancerulus, anas, anata, simul auca.
 sparow   larke   pye   revyn   colvyr
Passer, et alauda, pica, corvusque, columba ;
 parthyryd quayle   wodekok   jay
Perdix, coturnix, castrimargus, graculusque ;
     wodekoc pynok[1] sparowhawke wrenne
Gallus silvester, lirifa, nisus, regulusque,
  kyte   chowʒe   snyte hayron grype
Milvus, monedula, sic ibis, ardea, vulter.
  crane   owle   popynyay   swalow nyʒttyngale
Grus, bubo, psitagus, et irundo, sic philomena.
   flee   lowse   nete   mothe hond-werme worme
Pulex, pediculus, lens, tinea, curio, vermis ;
  flye gnatte bee dog-flye addurcop[2] drane
Musca, culex, apis, ciniphex, aranea, fucus.
  toode frogge addur   snayle water-addur foayle or a snayle
Bufo, rana, serpens, testudo, vipera,   limax ;
  wont[3] ematte   reremowse grashopper butturflye
Talpa, formica, vespertilioque, cicada, papilio.
  bawsin[4] conyng   hare   lyon   lebard
Castor, cuniculus, lepus, leo, vel leopardus.
  stokfyche wale   eyster lytul fiche   whelke
Fungia, cete, vel ostria, pisciculus quoque, concha ;
  fyche   neele   samoun lampray   heryng
Piscis, et anguilla, salmo, murena, vel allec.
  barlyche beene pyse rye   wheete   otyn
Ordium, faba, pisa, siligo, frumentum, avena ;

---

[1] *Pinnock* was a name for the hedge-sparrow. still in use in some of the provincial dialects.
[2] See before, p. 24.
[3] *Want*, or *wont*, the old name for a mole, is
[4] *Bawson, bawsin*, or *baustone*, was a common name for the badger.

METRICAL VOCABULARY.

        malte   vache   dragge   medylde corne
Et brasium, vicia, dragetum,[1] mixtilioque.
Worte siromellum, sed *growte* dicas agromellum;
  sycher   ale   wyne   drastys   methe
Sisera, cervisia, vinum, feces, ydromellum.
  botyr   whey dordus. curddys[2] chese   mylke
Butirum, serum, coagulum, casius, et lac;
  crayme sowre mylke whey poshoote[3] boystryg[4]
Quactum, exigalum, serum, balducta, colustrum.
  halle howse chamer garner grange schepyn
Aula, domus, camera, granarium, grandia, boscar;
  soler spence or botrye kychyn idem est
Solarium, promptuarium, coquina, popina;
  brewarne bakehouse stabulle stye, or a swyne holke
Pandoxatorium, pistrinum, stabulum,   ara.
  tempulle chyrche idem est synagoge chapelle
Templum, ecclesia, basilica, sinagogaque, capella;
  nawter oratory chyrche-haye[5] beryels
Ara, oratorium, cimiteriumque, sepulchrum.
  bedde schete chalon[6] quylte bedde-strawe[7]
Lectus, linthiamen, tapetum, culcitra, stratum;
  bolstar coverlyte pelowe blancketh celynge
Servical, toral, pulvinar, lodexque, velamen.
  brasyn potte posnette cawdrune brondyr[8] fryyn-panne panne or potte
Urceus, urceolus, cacabus, tripos, lebes,   olla;
  mortare pestelle gredyre broche nowle
Mortarium, pila, craticula, veruque, creagra.
  dysche ladylle crok-styke dobeler plater
Discus, metorium, contus, scutella, parapsis.
  sawsesere spone coop pece[9] salte
Salsarium, coclear, ciphus, crater, simul sal.
  borde-clothe towelle trenchere clothe broche
Gausape, manitergium, scissoria, mappa, verutum.
  spykkett[10] chese-wate oyle-pott tankard barelle
Clepsidra, casiarium, lechitus, amphora, cadus,
  basyn laver bancar spere schylde
Pelvis, lavatorium, bancarium, lancia, scutum.

---

[1] This word seems misplaced here. A *dragé*, as representing the Latin word *dragetum*, was a sort of comfit; but in English the word *dragge* was given to a mixed corn, called by Tusser *dredge*, which is evidently the meaning of it in this place. The Promptorium Parvulorum gives "Dragge, menglyd corne, *mixtio*."

[2] This is perhaps the meaning of *dorde* in the old ballad of the Feest,—
    Ther was castrell in cambys
    And capuls in cullys,
    With blandamets in *dorde*.

[3] A posset. The Prompt. Parv. has "Possot, *balducta*.".

[4] I have not met with this English word elsewhere. *Colustrum* is explained in an old glossary quoted in the Dictionary of Ducange by "*novum lac*."

[5] *Church-haye*, or *church-hawe*, was not an uncommon name for a churchyard.

[6] "Chalun, bedde-clothe, *thorale, chalo*." Prompt. Parv.

[7] Straw was the usual material of beds.

[8] A brandreth.

[9] A cup. The Catholicon has the word, "A pece of silver or metalle, *crater, cratera*."

[10] A spigot.

METRICAL VOCABULARY.

    perche   checur   tabeler   dyce   idem est
Pertica, scaccarium, alea, decius quoque, talus;
  kyng   roche   alphyn   kny3t   quene   pewne
Rex, rocus, alphinus, miles, regina, pedinus.
           hede   top   molde[1]   nolle   ere
Est capud et vertex, est cinciput, occeput, auris;
    templys   schede   lokke   here   idem est. here
Tempora, discrimen, coma, crinis, sive capillos.
    vesayge   scolle   brayne   werte   scrofe or scalle.
Est facies, cranium, cerabrum, papula quoque, glabra.
         the browe   lede of the eye   spac bytwene nostrelle
Est supercilium, cilium, sic palpebra, naris.
  white of the face   ye   happulle   ye, i. oculus
Albucies,   facies, oculus, pupillaque, talmus;
forehede nose nostrelle grystylle   poose
Frons, nasus, rinus, cartulagoque, caturrus;
  mowthe lyppe berde cheke gummys rofe of the mowthe
Os,   labrum, barba, faux, et gingiva,   palatum;
cheke-bone idem est chynne   tonge idem est
Mandula, mandibula, mentum, dens, glossaque, lingua,
schyny3t   thombe   schewyt fore-fyngur
Pollet enim pollex, res visas indicat index,
    medylle fyngur   leche-fyngur   acordyt
Stat   medius   medio, medicus jam convenit egro,
               ere   lytil-fyngur
Quas tua fert auris sordes trahit auricularis.
  brest   arme-pytt syde tete idem est idem est
Pectus, et acella, latus, uber, mamma, mamilla;
  hele foote too   hele   sole   hele
Calx, pes, articulus, calcanius, plantaque, talus.
bone flesche yuncte   marowe
Os, caro, junctura, medio fit in osse medulla;
werel-bone vayne /enew skyn idem est
Vertebra, cum vena, nervus, pellis, cutis atque.
  thye hepe the tendurnesse of the thye ham grete-too kne
Crus, femur,   et famen,   poples, alluxque, genu sit.
  body   hert gal mylt kedney myddereffe
Corpus sunt infra cor, fel, splen, ren, diafragma;
bowellys longys mawe bladdur ynwarde throte
Viscera, pulmo, jecur, vesica, precordia, guttur;
  lyndy   lyver i. stroma flyxrop blode   idem est
Lumbus, epar, matrix, lien, cruor quoque, sanguis.
rede blode. a gibelet   gotte
Exta   manent extra, sunt intestina sed intra.
the hoole of a prevay ars-wyspe gong idem est hoole
Gumphus,   menpirium, latrinam, cloaca, foramen.
Dum paro menpirium, sub gumpho murmurat anus.
  ars wolde woman   qwynsys rawe
Anus   anus   pedit, quia coctona cruda comedit.

[1] The suture of the skull.

METRICAL VOCABULARY.

       nappyt   hyssyt
Dum dormitat anus, velud ancer sibulat anus.
 corne mylle   mylston   bynne   kog
Far, mola, molaris, faricapsa, scariaballum;
 clakke¹   whele   flode-yate   spyndulle
Batillum, rota, sinoglostorium quoque, fusus.
 forge   fyre   tong   below   marchel   anfeld
Fabrica, pir, forceps, follis, marcollus, et incus;
 pynsors   nayle   cawser   horschoe
Pallatum, scalpum, clavus, incussoria, ferrus.
 schofylle spade   pycows   whelebarow   forke
Tribula, vanga, ligo, cenevecthorium quoque, furca;
 cracche   idem est   myxon
Presepe, cum precepio, starquiliniumque,
 flexe   wolle   hempe   selke-worme hordy²   selke
Linum, lana, canapus, bumbax, stupa, ceriumque;
                wase   stoppe
Cum grossa stupa rimas edis bene stupa.
 dystafe   spyndylle   warbe   threde   reele
Colus cum fuso, vertebrum, filum, alabrumque;
 3arne-wyne   clewe   warpe   offe³
Jurgillum, glomerus, subtegmen, sic quoque stamen;
 spole   webbe   clothe idem est   darte
Panus, cum tela, pannus, vestis quoque, telum.
        webbe   dartys
Nos vestit tela, gerimus ad prelia tela.
 brydylle   barnaculle⁴ cropyn⁵   paytrelle⁶
Frenum, cum chamo, postela, vel antela sit.
 solow-hunddul solow-heme solow⁷ culter chyppe   chare
Stiva,   buris, aratrum, culter, dentale, vomerque.
     extre   spokys   carte-nave   vely
Est axis duplex, radii sunt, timpana, canti;
 solow-borde 3oke   bonde   wythe
Barcha jugum jungas, hic demum vincula, retorta,
 bytylle   wegge
Mallus, intersimonium, meditiliumque.
 thombe   harpe   schare   vorow
Pollice tango liram, facio cum vomere liram,

---

¹ The clapper of the mill.

² I have not before met with the word *hordy* in the sense of *stupa*. The next line is added in the margin of the manuscript.

³ "Oof, threde for webbynge, *trama, stamen,*" *Prompt. Parv;* in illustration of which Mr. Way quotes from the Wicliffite version of Leviticus xiii. 47,—"A wullun clooth, or lynnen, that hath a lepre in the *oof (in stamine,* Vulg.) or in the werpe, it shall be holdun a lepre."

⁴ I have not before met with this word in the sense of a horse's bit *(camus)*.

⁵ *Cropon* occurs in the Promptorium Parvulorum as synonymous with crupper.

⁶ The strap across the horse's breast. In the early ballad of True Thomas (in the text of the Cambridge MS.), the caparison of the horse is described thus—

    Hir *paytrelle* was of a rialle fyne
    Hir crupur was of arafe,
    Hir bridulle was of golde fyne,
    On every side honge bellis thre.

⁷ The Anglo-Saxon name of the plow, preserved only in the dialects of the West of England. See before, p. 15.

METRICAL VOCABULARY. 181

  wayne chare the therrepyllis carte thylle
Plaustellum, currus, epredia, bigaque, reda;
barnaculle brydulle reyne idem est halter
Camus, cum freno, lorum, vel abena, capistrum.
 brode-axe persere axe hachet sawe
Est dolabrum, penitral, securis, ascia, cerra.
swerde idem est basselard[1]   daggar
Ensis, sic gladius, seca, sic sit armicudium.
 cordedenare sowter clowte of a schoo
Est alutarius, sutor quoque, pictacium sit;
clowter or cobeler tynker lether brystylle
Pictaciarius, incrustator, corria, seta.
 lest over-lether
Formipedia, licinia, impedia sit.
 baryng-sexe[2] sole nalle corduane
Sunt ansoria, solie, sibula, cordibanumque.
 blacche-pot blacche blacke
Attramentorium, sunt attromenta, sed atrum.
clowtyst corduane lest of a boote
Incrustas allutam, dic et quitibiale.
 tayler webster dyer tannar idem est
Est scissor, textor, tinctor, serdoque, frunitor;
 smyth towker[3] mason skynnere
Est faber, fullo, latamus, penularius atque
 carpynter dawber leche
Carpentarius, est cementarius, aleptes;
 karver lavender glover fowler
Cironomon, lotrix, cerotecarius, auceps.
appul-tre peere-tre hasyl note bannenote-tre[4] fygge
Pomus, pirus, corulus, nux, avelanaque, ficus;
plum-tre vyne qwyns-tre hepe-tre thewe-thornys[5] ellarne
Prunus, vitis, coctanus, cornus, morusque, sambucus.
wythy warden-tre aspe chasteyn oke
Salix, volemus, tremulus, castania, quercus;
 beche burche populere asche elme
Fagus, lentiscus, populus, six fraxinus, ulmus;
 ewe boxe ver-tre wythy mapulle
Taxus, sic buxus, abies, ciler, acer addes.
 busche idem est brere chery-tre wyld vyne
Et rubus, dumus, tribulus, cerasus, oliaster;
 yvy pyne-tre jenupyr-tre wylde-vyne masere
Edera, pinus, juniparus, labruscaque, mirra.
bay-tre tre bowe more[6] or roote levys
Laurus, lignum, ramus, radix sunt arbore, frondes,

---

[1] The baselard was a long dagger, usually worn suspended at the girdle.

[2] The Anglo-Saxon *seax*.

[3] A dyer.

[4] In the dialects of the West of England a walnut is universally called a *bannut*. This is by much the earliest example of the word I have met with.

[5] The A.-S. *hefe-þorn* is usually explained as meaning the wild-briar, or dog-rose, and *ramnus* is given as its Latin equivalent. Perhaps it is intended here for the blackberry.

[6] *More*, a root, is also a word peculiar to the West of England.

METRICAL VOCABULARY.

      smokke   brechys   schyrt   gowne   a chymere
Est interula, bracce, camisia, toga, et jupa;
 a bond   hoode   braygurdylle   taberde
Instita, capicium, perysomaque, collobiumque;
   keyfe   cappe   pyllyon   hoose   vampey
Thenaque, caleptra, pilius, caligaque, pedana.
   cloke   sleve   coote   kyrtylle
Est armilansa, manica, tinica, tinicella;
 kotyn or pak-clothe   dobelat   pancher
Est bumbicinium vestis, diploydis, epifemur,
 pope   patryarke   cardynalle   buschope
Papa, patriarcha, cardinalis, presul, atque
archebyschope prelatte or byschop   suffrygan
Archipresul, antistes, suffraganius sit,
   chapyllayne   prest   idem est
Atque capellanus, sacerdos, presbiter addes,
  decon   subdeacon   benott   idem est
Diaconus, subdiaconus, exorsista, benedictus.
kyng emparowre prynce duke a lord of thowsond kny3tes
Rex, imperator, princeps, dux, et   ciliarcha;
  erle   baron   kny3th   juge   deacon
Comes, et baro, miles, judex, diaconusque.
  reve   baylé   uplond-man   cherle
Prepositus, ballivus, rusticus, et colobertus;
 towne-man   gentylman   bondeman   gentylman
Villicus, et proceres, nativus, et est generosus.

Explicit liber Equus caballus,[1] *quod Spencer R.*

---

[1] These words commence a line on p. 177, which begins in the MS. with a large initial letter; but I do not know why they are here given as the title of the whole.

NAMES OF THE PARTS OF THE HUMAN BODY.[1]

(OF THE SAME DATE AS THE PRECEDING.)

---

 a mowthe face chyn tothe throto tonge rofe of the mowthe
Os, facies, mentum, dens, guttur, lingua, palatum;
 berde browe brye[2] forehede tempelle lyppe
Barba, supercilium, cilium, frons, tempora, labrum.
 the lede   syȝt ye whyte of the ye appulle of the ye
Palpebra sunt, acies, oculus, albugo, pupilla.
 cop of the nose snevel of the nose the brygge of the nose nostrelle
Purula, pus nasi sunt, interfinia, naris.
 fore party of the hede myddul party nolle the brayne
Sinciput, interciput, occiput, ac cerabrum, pars
 hede scolle fore-top schade of the here ere
Est capitis, cranium, vertex, discrimen, et auris.
 cheke gummes   here
Faux, et jungive, cum frontinella, capillis.
 grystyl of the nose lap of the ere cheke-tothe
Est cartilago, sic legia, sic genuinus.
 pame of the hond juntys handus   cubyte a feme
Palme, juncture manibus sunt, ulna, lacertus;
 nayle fyngurys schuldur breste nekke
Ungues cum digitis, humerus, cum pectore, collum.
 arme-pytt fyste cubyte   blodde tete
Acella, pugnus, cubitus, cum sanguine, mamma;
 wombe bladdur bakke rybbe-bone rybbe
Venter, vesica, tergum, spondilia, costa.
  navyle syede flesche skynne buttok
Est umbilicus, latus, et caro, pelle, nates sunt.
 hert mylte longes long gutte gal kydney mydrefe mawe
Cor, splen, pulmo, lien, fel, ren, diafragma, jecurque.
 a narce thye schare bakke backe-bone arce-hoole
Anus, crus, pubes, dorsum, sic spina, podexque.
 smal-pypys[3] stomake   inwarde   lyver
Arterie, stomacus, post intestina, sic epar.
 whyrle-bone kneys knee-panne zeneiw
Vertebra cum genibus, sunt internodia, nervus;

---

[1] This is printed from the same manuscript as the preceding more general vocabulary, which it follows immediately as a sort of supplement (MS. Harl. No. 1002, fol. 116, v°).

[2] The eyelashes.

[3] A rather curious name for the arteries.

Assez par my la mesoun
taken of gres tyme
De treste du fermeyson.
Pus avyent diversetez en rost,
Eit checun autre de cost,
cranes   pokokes   swannes
Grues, pounes, e cygnes,
wilde-ges   gryses (porceaus) (hennes)
Owes, rosées,[1] porceus, gelyns.
Au tercez cours avient conyns en gravé,
E viaunde de Cypre enfundré,
De maces, e quibibes, e clous de orré,
Vyn blanc e vermayl à graunt plenté.
wodekok
Pus avoyunt fesauns, assez,[2] et perdriz,
feldefares larkes
Grives, alowes, e pluviers ben rostez;
E braoun, e crispes, e fritune;
Ke soucre roset poudra la temprune.
Après manger avyunt à graunt plenté,
Blaunche poudre, ou la grosse dragé.[3]
E d'autre nobleie à fusoun,
Ensi vous fynys ceo sermoun;
Kar de Fraunceis i ad assez,
De meynte manere dyversetez,
Dount le vous fynys, seynurs, ataunt,
A fitz Dieu vous comaund.

Ici finist la Doctrine monsire Gauter de Byblesworde.

---

[1] For these two words, the Sl. MS. reads *chevrels*, glossed *kydes*, and the Camb. MS. *chevereaus*, with the gloss *kides*.

[2] *Ascies*, glossed *wudkokes*, MS. Sl., and the MS. Camb. has nearly the same reading.

[3] The Arundel MS. ends with this word rather abruptly; the subsequent lines and the colophon at the end are given from the Sloane MS.

METRICAL VOCABULARY.[1]

(PERHAPS OF THE FOURTEENTH CENTURY.)

     stumlyth   yn harneys   i. purpura i. superbus
Cespitat in phaleris yppus, blattaque suppinus;
i. lingua   i. vino   i. sermo i. stulto
Glossa velud themato labat emus infatuato,
s. ille i. bonus i. in operacione   i. fidelis i. sermone
Qui calus in praxi simul est, et pisticus emo,
     i. laus   i. loquitur vel predicat
Illius[2] oda placet, hic recte theologizat,
           tresory   i. divitis
Qui cupide servas ypogeum gazophilacis.
         i. celestis   i. altas sedes
Cerdus ad uranici scandes algalmata regni.
falsos homines i. devoratores qui stant in falsis causis i. depredantes
Pseustes, ambrones, sicophantes, vispiliones,
                                   i. circumbunt
Stix et Cochitus, Lethe, Flagitonque rotabunt.
the hanches i. cervi i. capre   i. quoqume
Terga   laphi dorceque latus delata popine,
      i. aqua cocta   rosste   a payge of the keschyn
An sint elixa, sint assave, scit bene   lixa.
a stode[3]   i. generosi   everey i. sponsas
Bulla velud proceres, stola sic eburnea nuptas;
      i. lectum i. coopertorium i. ornat borde-clothe
Utque cubile thoral decusat, gausape mensam,
   a kervere   a surgyon or a chamerleyne
Cironomon mensis, lectis assistit   aleptes.
      fowlere   a murtherer of men derke hernys
Dumetis auceps latet, et sicarius   antris,
gracilis puer bysnevyllyd   colte i. villosus   i. hirsutus
Puseo   reumaticus, pullus lappatus et hirtus,

---

[1] This curious vocabulary is printed from a manuscript of the fifteenth century (MS. Harl. 1002, fol. 113, r°), but the text is in all probability of an earlier date. The name of Spencer is subscribed to the end of it, but names signed in this way are those more usually of the copyist than of the author. From the occurrence in the interlinear gloss of several words, such as *nullow* and *bannut*, peculiar to the dialects of the West of England and the Welsh border, we may perhaps conclude that the MS. was written in that part of the island. The Latin contains a rather large number of words adopted from the Greek.

[2] A Latin commentator states in the margin that this word has "Media corrupta causa metri."

[3] i. nodus in cingulo, Latin gloss.

ENGLISH VOCABULARY.

Hoc frumen, A' code.
Hic humerus, A' schuldyre.
Hoc brachium, A' arme.
Hic cubitus, A' helbow.
Hic musculus, A' brawne.
Hec sura, idem est.
Hec pulpa, idem est.
Hec manus, A' hande.
Hec palma, bola, et ir, idem sunt.
Hic pollex, A' thowme.
Hic digitus, A' fynger.
Hoc corpus, A' body.
Hoc dorsum, A' bake.
Hic venter, A' wambe.
Hec caro, A' flesche.
Hic pectus, A' breste.
Hoc corium, A' hyde.
Hec cutis, idem est.
Hic sanguis, A' blode.
Hic humor, idem est.
Hoc os, ossis, A' bone.
Hec medulla, A' marow.
Hec febra, A' wayne.
Hec vena, idem est.
Hoc palatum, A' palate.
Hic orexis, est anelitus oris.
Hic polipus, A' snotte.
Hec ulna est spatium inter manum et capud.
Hic nodus, A' knokylle.
Hoc epilacium, A' honde-mowle.[1]
Hec junctura, A' joynte.
Hec unquis, A' nayle.
Hec ungula, idem est.
Hec mamma, A' pappe.

Hec mamilla, idem est.
Hoc uber, idem est.[2]
Hic torax, A' brest-bone.
Hic umbelicus, A' nawelle.
Hic clunis, idem est.[3]
Hec nates, A' thees.
Hic lumbus, idem est.
Hec piga, idem est.
Hec pinguedo, A' grese.
Hic pirtomen, A' ars-holere.
Hec vulva, A' cuntte.
Hoc oilinetum, (?) A' mygrayne.
Hec tentigo, A' kykyre.
Hoc epar, A' lywer.
Hoc splen, A' mylte.
Hoc fel, A' galle.
Hic pulmo, A' lunggys.
Hic stomacus, A' stomak.
Hoc gecur, A' maw.
Hoc diafragma, A' myddere.[4]
Hoc ren, A' nere.[5]
Hoc viscus, A' bowelle.
Hoc percordium, idem est.
Hoc veretrum, A' pyntylle.
Hic priapus, est finis veretri.
Hic cirbus, A' hars-tharme.
Hoc femur, A' thee.
Hic popler, A' hamme.
Hoc genu, A' knee.
Hec tubia, A' schanke.
Hic pes, -dis, A' fote.
Hic talus, A' hele.
Hic artuculus, A' tho.
Hec cavilla, A' ankylle.
Hec anta, A' kne-bone.

---

[1] The honde-mowle appears to have been the palm of the hand. It is the gloss on copinole in Walter de Biblesworth. See before, p. 161.

[2] Another vocabulary in the same volume of MS. (MS. Reg. 17 C. xvii., fol. 38 v°.) gives "uber, -is, Anglice hyddere," the latter word no doubt representing the modern udder.

[3] The glossator has misinterpreted this word and the next. The Nominale in the same MS. (Reg. 17 C. xvii., fol. 39, r°) explains, "hec natis, Anglice luddockes."

[4] For mydderede, the midriff.

[5] An old name for the kidney, still preserved in the dialects of East Anglia, though it is more usually employed popularly to denote the fat of the kidneys.

Hoc mandibilum, A⁴ chewylle.¹
Hec fragus, A⁴ kne-borde.
Hec matrix est in qua involvitur puer.
Hec homopleta, A⁴ schulder-bane.
Hec allux, A⁴ grete to.
Hec acella, A⁴ harm-ole.
Hec varex, -cis, est quedam vena tendens a vertice capitis usque ad plantam, que si bedatur reddet hominem curvum.

NOMINA ANIMALIUM.

Hic et hec bos, A⁴ neete.
Hic trio, idem est.
Hic boviculus, A⁴ bullok.
Hec vacca, A⁴ kowe.
Hec jumenta, A⁴ que.
Hec junix, idem est.
Hic taurus, A⁴ bulle.
Hic vitulus, A⁴ calfe.
Hic equs, A⁴ horse.
Hec equa, A⁴ mare.
Hic caballus, A⁴ cart-hors.
Hoc equicium, A⁴ harres.
Hic equiferus, A⁴ wyld hors.
Hic dextrarius, A⁴ stede.
Hic mannus, A⁴ rownse.²
Hic bladius, A⁴ hackenay.
Hic equilas, idem est.
Hic palifridus, A⁴ palfray.
Hic tradarius, idem est.
Hic emissarius, A⁴ stalon.
Hic pullus, A⁴ fole.
Hec porca, A⁴ sowe.
Hic porcus, A⁴ swyne.
Hic porcellus, A⁴ grysc.

Hoc aper, A⁴ bore.
Hic cingulus, idem est.
Hic oderinsicus, A⁴ spaneʒeole.³
Hic leporarius, A⁴ grayhownd.
Hec licesta, A⁴ byche.
Hic canis, A⁴ dogge.
Hic molosus, A⁴ band-dogge.
Hic ancer, A⁴ gandyr.
Hec auca, A⁴ gosse.
Hic ancerulus, A⁴ geslyng.
Hec aucula, idem.
Hic gallus, A⁴ cocke.
Hec gallina, A⁴ henne.
Hic pullus, A⁴ chekyn.
Hic capo, A⁴ capon.
Hoc altile, idem.
Hic spado, -inis, idem.
Hic catus, A⁴ catte.
Hic mureligus, A⁴ idem.*
Hic pilax, idem.
Hic juba, A⁴ horse-mane.
Hec caprona, idem.
Hic dromedarius, A⁴ drowmondere.
Hic rato, A⁴ raton.
Hic sories, idem.
Hic mus, A⁴ mowse.
Hic ovis, A⁴ schepe.
Hic aries, A⁴ wedyr.
Hic gargia, A⁴ gymbure.⁴
Hic agnus, A⁴ lamme.
Hec ambigua, est ovis portans duos agnos.

NOMINA ANIMALIUM FERARUM.

Hic leo, A⁴ lyon.
Hec liona, A⁴ lyonys.

---

¹ *Chewylle*, for *chowl*, or *jowl*, the jaw.
² *Rounse.* A rouncy is generally interpreted as meaning a common hackney horse. Thus, in the romance of Ipomydon (Weber, Met. R., vol. ii., p. 340), when the hero went to disguise himself as an half-witted and clownish fellow—

Armure he toke that was rusty,
And horsyd hym on an old rounsey

³ A spaniel.
⁴ In Lincolnshire, they still call a female sheep which has been twice shorn a *gimber*; in the north of England it is called a *gimmer*.

188   ENGLISH VOCABULARY.

Hic lupus, A^e wlfe.
Hic lepus, A^e hare.
Hic wlpes, A^e foxe.
Hec mustela, A^e weysyl.
Hic fetonarus, A^e fulmerd.
Hic erinacius, A^e hurchon.
Hec melota, A^e broke.[1]
Hic taxus, idem.
Hec talpa, A^e molle.
Hic pardus, A^e leparde.
Hec parda, est femella.
Hic pardus, est qui generat cum leona.
Hic cervus, A^e harte.
Hec cerva, A^e hynde.
Hic hinulus, A^e fawne.
Hec simea, A^e nape.
Hic ursus, A^e bere.
Hic urcus, A^e buke.
Hoc elephas, -tis, A^e elyfawnte.
Hec pantera, A^e pantere, cum multis coloribus.*
Hic et hec linx, est animal habens oculos acutos.
Hic scurellus, A^e a squyrylle.
Hic sirogrillus, idem.
Hic cuniculus, A^e conninge.
Hic zenozephalus, A^e maremusset.
Hic furestus, vel forestus, A^e forest.[2]

NOMINA AVIUM.

Hic fornix, A^e wodekok.
Hec orna, idem.
Hec philomena, A^e nyghtyngale.
Hec lucar, i. lucia.
Hec nicticorax, A^e nyght-crake.[3]
Hec avia, idem.

Hec ardua, A^e heyrune.
Hec columba, A^e dowwe.
Hic palumbus, A^e stoke-dowef.
Hic maviscus, A^e mawysse.
Hec fidedula, idem.
Hec merges, A^e cote.
Hic sturnus, A^e sterlyng.
Hic regulus, A^e wrenne.
Hic sperrus, idem.
Hic carduelis, A^e goldefynche.
Hic corvus, A^e crawe.
Hec aquila, A^e neggle.
Hec milvus, A^e glede.[4]
Hic pascer, A^e sparow.
Hec upipa, A^e wype.[5]
Hic tercellus, A^e hawke.
Hic prepes, idem.
Hic nisus, A^e sperhawke.
Hic ancipiter, A^e goshawke.
Hic erodius, A^e gerfawcune.
Hic graculus, A^e jay.
Hic citacus, A^e papinjay.
Hec alauda, A^e larke.
Hic arundo, A^e swalo.
Hec nodula, A^e kaa.[6]
Hec bubo, -is, A^e nowle.
Hic corvus, A^e rawyn.
Hic frondator, A^e tytmase.
Hec olor, A^e swane.
Hic signus, idem.
Hic grus, A^e crane.
Hic cuculus, A^e cucko.
Hec frigella, A^e robynet red-brest.[7]
Hec ciconia, A^e storke.
Hec marula, est avis habens nigrum rostrum.

---

[1] The *broke* was the badger.
[2] The ferret.
[3] The *caprimulgus Europæus*, still called in Yorkshire a *night-crow*. Its more usual name is *night-jar*.
[4] A kite. The Anglo-Saxon name. See p. 29.
[5] The lapwing.
[6] A chough. The A.-S. *ceo*.
[7] *i. e.*, "little Robin" redbreast. It is the earliest instance of the use of this popular name that I have met with. Robin was a common appellation of affectionate familiarity.

Hic pellicar, A⁶ pellicane.
Hic rostellus, A⁶ spynke.
Hec frugella, A⁶ roke.
Hec agalauda, A⁶ plowere.
Hic perdix, A⁶ pertrycke.
Hec fuliga, A⁶ semawe.
Hic campester, A⁶ feldfare.
Hic merulus, A⁶ marlyon.
Hic cornix, A⁶ crawe.
Hic pavo, A⁶ pacok.
Hic coturnix, A⁶ more-hene.
Hic vultur, A⁶ grype.[1]
Hic fasianus, A⁶ fesant.
Hoc rustrum, A⁶ nebbe.[2]
Hic mergus, A⁶ cote.
Hec qualia, A⁶ quayle.
Hic pellicanus, A⁶ pellycane.
Hic fenix, A⁶ fenys.
Hic capus, A⁶ muskett.[3]

NOMINA PISCIUM.

Hoc allec, A⁶ heryng.
Hic salmo, A⁶ salmon.
Hoc mugyl, idem.
Hic uronoscopus, A⁶ thornbak.
Hic fundulus, A⁶ playsse.
Hic pecten, id.
Hic luceus, A⁶ pyke.
Hic dentrix, idem.
Hic lucellus, A⁶ pyckerylle.
Hic gamerus, A⁶ spyrlyng.
Hic silurus, A⁶ loche.
Hic scorpio, A⁶ stytlyng.[4]
Hec muprena, A⁶ lamprune.
Hec lampada, A⁶ lampray.
Hic caput, A⁶ caboche.[5]

Hec anguilla, A⁶ nele.
Hic cancer, A⁶ crabbe.
Hec balena, A⁶ qwalle.
Hic cetus, idem.
Hec ceta, idem.
Hoc cete, idem.
Hic congruus, A⁶ conggyre.
Hic epimora, est piscis qui moritur eodem die quo nascitur.
Hoc cochile, est quilibet piscis obtecta.
Hoc ostrium, A⁶ ostyre.
Hic megarus, A⁶ makyrelle.
Hic ypotamus, est marinus.
Hec rochea, A⁶ roche.
Hic brumillus, A⁶ brone.[6]
Hec tortuga, A⁶ wylke.
Hic rumbus, A⁶ storjon.
Hic clamitus, A⁶ wytyng.
Hic torpedo, est piscis habens multos pedes.
Hec phoca, A⁶ porpas.
Hec delphin, A⁶ sawmone.
Hec merula, A⁶ lamprone.
Hec rogaterea, A⁶ thornbacke.
Hic textus, A⁶ tenche.
Hic mullus, A⁶ codlyng.
Hic codlingus, idem.
Hec perca, A⁶ perche.
Hec gamorus, A⁶ hornebek.
Hic gobio, A⁶ gojune.
Hoc turtur, A⁶ turbote.
Hic polipus, A⁶ lopstere.
Hec conca, A⁶ cochilt.

---

[1] *Grype* was an old name for the vulture, and is not unfrequently found in that sense in the early metrical romances, though it is sometimes used to signify a griffin.

[2] A bird's neb or beak.

[3] The male of the sparrowhawk.

[4] The stickleback.

[5] The bulhead, or miller's-thumb, called in old French *chabot*.

[6] *Brone*, the bream.

NOMINA VERMIUM.

Hec cerpigo, -nis, A*ᵉ* regworme.
Hec lacerta, A*ᵉ* newte.
Hec uria, est pediculus porci.
Hec lens, -dis, A*ᵉ* nyte.
Hec salamandra, A*ᵉ* cryket.
Hic grillius, idem.
Hec apes, A*ᵉ* bee.
Hec saguisuga, i. irundo.
Hec pala, A*ᵉ* wode.
Hec sicada, A*ᵉ* gyrssoppe.
Hec irania, A*ᵉ* erane.[1]
Hec amittena, A*ᵉ* schep-tyke.
Hec culex, A*ᵉ* knate.
Hic fucus, A*ᵉ* drane.
Hec vaspa, A*ᵉ* waspe.
Hic papilio, A*ᵉ* butterfle.
Hec teredo, est vermis corodens ligna.
Hic cimex, A*ᵉ* mawke.[2]
Hec tinea, A*ᵉ* moke.[3]
Hic cirus, A*ᵉ* hand-worme.
Hic scarabeus, A*ᵉ* wode.
Hec incedula, A*ᵉ* glyde-worme.[4]
Hec noctirula, A*ᵉ* idem.
Hec noctuluca, idem.
Hec tanterida, est vermis terre.
Hic emigramus, est vermis capitis.
Hic lumbricus, est vermis ventri.
Hic tarus, est vermis lardi.
Hic bombex, A*ᵉ* sylk-worme.
Hic bufo, A*ᵉ* tade.
Hic erinacius, A*ᵉ* nurchon.
Hic glis, -ris, A*ᵉ* dormowse.
Hec formica, A*ᵉ* pysmyre.

Hec testugo, A*ᵉ* snele.
Hic limax, -cis, idem.

NOMINA HERBARUM.

Hoc petrocillum, A*ᵉ* percylle.
Hoc ciler, A*ᵉ* mynte.
Hec menta, idem.
Hoc nausticium, A*ᵉ* water-kyrs.
Hoc milifolium, A*ᵉ* mylfoile.
Hec beta, A*ᵉ* bete.
Hic ysopus, A*ᵉ* ysoppe.
  Ysopus est harba, ysopo spergitur unda.
Hec altea, A*ᵉ* wyld malle.
Hec saliunca, A*ᵉ* wyne.
Hec vepres,
Hec uva, A*ᵉ* grapys.
Hic calamus, A*ᵉ* rede.
Hec rosa, A*ᵉ* rose.
Hoc lilium, A*ᵉ* lylle.
Hec minifera, A*ᵉ* water-lylle.
Hec embroca, A*ᵉ* maythe.[5]
Hic daucus, A*ᵉ* clap-wype.[6]
Hoc olus, -ris, A*ᵉ* worte.
Hoc nugudere, A*ᵉ* calstok.
Hic caulus, A*ᵉ* uwle (?) or thyme.
Hec cuna, A*ᵉ* croppe.[7]
Hec saliva, A*ᵉ* salwe.
Hec urtica, A*ᵉ* nettylle.
Hec pimpinella, A*ᵉ* primerolle.
Hoc ligustrum, idem.
Hoc pringrius, idem.
Hec viola, A*ᵉ* wyolet.
Hoc vaccinium, A*ᵉ* cowsokulle.[8]
Hec papaver, A*ᵉ* chesbolle.[9]

---

[1] *Erane*, or *irane*, from the A.-N., was a common name for a spider.

[2] *Mawke*, a maggot, still in use in the northern dialects.

[3] A moth.

[4] The glow-worm.

[5] Camomile (the *anthemis cotula* of botanists), still called in some districts *may weed*; the A.-S. *mageða*. See the A.-S. Vocabularies.

[6] *Clap-wype*. *Daucus* is understood to mean the parsnip.

[7] Perhaps it should be *cima*, the crop, or top, of a plant. The Catholicon has "a croppe, *cima*."

[8] Apparently another name for the cowslip.

[9] *Chesbolle* was an old name for the poppy.

Hoc omella, idem.
Hic felix, -cis, A^e brakyn.
Hoc solsequium, A^e sawsykylle.
Hoc ditaneum, A^e dytan.
Hoc columbina, A^e colybyn.
Hec lactuca, A^e letys.
Hic muscus, A^e muske.
Hic carduus, A^e thystylle.
Hoc gramen, A^e bent.[1]
Hec murica, A^e wormine brome.
Hec edera, A^e iwyn.
Hec licoricia, A^e licorys.
Hoc alleum, A^e garle.
Hoc sinapium, A^e warkecok.
Hec sepula, A^e chesbolle.
Hec salgea, A^e sawge.
Hec selidonia, A^e solydyne.
Hoc feniculum, A^e fynkylle.
Hec malva, A^e malle.
Hoc apium, A^e the.
Hoc trifolium, A^e hart-claver.
Hic sicassis, idem.
Hoc pentifolium, A^e filife.
Hoc sirpillum, A^e petergrys.[2]
Hoc piper, A^e pepyre.
Hoc siminum, A^e comyne.
Hoc synamomum, A^e canelle.
Hoc strigillum, A^e morelle.
Hoc solatrum, idem.
Hec vervena, A^e warwayn.
Hec agremonia, A^e agremoyne.
Hec pimpernella, A^e pimpernolle.
Hec sintecula, A^e synthon.
Hec scandur, A^e madyr.
Hic sendo, idem.
Hec pionia, A^e pyon.

Hic tintimalius, A^e spowrge.
Hec rapa, A^e rape.
Hoc bacar, A^e nepe.
Hic crocus, A^e safurroun.
Hic plantago, A^e waybred.
Hoc raparium, A^e raddyk.
Hic tipus, A^e homelok.
Hec secuta, idem.
Hic cardo, A^e cardoun.[3]
Hic carduus, A^e tasylle.
Hic arundo, A^e rede.
Hec canna, A^e cane.
Hec carix, -cis, A^e segge.
Hec papirio, A^e resche-busk.
Hic junccus, A^e resche.
Hic sirpus, idem.
Hic papirius, idem.
Hoc borago, A^e borage.
Hoc sepe, A^e honʒon.
Hec concilida, A^e consaude.
Hoc absinthium, A^e wormode.
Hec costus, A^e coste.
Hec febrifuga, A^e fevyrfew.
Hec gensta, A^e gromylle.[4]
Hec lappa, A^e clete.[5]
Hec endiva, A^e endywe.

NOMINA ARBORUM.

Regula est quod omnia nomina arborum sunt feminini generis exceptis quatuor, hic oliaster, et hic piaster, hic rubus, et hic dumus. Hic oliaster est uva sterilis.

Hec quarcus, A^e ake.
Hec volemus, A^e permayn-tre.
Hec ilex, est juvenis quarcus.
Hec sambuca, A^e hyllor-tre.[6]

---

[1] The word *bent* was applied usually to the long coarse grass growing on the moors, but often in a more general sense to grass of all kinds.

[2] *Serpillum* is understood as meaning, in the older vocabularies, wild thyme.

[3] *Cardon* (Lat. *carduus*), the old French name for the thistle; in modern French, *chardon*.

[4] *Gromylle*, the plant now called *gromwell*, the *lithospermum officinale* of botanists.

[5] The clote, or yellow water-lilly.

[6] *Hyllor*, the elder, still called in some parts of England a *hilder-tree*.

Hec taxus, A^c haw-tre, new-tre.
Hec corolus, A^c hesylle-tre.
Hec avelana, A^c walnot-tre.
Hec arbutus, A^c crab-tre.
Hec fraxinus, A^c hesche-tre.
Hec pepulus, A^c popul-tre.
Hec ascer, -ris, A^c mapulle-tre.
Hec abies, A^c fyrre-tre.
Hec prunus, A^c plum-tre.
Hec castania, A^c chestan-tre.[1]
Hec ficus, A^c fyke-tre, *vel fructus*.

Nux, avelana, pirus, glans, et castania, ficus,
Fructum cum ligno sub eodem nomine signo.

Hec mesculus, A^c mcle-tre.
Hec sorbus, A^c opynhars-tre.[2]
Hec sirasus, A^c cheri-tre.
Hec oliva, A^c olyf-tre.
Hec sentis, est spina.
Hec silex, A^c wyllo-tre.
Hec lentiscus, A^c byrke-tre.
Hec coccinus, A^c quoyne-tre.
Hec tremulus, A^c hespe-tre.
Hec malus, A^c apul-tre.
Hec pomus, idem.
Hec tribulus, A^c brame.[3]
Hec vepres, idem.
Hec singinerperus, est quedam arbor cujus cyneres volunt ignem servare per annum.

Signiperus quod glens pir tibi dicitur arbor,
De gigno, -is, et pir, quod dicitur ignis,
Et cujus cyneres involent ardere per annum.

Hoc vimen, A^c oscre.
Hic viburius, A^c idem.
Hec cornus, A^c pet-tre.
Hec morus, A^c mulbery-tre.
Hec tilia, A^c baste-tre.

Hec ussis, A^c olyn-tre.
Hec damasenus, A^c **damyssyn-tre.**
Hec cedrus, A^c **sydyre-tre,** *et est talis nature quod nunquam putrescet in aqua nec in terra*.
Hec cipressus, est arbor odorissimus et tepida, et habet naturam et rubrum colorem, A^c cypyr-tre.

NOMINA FRUCTUUM.

Hoc pomum, A^c apulle.
Hec nux, A^c notte.
Hic nuclius, A^c kyrnelle.
Hec avelena, A^c walnot.
Hoc pirum, A^c pere.
Hec glans, A^c acorne.
Hoc ciresum, A^c chery.
Hoc volemum, A^c permayne.[4]
Hoc prunum, A^c plumme.
Hoc stragum, A^c strabery.
Hic ficus, A^c fyke.
Hec racemus, A^c rasyn.
Hec uvapassa, A^c idem.
Hec uva, A^c grape.
Hoc sorbum, A^c hopynhars.
Hoc malum granatum, A^c **pounkarnet.**[5]
Hoc malum punicum, idem.
Hoc coccinum, A^c quoyne.[6]
Hoc masculum, A^c orange.
Hoc cornum, A^c pete.

NOMINA PERTINENCIA ECCLESIE.

Hoc delebrum, i. ecclesia.
Hoc altare, i. ara.
Hic calix, A^c chalys.
Hec patena, A^c patent.

---

[1] *Chestan-tre*, the chestnut. See before, the note on p. 33.
[2] See before, p. 32.
[3] *i. e.*, a bramble.
[4] A sort of apple, of which Drayton speaks as being a modern importation into our **island**.

The **pearemaine**, which to France long ere to us was knowne,
Which careful frut'rers now have denizend our owne.
Polyolb., Song xviii.

[5] The pomegranate.
[6] *Quoyne*, or *coyne*, the quince.

ENGLISH VOCABULARY.

Hic sercophagus, i. petra.
Hec tumba, idem.
Hec libitina, A^c bere.
Hoc feretrum, idem.
Hoc tribulum, A^e sensours.
Hoc tus, A^e cense.
Hec ascera, A^c a lytil chyp.
Hec campana, A^e belle.
Hoc tintinabilum, A^e lytylle belle.
Hoc ventilogium, A^e wedercok.
Hec ymago, A^e ymage.
Hoc semitorium, A^c kyrgarth.[1]
Hoc marmor, A^e marbulle.
Hec candela, A^e candylle.
Hoc candelabrum, A^c candylstyk.
Hoc campanile, A^e stepulle.
Hoc aspersorium, A^e strynkylle.[2]
Hic ysopus, A^c idem est.
Hic ambo, -is, A^e letrune.[3]
Hoc campanare, A^e bel-howse.
Hoc oblatum, A^c obley.
Hoc antiphonarium, A^c anfenare.
Hoc missale, A^c mes-bok.
Hoc gradale, A^c grayel.
Hoc troperium, A^c tropure.
Hoc martilogium, A^c martilage.
Hec bibleoteca, A^c bybulle.
Hoc armariolum, A^e almery.
Hoc sacrarium, A^c sacrary.
Hoc orologium, A^c orlage.
Hoc vitrum, A^c glasse.
Hoc sudarium, A^c sudary.
Hec cera, A^c wax.
Hec cancella, A^c chawnsylle.
Hic corus, idem est.
Tres sunt partes columne, talus, stilus, et epistilium; vasis est fundamentum, stilus est media pars, epistilium est superior pars.

Hoc superpelicium, A^c surplys.
Hec crisma, A^c creme.[4]
Hoc crismatorum, A^c crismator.
Hec alba, A^c haube.
Hec stola, A^c stole.
Hec crux, A^c crosse.
Hoc lavatorium, A^c lavatory.
Hec fons, A^c welle.[5]
Hic cereus, A^e serge.
Hic lampas, A^c lampe.
Hic absconsus, A^c sconse.[6]
Hec lucerna, A^c lantyrne.
Hoc pulpitum, A^c polepyt.
Hec fiola, A^c fiolle.
Hoc oleum, A^c oyle.
Hec pixis, A^c boyst.[7]
Hoc alabaustrum, idem est.
Hec hostia, est corpus Christi.
Hoc viaticum, idem est.
Hoc restiarium, A^c rewystre.
Hec restis, est corda.
Hoc fedus, idem.
Hic laqueus, idem.
Hic funiculus, idem.
Hic batillus, A^c clapyre.
Hoc manutergium, A^c towelle
Hec peruria, A^c perrore.
Hoc velum, A^c wayle.
Hic amittus, A^c amytte.
Hic tiera, idem est.
Hec fanulla, A^c fanone.
Hic manipulus, idem est.
Hec zona, A^c gyrdylle.
Hec poderis, A^c rochytt.
Hec infula, A^c chesibylle
Hoc ostrum, i. purpura.
Hoc ordinale, A^c ordinalle.
Hic ordinarius, idem est.

---

[1] The churchyard, still called a *kirk garth* in the north.
[2] The holy-water sprinkler, or *aspersoir*.
[3] The lectern, or reading desk.
[4] The crism, or consecrated oil.
[5] More correctly the font.
[6] A sort of candlestick made to be attached to the wall. The word is still in use for such candlesticks in the north of England. The box for holding the oil &c., a p. ?.

NOMINA ARTIFICIORUM.

Hic excubus, A^e wayte.
Hic liricen, qui canit in lira.
Hic secuticen, qui canit in scituta.
Hic tibicen, qui canit in tubia.
Hic monetarius, qui facit monetam.
Hic aurifaber, A^e goldesmythe.
Hic candidarius, A^e lawnder.
Hic, hec formicapola, venditor unguentorum.
Hic sementarius, A^e mason.
Hic littamus, idem est.
Hic mango, A^e horse-mownger.
Hic mores, i. quod stultus.
Hic sissor, A^e tayleȝour.
Hic carpentarius, A^e kart-wryght.
Hic molendinarius, A^e mylur.
Hic frunes, A^e barkare.[1]
Hic tannator, idem est.
Hic serdo, idem est.
Hic pandoxatrix, A^e bacstare.
Hic architector, A^e thekare.[2]
Hic cuparius, A^e cowpare.
Hic aliator, A^e hussardore.
Hic triculator, A^e tresorre.[3]
Hic tesaurarius, idem est.
Hic figulus, A^e potter.
Hic pistor, A^e backstare.
Hic carnifex, A^e bochere.
Hic seroticarius, A^e glowere.[4]
Hic pelliparius, A^e schynnere.
Hic scriba, A^e chaunsyllere.
Hic cancellarius, idem est.
Hic sinescallus, A^e stewered.
Hic vicecomes, A^e scheryf.
Hic comes, A^e herrylle.

Hec comitissa, A^e cowntasse.
Hic baro, A^e baron.
Hec baronissa, A^e baronys.
Hic abbas, A^e abott.
Hic prior, A^e pryor.
Hic monacus, A^e monk.
Hic canonicus, A^e chanon.
Hic opilio, A^e scheperd.
Hic subulcus, A^e swynard.
Hic bubulcus, A^e hoxhard.
Hic ortolanus, A^e gardyner.
Hic nugator, A^e trifulere.
Hic pincerna A^e botelere.
Hic, hec advena, A^e comelyng.[5]
Hic temerarius, A^e folehardy.
Hic cocus, A^e coke.
Hic coquinarius, idem est.
Hic lixa, idem est quod lixo, A^e quystrone.
Hic barbitansor, A^e barbur.
Hic auceps, A^e fowlere.
Hic piscator, A^e fyschere.
Hec pectrix, A^e kemster.
Hic textor, A^e webstere.
Hic fullo, A^e fullare.
Hic faber, A^e smythe.
Hec fabrissa, A^e smyt-wyfe.
Hic recors, A^e cowharde.
Hic apotecarius, A^e spycere.
Hic ninarius,[6] A^e cokwalde.
Hic triumphus,[7] A^e constabulle.
Hic alutarius, A^e cordewenere.
Hic scellarius, A^e sadyllar.
Hic pustularius, A^e botullere.
Hic lorimarius, A^e gyrdylhar.
Hic capistrius, A^e helterer.[8]

---

[1] *i.e.*, a tanner.
[2] Literally a thatcher.
[3] *Tresorre*, a treasurer.
[4] A glover. The Latin word should be *cirotecarius*, for *chirothecarius*.
[5] The common name for a stranger or guest.
[6] *Ninnarius.* This low-Latin word, sometimes spelt *minarius*, is usually employed to signify what we call a *wittol*, or contented cuckold.
[7] *Triumphus.* This word is not found in this sense in Ducange.
[8] *Helterer*, one who makes halters.

ENGLISH VOCABULARY.

Hic archarius, A^e bowere.
Hic pannarius, A^e drapure.
Hic cicarius, est ille qui facit cicas.[1]
Hic mercator, A^e marchand.
Hic institor, idem est.
Hic fleobotomator, A^e blode-later.
Hic scarificator, A^e carsare.[2]
Hic tonsor, A^e cuttere.
Hic rasor, A^e shawere.
Hic sitator, A^e somundare.[3]
Hic edituus, est custos domus.
Hic sortilegus, A^e wyche.
Hec siren, A^e meremaydyn.
Hic eruginator, A^e forbushere.[4]
Hic armiger, A^e sqwyere.
Hic latro,[5] idem est.
Hic scutifer, idem est
Hic sitharista, A^e harpure.
Hic sitharizo, idem est.

NOMINA FLUMINUM.

Hoc mare, A^e see.
Hoc pelagus, idem.
Hoc fretum, idem.
Hoc equor, idem.
Hoc altum, idem.
Hic fluvius, idem.
Hic cathaclismus, inundacio aque.
Hic fons, A^e welle.
Hic puteus, A^e pytt.
Hec limpha, A^e water.

Hec latex, idem.
Hic rivus, A^e syke.[6]
Hoc vivarium, A^e wywere.
Hoc stagnum, A^e poynde.
Hoc medianum, est spacium inter aquas.
Hec piscina, A^e pole.
Hoc amnis, est aqua tantum precens.

NOMINA METALLORUM.

Hoc aurum, A^e golde.
Hoc argentum, A^e sylwor.
Hoc es, -ris, A^e brasse.
Hoc plumbum, A^e lede.
Hoc ferrum, A^e yryn.
Hoc electrum, A^e pewtyre.
Hec calibs, A^e stele.
Hoc stagnum, A^e tyne.
Hoc auricalcum, A^e latone.[7]
Hoc cuprum, A^e copurre.

NOMINA ARMORUM.

Hec spata, A^e fawchon.
Hic pugio, A^e myscrecord[8]
Hec fustis, hic baculus, idem sunt.
Hec sudes, idem.
Hec lorica, A^e hawbyrgon.
Hec clava, A^e mase.
Hec galea, A^e helme.
Hec cassis, idem.
Hec ensis, A^e swerde.
Hic gladius, idem.

---

[1] *Sicarius* (incorrectly written *cicarius*) is here used for one who makes *sicas*, or daggers.

[2] *Carsare.* I have not met with this word before. The practice of scarification was extensively employed by the mediæval surgeons.

[3] *i. e.*, a somner.

[4] *Forbushere.* This was a business of considerable importance when armour and arms were in general use, and were in continual need of furbishing, or scrubbing. The name Frobisher is probably derived from it. See before, p. 124.

[5] This is a very extraordinary use of the word *latro*.

[6] *Syke* is still used in the dialects of the north of England to signify a small stream or gutter.

[7] The metal formerly called in English *laten*, or *latten*, from the French *laiton*, was a compound of copper, very much resembling brass, which was extensively used in the middle ages, but the exact composition of which seems not now to be known.

[8] *Myscrecord.* This name was given to a thin bladed dagger worn by the warrior, and used to dispatch one who was dangerously wounded, intended, as it is said, to imply that this was an act of mercy.

Hec gesa, A^e gysserne.[1]
Hoc telum, A^e darte.
Hoc jaculum, idem.
Hoc missele, idem.
Hoc pilum, idem est.
Hec balista, A^e awblast.[2]
Hoc petillum, A^e bolte.
Hec petulio, idem.
Hic tripolus, idem.
Hic bipennis, A^e twybyl.
Hic clipeus, A^e scholde.
Hoc scutum, idem.
Hec lancea, A^e spere.
Hec hasta, idem.
Hic cuspis, A^e poynte.
Hec catepulta, a brad-harrow.[3]
Hec feretra, A^e qwywere.
Hec pelta, A^e boculere.
Hec umbo, -nis, A^e bose.
Hec antile, A^e hulnase.
Hec cathena, idem.
Hic arcus, A^e bow.
Hic tropheus, A^e bawdryk.
Hec cica, A^e misericord.
Hec funda, A^e slyng.
Hec lorax, A^e haburjone.
Hic mucro, A^e swerd.
Hec securis, A^e axe.
Hec securicula, A^e hachytt.
Hoc braciolum, A^e brasor.[4]
Hoc brachiale, idem.
Hec targea, A^e targett.

NOMINA ORNAMENTORUM.

Hec camicia, A^e sarke.

Hec inchila, A^e rochett.
Hoc femorale, A^e breke.
Hec bracce, -arum, idem.
Hec tunica, A^e cote.
Hec supertunica, A^e surkote.
Hec caliga, A^e hose.
Hec pedana, A^e wampe.[5]
Hec formula, A^e last.
Hoc formipedium, idem.
Hoc perplicar, A^e gartere.
Hoc subligar, idem.
Hoc lumbare, A^e brekgyrdylle.
Hoc perizoma, idem.
Hec toga, A^e gowne.
Hec linistema, A^e tarteryne.[6]
Hec lacuna, est extremitas vestis.
Hoc gremium, A^e scyrtte.
Hoc fimbrium, A^e hemme.
Hec pera, A^e strype.
Hoc presegmen, A^e screde.
Hec armilansa, A^e cloke.
Hec astita, A^e rokytte.
Hec tena, A^e howe.
Hec tenea, A^e tappe.
Hoc reticulum, A^e kelle.[7]
Hoc sertum, A^e garland.
Hoc capellum, A^e hatte.
Hec mitra, A^e mytyre.
Hec galliare, idem.
Hec nata, idem.
Hec laurea, A^e crowne.
Hoc dyadema, idem.
Hec corona, idem.
Hec manica, A^e myttan.
Hoc epitogium, A^e cowrteby.[8]

---

[1] The *gisarme,* or *giserne,* was the bill or battle-axe. It has been identified with the Latin *gesa* by an older authority, the commentator on John de Garlande. See before, p. 131.

[2] *Awblast,* the arbalest, or crossbow.

[3] A broad-arrow was distinguished by a large forked head.

[4] *Brasor,* the brasser, or armour for the arm.

[5] *Vampe,* or *vampy,* bottoms of hose covering the foot; or, perhaps here, the upper leather of a boot.

[6] Tarterine is described as a kind of silk stuff, said to have been so named because it was obtained from the Tartars.

[7] *Kelle,* a covering of network for the head.

[8] A *courtby,* or *courtpy,* was a short cloak of coarse cloth.

ENGLISH VOCABULARY.

Hoc limpidium, idem.
Hoc bombacilium, idem.
Hec capa, A⁵ cope.
Hec clavus, A⁵ mantylle.
Hoc pallium, idem.
Hec lacerna, idem.
Hec carelta, A⁵ lasse.[1]
Hec caxacalla, idem.
Hoc stropheum, A⁵ gyrdylle.
Hic balteus, idem.
Hoc singulum, idem.
Hec ligula, A⁵ garter.
Hec corigia, A⁵ thowyng.[2]
Hoc braccale, A⁵ brygyrdylle.
Hic loculus, A⁵ purse.
Hoc marsupium, idem.
Hic ocria, A⁵ bote.
Hic sotularis, A⁵ scho.
Hoc antepedale, A⁵ wampe.
Hoc pedium, idem.
Hic pero, -ri, A⁵ wolyng.[3]
Hec mantica, A⁵ male.
Hec zonata, idem.
Hoc redimentum, est ornamentum mulieris.
Hoc discriminale, est ornamentum capitis.
Hec caracalla, A⁵ kelle.[4]
Hoc peplum, A⁵ wympulle.
Hoc tricatorium, A⁵ tressure.
Hec vitta, A⁵ bend.
Hoc servale, idem est quod sertum.
Hec inauris, est annulus in aure.
Hoc armillum, est ornamentum.

NOMINA INSTRUMENTORUM AULE.

Hec aula, A⁵ halle.
Hec mensa, A⁵ borde.
Hic tristellus, A⁵ tresto.
Hoc bancarium, A⁵ banquere.
Hoc dorsarium, A⁵ dosur.
Hec buda, A⁵ natte.
Hoc scorium, idem.
Hec cillaba, A⁵ tabulle dormawnd.[5]
Hec pelvis, A⁵ basyn.
Hoc lavatorium, A⁵ laworre.
Hic ignis, A⁵ fyr.
Hic focus, idem.
Hic pir, idem.
Hoc focarium, A⁵ harthe.
Hec fax, -cis, A⁵ brande.
Hec torris, idem.
Hec teda, idem.
Hic tissio, idem.
Hoc ricrepoforilium, A⁵ 30le-stok.[6]
Hic, hec ciner, A⁵ askys.
Hec andena, A⁵ awndyren.
Hoc sedile, A⁵ lang-sedylle.[7]
Hec cathedra, A⁵ chayere.
Hec forceps, A⁵ tungges.
Hoc scannum, A⁵ bynke.[8]
Hoc stabellum, A⁵ stole.
Hoc fultrum, A⁵ cosyn.
Hoc focale, A⁵ wode to the fyre.
Hic culigna, A⁵ pare belows.
Hec antipera, A⁵ serene.

NOMINA PERTINENCIA AD PISCERNAM.

Panis fluentatus. A⁵ gur-bred.

---

[1] *Lasse*, a cassock.
[2] *Thowyng*, a thong.
[3] *Wolyng*, a leathern sack.
[4] *Kelle* signifies properly a smock, or petticoat; perhaps it is used here for what we call a smock-frock.
[5] *Table dormaunt* appears to have been the name for a permanent table in the hall, as distinguished from the board which was placed temporarily upon trestles. The Latin *cillaba* appears to have been applied to a round table.
[6] What is still called in the north a *yule-clog*, or *yule-log*.
[7] The long wooden seat with back and arms, which is still called a *settle*.
[8] *Bynke*, a bench—the usual seat in the hall.

Panis furfurius, A^e bran-bred.
Panis ordiccius, A^e barly-bred.
Panis triticius, A^e whet-bred.
Panis similaginius, A^e payn-mayn.¹
Panis fabicius, A^e bene-bred.
Panis pisacius, A^e pes-bred.
Panis avenacius, A^e hafyr-bred.²
Panis siliginius, A^e tharf-bred.³
Panis sigalinus, idem.
Panis muscidus, A^e mowlde-bred.
Hoc libum, A^e wastelle.⁴
Hic artocopus, A^e symnelle.⁵
Hic panis, A^e lof of bred.
Hic lesca, A^e scywe.⁶
Hic torcellus, A^e cake.
Hoc minutal, A^e cantelle.
Hic mucor, A^e mowlde.
Hec briba, A^e lumpe.
Hoc frustrum, A^e mese, gobyt.
Hoc ferculum, idem.
  Farcla sunt frustra, dicuntur fercula vasa.
Hec mica, A^e crowm.
Hec mappa, A^e borde-clathe.
Hoc gausape, A^e sanap.⁷
Hic morsus, A^e bytte.
Hoc manutergium, A^e towelle.
Hoc selarium, A^e celare.⁸
Hoc sal, A^e salte.

Hoc cocliar, A^e spone.
Hec sporticula, A^e relef.⁹
Hoc dolium, A^e townne.
Hic uter, A^e buffylle.¹⁰
Hic collator, A^e costylle.¹¹
Hoc murra, A^e masere.
Hoc vinum, A^e wyne.
Hoc merum, A^e mede.
Hoc claretum, A^e clarett.
Hec servicia, A^e ale.
Hec selia, idem est.
Hic ciphus, A^e coppe.
Hoc cooperculum, A^e cowerkylle.
Hec fex, A^e dregges.
Hoc nectar, A^e pyment.
Hoc armariolum, A^e almere.
Hoc sissorium, A^e trenchur.
Hic casius, A^e chese.
Hoc cepe, A^e honʒon.¹²
  Casius et cepe veniunt ad prandia sepe.
Hoc butirum, A^e buttyre.
Hic cadus, A^e barylle.
Hic ducellus, A^e dosylle.¹³
Hoc poculum, A^e drynk.
Hic potus, idem est.
Hic cophinus, A^e hampere.
Servicia nova, A^e new ale.
Servicia deficata, A^e stale ale.

¹ *Payn-mayn* was the name given to the bread of finer quality.

² *Hafyr-bred*, bread made of oats; oat-cakes.

³ This term is now used in the north for unleavened bread.

⁴ *Wastelle*, a cake, the Fr. *gâteau*.

⁵ *Symnelle*. See before, p. 127.

⁶ *i. e.*, a shive, or slice.

⁷ *Sanap*, a napkin. The romance of Sir Degrevant, l. 1387, speaks of—
  Towellus of Eylyssham,
  Whyʒth as the secs fame,
  Sanappus of the same,
    Thus servyd thei ware.

⁸ *Celare*, a salt-sellar.

⁹ *Relef*, a small basket.

¹⁰ *Buffylle*, a leather bottle, for liquors, as would appear from the Latin equivalent. See before, p. 98.

¹¹ *Costylle*. A costrel was a bottle or vessel of wood, resembling that which the labourers still carry with them in harvest time.

¹² *i. e.*, an onion. From the verse which follows we may perhaps conclude that it was usual to eat onions with cheese.

¹³ *Dosylle*, the faucet of a barrel. Robert of Gloucester, describing the disturbances in Oxford in the thirteenth century, and the mischief the scholars did in the townsmen's houses, (ed. Hearne, p. 542), says—
  Vor the mer was vinter, hii breke the viniterie,
  And alle othere in the toun, and that was lute maistrie;
  Hii caste awei the *dosils*; that win orn abrod so,
  That it was pité gret of so much harm ido

ENGLISH VOCABULARY.

Servicia acerba, A^e sowre ale.
Hoc placentum, A^e wastelle.

NOMINA PERTINENCIA AD CAMERAM.

Hoc pecten, A^e combe.
Hoc colobium, A^e tabarde.
Hec armilansa, A^e cloke.
Hic clavus, idem.
Hoc capicium, A^e hode.
Hec supertunica, A^e furd-cote.
Hec tunica, A^e cote.
Hec toga, A^e gowne.
Hec manica, A^e slewe.
Hec glitella, A^e kostyr.[1]
Hec sista, A^e kyst.
Hec arca, A^e arke.
Hec teca, idem.
Hec capsa, idem est.
Hic nodulus, A^e boton.
Hoc calcar, A^e spore.
Hec stupa, A^e barre.
Hoc monile, A^e broche.
Hec agnaria, A^e nedyl-hows.
Hec pustula, A^e bokylle.
Hoc speculum, A^e meror.
Hic fusus, A^e spyndylle.
Hec madula, A^e jurdan.
Hic jurdanus, idem est.
Hoc tapetum, A^e tapyt.
Hoc coopertorium, A^e coverlyde.
Hoc carentrevillum, A^e canwas.
Lectus plumalis, A^e fedyr-bed.
Hic lectus, A^e bede.
Hoc stratum, A^e bed-lytter.
    Est lectus stratum, via regia sit tibi strata.

Hoc epicaustorium, A^e chymne.
Hic caminus, idem est.

NOMINA PERTINENCIA AD COQUINAM.

Hic coqus, A^e coke.
Hic, hec lixa, A^e quystron.[2]
Hoc mortarium, A^e morter.
Hic pilus, A^e pestylle.
Hoc micatorium, A^e myowre.[3]
Hoc mortorium, A^e postyk.
Hec olla, A^e potte.
Hec anca, A^e pot-ere.
Hic urceus, A^e posnett.
Hic urciolus, A^e idem.
Hec ollula, A^e idem.
Hec patella, A^e panne.
Hec tripes, A^e burnderthe.[4]
Hec scapha, A^e bolle.
Hoc frixorium, A^e friyng-pan.
Hic limas, A^e naprune.
Hoc succidium, A^e sowsse.
Hoc ramentum, A^e ramayle.[5]
Hoc sepum, A^e tallo.
Hoc veru, A^e spytt.
Hoc verutum, A^e spit with mete.
Hic fumus, A^e reke.
Hec flamma, A^e low.
Hec fuligo, A^e sote.
Hoc brodium, A^e brothe.
Hoc ferculum, A^e mese.
Hoc potagium, A^e potage.
Hoc edulium, A^e sowle.[6]
Hoc adipatum, A^e browys.
Hoc lacticinium, A^e wytte-met.
Hoc lac, A^e mylke.

---

[1] *Kostyr*, the hanging of the wall of the room —*aulæum*.

[2] *Quystron*, the cook's assistant, or scullion.

[3] *Myowr*, an implement for reducing bread into crumbs, in old French *esmieure*.

[4] *Burnderthe*, a brandreth, or iron tripot, to place over a fire for supporting a pot or kettle.

[5] *Ramayle*, scrapings.

[6] *Sowle*, anything eaten with bread, like cheese, &c., still called in some of the English dialects *soul* or *sowl*. Thus, in the romance of Havelok, l. 767—

    Kam he nevere hom handebare,
    That he ne broucte bred and *sowel*

Hoc serum, A^c way.
Hoc coagulum, A^c crodde.
Hoc coactum, A^c reme.
Hec perapsis, A^c doblere.
Hoc sallarium, A^c sowser.
Hec taleteca, A^c blawmunger.
Hoc pepe, A^c mortrus.
Hic garrus, A^c brewett.
Hoc sepulatum, A^c sewe.
Hic pastillus, A^c pastyth.
Hic baco, A^c bacon.
Hec perna, A^c flyk.
Hoc lardum, A^c lardyre.
Hoc fertum, A^c podyng.
Hec salucia, A^c sauseyre.
Hoc tunsetum, A^c hagase.[1]
Hec olda, A^c hyspyn.
Hic omasus, A^c trype.
Caro recens, fresche flesche.
Caro salsa, salt flesche.
Caro bovina, beyf-flesche.[2]
Caro porcina, swyne-flesche.
Caro vitulina, calf-flesche.
Caro mutulina, chepe-flesche.
Caro aucina, gose-flesche.
Caro spadonia, capune-flesche.
Caro caponina, capon-flesche.
Caro gallinaria, hene-flesche.
Caro grossa, grete flesche.
Caro assota, rost flesche.
Caro in brodio, in broth.
Caro cocta in pasta, bakyn.
Hic pugio, A^c pejon.
Hoc caldarium, A^c caldron.

Hec ferina, A^c wenyson.
Hoc senapium, A^c mustarde.
Hoc alleum, A^c garly.
Hoc jus viride, A^c warins.
Hec emulaga, A^c batyre.
Hic chalaphus, A^c pan3ere.
Caro cruda, A^c ra flesche.
Caro rancida, A^c rest flesche.
Hic scamellus, A^c dressyn-knyf-bord.
Hic nidor, sapor coquine.
Hic afingea, pinguedo porci.
Hoc abdomen, idem est.
Hec nebula, A^c noble.
Hec rafra, A^c wayfyre.
Hic flato, A^c flaune.[3]
Hec cratericula, A^c rost-yryn.
Hec artocria, a pie de pundio.

NOMINA PERTINANCIA AD BRASORIUM.

Hec brasiatrix, A^c brewster.
Hec cima, A^c kymnelle.[4]
Hec tina, A^c sa.
Hic fornax, A^c furnasse.
Hoc alveum, A^c trogh.
Hoc brasium, A^c malte.
Hec barzisa, A^c wortte.
Hoc dragium, A^c draf.
Hoc calderium, A^c caldron.
Hic cacabus, idem.
Hoc taratantarum, A^c temse.[5]
Hec curella, A^c kunlioun.[6]
Hoc cilicium, A^c hayre.
Hoc ydromellum, A^c growte.
Hec mola, A^c quernes.

---

[1] *Hagase.* The hagas was the paunch, or stomach, of the animal, stuffed with minced meat, &c., something in the manner of a sausage; the origin of the modern Scottish *haggis*.

[2] These interpretations would seem to show that the Anglo-Norman terms, beef, pork, &c., had not yet entirely superseded the names of meat of Anglo-Saxon derivation.

[3] *Wayfire ... flaune.* Wafers were a very light kind of cakes; in old French *gauffres*: flauns were custards.

[4] *Kymnelle,* a tub for household purposes; a vat.

[5] *Temse,* a sieve. The word is still in use in the North of England.

[6] *Curella* signifies a small tub.

Hec pruera, lingge.¹
Merica, idem est.

NOMINA PERTINENCIA AD PISTRINUM.

Hic pistor, A^e bacster.
Hec ferina, A^e mele.
Hic furfur, A^e bran.
Hic flos, A^e flowre.
Hec similago, est purissimus flos.
Hec pasta, A^e dagh.
Hoc levamentum, A^e lewan.²
Hoc fermentum, A^e sur-dagh.³
Hoc crebrum, A^e syfe.
Hoc pellen, A^e floure.
Hoc pollitridium, A^e bult-clathe.
Hec falanga, A^e satre.
Hec pela, A^e pele.
Hec vertebra, A^e cobarde.
Hoc tresorium, A^e scomure.
Hic furnus, A^e oven.
Poletriduare, to bulte.
Hoc sinarium, A^e sotre.
Hec casta, A^e rybbe.
Hic cultellus, A^e knyfe.
Hec sindula, A^e blade.
Hoc manubrium, A^e hefte.
Hoc penum, A^e egge.
Hic perrasmus, A^e tong.
Hec cuspis, A^e poynte.
Hec sperula, A^e werylle.

NOMINA PERTINENCIA AD ORRIUM.

Hec garba, A^e chef.
Hic manipulus, A^e repe.
Hec corbex, A^e lepe.
Hoc ventilabrum, A^e wyndylle.
Hic modius, A^e buschelle.
Hic corus, A^e mesure.

Hec prebenda, A^e probend.
Hic abbatis, A^e prowande.
Abbatis avenam dat equis abbatis avenam.
Hec avena, A^e otys.
Hoc ostorium, A^e stryke.*⁴
Hec ala, A^e wenge.
Hoc flagellum, A^e flayle.
Hoc rastrum, A^e rake.
Hoc granum, A^e corne.
Hec spica, A^e corne-here.
Hoc frumentum, A^e wete.
Hoc triticum, A^e whete.
Hec pisa, A^e pese.
Hec faba, A^e bene.
Hec vicia, A^e feche.
Hec lens, A^e lentylle.
Hoc ordium, A^e barly.
Hec siligo, A^e rye.
Hoc sigalum, idem.
Hec curalis, A^e crappys.
Hoc lollium, A^e populle.
Hic cratis, A^e fleke.
Hoc tribulum, A^e schowulle.
Hec solea, A^e sole.
Hec pedana, A^e wampay.⁵
Hoc intercucium, A^e weltte.
Hoc pictacium, A^e clowte.

VERBA SOLI DEO PERTINENCIA.

Pluit, raynes, *Deus meus.*
Gelat, freses, *Deus tuus.*
Degelat, thowes, *Deus suus.*
Floctat, snawes, *Deus illius.*
Ningit, snawes, *Deus ipsius.*
Tonat, thoneres, *Deus sanctus.*
Grandinat, hayles, *Deus omnipotens.*
Fulgurat, lewnes, *Deus creator.*
Fulminat, idem, Deus dat omnia.

---

¹ *Pruera* is a corruption of *bruera,* and *merica* of *mirica.* Ling, the *calluna* of modern botanists, is introduced here because it was used largely for making brooms, and other domestic purposes.

² Leaven.
³ *Sur-dagh,* i. sour dough.
⁴ A strike, or bushel measure.
⁵ *Wampay.* See before, p. 196.

NOMINA PERTINENCIA AD CARECTARIAM.

Hec beta, est secundus panis.
Hec gerusia, A' gadde.
Hec mantica, A' male.
Hec mastiga, A' wyppe.
Hec reda, A' chare.
Hic aculeus, A' brode.[1]
Hoc plaustrum, A' wayne.
Hec tema, A' teme.
Hec torques, A' wythe.[2]
Hic currus, A' karte.
Hec bina, est currus habens duos equos.
Hec rota, A' qwele.
Hic radius, A' spake.
Hoc meditulium, A' nawef.
Hic axis, A' axyl-tre.
Hoc humullum, A' lyn-pyne.
Hic limo, A' thyllys.
Hoc fricsorium, A' pynne.
Hic viredus, A' thyl-hors.
Hoc dorsilollum, A' cart-sadylle.
Hec singula, A' garthe.
Hec postela, A' tayle-rape.
Hec antela, A' paytrylle.
Hec trane, -arum, A' trays.
Hoc capistrum, A' heltyre.
Hoc scansile, A' styroppe.
Hec stropa, idem.
Hec strigilis, A' hors-combe.
Hoc aratrum, A' plogh.
Hoc jugum, A' yokke.

NOMINA PERTINENCIA AD LACTITIUM.

Hoc multrum, A' ches-fat.[3]
Hoc lac, A' mylk.
Hoc butirum, A' buttyr.
Hic caseus, A' chese.

Hoc coagulum, A' crodes.
Hec bedulta, A' possyt.
Hoc serum, A' way.
Hic lacsugo, A' way.
Hec antipera, A' kyrne.
Hoc almariolum, A' almary.
Hoc torcular, A' prassur.
Hoc coactum, A' reme.
Hec multra, A' payle.
Hec lactis, -cis, A' cheslyppe.[4]

NOMINA LUDORUM.

Hoc hastiludium, A' justyng.
Hoc tirocinium, A' turnament.
Hoc interludium, A' entyrlute.
Hic trocus, A' toppe.
Hec scutica, A' scowrge.
Hec pila, A' balle.
Hoc pedum, A' cambok.[5]
Hic pirrus, A' chekyr.
Hic scaccarius, idem.
Hic scaccus, A' chesse.
Hic talus, A' dyse.
Hec alea, idem.
Hec tabella, A' tabulles.
Hec tuba, A' trumpe.
Hec buccina, idem.
Hec fistula, A' pype.
Hec idraulis, A' water-pype.
Hec cithera, A' harpe.
Hec lira, A' harpe-string.
Hor plectrum, A' wrastt.
Hoc tympanum, A' taburne.
Hic sambucus, A' sytholle.
Hec vetella, A' rybybe.
Hec symphonia, A' symphane.
Hec palpita, A' sawtre.
Hec viella, A' fythylle.

[1] Brode, a prick, or goad.
[2] A with, or twisted rod.
[3] Ches-fat, a milkpail.
[4] Cheslyppe. Perhaps runnet, which is still called cheeselop in the north.
[5] Cambok, an old game at ball played with a crooked stick, mentioned under this name by Stowe.

ENGLISH VOCABULARY.

Hoc symbalum, A^e symbale.
Hoc organum, A^e organs.

NOMINA PERTINENCIA DOMORUM.

Hoc fundum, A^e grownd-walle.[1]
Hec bassis, idem.
Hec paries, A^e walle.
Hic murus, idem.
Hic cardo, A^e thriswald.
Hoc limen, idem.
Hoc sublimen, idem.
Hec postis, A^e post.
Hoc laquear, A^e post-band.
Hec fania, A^e pautre.
Hec trabes, A^e balk.
Hec tegula, A^e teylle.
Hoc later, idem.
Hoc laquear, A^e postband.
Hec cavilla, A^e pynne.
Hic cuneus, A^e wegge.
Hec tingnus, A^e howse-hessyng.
Hoc domicilium, idem.
Hoc edificium, idem.
Hec columna, A^e pelere.
Hec volta, A^e wowte.
Hoc lodium, A^e lowere.[2]
Hoc spelare, A^e wyndow.
Hec fenestra, idem.
Hoc ostium, A^e dore.
Hec sera, A^e lok.
Hec victinella, A^e stapulle.
Hec clavis, A^e kay.
Hoc repagulum, A^e dore-bar.
Hoc pessulum, idem.
Hec vectis, idem.
Hic clatrus, idem.

Hic obex, idem.
Hoc ostiolum, A^e hek.[3]
Hoc superliminare, A^e ouver-slay.
Hoc superlimen, idem est.
Hoc tignum, A^e spere.
Hoc tigillum, idem.
Hoc festum, est lignum ad quod omnia tigna conveniunt.
Hec trapecula, A^e bynd-balk.
Hoc doma, A^e rofe.
Hic hamus, A^e hoke.
Hec sericula, A^e clykyt.

NOMINA AD NUTRIARIUM.[4]

Hec obstatrix, A^e mydwyfe.
Fassiatus, A^e swathild.
Hoc cunabulum, A^e credylle.
Reperre, to crepe.
Salmare, to slawor.
Hec salmacio, A^e slaveryng.
Hoc salmarium, A^e slaveryng-clout.
Alutare, to fyle.
Mutulare, to mamere.
Hec mutulatio, A^e mameryng.
Vagire, i. clamare sicut infans.
Hec ancilla, A^e maydyn.
Hec puella, idem.
Hec trocus, A^e toppe.
Hec mataxa, A^e hekylle.
Hic limphus, A^e topflax.
Hec fascia, A^e credyl-bande.
Hic colus, A^e roke.
Hic fusus, A^e spyndylle.
Hec lacrima, A^e tere.
Surdus, -a, -um, deffe.
Surdaster, -a, -um, A^e halfe-deffe.

---

[1] *Ground-walle;* this is the old Anglo-Saxon term. See before, p. 81.

[2] *Lowere,* a louver. The open turret, or lantern, on the roof of a building, especially on the old baronial halls, the original object of which was to carry off the smoke from the fire in the middle of the hall.

[3] *Hek* is perhaps used in the same signification which it still bears in the north, the lower half of the door, which remains shut while the other half opens.

[4] The words follow each other in this chapter as though they had been taken from the "tretise" of Walter de Biblesworth.

NOMINA PERTINENCIA AD BOVARIUM.

Hic bibulcus, A' ox-arde.
Hic, hec bos, A' ox.
Hic taurus, A' bulle.
Hec vacca, A' cow.
Hic boriculus, A' styrk.
Hec juvenca, A' quee.
Hic vitulus, A' calfe.
Hoc presepe, A' crybe.
Hoc boverium, A' ox-stalle.
Hic palus, A' stak.

NOMINA SERPENTUM.

Hic idrus, serpens antiqua.
Hec emfimenia, serpens cum duobus capitibus.
Hic cholendrus, serpens qui moritur in aquis.
Hic seps, serpens exiguus.
Hic dipsas, serpens magne malicie
Hec salpia, serpens qui non videtur.
Hic coluber, A' snake.

NOMINA PERTINENCIA AD SUARIUM.

Hic porcarius, A' swyne-herd.
Hic aper, A' bore.
Hic, hec sus, A' sowe.
Hec porca, i. quod scrofa.
Hic frendis, A' galt.[1]
Hic neufrendis, A' gylt.
Hic porcellus, A' gryse.

NOMINA PERTINENCIA DOMORUM.

Hoc monasterium, A' mynstre.
Hec ecclesia, A' kyrk.
Hic cancellus, A' chawnsylle.
Hic chorus, idem est.
Hec capella, A' chapylle.
Hoc oratorium, A' oratory.
Hoc refectorium, A' frature.
Hoc dormitorium, A' dorture.

Hoc capitulum, A' chapytur.
Hoc locutorium, A' parloure.
Hoc claustrum, A' clostyre.
Hec porticus, A' porche.
Hec proaula, idem est.
Hec aula, A' halle.
Hec camera, A' chawmbur.
Hec talamus, idem est.
Hec latrina, A' wardroppe.
Hec cloaca, idem est.
Hoc solarium, A' selare.
Hec panteria, A' pantre.
Hec botelaria, A' botelary.
Hoc lardarium, A' lardyr-howse.
Hec quoquina, A' kechyn.
Hoc pistrinum, A' bac-house.
Hoc brasorium, A' brew-house.
Hoc torale, A' kyln-howse.
Hoc furnium, A' oven-house.
Hoc orreum, A' lathe.
Hoc granarium, idem est.
Hoc palare, A' chaf-house.
Hoc boster, A' schyppune.
Hoc stabulum, A' stabulle.
Hoc columbare, A' dowe-cote.
Hec barcaria, A' schepe-house.
Hec porcaria, A' swyn-cote.
Hoc suarium, idem est.
Hec ara, idem est.
Hoc orile, A' fald.
Hoc tigurrium, A' cheperd-howse.
Hoc gallinarium, A' hene-cote.
Hec salina, A' salte-cote.
Hoc repositorium, A' horde-house.
Hec garbana, idem est.
Hoc argastulum, A' prisoun.
Hic bocardo, idem est.
Hoc prostipulum, est domus meretricis.
Hoc lupanar, idem est.
Hec quinquatria, est domus habens quinque porticus sub se.

---

[1] Galt, a boar-pig.

NOMINA CONSANGUINIORUM.

Hic pater, A*ᵉ* fadyre.
Hic genitor, idem est.
Hic, hec parens, est pater vel mater.
Hic victricus, A*ᵉ* step-fadyre.
Hec victrica, A*ᵉ* step-modyre.
Hic filiaster, A*ᵉ* step-sone.
Hec previgna, A*ᵉ* step-doghter.
Hec filiaster, idem est.
Hic compater, A*ᵉ* godefader.
Hec commater, A*ᵉ* godemoder.
Hic filiolus, A*ᵉ* godeson.
Hec filiola, A*ᵉ* goddoghter.
Hic frater, A*ᵉ* brother.
Hic germanus, idem est.
Hec soror, A*ᵉ* syster.
Hec germana, idem est.
Hic sororius, A*ᵉ* syster hosband.
Hic socer, A*ᵉ* pater-in-lege.
Hec socrus, A*ᵉ* mater-in-lege.
Hec nurus, A*ᵉ* filia-in-lege.
Hic gener, A*ᵉ* sone-in-law.
Hec amita, soror patris.
Hec matertera, soror matris.
Hic avus, A*ᵉ* eld-fader.
Hec avia, A*ᵉ* eld-moder.
Hic proceser, pater patris-in-lege.
Hic nepos, est filius filii.
Hec neptis, est filia filii vel filie.
Hec glos, -ris, est soror-in-lege.
Hic levir, est frater-in-lege.

NOMINA TEMPORA ANNI.

Hic yemps, A*ᵉ* wyntyre.
Hoc ver, -ris, vere.
Hec estas, A*ᵉ* summure.
Hic autumnus, A*ᵉ* harwest.

A NOMINALE.[1]

(OF THE FIFTEENTH CENTURY.)

Incipit nominale sub compendio compilatum tam de fixis quam de mobilibus.

DE VOCABULIS AD SINGULA MEMBRA
HUMANI CORPORIS SPECTANTIBUS.

Hoc principium, ⎫
Hoc inicium, ⎪
Hoc exordium, ⎬ *A* begynnyng.
Hoc primordium, ⎪
Hic origo, ⎭
Hoc caput, A^{ce} hede.
Hoc occiput, a nodyle.
Hoc cinciput, i. pars anterior.
Hoc interciput, i. media pars.
Hoc ffrontispicium, a for-tope.
Hec vertex, A^{ce} hatrelle.
Hoc discrimen, the schade of the hede.[2]
Hic crinis, ⎫
Hic capillus, ⎬ *A^{ce}* hare.
Hec coma, ⎪
Hic pilus, ⎭

Hoc cerebrum, a brayn.
Hoc crinium, a harn-pane.
Hec ffacies, a face.
Hec ffaciecula, i. parva facies
Hoc tempus, a tunwonge.[3]
Her macula, a spote.
Hec papula, a blane.
Hec maxilla, ⎫
Hec mola, ⎬ *A* chek-bone.
Hec jaux, ⎭
Hec frons, a forete.
Hoc cilium, a brow.
Hoc supercilium, a brow-bone.
Hoc intercilium, the space betwene the eyn.
Hic oculus, ⎫
Hic talmus, ⎬ *A^{ce}* ne.[4]
Hec palpebra, the ee-lyde.

[1] A common title for the vocabularies of the fifteenth century was that of *Nominale*, intimating that it was strictly a vocabulary of nouns, or names of things, classified under their different heads. The nominale here printed is taken from a very curious MS. of the fifteenth century, in the collection of Joseph Mayer, Esq., F.S.A., of Liverpool, which had no doubt belonged to the schoolmaster who taught with it, and remains in its original cover of vellum, contrived so as to roll up to make it more portable, with a string attached, to tie it when rolled. It is unfortunately not quite complete, a leaf having been lost; but to judge from the part which remains, that which is lost was probably the least important part of it, and may be supplied from the complete vocabularies of the fifteenth century, printed in the present volume.

[2] Schede, or shed, was the common name for the separation of the hair on the top of the head, from which it spread down on either side.

[3] The Anglo-Saxon þunwang, a temple. See the A.-S. vocabularies in the present volume.

[4] *Ne*, an eye. This practice of prefixing the final *n* of the article to the noun, when the latter commences with a vowel, is of constant recurrence in these vocabularies of the fifteenth century.

A NOMINALE.

Hec pupilla, the appylle of the ee.
Hec albedo, ⎫
Hec albucies, ⎬ the whyte of the ee.
Hoc albumen, ⎭
Hec acies, the scharpnes of the ee.
Hic nasus, a nese.
Hec naris, a nes-thyrylle.
Hoc interfinium, the bryg of the nese.
Hec purila, the poynt of the nese.
Hec cartilago, a grystylle.
Hoc rostrum, a bylle.
Hic cirrus, a topylle.[1]
Hic polipus, the fylth of the nese.
Hec saliva, a spyttynge.
Hec orexis, a spewynge.
Hec glabra, a scale.
Hoc mentum, a chyn.
Hec uteelaris, a wong-tothe.[2]
Hoc os, -ris, a mowthe.
Hec gena, ⎫ cheke.
Hec bucca, ⎭
Hec lingua, ⎫ a tonge.
Hec glossa, ⎭
Hoc labium, ⎫ a lype.
Hoc labrum, ⎭
Hic dens, -tis, a tothe.
Hec jungiva, a gume.
Hec auris, a nere.
Hec auricula, i. parva auris.
Hec colera, the er-sope.[3]
Hec mandibula, a cheke-bone.
Hic porrigo, a poke.
Hec veruka, a warte.
Hoc ulcus, a kylle.[4]
Hic gibbus, a byle behynde.
Hic gibber, a byle before.
Hec struma, idem est.
Hoc collum, a neke.

Hec gula, ⎫ a throte.
Hoc guttur, ⎭
Hec frontinella, the pyte in the neke.
Hoc frumen, i. summa pars gutturis.
Hec ructa, ⎫ idem est.
Hoc rumen, ⎭
Hic ysophagus, a wesande.
Hoc epiglotum, a thote-gole.
Hic stomacus, a stomake.
Hoc brachium, a narme.
Hec acella, a narme-hole.
Hic cubitus, a cubyte.
Hic humerus, a chwdyr.
Hic manus, a hande.
Hic digitus, a fyngyr.
Hec palma, ⎫
Hoc ir, irris, ⎬ the lone of the hande.
Hec vola, ⎭
Hic pollex, a thome.
Hic index, the secunde fynger.
Hic medius, the longe fynger.
Hic medicus, the therde fynger.
Hic auricularis, the lytyle fynger.
Hic pugnus, a fyste.
Hec unguis, ⎫ a nayle.
Hec ungula, ⎭
Her junctura, a joynt.
Hoc corpus, a body.
Hec cutis, ⎫ a skyne.
Hec pellis, ⎭
Hoc tergum, ⎫ a bake.
Hoc dorsum, ⎭
Hoc spondile, a bake-bone.
Hic torax, a breste-bone.
Hic venter, ⎫ a wame.
Hic alvuus, ⎭
Hic umbelicus, a navyle.
Hec natis, a bottoke.

---

[1] *Topple* was used by old writers to signify a tuft or crest.

[2] *Wong*, or *wang*, was the A.-S. word for a cheek; *wang-toð* meant a grinder. *Wangtooth* is, I believe, still used in this sense in the north.

[3] A Nominale in MS. Reg. 17, C. xvii., fol. 38, v°, gives, " *colera, Anglice* arwax."

[4] A kile, or ulcerated sore.

Hec cawda,
Hec dica, } a tayle.
Hic lumbus, a hype.
Hoc uber,
Hec mamma, } a pape.
Hec mamilla,
Hoc pectus, a breste.
Hoc latus, a syde.
Hec costa, a rybe.
Hec pubes, ʒong hore.[1]
Hoc femur,
Hoc crus, } a the.
Hoc veretrum,
Hic priapus, } a pyntyle.
Hec vulva, a cunte.
Hic testiculus, a balloke.
Hic ramex, locus genitalium.
Hoc genitale, a balloke stone.
Hec piga, a balloke code.
Hic anus,
Hic culus, } a ners.
Hec poplex, a hame.
Hec matrix,
Hec stera,
Hec secundina, } *pellis in qua concipitur infans.*
Hec secunda,
Hoc viscus,
Hoc intestinum, } a bowyle.
Hoc extum,
Hoc scrutum, a trype.
Hec diafragma, a mydrede.
Her pulpa, A^c brawne.
Hoc epat, -tis, a lyver.
Hoc splen, a mylte.
Hoc cor, -dis, a herte.
Hoc ren, -is, a nere.[2]
Hic lien, -nis, a longe-gute.
Hic pulmo, the lownges.

Hoc jecor, a mawe.
Hoc cadaver, a caryoun.
Hoc burburium, owmlys.[3]
Hoc cepum, talow.
Hoc adumen, } A^{ce} gres between the skyn
Hic pinguedo, } and the ...
Hic adeps, idem est.
Hic sanguis,
Hic cruor, } A^{ce} blode.
Hec omomestra, a medryn.[4]
Hoc fel, -lis, a gale.
Hoc sperma, A^{ce} fry.
Hoc stercus,
Hec merda, } a torde.
Hoc cirbrum, a gute.
Hoc genu, a kne.
Hoc internodium, the knope of the kne.
Hec tibia, a lege.
Hec sura, a chyn-bone.
Hic nervus, a synow.
Hec vena, a vayn.
Hoc os, -sis, a bone.
Hec medulla, margthe.[5]
Hoc crus, -ris, a the.
Hec cavilla, a nankyle.
Hic musculus, the calfe of the lege.
Hic fragus, a wyrste.[6]
Hic talus,
Hic cals, -cis, } a hele.
Hec duricies, hardnes of the hande.
Hic pes, -dis, a fote.
Hec planta, the sole of the fote.
Hec apostema, a postym.
Hec vertebra, the wherl-bone.
Hic sinus, a bosome.
Hoc grabatum, penultima corrupta, a skyrte.

---

[1] *i. e.*, young hair. The Nominale in MS. Reg. 17, C. xvii, fol. 38, v°, explains *pubes* and *picten* (pecten) by "*Anglice* rawne."

[2] The kidneys. See before, p. 186.

[3] The umbles.

[4] The midriff.

[5] The marrow; A.-S. *mearh*, or *mearg.*

[6] The bend of the knee.

Hoc gremium, a heme.
Hic allux, -cis, a grete too.
Hic articulus, a lytyle too.
Hoc vulnus,
Hec plaga, } a wonde.
Recia, regna plage dicuntur, vulnera plage.
Hic sudor, -ris, A^{cc} swete.
Hec lacrima, a tere.
Hic porus, a swete-holle.
Hec scabia, a skale.
Hic corona, a crowne.
Hec vesica, a bledyr.
Hec urina, A^{cc} pysse.
Hec urinula, idem est.
Hoc bumbum, a ferte.
Hec lirida, a fyse.
Hic passus, a rayke.[1]
Hoc progressus, a goynge forthe.
Hic regressus,
Hec revercio, } a tornyng agayne.
Hic adventus,
Hic accessus, } commyng to.
Hic recessus,
Hec discessus, } a departynge.
Hic gustus, a taystyng.
Hic olfactus, a smellyng.
Hic auditus, a heryng.
Hic visus, a syghte.
Hic tactus, a towchyng.
Hec anima, a salle.
Hic spiritus, a spret.
Hec mens, a mynde.
Hic sensus, a wyte.
Hoc factum, a dyde.
Hec vita, A^{cc} lyfe.
Hec conversacio, idem est.
Hec voluntas, a wyle.
Hoc carecter,
Hoc cicatrix, } a nerre.[2]

Hec lenticula, a frakyn.[3]
Hec omoplata, a schuldyr-bone.
Hoc pollicium, a nynche.

CAPITULUM 2^{м}.
NOMINA DIGNITATUM CLERICORUM.

Hic papa, a pape.
Hic apostolus, A^{cc} apostyle.
Hic patriarcha, a patriarke.
Hic cardinalis, a cardynale.
Hic archyepiscopus, an ersbychope.
Hic episcopus, a byschope.
Hic archidiaconus, a narsdekyn.
Hic diaconus, a dekyn.
Hic decanus, a dene.
Hic legatus, a legate.
Hic propheta, a profete.
Hic officialis, an offycyale.
Hic poeta, a poyte.
Hic archisinagogus, i. princeps sinagogie.
Hic cancellarius, a chanceller.
Hic suffraganus, a suffrykayn.
Hic abbas, a abbote.
Hic prior, a pryor.
Hic subprior, a subprior.
Hic causidicus, a vokyte.
Hic philosofus, a fylysofer.
Hic monachus, a monke.
Hic canonicus, a chanoun.
Hic celerarius, a celerer.
Hic sacrista, a secristoun.
Hic comissarius, a comyssari.
Hic rector, a person.
Hic vicarius, a vyker.
Hic presbiter,
Hic sacerdos, } a preste.
Hic doctor, a dotyr.
Hic legista, a legistery.

---

[1] A step. This word is no doubt connected with the old English word *rayke*, or *rake*, to proceed, or go.

[2] *Nerre*, a scar, or pock-mark, still called an *ar* in the north.

[3] A spot, or freckle.

Hic bacularius, a bachyler.
Hic sophista, a sovyster.
Hic preco, -nis, } a bedylle.
Hic bidellus, }
Hic diaconus, } a dekyn.
Hec levita, }
Hic subdiaconus, a subdekyn.
Hic acolitus, a colyte.
Hic exorcista, a benyte.
Hic magister, } a mastyr.
Hic pedagogus, }
Hic ostiarius, a uscher.
Hic, hec scolarius, a scoler.
Hic clericus, a clarke.
Hic discipulus, a dyscyple.
Hic scriptor, a wryter.
Hic minister, a mynester.
Hic gubernator, a governer.
Hic instructor, a submastyr.
Hic frater, a frere.
Hic novellus, } a novys.
Hic novicius, }
Hic succellerarius, a sowthselerer.
Hic templarius, a templer.
Hic, hec heremita, a ermyte.
Hic, hec anacorita, a ancoryse.
Hic gramaticus, a gramaryonn.
Hic citator, } a summunder.
Hic aparator, }
Hic judex, a domsman.
Hic notarius, } a noterer.
Hic arbiter, }
Hic lector, a redere.
Hic cantator, a synger.

Hic musicus, a musyker.
Hic modulator, } a endyter.
Hic dictor, -ris, }
Hic versificator, a versyfyer.
Hic ebdomidarius, } a cerg-berare.
Hic ceroferarius, }
Hic chorista, } a qwalester.[1]
Hic paraphonista, }
Hic hospitelarius, a hosteler.
Hic patronus, a patrone.
Hic sequestarius, a sequesterer.
Hic latinista, a Latyn-maker.

CAPITULUM 3ᵐ.

NOMINA RERUM PERTINENCIUM CLERICO.

Hic cornu, indeclinabile, a horne.
Hoc pennare, a pener.
Hoc incaustum, Aᶜᶜ ynke.
Hic calamus, a stalke.
Hec penna, a pen.
Hoc acuperium, } a wheston.
Hic cos, -tis, }
Hic artavus, a penknyfe.
Hec vagina, a schethe.
Hec bursa, a purs.
Hoc percaminum, perchement.
Hic papirus, paupere.
Hec sidula, a scrowle.
Hec zona, } a gyr-
Hoc tropheum, media corrupta, } dyle.
Hic pumex, Aᶜᶜ pomege.
Hic quaternus, a quare.[2]
Hec diptica, a smale tabyle.[3]

---

[1] A querister, or chorister. It is a very unusual form of the word.

[2] A quire of vellum or paper. See before, pp. 75 and 116.

[3] A tablet, or table-book. The common use of table books in the middle ages has been alluded to more than once in the present volume. According to the Boke of Curtasye (p. 22), the steward of the baronial household set down his accounts in a table-book before they were entered in the regular books—

At countyng stuarde sehalle ben,
Tylle alle be brevet of wax so grene
Wrytten inte bokes, without let,
That be fore in tabuls have ben sett.

For the wax, or other similar substance, a composition was substituted in the course of the fifteenth century, which eventually gave place to what is known as asses' skin.

Hic stilus,
Hic graphus, } a poyntyle.[1]
Hoc plumbum, A^{ce} lede.
Hoc regulare, a rewler.
Hec crota, A^{ce} calke.
Hoc punctorium, a prykker.
Hoc rasorium,
Hec novacula, } a rasure.
Hic pulver, -ris, powdyr.
Hoc fulgur, A^{ce} bornston.[2]
Hec rosina, A^{ce} rosyle.

CAPITULUM 4ᵐ.

NOMINA DIGNITATUM LAICORUM.

Hic imperator,
Hic induperator, } a emperowre.
Hic rex, -gis,
Hic regulus, } a kynge.
Hic princeps, a prynce.
Hic dux, -cis, a duke.
Hic comes, A^{ce} nerle.
Hic dominus,
Hic herus, } a lorde.
Hic baro, a barone.
Hic miles, -tis,
Hic eques, } a knyght.
Hic tiro, -nis,
Hic neoptolemus, a 30ng knyght.
Hic principatus, a prinshode.
Hic vicecomes, a scheryfe.
Hic siniscallus, a stewerde.
Hic armiger,
Hic scutifer, } a squyere.
Hic heres, an are.
Hic ballivus, a baylé.
Hic villicus,
Hic prepositus, } a grafe.[3]

Hic major,
Hic prefectus, } a mayr.
Hic senior,
Hic decrepitus, } a nald-man.
Hic, hec homo,
Hic mas, } a man.
Hic homunculus, a lytyl-man.
Hic paterfamilias,
Hic iconimus, } husbandman.
Hic, hec burgensis, a burgys.
Hec civis, a cyttenere.
Hic arculius, a wayte.
Hic constabularius, a constabyle.
Hic lictor, a sargent.
Hic camerarius, a chamerlane.
Hic aresponsis, i. qui respondit pro principe.
Hic claviger, a kay-berere.

Clava ferit, clavis aperit, clavus duo jungit.
Clavis nos vel vas qui fert sit claviger;
Indue te clavo, rege clavo, percute clavo.

Hic centurio, qui habet centum milites.
Hic quaternio, qui habet iiij^{or} milites.
Hic decurio, qui habet x. milites.
Hic tetrarcha, princeps 4^{or} regionum.
Hic proditor, a traytore.
Hic assecretis, a cowncellere.
Hic archimentrita, i. princeps omnium.
Hic panterius, a pantrer.[4]
Hic pincerna, a botler.
Hic cokus, a kuke.
Hic, hec lixa, a kychyn page.[5]
Hic archemerus, a master cuke.
Hic janitor, a porter.
Hic Romanus, a Romayn.
Hic Judeus, a Jew.
Hic Saracenus, a Sarzyn.

---

[1] The Roman *stylus*, and Anglo-Saxon *græf*. See before, p. 75.
[2] *Bornston*, perhaps brimstone.
[3] The Anglo-Saxon *geréfa*, a reeve.
[4] The panter, pantrer, or pantner, was properly the officer of the household who had the care and distribution of the bread (*panis*); and the pantry was especially the bread department of the household.
[5] Or a quistron.

Hic predo, } a robber.
Hic vespilio,
Hic primiplus, qui habet primam berbam.
Hic primipilus, qui fert pila ad prelia.
Primipilus berbam primam desingnat habentem,
Ast primipilus qui fert ad prelia pila.

Hic venator, a hunter.
Hic ephebus, a ȝung man.
Hic cimiflo, a nask-kyste.[1]
Hic mango, a cosyr.
Hic stabularius, a stabyler.
Hic macercator, a pleter.
Hic exelerarius, a byrler.[2]
Hic tribunus, a sawdyn.

CAPITULUM 5.
NOMINA ARTIFICIUM.

Hic emptor, a byer.
Hic venditor, a seller.
Hic mercator, a merchande.
Hic mercinarius, a mercer.
Hic pannarius, a draper.
Hic figalus, a potter.
Hic membrarius, a perchmenter.
Hic campanarius, a bel-maker.
[*Hic apo*]*ticarius,* a spycer.
[*Hec a*]*poteca,* a spycer schope.
Hic revelus, a peder.[3]
Hic faber, a smythe.
Hic aurifaber, a goldsmyth.
Hic carpentarius, a wryghte.
Hic tector, a theker.
Hic tegularius, a tyller.

Hic auceps, a fowler.
Hic sissor, a taylȝor.
Hic piscator, a fychere.
Hic piscarius, a fychmanger.
Piscator prendit quod piscarius bene vendit.
Hic textor, a webster.
Hic versor, a tornere.
Hic berbetonsor, a berbor.
Hic reciarius, a net-maker.
Hic fleobotomator, a blod-letter.
Hic monetarius, a mony-maker.
Hic serdo, } berkere.[4]
Hic frunitor,
Hic sellarius, a sadyler,
Hic urigenator, a frobycher.[5]
Hic sarrator, a sawer.
Hic fullo, a walker.
Hic tinctor, a lytster.[6]
Hic plumbarius, a plumber.
Hic sutor, } a sowter.[7]
Hic aluterius,
Hic picticiarius, a cobbeler.
Hic funerius, a ropere.
Hic restio, id.
Hic cribrarius, A^{cce} fys-maker.[8]
Hic pelliparius, A^{cce} skynner.
Hic molendinarius, a milner.
Hic farrator, a ferrur.
Hec murida, a ratunner.[9]
Hic cuperius, a cowper.
Hic victillarius, a hukster.
Hic capillarius, a bokyl-maker.
Hic scutarius, a scheld-maker.
Hic corrigiarius, A^{cce} gyrdil-maker.

---

[1] Called more usually an *askfyse,* the servant who made and blew the fire.

[2] The attendant who served the wine. The verb *birle,* (A.S. *birlian*) to draw or pour out wine, is not an uncommon word in the old writers. In the metrical romance of *The Avowynge of King Arther* (Robson's Metr. Rom., p. 80), we are told that there was at a great feast—

— rialle servys and fyne,
In bollus *birlutte* thay the wyne

[3] *Pedder* was the old name for a pedlar.

[4] *i. e.,* a tanner.

[5] See before, p. 195.

[6] *Lıtster,* a dyer.

[7] *Sowter,* a shoemaker; the Latin *sutor.* It is preserved in the Scottish dialect.

[8] From the Latin word, this would seem to mean a maker of sieves. Perhaps it should be *syf-maker.*

[9] A rat-catcher.

A NOMINALE.

Hic *lorinarius*, a loryner.[1]
Hic *cipharius*, a cop-maker.
Hic *sirotecarius*, A^{cce} gloyfer.
Hic *firmacularius*, a broch-maker.
Hic *nauta*, A^{cce} schypman.
Hic *medicus*, a leche.
Hic *carnifex*, a bocher.
Hic *circulator, qui amputat vites.*
Hic *tibiarius*, A^{cce} leg-maker.
Hic *carbonerius*, a col3er.[2]
Hic *pectinarius*, a come-maker.
Hic *cordex*, a stryng-maker.
Hic *plummarius*, a plumstere.
Hic *salinarius*, a salter.
Hic *anularius*, a ryng-maker.
Hic *corbio*, a pan3er-maker.
Hic *citaciarius*, a rel-maker.
Hic *circumforarius*, a mycher.[3]
Hic *vascularius*, a turner.
Hic *ursarius*, a ber-warde.
Hic *fossarius*, a dyker.
Hic *plantator*, a nymper.[4]
Hic *ortilanus*, a gardyner.
Hic *avigerulus*, a pulter.
Hic *tolonarius*, a toller.
Hic *rusticus*, a fyld-man.
Hic *villicus*, a town-man.
Hic *messor*, a scherer.
Hic *fulcator*, a mawer.
Hic *fugator*, a dryfer.
Hic *stinarius*, a halder.[5]
Hic *arator*, a tyller.
Hic *harpicator*, a haroer.
Hic *bigarius*, a cartter.
Hic *pastor*, a hyrd-man.
Hic *vaccarius*, a cow-herd.

Hic *equinarius*, a hors-harde.
Hic *mulundinarius*, a mul-harde.
Hic *asinarius*, a nas-hard.
Hic *bubulcus*, a swyn-herde.
Hic *aucarius*, a gos-herd.
Hic *pictor*, a panter.
Hic *sculptor*, a grafer.
Hic *smigmator*, a sop-seler.[6]
Hic *pugillus*, a schampyon.
Hic *latamus*, a mason.
Hic *simentarius, idem est.*
Hec *latomega*, a mason ax.
Hic *petro, -nis*, a mason schype.
Hec *regula*, a mason rewlle.
Hoc *perpendiculum, idem.*
Hec *amussis*, a mason lyne.
Hec *troclea*, a wyndas.
Hic *hostiarius*, a nostyller.
Hic *architenens*, a narcher.
Hic *pugnator*, a fyghter.
Hic *vestigator*, a trufer.
Hic *gemellus*, a twynlynge.
Hic *tortor*, a turmenter.
Hic *lictor, idem est.*
Hic *disculus*, a trowean.
Hic *trutannus, idem.*
Hic *cancellator,* }
Hic *alumnator,* }
Hic *ligator*, a bynder.
Hic *bajulator*, a berer.
Hic *cultellarius*, a cuteler.
Hic *balistarius, qui facit balistas.*
Hic *murator*, A^{cce} waller.
Hic *rotarius*, A^{cce} whel-maker.
Hic *cassarius*, a cas-maker.
Hic *ceparius*, A^{cce} un3on-seller.[7]

---

[1] A maker of horses' bits.
[2] i. e., a collier.
[3] A *micher* means one who goes sneaking about for improper purposes, as to steal on the sly, to act as a messenger in illicit amours, &c. In the latter sense, the verb *to mich* was in common use among the Elizabethan writers.
[4] Properly one who grafts, or who plants settings of trees. From the A.-S. *impian*, to graft, or plant.
[5] The man who held the plow.
[6] A dealer in soap. *Smigma* is usually taken for an unguent for perfuming, or pomatum.
[7] i. e., a seller of onions.

Hic pomilio, A^{cce} apul-seler.[1]
Hic tabernarius, A^{cce} taberner.
Hic caupo, idem est.
Hic candelarius, a candeller.
Hic cerarius, A^{cce} whax-maker.
Hic archonista, a bower.
Hic metellus, A^{cce} reve.
Hic inclusor, a pynder.
Hic mendicus, A^{cce} beggere.
Hic ruscator, a tylkyllere.
Hic naucherus, qui regit navym.
Hic polentradinator, A^{cce} a bulter.
Hic pistor, A^{cce} a baxter.
Hic pandoxator, A^{cce} brewster.
Hic focarius, a fewyller.
Hic ignarius, idem est.
Hic fauconerius, a fawconer.
Hic prebitor, qui dat prebenda.
Hic prebendarius, cujus sunt prebenda.
Hic dapifer, A^{cce} mettes gyffer.
Hic depositor, a serofer in halle.
Hic depositarius, ille qui commedit.
Hec familia, a menȝe.[2]
Hic peregrinus, A^{cce} a pylgrym.
Hic alienigena, A^{cce} a cumlynge.
Hic, hec comes, A^{cce} a felow.
Hic, hec sodalis, idem est.
Hic infans, ⎫
Hic pucio,   ⎬ A^{cce} a chylde.
Hic puer,   ⎭
Hic adolescens, est puer xiiij^{cem} annorum.
Hic decrepitus, ille qui radit cum baculo.
Hic tantillus, a dwarf.
Hic verbius, -ui, qui est beatus vel qui habet uxorem.
Hic perhendinator, A^{cce} a sogorner.
Hic liber, A^{cce} freman.

Hic libertinus, A^{cce} ille qui fit liber.
Hic gigas, a gyawnte.
Hic, hec pifundabalista, A^{cce} a slynger.
Hic texillaris, a spy in batylle.
Hic bestiarius, a pes-cryere.
Hic solenciarius, idem est.
Hic apprenticius, a prentys.
Hic cathecuminus, noviter conversus et non baptizatus.

CAPITULUM 6.
NOMINA CONSANGUINITATIS ET AFFINITATIS.

Hic triavus, the thyrde fadyre.
Hec triava, the thyrd fro the modyre.
Hic attavus, the thyrde fadyre.
Hec attava, the thyrd modyre.
Hic abavus, the secund fro thy fadyr.
Hec abava, the secunde fro the modyr.
Hic proavus, the forne fadyre.
Hec proava, the forne modyre.
Hic avus, A^{cce} a neld fadyre.
Hec ava, a nold modyre.
Hic pater, a fadyr.
Hec mater, a modyre.
Hic compater, a godfadyre.
Hic paternus, idem.
Hec commater, a godmodyre.
Hec materna, idem est.
Hic filius, ⎫
Hic natus, ⎬ a sune.
Hec filia, ⎫
Hec nata,   ⎬ A^{cce} a dowghter.
Hic filiolus, a godsune.
Hec filiola, A^{cce} a goddowghter.
Hic frater, a brodyr.
Hic germanus, A^{cce} a halfe-brodyre.
Hec soror, a syster.
Hec germana, a halfe-syster.
Hec fraternitas, a brotherode.

---

[1] i. e., a seller of apples.
[2] More properly written maisnie (from the Anglo-Norman), the household; the whole attendance upon the personal establishment of the feudal lord. It has no connection whatever with the word many (the Anglo-Saxon manig).

Hic fratruelis, filius patris.
Hec fraterna, filia fratris.
Hic sorarius, i. filius sororis.
Hec sororia, i. filia sororis.
Hic cognatus, a cosyne.
Hec cognata, a nese.
Hec neptis, idem est.
Hic affinis, a syb-mane.
Hic consanguinius, idem.
Hec consanguinia, a syb-womane.
Hic avunculus,
Hic patruus, } a neme.
Hec ameta,
Hec matertera, } a nawntt.
Hec abamita, soror avi.
Hic victricus, stepfadyr.
Hic patriarchus, idem.
Hic prevignus, a stepsune.
Hec filiaster,
Hec previgna, } a stepdowghter.
Hic gemellus, a twynlynge of men.
Hec gemella, a twynlynge of women.
Hic pupillus, a modyrles chylde.
Hic orphanus, a fadyrles chylde.
Hic orbus, qui privatur prole.
Hic aborticus, i. non suo tempore ortus.
Hic postimus, he that is born aftyr the deth of hys fadyre.
Hic proculius, est filius natus patre existente procul.
Hec pupilla, que caret parentibus.
Hec orba, que privatur prole.
Hec proculia, est nata patre existente procul.
Hic sponsus,
Hic conjunx, } a husband.
Hec sponsa,
Hec conjunx, } a wyfe.
Hec domiduca, a bryde.
Hoc conjugium,
Hoc sponsale, } a maryage.

Hec affinis, a lyans.
Hic socer, a neld-fadyre.
Her socrus, a nold-modyre.
Hic gener, a dowghter husband.
Hec nurus, i. uxor filii.
Hic sorarius, sponsus uxoris.
Hec glos,
Hec fratrissa, } *i. uxor fratris.*
Hic levex, i. frater mariti uxoris.
Hec noverca, a stepmodyr.

CAPITULUM 7.
NOMINA DIGNITATUM MULIERUM.

Hec imperatrix, a e[m]prys.
Hec induperatrix, idem.
Hec regina, qwen.
Hec ducissa, a duches.
Hec regula, idem.
Hec comitissa, a comytiss.
Hec baronissa, a baronyss.
Hec domina,
Hec hera, } a lady.
Hec abra,
Hec ancilla, } a bur-woman.[1]
Hec puella,
Hec ampha. } a madyn
Hec adolescentula, puella xiiij^cem [annorum].
Hec materfa[mi]lias, huswyf.
Hec nutrix, A^cce norysch.
Hec ridua, a wydo.
Hec equitrissa, que equitat.
Hec anus, a nold wyff.
Hec claviger, que portat c[laves].
Hec ignaria, que facit i[gnem].
Hec ostiaria, a ostylle[re].
[Hec fem]ina, a woman.
[Hec f]abrissa, A^cce a smyth wyfe.
Hec rustica, A^cce a feldman wyfe.
Hec obstetrix, a mydwyfe.
Hec abatissa, A^cce a abatyse.

---
[1] *i. e.*, a chambermaid.

Hec monialis, a nune.
Hec patronissa, idem est.
Hec sacerdotissa est femina dans sacra.
Hic, hec sinobita, qui vel que manet in sinobio.
Hec anacorita, a ankrys.

NOMINA ARTIFICIUM MULIERUM.

Hec pectrix, a kempster.
Hec textrix, a webster.
Hec scutrix, a sewster.
Hec tontrix, a barbor.
Hec pistrix, a baxter.
Hec pandoxatrix, a brewster.
Hec filatrix, A^{cce} a spynner.
Hec carpetrix, a carder.
Hec lotrix, a lawnder.
Hec siccatrix, a dryster.
Hec reciaria, A^{cce} a kel-maker.
Hec palmaria, a brawdster.
Hec salinaria, a salster.
Hec avigerula, que vendit aves.
Hec sereatrix, a sylk-maker.
Hec androchia, a dayre.
Hec apoticaria, A^{cce} a spyser wyfe.
Hec auxiatrix, a hukster.

NOMINA JUGULATARUM MULIERUM.[1]

Hec citharista, a herper.
Hec lericina, idem est.
Hec tubicina, A^{cce} a trumper.
Hec fistilatrix, a piper wyfe.
Hec jugulatrix, a jugoler.
Hec saltatrix, a tumbler.
Hec secutissina, que canit in secuta.
Hec tripudiatrix, a dawnser.
Hec timpanizatrix, A^{cce} a tymburnar.

NOMINA REPREHENSIBILIUM VIRORUM.

Hic gulo, a gluton.
Hic ego, -nis, idem.
Hic leno, -nis, baustrott.[2]
Hic adulter, a spowsbreker.
Hic mecus, A^{cce} lechowr.
Hic fornicator, idem est.
Hic fenerator, } a usurer.
Hic usurator,
Hic et hec scurra, a rebalde.
Hic et hec fur, a theffe.
Hic, hec latro, idem.
Hic ereticus, } a herytik.
Hic sismaticus,
Hic spoliator, A^{cce} a robber.

---

[1] A Nominale in MS. Reg. 17, C. xvii., fol. 43, v°, gives the following rather curious list relating to minstrelsy and games :

Hic castrator. Anglice lybbere.
Hic prestigiator, Anglice mynstralle.
Hec cithera, Anglice harpe.
Hec lira, Anglice harpe-stryng.
Hoc plectrum, Anglice warete.
His citheredus, } *Anglice* harpure.
Hec cithereda,
His tubicen, } *Anglice* troumpe.
Hec tuba,
Hic fidis, Anglice fydellere.
Hec viella, Anglice fedylle.
Hic arculus, Anglice fydyl-styk.
His gigator, Anglice getyrnere.
Hec giga, Anglice getyrne.
His simbolisator, Anglice crowde.
Hoc simbolum, Anglice scotnyng.
Simbolisare, to crowde or scotnyg.
His simphonia, Anglice mynstrylay.
His corallus, Anglice crowdere.
Hec coralla, Anglice crowde.
Hoc psalterium, Anglice sawter.
Hoc organum, Anglice orguna.
Hoc simpharium, Anglice synfan.
Hic joculator, } *Anglice* jogulour.
Hic mimus,
Hic tripidiator, Anglice dawnsere.
Hoc tripudium, Anglice dawnse.
Hec corea. Anglice carolle.
Hec fascia, Anglice credil-sang.
His fistulator, Anglice pypere.
Hec fistula, Anglice pype.
Hic escubius, } *Anglice* wayte.
His expoliator,
Hec colomaula, Anglice wayte-pype.
Hoc expiridium, Anglice rede.
Hec saltatrix, Anglice tumbullere.
Hic gestiarius, Anglice gester.
Hic scurra, Anglice harlot.
Hic nugator, Anglice japer.
Hec nuga, Anglice jape.
Hic nugigerulus, Anglice trifulere.

[2] *Baustrott,* a bawd.

A NOMINALE.

Hic explorator, a spyer.
Hic muricidus, a losynge.[1]
Hic bilinguis, qui habet binas linguas.
Hic pelinguis, a hor-coppe.[2]
Hic murmurator, a grocher.
Hic garcio, a knave.
Hic sacerdotulus, i. filius sacerdotis.
Hic spirius, a basterde.
Hic nothus, contrarius spirio.
Hic, hec homicida, a man-sleer.
Hec, hic patricida, A^{cce} que vel qui occidit patrem.
Hec, hic matricida, que vel qui occidit matrem.
Hec, hic parenticida, qui vel que occidit parentes.
Hic duribuctus, a dasyberd.[3]
Hic aliator, a haserder.
Hic sarberus, i. janitor inferni.
Hic aquariolus,
Hic, hec exul, a nowtlay.
Hic tortor, a turmentur.
Hic et hec armifraudita, a skratt.[4]
Hic, hec apostita, qui bene incipit et statim recedit.
Hic antechristus, ancryst.
Hic zelotopus, a kukwald.
Hic nerenus, idem est.
Hunc dico zelotopum cui non sua sufficit uxor.

NOMINA REPREHENSIBILIUM MULIERUM

Hec meritrix,
Hec tabernaria, } a strumpytt.
Hec saga, a wech.
Hec fornicatrix, a sinner.

Hec pronuba, a bawdstrott.[5]
Hec sacerdotula, i. filia sacerdotis.
Hec adulteria, a spowsbrekere.
Hec elena, A^{cce} a strumpytt.
Est meretrix elena, virgo vocatur Elena.

Hec caupana, A^{cce} a taverner wyffe.
Hec taberna, idem est.
Hec caricia, i. fallax ancilla.
Hec concubina, a leman.

NOMINA RERUM PERTINENCIUM UXORI.

Hic colus, a roke.
Hic fusus, a spyndylle.
Hoc alabrum, a relle.
Hec mataxa, a hekylle.
Hoc virgilium, a par garnwyndil-blades.
Hoc canabum, a hemp.
Hoc linum, A^{cce} lyn.
Hoc filum, A^{cce} threde.
Hoc glomus, a clewe.
Hoc lapsum, a top of lin.
Hic folliculus, a betylle.[6]
Hoc linerium, A^{cce} lyn-sed.
Hec rupa, a brake.
Hoc exculidium, A^{cce} a swyndyl-stoc.
Hoc excudium, a swyndil-land.
Hec stupa, a hardes.
Hoc rectubrum, a whelle.
Hec rota, idem est.
Hic linipolus, a stric of lyne.[7]
Hec troilia, a trindylle.[8]
Hoc multrum, a kytt.[9]
Hec lamia, slay.[10]
Hoc pecten, idem.

---

[1] *Losynge*, a worthless fellow.
[2] i. e., a bastard.
[3] *Dasyberd*, a simpleton, or fool.
[4] *Skratt*, a hermaphrodite. The word is still in use in the dialects of the north of England. It is the pure Anglo-Saxon word. See before, p. 45.
[5] *Bawdstrott*. The meaning of the word is here identical with that in which it is used in a preceding chapter.
[6] *Betylle*, the instrument with which the flax was beaten.
[7] *Stric*, perhaps *strike*, a measure.
[8] The wheel. It is still in use in the dialect of Derbyshire.
[9] A pail.
[10] The name for a part of the weaver's loom.

Hoc multrale, A^{cce} a mylk-sele.
Hoc lacinatorium, a slek-stone.¹
Hoc laciatorium, A^{cce} a web-beme.
Hoc stamen, a warpe.
Hec trama, A^{cce} a wefte.²
Hec forigo, a lystynge.³
Hoc ventilabrum, a wyndyllynge.
Hic saccus, a seke.

NOMINA JUGULATORUM.

Hic jugulator, A^{cce} a jogoler.
Hic citharista, A^{cce} a herper.
Hic tubicen, A^{cce} a trumper.
Hic fistilator, A^{cce} a piper.
Hic ridulator, a fydeler.
Hic secuticen, qui canit in secuta.
Hic cornuten, qui canit a cornu
Hic saltator, a tumbler.
Hic timpanizator, a taberner.
Hic gladiator, a swerd-plaer.
Hic choricista, qui canit in choro.
Hic barbatissa, qui canit in barbita.
Hic simphonista, A^{cce} a simphoner.
Hic tripudiator, a dawnser.
Hic et hec lerecen, a herper.
Hic, hec coraula, qui vel que ducit coria in aula.
Hic organista, qui ludit ad organa.
Hic buccinator, a trumper.
Hic simphonizator, a simphoner.
Hic citolator, a cytolerer.

NOMINA OPERARIORUM.

Hic cultor, a tylman.
Hic, hec agricola, idem est.
Hic rusticus, a churle.

Hic frondator, a wod-feller.
Hic vector, A^{cce} a berer.
Hic triturator, A^{cce} a tasker.⁴
Hic vinitor, a wyn-maker.
Hic septor, a heg-maker.
Hic litor, A^{cce} a dowker.
Hic aqueductor, a water-leder.
Hic aquebajulus, a holi-water clerke.
Hic runcator, ⎱ lowker.⁵
Hic circulator, ⎰
Hic colibertus, A^{cce} a carle.⁶
Hic operarius, A^{cce} a werkman.

NOMINA ANIMALIUM DOMESTICORUM.

Hic equus, a hors.
Hec equa, a mer.
Hoc jumentum, quoddam animal adjuvans.
Hic dextrarius, A^{cce} a stede.
Hic succussarius, a trotter.
Hic gradarius, a hawmbler.
Hic emissarius, a stalan.
Hic caballus, A^{cce} a cabylle.⁷
Hic spado, -nis, a haknay.
Hic veredus, A^{cce} a cartt-hors.
Hic admissarius, equus qui portat arma.
Hic pullus, a folle.
Hic equiferus, a wyld.hors.
Hec equifera, a wyld mer.
Hoc equicium, a hares.
Hic, hec bos, -vis, a nox.
Hic taurus, a bulle.
Hec vacca, a kowe.
Hic buculus, a stott.
Hec juvenca, a qwye.⁸

---

¹ Perhaps for *flek-stone.* The Latin *liciatorium* is interpreted in later vocabularies as the *yarn-beam.*
² The woof.
³ The list of cloth.
⁴ *Tasker, i. e.,* a thrasher. The word is now used in some dialects for a reaper; perhaps so named as working by *task,* or piece.
⁵ A weeder.
⁶ The sense here given to the word *carle,* as synonymous with *collibertus,* generally taken to signify a freedman, is curious.
⁷ *i. e.,* a capul, or horse of burthen.
⁸ *Quye,* a female calf.

Hic vitulus, a calfe.
Hec vitula, qwye calffe.
Hoc armentum, a drowe.
Hec ovis, a schepe.
Hec ovicula, idem est.
  Que male fetet ovis non est melior tribus ....
Hec adacia, i. ovis vitula.
Hec apica, a scabbyd ewe.
Hic titerus, A^{cce} a bel-wether.
Hec bidua, a gymbyre.
Hic agnus, a lame.
Hec agna, a new lame.
Hec cenaria, A^{cce} a cad.[1]
Hec aries, }
Hec berber, } *A^{cce}* weder.
Hic vervex, A^{cce} a tuppe.
Hic grex, a floke.
Hic singulus, }
Hic aper, } *A^{cce}* a bore.
Hic nefrendus, a galtte.
Hec sus, suis, a sowe.
Hec scropha, idem est.
Hic porcus, A^{cce} a hoge.
Hic porcellus, idem est.
Hic ircus, a gat.
Hec capra, idem est.
Hec caprella, a sche gatt.
Hic capriolus, a lytil gatt.
Hic asinus, A^{cce} a nas.
Hec asina, uxor ejus.
Hic burdo, i. genitum inter equum et asinam.
Hic mulus, A^{cce} a mule.
Hec mula, a mule.
Hic camelus, a camylle.
Hec camela, uxor ejus.
Hic dromedarius, a dromedary.

Hic dromedus, a dromund.
Hic, hec canis, a hunde.
Hic catellus, a whelpe.
Hec canicula, a byche.
Hic adorrinsicus, a spanȝelle.
Hic leporarius, a grayhund.
Hic molosus, a band-doge.
Hic aggregarius, a scheperd dog.
Hic luciscus, est canis genitus inter canem et vulpem.
Her lucisca, est canicula similiter nata.
Hic caniculus, a kenet.[2]
Hic mureligus, a catt.
Hir catus, idem est.
Hic catulus, a kytylyng.[3]
Hic catellus, idem.
Hec polea, est colleccio vel pluralitas quorumcunque bestarum.

NOMINA FERARUM.

Hic leo, A^{cce} a lyon.
Hec lea, }
Hec leena, } *A^{cce}* a lyonys.
Hic leopardus, A^{cce} a leberde.
Hec leoparda, uxor ejus.
Hic, hec elephas, -antis, a clephawnt.
Hic unicornus, A^{cce} a unycorne.
Hec simia, A^{cce} a nappe.
Hic cervus, a hertt.
Hec cerva, A^{cce} a hynde.
Hec capra, }
Hec davas, } *A^{cce}* a ra-buke.
Hec doma, A^{cce} a doo.
Hic enulus, A^{cce} a fawne.
Hic lupus, A^{cce} a wolffe.
Hec lupa, uxor ejus.
Hic vulpes, A^{cce} a fox.

---

[1] *Cad.* This word is at present used in the dialect of the eastern counties to signify a very small pig.

[2] A small species of hunting dog, mentioned often in the old writers on the chase, and not uncommonly in the metrical romances, and supposed by some to be equivalent with our harrier. The word, however, seems to be often used as the simple equivalent of a hound.

[3] A kitten.

Hic ursus, A^{cce} a bere.
Hec ursa, uxor ejus.
Hic urunacius, A^{cce} a urchen.
Hic castor, A^{cce} a bever.
Hic canisponticus, idem.
Hic cirogrillus, a sqwerylle.
Hic taxus, A^{cce} a broke.
Hec melota, idem est.
Hic lutricius, a notyre.
Hec mustela, wesylle.
Hic sorex, A^{cce} a raton.
Hic mus, -ris, A^{cce} a mows.
Hic glis, } *A^{cce}* a dormows.
Hic sorex,
Hic nex, -cis, media producta, animal simile capre.
Hic ferutus, A^{cce} a forytt.
Hic sinozephalus, a mancowe.[1]
Hic fetoutrus, A^{cce} a fulmard.[2]
Hic tigris, -ris vel -dis, velox animal.
Hic linx, animal penetrans parietes visu oculorum suorum.
Hic panter, animal diversi coloris.
Hic gamelion, animal varii coloris et sola aere vivit, a buttyrfle.
Hic onager, A^{cce} a wyld has.
Hic tragelaphus, } *parte cervus parte*
Hic hircocervus, } *ircus.*
Hic effimatus, animal inpungnans serpentes.
Hic cocadrillus, A^{cce} a cocadrylle.
Hec talpa, A^{cce} a molle.
Hic spinx, vermis lucens in noctibus.
Hic lepus, A^{cce} a hare.
Hic cuniculus, A^{cce} a conynge.

NOMINA VOLATILIUM DOMESTICORUM.

Hic gallus, a coke.

Hec gallina, A^{cce} a henne.
Hic capo, A^{cce} a capon.
Hic pullus, A^{cce} a chekyn.
Hic, hec natis, -tis, A^{cce} a malerde.
Hec anas, -tis, A^{cce} a duke.
Hic ancer, A^{cce} a gander.
Hec auca, A^{cce} a gose.
Hic ancerulus, a geslynge.
Hec columba, a dowfe.
Hic pavo, A^{cce} a pecoke.
Hic signus, } *A^{cce}* a swanne.
Hic olor,

NOMINA VOLATILIUM INCOMESTILIUM.

Hec ales, A^{cce} a byrde.
Hec volucris, idem est.
Hec aquila, A^{cce} a negylle.
Hic grifes, a grefyne.
Hic falco, a fawkon.
Hic erodius, A^{cce} a jarfawkon.
Hic ancipiter, A^{cce} a goshawke.
Hic tercellus, a tercelle.
Hic nisus, a sperhawk.
Hic capus, A^{cce} a muskytt.
Hic milvus, a glede.
Hic condulus, A^{cce} a busherde.
Hic corvus, a rawyn.
Hic cornix, A^{cce} a crawe.
Hic nicticorax, a nyght-craw.
Hic struccio, a nostryche.
Hic bubo, A^{cce} a nowlle.
Hic castrimergus, a wodkoke.
Hic ibis, -dis, } a snype.
Hic ibex, -cis,
Hic onocrotalus, a butturre.[3]
Hic pelicanus, A^{cce} a pelican.
Hec upipa, A^{cce} a wype.[4]
Hec vespertilio, a bake.[5]

[1] *Mancowe,* a baboon.
[2] A polecat. The word is still in use in the northern dialects.
[3] The bittern.
[4] *Wype,* the lapwing.
[5] *Bake* was the old form of bat.

A NOMINALE.

Hec monedula, a kowe.
Hic picus, }
Hec pica, } a pye.
Hic graculus, A^{cce} a jaye.
Hic irundo, a swalo.
  Crescit harundo, sugit hirudo, canit hirundo.
Hec toda, a wagsterd.[1]
Hic regulus, a wrenne.
  Regulus est serpens, avis, et rex parvulus omnis.
Hec frigella, a roberd.[2]
Hic psitacus, A^{cce} a papynjay.
Hic cuculus, A^{cce} a cauko.
Hec philomena, a nyghtynggale.
Hic phenix, media producta, a phenes.
Hec arpipia, i. rapax.
Hec alcedo, a wodwale.
Hec lucinia, }
Hic carduelis, } a goldfynche.
Hic turtur, A^{cce} a turtyl-dowff.
Hec alauda, A^{cce} a larke.
Hic palustris, a rede-sparowe.[3]
Hec calendula, a plovere.
Hic conturnix, a qwaylle.
Hic fecianus, a fesantt.
Hic maviscus, a thyrstylle.
Hic sturnus, a sterlynge.
Hic frondator, a sterkyng.
Hic perdix, a partryke.
Hic ficedula, a nuthage.[4]
Hec ardia, a haron.
Hic palumbus, a cowscott.[5]
Hec fulceca, a semawe.[6]
Hic passer, a sparowe.
Hec merges, a cott.
Hic ruruscus, a feldfare.
Hic garulus, a thrus.

Hic pratellus, a buntyle.[7]
Hic virudiarius, a ruddoke.[8]
Hec sarra, a wyld drake.
Hic, hec grus, a crane.
Hic conturnix, a kyrlewe.
Hec campestrer, a feldfare.
Hic viscus, a byrd-lyme.
Hoc viscerium, a lyme-pott.
Hec vitubila, a pytt-falle.
Hec discipula, a swyke.[9]
Hoc falconerium, a fawconere moe.
Hoc aucipium, a hawkynge.

PARTES ANIMALIUM BRUTORUM.

Hoc stirillum, a gaytt berde.
Hec juba, a hors mane.
Hec cornu, indeclinabile, a horne.
  Corna gerit cornus, pecudum sunt cornua . . .
  Militis est quando properat sua bella gerendo.
Hoc rostrum, a bylle.
Hec ceta, a brystille.
Hec crista, est crinis vel quod eminet super galeam et super capita quorundam animalium, the cokcome.
Hec galla, idem est.
Hic pugio, -nis, a tange.[10]
Hec ungula, a clee.
Hec calcar, a spure.
Hoc paliare, a dewlappe.
Hec cauda, a taylle.
Hec ala, a wenge.
Hec pinna, a fynne.
Hec pluma, a fedyre.
Hec penna, a penne.
Hoc ilum, the pyf of the penne.
Hec lana, wolle.

---

[1] *Wagsterd*, probably the water-wagtail.
[2] The chaffinch.
[3] The reed-sparrow.
[4] *Nuthage*, the nuthatch.
[5] See before, p. 62.
[6] *Semawe*, probably the sea-mew.
[7] *Buntyle*, the bunting, or woodlark.
[8] The robin. See, on the popular name of this familiar bird, a former note, p. 188.
[9] *Swyke*, a trap, or snare, for birds.
[10] *Tange*, a sting, still used in the north of England.

Hoc vellus, a fleys.
Hic villus, a lok of wolle.
Hec brunda, a harte horne.
Hec suama, a scalle.
Hec brancia, } a gylle.
Hec senecia,
Hec lactis, a cheslepe.[1]
Hoc cepum, talowe.
Hic armus, a spawde.
Hec vicecolla, a gragge.
Hec membrana, est pellis ale vespertilionis.
Hoc jecor, a mawe.
Hoc reticulum, pinguedo circa jecur.
Hoc pectusculum, a bruskette.

NOMINA PISCIUM.

Hic piscis, a fyche.
   Hic editur piscis, hec servat aromata pixis.
Hec belua, i. animal magnum m[a]ris.
Hic cetus, a whalle.
   Est hominum coetus, set vivit in equore cetus.
Hec balena, a balene.
Hic salmo, -nis, a sawmun.
Hec amphinia,
Hic delfinis, } a porpas.
Hec foca,
Hoc allec, a herynge.
Hic congruus, a cungyre.
Hic megarus, a macrelle.
Hec lampreda, a lampray.
Hec murenula, a lamprun.
Hec anguilla, a nele.
Hic polanus, } a place.
Hic pecten,
Hic molanurus, piscis qui magnam caudam.
Hic dentrix, a pyke.
Hic lucius, a lewse.
Hic luticulus, a pyke.
Hic turbo, -nis, a turbott.

Hic uronoscopus, a thornbake.
Hec ragadia, raye.
Hec epimera, a sprott.
Hec truta, a trowte.
Hic capito, a bulhede.
Hic morus, a haddoke.
Hic gulio, -nis, a goryone.
Hic solimicus, a menawe.
Her alosa, a loch.
Hic gamerus, a styklynge.
Her tenia, a tenche.
Hic brimellus, a breme.
Hic pelanius, a flewke.
Hic ipotamus, i. equus marinus.
Hic suamatus, a hund-fych.
Hec squilla, piscis delecatus.
Hec sirena, a mermaydyn.
Hoc ostrium, } a nostyre.
Her ostria,
Hic musculus, a muscul.
Hic cancer, a crabbe.
Hic polipus, } a lopster.
Hec gorra,
Her cepia, est piscis de quo fit caustum.
Hic sperlyngus, } a sperlynge.
Hic thimalus,
Hic rumbus, a sturyon.
Hec fungia, stok-fyche.
Hic mulus, a mulett.
Her folea, a fol-fyche.
Hic glaucus, a whytynge.
Her balbena, a balbene.
Hic norus, a melle-welle.
Hoc conchile, -lis, alle manner schel-fyche.

NOMINA VERMIUM ET MUSCARUM.

Hic vermis, a worme.
Hic drago, a dragone.
Hic serpens, a nedyre.

---

[1] Rennet is still called *cheeselope* in the north.

A NOMINALE.

Hic basiliscus, rex serpencium.
Hic idrus, a watyr-nedyre.
Hic natrix, -cis, violator aquarum.
Hic hispis, -dis, quoddam genus serpentis.
Hic ibis, -dis, } a neddyre.
Hic coluber, }
Hic ferastrix, a hornyde eddyre.
Hoc amphibim, est serpens cum tribus capitibus.
Hic jaculus, } a flyande eddyre.
Hic biceps, }
Hec arena, } a neranc.
Hec aranea, }
Hic bufo, a tode.
Hec rana, a frosche.
Hec lacerta, a newtt.
Hic scorpio, a scorpyone.
Hic pulex, a flye.
Hic lens, -dis, a nyte.
  Lens, -dis, capiti, lens, -tis, convenitur ori.
Hic multipes, a welbode.[1]
Hec cencipita, idem est.
Hec scutula, a blynd-worme.
Hoc tumultum, est vermis in cornubus arietum.
Hec tinia, a moke.
Hec terudo, -nis, a tre-worme.
Hic trunos, idem est.
Hic ciro, -nis, a hande-worme.
Hic limax, a snyle.

Hec eruca, a cole-worm.
Hec sanguissuga, a hors-leche.
Hic pediculus, a lows.
Hic pedicus, idem est.
Hec ascarida, a schep-lows.
Hic tramus, a mowght.
Hec lendex, -cis, idem.
Hic serastes, i. serpens cornutus.
Hic dipsas, -dis, i. quidam serpens.
Hec musca, a flye.
In plurali numero hee serene sunt serpentes volantes.
Hec musio, -nis, a grett flye.
Hec apes, -is, a bee.
Hic fucus, a drane.
Hoc examen, a swarme.
Hec juxura, a hyfe.
Hec vaspa, a waspe.
Hic rambricus, a paddoke.[2]
Hoc orameum, i. collectio apum.
Hic papilio, a buttyrflye.
Hec polemita, a somer-boyde.[3]
Hec sicoma, a myge.[4]
Hic culex, a gnaytt.
Hic brucus, a breas.[5]
Hec cicada, a grysope.
Hec salamandra, a crekytt.
Hic crabius,[6] a cercole.
Hic bumbio, a hund-flye.
Hic ariax, a hert horne.
Hec formica, a pysmyre.

---

[1] *Welbode,* a woodlouse.
[2] *Paddoke.* Possibly the Latin should be *lumbricus*, which is explained in the next glossary as signifying a tadpole. There appears to have been always some little diversity in the use of the word *paddock*. In some of the modern English dialects it is applied to a frog. We might naturally suppose it to be a diminutive of *pade*, which was also a name for a toad; and a passage in the Coventry Mysteries, p. 164, evidently makes a distinction between the two words—

I seal prune that *paddok*, and prevyn hym as a pad
An English gloss of the latter part of the fourteenth century (Reliq. Ant. vol. i., p. 8,) explains the Latin *rana* by a *paddoke*, which agrees with the English provincial use of the word just alluded to.

[3] The same Latin word is explained in the next glossary by a *bude*—apparently a species of beetle.
[4] A midge, or gnat.
[5] The breeze, or gadfly.
[6] Perhaps for *crabro*, a hornet.

Hec apaphsibena, a nedyr with ij. hedes.
Hec urma, a eges-worme.
Hic papheas, serpens cum grosso capite.
Hec bredraca, serpens habens faciem hominis.

NOMINA MORBORUM ET INFIRMORUM VIRORUM.

Hec lepra, a mesylery.
Hec serpedo, a mesylle.
Hic cancer, the cankere.
Hec porigo, a poke.
Hec papula, a red-spott.
Hoc glandulum, a wax-kyrnylle.[1]
Hec pustula, a blane.
Hec scabies, a scabbe.
Hec glabra, a scalle.
Hec podegra,
Hic perneo, } a mowlle.
Hec sinnancia, a swynacye.
Hic gibbus, a boche in bake.
Hic figus, the fyge.
Hec struma, a boch in the brestes.
Hec siragra, i. nodositas manuum.
Hec tussis, -sis, the host.
Hic caterrus, the pose.
Hec spasma, the cramppe.
Hec tisis, the tyssyke.
Hec ypomanes, the fransey.
Hic bubo, -nis, i. morbus sub ano.
Hic frebris, the fevere.
Hic fluxus, the flux.
Hoc ulcus, -ris, a kyle.
Hec apostema, a postem.
Hoc vulnus,
Hec plaga, } a wonde.
Hec cicatrix, a festyre.
Hic, hec intereus, est morbus inter carnem et cutem.
Hec muliebria,

In plurali hec menstrua, sunt infirmitates mulierum.
Hec idropis, -dis vel -pis, dropsye.
Hic pruritus,
Hec prurigo, } a 3ekynge.
Hec extisis, -is, a swoynyng.
Hic litergus,
Hec litergia, } *i. infirmitas.*
Hec surditas, a defnes.
Hic tumor, -ris, bolnynge.
Hec cecitas, -tis, a blyndnes.
Hec dissentaria, est divicio vel ulceratio intestinorum.
Hec lippitudo, est infirmitas occulorum.
Hec paralisis, pallsay.
Hec lentigo,
Hec lenticula, } a frakkyne.[2]
Hec gutta, a gutt.
Hec impetico, sicca scabies.
Hec sinax, -cis, pursenes, *vel quoddam festum.*
Hec gutturna, the qwynse, *et inde* gut.
Turnosus, -a, -um, full off that ewelle.
Hec commissialis, i. morbus caducus.
Hec glaucoma, a the gowyl sowght.
Hec ictaricia, the jandis.

NOMINA INFIRMORUM.

Hic infirmus, a sek mane.
Infirmus, -a, -um, seke.
Morbosus, -a, -um, full of ewylle.
Languidus, -a, -um, sorounde.
Leprosus, -a, -um, leperus.
Limatygus, -a, -um, lymatyke.
Limphaticus, -a, -um, hafande the fransey.
Hic erecticius, qui vexatur multis demonibus.
Surdus, -a, -um, defe.
Mutus, -a, -um, dowme.

---

[1] *Wax-kyrnylle*. Palsgrave has the word *waxenkernel*, which is explained as meaning an enlarged gland in the neck.

[2] A freckle.

A NOMINALE.

Hec stroba, a woman glyande.[1]
Mutulatus, -a, -um, handles.
Cardiacus, -a, -um, purse.
Idropicus, -a, -um, hafand the dropsy.
Cecus, -a, -um, blynd.
Claudus, -a, -um,
Hic et hec loripes, qui habet pedem ligneum.
Extalus, media producta,
Litergitus, -a, -um, } *i. obliviosus*.
Hic strabo, -nis, a glyere.
Luscus, -a, -um, he that is sand-blynde [2]
Lippus, -a, -um, blere-yed.
Hic monoculus, a one-eyd man.
Hic lanaculus, qui fert lanam ad oculos tergendos.
Paraliticus, -a. -um, hafand the pallsy.
Harniosus, -a, -um, burstyn.
Calculosus, -a, -um, hafand the stone.
Gutturnosus, -a, -um, hafand the qwynsy.
Semicecus, -a, -um, half-blynd.
Gibbosus, -a, -um, bochy.

NOMINA ARBORUM ARABILIUM ET FLORUM.

Hec arba, a herbe.
Hec arbula, idem.
Hec salgia, a sawge.
Hec minta, mynt.
Hoc petrocillum, persylle.
Hic ditamnus, detane.
Hoc feniculum, fynkylle.
Hic isopus, -pi, ysope.
Hoc cerbellum, pellatur.
Hoc olus, -ris, cole.
Hec maguderis, a calstok.[3]
Hec beta, idem est.

Hec borago, -nis, borage.
Hoc porrum, a leke.
Hic bilbus, a lekes hed.
Hoc porrulum, a portte.
Hoc sepe, a nonʒone.[4]
Hec sepa, a chesbolle.[5]
Hec hinnula, a scalyone.
Hec fantula, idem est.
Fantulus est filius, sed fantula crescit in ortis.
Hec ascolonia, a holleke.
Hec allia, garleke.
Hoc allium, idem est.
Hec columbina, a columbyne.
Hic crocus, sapherone.
Hec ruta, rewe.
Hoc caliandrum, a caliawndyre.
Hoc cinamonum, canylle.
Hoc piper, pepyre.
Hoc seminum, comyne.
Hec eruta, whytte pepyre.
Hec lactuca, letys.
Hoc lens, -tis, quoddam genus liguminis.
Hic sinollus, a chesbolle.
Hec rapa, a neppe.
Hoc rapum, idem.
Hec napus, genus liguminis.
Hec sinapis, herba ferens sinapia.
Hoc sinapi, indeclinabile, semen sinapis.
Hec camamilla, camamelle.
Hec sandax, -cis, maddyre.
Hoc sinicium, a tasylle.
Hec pionia, a pione.
Hoc lilium, a lylye.
Hoc apium, smalege.[6]
Hoc melo, -nis, genus liguminis.
Hic cucumer, cel -mis, a palmer-nutte.[7]

---
[1] *Glyante*, squinting.
[2] Sand-blind, *i. e.* dim-sighted.
[3] *Calstok*, called in the Prompt. Parv. a *calke-stoke*, is explained by Palsgrave *pié de chou*, and is supposed to mean the stalk of the cale, or colewort.
[4] An onion.
[5] The word can hardly mean here a poppy.
[6] Smallage, or wild celery (the *apium grave olens* of botanists).
[7] *Palmer nutte*. The next vocabulary explain cucumer by a *flage*.

Hoc cucumerium, locus ubi crescunt.
Hec betonia, betony.
Hic flos, -ris, a flowre.
Hoc floretum, locus ubi crescunt.
Hec verveta, a verveyn.
Hec egrumonia, egromonyn.
Hoc absinthium, wormwod.
Hec artemesia, mugwortt.
Hoc millefolium, A^{cce} ʒarow.
Hic costus, rybbe.
Hec plantago, -nis, waybrede.
Hec paradilla, a doke.
Hec urtica, a netylle.
Hoc urticetum, a netyl-buske.
Hec arundo, -nis, a red.
Hec buglossa, oxtunge.[1]
Hec secuta, a humloke.
Hec anacia, anas.
Hec genciana, a gencyan.
Hoc polipodicum, a pollypod.
Hoc folium, est herba natans sine radice.
Hec felix, -cis, media corrupta, brakyne.
Hoc felicetum, } a brakyn-buske.
Hoc filacerium, }
Hec viola, a vyolytte.
Hic cardo, -nis, media corrupta, thystylle.
Hic cirpus, hic junccus, a rysche.
Hic papirus, a sene.[2]
Hic papirio, locus ubi crescunt.
Hec carex, -icis, a flege.
Hoc carecetum, locus ubi crescunt.
Hic scabius, -ii, scabryge.
Hec malva, a maloo.
Hec celidonia, celydoun.

Hec filago, quedam herba.
Hoc vastucium, welcresse.
Hoc ligustrum, a primerose.
Hec elenacampana, horshalle.[3]
Hec uticella, haryffe.[4]
Hic fragus, a strebere-wyse.
Hoc fragum, a strebere.
Hec cimnicia, hund-fynkylle.
Hic ebolus, wal-wortte.
Hoc albatorium, sothernwode.
Hec amarusa, donfynkylle.[5]
Hoc consolidum, a daysey.
Hec hastula, wodruffe.
Hec lavendula, lavandyre.
Hec ipia, chekyn-mette.
Hec loriala, loryalle.
Hec scurera, saveray.
Hoc tansetum, tansaye.
Hoc epitimeum, tyme.
Hec vermicularis, ston-croppe.
Hec valmaria, pene-grysse.
Hoc glustrum, flowrd of feld. *Unde invenitur metrice de beata virgine:*

O mater, glustri decor, candorque ligustri,
Labe cadens lustri, necnon et sorde palustri,
Nato prelustri me jungas more colustri,
Ne regar amplustri Satane per lirida lustri.

Hec spurgia, a sporge.
Hec tormentilla, tormentyne.
Hec alcia, est magna silvestris.
Hec caperis, i. herba frutex spinosus.
Hec bursa pastaris, hare-belle.
Hec centaria, centarye.
Hoc ligustrum, a cowslowpe.
Hoc porarium, a lek-bed.
Hoc subterrarium, a debylle.
Papaver, A^{c} a chespolle.[6]

---

[1] Bugloss, the *lycopsis arvensis* of botanists.
[2] The wild nasturtium.
[3] Called elsewhere *horsehelin*.
[4] *Haryffe.* In Gloucestershire the name *hairiff* is given to the plant called more usually cleavers, or goose-grass (*apium aparine*); in the north it is applied to catchweed.
[5] Perhaps *amarusa* is a corruption of *amaracus*, which is explained differently as meaning sweet marjoram (*origanum vulgare*), or feverfew (*pyrethrum parthenium*).
[6] A poppy. See the preceding page.

DE NOMINIBUS SPECIERUM.

Hic apoticarius, a spyere.
Hec species, -ei, spyce.
 Est species logicus, est altera grammaticorum,
 Estque genus species, species est forma virorum,
 Est eciam species gratum quod prestat odorem;
 Totque modus species viriatur quot monitorem.
Hoc piper, -ris, peper.
Hic crocus, saferon.
Hoc amigdalum, a almunde.
Hoc amigdalatum, almund-mylk.[1]
Hec ficus, a fyke, or a fykes.
 Hic ficus morbus, hec ficus fructus et arbor.
Hoc ciminium, comyn.
Hoc zinzibrum, gyngyre.
Hec liquirisia, lycorys.
Hoc amomum, canylle.
Hec galanga, galyngaye.
Hic gariofilus, a cloyfe.[2]
Hec masia, a mace.
Hoc quiperium, a quybybe.
Hec zucura, zugure.
Hoc anisium, anys.
Hoc feniculum, fynkyl-sede.
Hic racemus, a rasyn.
Hoc risi, indeclinabile, ryse.
Hoc alexandrum, alysandyre.
Hoc granellum, granes.
Hoc zeduarium, zeduarye.
Hoc electuarium, letwerye.
Hoc balsamum, bawme.
Hoc ponderale, haburdepays.
Hic census, rychenes.
Hoc unium, vyncloun.[3]

Hec asura, asyre.
Hoc gummi, indeclinabile, gume.
Hoc dragetum, drage.
Hic pulver, vel -ris, powdyre.
Hoc pinetum, a pyoun.
Hec uncia, a nowns.
Hec semiuncia, half a nouns.
Hoc pondus, a wehgt.
Hec statera, idem est.
Hic bilanx, -cis, belans.
Hoc stateris, idem.
Hoc examen, lingua bilancis.
 Est examen apum colleccio, lingua bilancis.
Hec dragma, est octava pars uncie.
Hec rosina, rosyn.
Hoc butumen, terre.
Hec pix, -cis, pyk.
Hoc ponde, a fowdrelle.
 Res sit vera staterem portate statera.
Hic bipondus, i. genus ponderis ex duabus assibus appositum.
Hec urapassa, a raysyn.
Hec massa polatarum, a frayle ful of fyks.
[*Hic dactilis, A^{cc}* an almonde].[4]

NOMINA ARBORUM ET EARUM FRUCTUUM.

Hec arbor, vel -bos, a tre.
Hec pirus, a per-tre.
Hoc pirum, a pere.
Hoc piretum, est locus ubi crescunt.
Hec pomus, a nappyl-tre.
Hoc pomum, a nappylle.

---

[1] Almond-milk, or almond-cream, appears to have been a favourite article in the pastry and dessert department during the middle ages. The Forme of Cury (p. 17) gives the following receipt for making a "cawdel of almand-mylk": "Take almandes blanched, and drawe hem up with wyne; do thereto powdor of gynger, and sugar, and color it with saffron; boile it and serve it forthe." It seems to have continued in fashion until at least the end of the seventeenth century, as would appear from the following extract from one of the popular dramatists of that age:

"The devil take me, I love you so, that I could be content to abjure wine for ever, and drink nothing but almond-milk for your sake."—*Shadwell, Epsom-Wells*, 1673.

[2] *Cloyfe*, a clove.
[3] *Vyncloun*, a sort of spice.
[4] This line is written in a rather later hand than the rest of the manuscript.

228   A NOMINALE.

Hoc pometum, locus ubi crescunt.
Hec taxus, ew.
Hec serasus, a chere-tre.
Hoc serasum, a chere.
Hec prunus, a plum-tre.
Hoc prunum, a plum.
Hec pepulus, a bolys-tre.
Hoc pepulum, a bolysse.[1]
Hec corulus, a hesyl-tre.
Hoc coruletum, ubi habundant.
Hec nux, -cis, a nutte.
Hec arelana, a walnutte and the nutte.
Hec ficus, -ci vel -cus, a fyg-tre or a fig.
Hec cariga, a fyg
Hec castania, a cheston, or the tre.
Hec cornus, -ni vel -nus, a slo-tre.
Hoc cornum, a slo.
Hoc cornetum, ubi habundant
Hec ramnus, -ni, a thethorn-tre.[2]
Hoc ramnum, -ni, fructus ejus.
Hec ema, i. alba spina.
Hec arbitus, wod-crab-tre.
Hoc arbitum, a crabe.
Hec amigdalus, a almund.
Hec morus, a fylberd-tre.
Hoc morum, fructus ejus.
Hec cicomonis, a cycomyr-tre.
Hoc cicomonium, fructus ejus.
Hec ritis, a vyn-tre.
Hec ura, a grape.
Hec pinus, -ni vel -nus.
Hoc pinum, fructus ejus.
Hoc pinetum, locus ubi crescunt.
Hec quercus, -ci vel -cus, a nak.
Hec glans, -dis, a nacorun.
Hec galla, a nake-appylle
Hec ibex, -cis, a sapplynge.
Hec laurus, -ri vel -rus, a loryl-tre
Hec fraccinus, a nesch-tre.

Hoc fraccinum, a kay of a nesche.
Hoc fraccinetum, locus ubi habundant.
Hic oliaster, i. oliva silvestris.
Hec abies, -etis, a fyrre.
Hec acer, -ris, a mapul-tre.
Hec cedrus, a cedyr-tre.
Hec salix, -icis, a welogh.
Hec tremulus, a nespe.
Hec ulnus, a nellyr-tre.
Hec buxus, A^{cce} a box-tre.
Hec sambucus, a bur-tre.
Hec ussus, a holyn-tre.
Hec lentiscus, a byrk-tre
Hoc bidellium, i. arbor dans bonum o[dorem].
Hec spina, a thorn.
Hoc spinetum, locus ubi crescunt.
Hec plantacius, a plan-tre.
Hec fagus, -gi, a bech-tre.
Hec cilia, a lynde.
Hec cocianus, a coven-tre.[3]
Hoc socianum, fructus ejus.
Hec percitus, arbor quedam.
Hoc malagranatum, fructus . . . . .
Hec mespulus, a mel-tre.[4]
Hoc mespulum, fructus ejus.
Hec esculus, fructus ejus.
Hec populus, a popyl-tre.
Hec cipressus, a cypyr-tre.
Hec maluspunicus, quedam arbor.
Hoc malumpunicum, fructus ejus.
Hec juniperus, parva arbor spinosa.
Hec sanguinus, arbor coloris sanguinii.
Hoc sanguinetum, locus ubi crescunt.
Hec nucliarius, est quelibet arbor ferens nuces.
Hoc nucliarium, locus ubi crescunt.
Hec silva, } a woyd.
Hec indago,

---

[1] *i. e.,* a bullace (*prunus insititia*).
[2] Generally interpreted as the dog rose, or wild briar, called *befe-born* by the Anglo-Saxons.

See before, pp. 33, 68, 141, 181.
[3] The coigne-tree, or quince.
[4] The medlar, *mespilus germanica.*

A NOMINALE.

Hec *subuscus*, undyr-wod.
Hic *titrus, arbor que cito surgit.*
Hec *volemus*, a wardun-tre.[1]
Hoc *volemum, fructus ejus.*
Hec *merica, media producta*, a brome.
Hoc *succetum, ubi crescunt frutices.*
Hic *rubus, -i*, a buske.
Hoc *rubietum, ubi crescunt vel rubiant.*
Hic *dumus*, a thorn-buske.
Hic *tribulus*, ⎫
Hec *repres*, ⎬ a brere.
Hec *reprecula*, ⎭
Hoc *virgultum*, a halte.[2]
Hec *virga*, a wand.
Hec *viprex, -icis*, a schyd.[3]
Hoc *vimen, -nis*, qwykyr.
Hoc *vimitum, locus ubi crescunt.*
Hec *saliunca, -ce*, a whyn.
Hec *aborigo*, ⎫
Hec *abories*, ⎬ *sunt superflue faucies.*
Hec *stipes, -tis, i. arbor.*
Hec *radix*, a rot.
Hic *trunccus*, a stok.
Hic *vel hec cortex, -cis*, bark.
Hic *liber, interior pars corticis.*
Hoc *suber, intima pars corticis.*
Hoc *abdomen*, grund-sope.[4]
Hic *frons, -dis*, a gren bught.
Hoc *folium*, a lefe.
Hic *ramus*, ⎫
Hic *ramusculus*, ⎬ a braunche.
Hoc *ramale*, a dry brawnche.

Hec *palmes, -tis*, a brawnch of vyne.
Hic *pampinus, folium vitis.*
Hic *botrus, -i, flos vitis.*
Hic *racemus*, a brawnch of grapys.
Hec *acinus, est granellum uva.*
Hec *labrusca, est agrestis vitis, vel botrus amarus.*
Hoc *germen*, ⎫
Hec *pululacio*, ⎬ a burjonyng.
Hec *astula, -e*, ⎫
Hec *quisquilie*, ⎬ a chype.
Hic *saltus*, a lawnd.
Hic *rogus*, ⎫
Hic *fax, -cis*, ⎬ a bronde.
Hec *ticio, -nis*, a col-pytte.
Hec *fala*, a fagot.
Hic *faciculus*, a kynch.[5]
Hec *cima*, the crop of a tre.
   Cima caput virge, verborum gloria sema.
Hic *fullus*, a fylberd-tre.[6]
Hec *condimus*, a wardun-tre.
Hoc *condimum*, a wardun.
   Arborum nomen femininum dic fore semper,
   Ni rubus, dumus, oliaster, sive piaster,
   Adda viburnum predictis, addito vimen.

HEE SUNT PARTES FRUCTUUM.

Hoc *nauci, indeclinabile*, defe.
Hic *nuclius*, a kyrnyl.
Hec *moraria*, a cobyng nut.
Hec *perima*, ⎫
Hec *peripsima*, ⎬ a paryng.

---

[1] The warden was a large coarse pear used for baking.
[2] A holt, or copse.
[3] *Schyd* means usually a billet of wood.
[4] *Grund-sope*. This appears to be a different meaning of the word to that which it usually bears. The Prompt. Parv. gives, "Growndesope of any lycoure, *fex, sedimen.*"
[5] *Kynch* must here mean a small bundle.
[6] The Latin should be *fillis*. "Filberde-tree, *phillis*," Prompt. Parv. Gower, *Confes. Amant.* vol. ii., p. 30 (ed. Pauli), has misrepresented the story of Phillis and Demophoon, in Ovid, in order to give a derivation of this word—
   And Demephon was so reproved,
   That of the Goddes providence
   Was shape suche an evidence
   Ever afterward ayein the slowe,
   That Phillis in the same throwe
   Was shape into a nutte-tre,
   That alle men it mighte se,
   And after Phillis phillıberde
   This tre was cleped in the yerde.

Hec pulpa, the mett.
Hec arula, the crok.
Hec pertica, the sterte[1] of a napulle.
Hec testa, a schelle, *vel cortex nucis*.

NOMINA DOMORUM ET RERUM ECCLESIASTICARUM.

Hoc monasterium, a mynster.
Hec cenobium, a nabbay.
Hec abathia, idem est.
Hoc hospitale, a nospytalle.
Hoc sinodogium,
Hoc diverticulum, } *i. diversorium.*
Hec ecclesia,
Hoc templum,
Hoc delubrum, } a kyrk.
Hoc fanum,
Hec basilica,
Hic cancellus,
Hic chorus, } a chawnsylle.
Hoc vestibulum, a revestre.
Hic porticus, a porche.
Hoc pulpitum, a pollepyt.
Hoc campanile, a stepulle.
Hoc oratorium, a oratory.
Hoc portiferium, a portas.
Hoc gradale, a grale.
Hoc missale, a myssalle.
Hic troporius, a tropery.
Hic calendarius, a calendar.
Hic ymnerius, a ymner.
Hoc ymnare, idem est.
Hic antiphonerius, a antyphonere.
Hec letania, letony.
Hoc alphabetum, a nabse.[2]
Hec gracia, a grace.
Hoc premorium, a primer.
Hoc psalterium, a sawtyr.
Hoc brevarium, a brevyar.
Hoc processionale, a processyonar.

Hoc martilogium, a mertilloge.
Hec biblioteca, a bybulle.
Biblioteca mea servat meam bibliotecam.
Hoc manuale, a manuelle.
Hic passionerius, a passyonar.
Hoc regestrum, a regyster.
Hoc ordinale, a ordynalle.
Hic crucifixus, a crucyfixe.
Hec crux, -cis, a cros.
Hec ymago,
Hec statua, } a ymage.
Hec eucaristia, hostia sacrata.
Hoc altare, a nawtyr.
Hoc superaltare, a hye awtyr.
Hic fons, -tis, a font.
Hoc carisma, -tis, creme.
Hoc oleum, oylle.
Hic baptismus, a batym.
Hec extremaunccio, a nentment.
Hec confirmacio, a confyrmynge.
Baptismum proprie fertur mundacio mentis,
Exterior querit per aquam, baptisma vocatur.
Hec vox baptismus signat utrumque simul.
Hic catecuminus, est ille qui est conversus ad fidem et non est baptizatus.
Hoc vexillum, a banere.
Hic calix, -cis, a chalys.
Vas cleris vinique calix est et nomen inertis.
Hoc corperarium, a corperax.
Hec fiola, a crewyt.
Hec pixis, -dis, a box.
Hic editur pissis, hic servat aromata pixis.
Hoc ostiarium, a obley, or a box.
Hec ostia, a cyst.
Hoc thus, -ris,
Hoc thimiama, } encens.
Hoc incensum,
Hoc aspersorium, a strynkylle.
Hoc turibulum, a sensyr.
Hec acerra, a schyp for censse.[3]
Hoc sacrarium, a sacrear.

[1] The stalk.
[2] *i. e.*, an ab-c.

[3] The *nef*, a vessel in the form of a ship, used in the church from an early period to hold the in-

Hoc lectrinum, a letyrn.
Hoc vitrum, glasse.
Hoc feretrum, ⎫
Hic loculus,   ⎬ a ber.
Hec libitina, ⎭
Hoc facitergium, a towylle.
Hoc manutergium, a sanope.
Hoc velum, a vayle.
Hoc crismale, a crisome.
Hec lucerna, a lantron.[1]
Hec absconsa, a scons.[2]
Hec lampas, -dis, a lawmpe.
Hoc lurthium, a nawtyr-cloth.
Hoc organum, a organ.
Hec decima, tythe.
Hec oblacio, a offeryng.
Hec alba, a nawbe.
Hic amictus, a namyt.
Hec fanula, a fanune.[3]
Hec casula, ⎫
Hec poderis, ⎬ a chesapulle.
Hoc spectaculum, a spectakylle.
Hoc pedum, a clappe.[4]
Hec capa, a cape.
Hec dalmatica, a canturcope.[5]
Hec zona, a belt.
Hec tunicula, tunakyl.
Hec mitra, a mytyre.
Hec patura, a parur.
Hec stola, a stolle.
Hoc superpellicium, a surplys.
Hoc orilegium, a norlyge.
Hic oronoscopus, a orlegge.
Hoc aurifigium, a gold-fre.
Hoc superfemorale,
Hec caleptra, a coppe.
Hoc pedum, a crowche.

Hic cerius, a serge.
Hic torticus, ⎫
Hec teda, -e, ⎬ a serg-berer.
Hec candela, a candyle.
Hic lichinus, a weke.
Hoc candelabrum, a candylstyk.
Hec secula, a rysch.[6]
Hic stilus, a peller.
Est stilus unde scribit puer, stilus esto columna,
Dictandique modus dicitur esse stulus.
Hoc circinatorium, a circynatory.
Hoc claustrum, a clostyr.
Hoc valitudinarium, a fermery.
Hoc ventilogium, ⎫
Hec cheruca,   ⎬ a wedyrcoke.
Hoc semitorium, ⎫
Hoc atrium,   ⎬ a kyrk-3erd.
Atria die aulas, eadem semitoria dicas.
Hoc sudarium, a sudary.
Hic gradus, a degre.
Hic certofagus, ⎫
Hoc mauseolum, |
Hic tumulus, |
Hec tumba,   ⎬ a grave.
Hoc poliandrum, |
Hoc bustum,   ⎭
Hoc glossum, a schryn.
Manda vetat mandrum lieos intrare meandrum;
Clausit Alexandrum magnum parvum poliandrum.
Hec reliquie, -arum, relyks.
Hic bostarius, a graf-makere.
Hec capsa,   ⎫
Hec capsula, |
Hec capcella, ⎬ a kyst.
Hec cista,   ⎭
Hec crupta, a hol in the erthe.
Per quem fit crupta, non fiunt carmina scripta.

---

cense, as well as other articles. A similar vessel was used at the baronial table to hold wine, &c.

[1] A lantern.
[2] See before, p. 193.
[3] The priest's maniple.

[4] *Pedum* occurs again below, where it is explained as a *crowche,* or pastoral staff.
[5] We must conclude, from the Latin equivalent, that this word signifies a maniple.
[6] *Rysch,* a rushlight.

Hoc consistorium, a constre.
In plurali hec sacerdotorum dicuntur loco inferiora, ad que omnis erit a . . . . nus sacerdotibus,
Hoc dormitorium, a dortore.
Hec cella, a celle.
Hoc capitulum, a chapyture.
Hoc centorium, }
Hoc tabernaculum, } a tabernakylle.
Hec regia, est domus regis.
Hoc castellum, a castylle.
Hoc palacium, a palas.
Hoc atrium, a hawlle.
Hec aula, idem est.
Hic turrus, }
Hec arax, } a towre.
Hec phalea, turris lignea.
Hic citus, est passio vel mari domus.
Hec mancio, -nis, a dwellynge plas.
Hoc messuagium, a messe.[1]
Hoc coutagium, a cotage.
Hoc opidum, a caystelle.
Hoc penetrale, a chawmbyre.
Hoc Syon, indeclinabile, Syon.
Montem dic Syon, die ecclesiam fore Syon.
Tres sunt partes columne, s. basis, stilus, et epistilium; basis est fundamentum, stilus est media pars, et epistilium est supprema pars.
Hec heremus, A^{ree} armyteghe.
Hoc heremum, scitum illius loci.

NOMINA DOMO PERTINENCIA.

Hoc scamnum, a bynk.
Hec mensa, a tabylle.
Hec fultra, a cuschoun.
Hec cathedra, a chare.

Hic tristellus, a trestylle.
Hec pelvis, a basyn.
Hoc lavatorium, a lavyre.
Hoc mantile, a towylle.
Hoc sedile, a long-setylle.
Hec forceps, tange.[2]
Hec tripos, a brandrythe.
Hoc manutergium, a sauope.
Hoc selarium, a selere.
Hic sal, -lis, salt.
Hec cambuca, a cambok.[3]
Hoc coclier, a spon.
Hic calathus, a baskyt.
Hic corbes, }
Hoc dolium, } a tune.
Hoc uter, -ris, a busche.
Hic colateralis, a costrille.
Hec clipsidra, a spygotte.
Hic ciphus, a cope.
Hec servicia, ale.
Hoc vinum, }
Hoc merum, } wyn.
Hec fex, -cis, dregges.
Hoc claretum, a clarete.
Hoc nectar, -ris, pyment.
Fex vini tibi sit, olei dicatur amurca.
Hoc scabellum, a stolle.
Hoc monile, a broche.
Hoc acuare, a nedyl-hows.
Hec pluscula, a bokylle.
Hoc speculum, a myrrore.
Hoc scissorium, a trencher.
Hic bino, a cart-staffe.
Hec traha, a sled.
Hec buris, a plugh-beme.
Hec formepedia, a last.
Hoc senvectorium, a barow.
Hoc serculum, a wed-hoc.

---

[1] A mansion, or manor.
[2] Tongs.
[3] *Cambuck*, and the medieval Latin words *cambuca*, or *cambuta*, were used in the sense of a bent or crooked staff or beam, and here perhaps means some implement for supporting or suspending articles, like those by which butchers hang up carcases of slaughtered animals.

A NOMINALE.

Hec mensacula, a bord-knyf.[1]
Hec olla, a potte.
Hec idria, a watyr-potte.
Hic contus, } a postyke.[2]
Hec pila, }
Hic ursiolus, a posnet.[3]
Hec ampulla, est olla cum duabus auribus.
Hic discus, a dische.
Hic perapsis, -dis, a dobler.[4]
Hec pila, a pestylle.
Hic fornax, a fornes.
  Et pila pes pontis, pila ludus, pila taberna:
  Pila terit pultes, sed pila jeruntur in hostes.
Hoc veru, a spytt.
Hoc pepe, moteryls.
Hoc striaballum, a cog of a welle.
Hic assicus, a mylner-pyt.
Hoc emolimentum, a mel-tyre.
Hec ferricapsa, a hopyr.
Hoc sinoglossotorium, a flod-ʒat.
Hoc terratorium, a clape.
Hic alvus, a trowght.
Hec pala, a pele.
Hec vertybra, a col-rak.[5]
Hic pastellus, a pastethe.
Hec mebula, a mekylle.
Hec vafra, a wafron.
Hoc placentum, a wastylle.
Hic artocopus, a symnylle.
Hoc fermentum, sur-dowght.
Hoc furfur, branne.
Hec costa, a rybe.
Hec mola, a qwern-ston.
Hoc cilicium, a hare.

Hoc idromellum, growtt.[6]
Hoc ciromellum, wort.
Hoc sigisterium, draf.
Hec cuva, } a fat.
Hec uva, }
Hec congelima, a scowk.
Hic arcomus, a hay-stak.
Hec arista, a nawn.
Hec spica, a ner.
Hec febula, a ben-codde.
Hec tina, a soe.
Hoc tinarium, a so-tre.
Hic corbis, } a lepe.
Hec sporta, }
Hec garba, } a schaffe.
Hec merges, }
Hic manipulus, a repe.
Hic modius, a buschylle.
Hic corus, a mesur.
Hoc osorium, a strikylle.[7]
Hic vannus, a fanne.
Hec ala, a weng.
Hoc ventilabrum, a scotylle.[8]
Hoc flagellum, a flaylle.
Hoc rastrum, a rak.
Hoc granum, corn.
Hoc frumentum, whet.
Hoc ordium, barly.
Hec pise, a pese.
Hec faba, a ben.
Hec vicia, a fech.
Hec cruralis, craps.
Hoc exaticum, byge.[9]
Hec mixtilio, -nis, idem est.
Hec avena, hafyr.

[1] *i. e.*, a carving-knife. See before, p. 123.
[2] A pestle.
[3] A skillet, or small pot.
[4] A *dobler*. The same Latin word is explained in the next vocabulary a *platter*.
[5] A coal-rake, or implement for raking the ashes of a fire.
[6] *Growtt*, a sort of ale In the old play of Tom Tyler and his Wif, this liquor is mentioned in the two verses of a song—
  This jolly *grout* is jolly and stout,
  I pray you stout it still-a.
[7] A strickle, or piece of wood for levelling the corn in the measure.
[8] *Scotylle*, a winnowing-fan.
[9] A kind of barley

Hec siligo, ry.
Hoc lolium, a popylle.
Hec cratis, a flek.
Hoc tugurrium, a hollek.
Hoc ovile, a fald.
Hic vomer, vel hec, -mis, a seke.
Hoc cultrum, a cultyr.
Hoc jugum, a ʒok.
Hec harpica, a harowe.
Hoc bidens, a mattok.
Hec liga, vel mera, a pyk.
Hec vanga, a spathe.
Hec furca, a fork.
Hoc tribulum, a scowule.
Hoc dolubrum, a brod-ax.
Hec securis, a nax.
Hec serucula, a hachyt.
Hec acia, a thyxylle.
Hoc terubrum, ⎱ a wymbylle.
Hoc penetrale, ⎰
Hoc sumen, tharne.
Hoc armoriolum, a nalmry.[1]
Hoc orium, a lath.
Hoc bostare, a nox-hows.
Hoc stabulum, a stabylle.
Hec arena, gravylle.
Hec mantica, a malle.
Hic mergus, ⎱ a bokytt.
Hec situla, ⎰
Hec postica, a posturne.
Hoc perforale, a persure.
Hec lima, a fylle.
Hic cirrinus, a compas.
Hic folus, a bolle.
Hoc clavarium, i. repositorium clavorum.
Hec revictica, a grawyng-ern.
Hec sarra, a sawe.
Hoc repagulum, a barre.
Hec gerula, a gad.

Hec mastica, whypcord.
Hic aculius, a brad.
Hoc plaustrum, a wayn.
Hec quadriga, a charʒott.
Hec biga, a cart.
Hic currus, idem est.
Hec rota, whele.
Hec axis, a naxyltre.
Hic radius, a spak.
Hoc meditollium, a nar.
Hic cantus, a felowe.
Hec cavilla, a nayle or a pyn.
Hic temo, a teme.
Her torques, a wythe.
Hic limo, a thylle.
Hic limarillum, a thyl-pyn.
Hic viredus, a thyl-hors.
Hoc dorsolallium, a cart-sadylle.
Hec singula, a hors-garthe.
Scingula scingit equum, singula sunt hominum.
Hoc postela, a croper.
Hee trahivie, trays.
Her antela, a pettrylle.
Hee opisie, -arum, harnes.
Hoc capistrum, a heltyr.
Hoc scansile, a styroppe.
Hoc calamistrum, a hors-kame.
Hoc ligatorium, a tedyre.[2]
Hic cacabus, a cawdrun.
Hic urcius, a bras pott.
Her sterago, a fryng-panne.
Her creagra, a fleschok.
Hec sertago, a fryng-panne.
Hec cratis, a rost-ʒern.
Hoc ipopirgium, a nawndyrn.
Hoc spumatorium, a scomur.
Hoc ireposimum, a hors-hamer.
Hic arquelus, a nox-bowe.
Her lanea, a slaye.

---

[1] An aumbry, or cupboard, formed from the Low Latin word *almariolum*.

[2] *Tedyre*, a cord to tie an animal to a stake, still called in Kent a *tether*.

Hoc *hausorium*, a ladylle.
Hoc *scorium*, a natt.
Hec *navecula*, schetylle.
Hoc *jubar*, a neppe.
Hoc *licium*, a throm.
Hic *cathinus*, a gret doblere.
Hoc *micatorium*, a myere.
Hoc *trajecterium*, a pot-lyd.
Hoc *omentum*, a stren3erd.
Hoc *bolideum*, a plum of lede.
Hec *conspica*, a glen.
Hec *iberna*, i. *tempestas maris*.
Hic *palus*, a stak.
Hoc *abditorium*, a cofyr.
Hec *clitella*, a pak.
Hec *cupa*, a stope.
Hec *trolla*, a trowylle.
Hic *rogus*, a fyre.
Hic *ignis*, idem.
Hec *roga*, almus.
  Hic rogus est ignis, elemosina sit roga dicta.
Hoc *cunabilum*, a credylle.
Hec *rubigo*, a rust.
Hoc *torcular*, a pressur.
Hoc *falcastrum*, a bylle.
Hic *faux*, a chek.
Hec *falx*, a sykyl, or a seth.
Hec *scopa*, a besum.
Hec *paries*, a walle.
Hec *scala*, a leddyr.
Hoc *foramen*, a hole.
Hic *later*, *-ris*, a tylle.
Hic *marmor*, *-ris*, a marbylle.
Hoc *gipsum*, morter.
Hoc *cementum*, cyment.
Hic *simentarius*, a waller.
Hic *asser*, a latt.
Hec *latta*, idem.

[1] *Bygyng*, a building; from the A.-S. *biegan*, to build.
[2] The spense, or buttery.
[3] A stable for cattle.

Hec *cratis*,
Hec *escaria*, a met-tabylle.
Hic *escarinus*, a met-dysch.
Hoc *lorum*, a brydille.
Hec *abena*, a rayn.

JAM DE EDIFICIIS DOMORUM.

Hoc *edificium*, a bygyng.[1]
Hec *domus*, a hows.
Hec *casa*, a lytille-hows.
Hec *talamus*,
Hec *camera*,
Hic *conclavis*, } a chambyre.
Hec *zeta*,
Hoc *tristegum*, i. *domus tricamerata*.
Hoc *pretorium*, a moyt-halle.
Hoc *celarium*, a spens.[2]
Hoc *dispensorium*, idem est.
Hoc *lardarium*, a lardyr-hows.
Hec *coquina*, a kychyn.
Hoc *pistrinum*, a bak-hows.
Hoc *molendinum*, myln.
Hec *forica*, a prevy.
Hec *pennates*, *-cium*, idem est.
Hoc *stabulum*, a stabulle.
Hoc *boster*, a bose.[3]
  Noster erit, nomen proprium, stabulum quoque boster;
  Bostaris facit hec gero, bostaris ille.
Hec *amissis*, a swyer.[4]
Hec *fabrica*, a forge.
Hec *carcer*, a presun.
Hoc *argastulum*, a denjon.
Hec *taberna*, a tabyrn.
Hec *teges*, parva domus.
Hec *fornix*, *-icis*, a bordyl-hows.[5]
Hoc *scortorium*, idem est.
Hec *opella*, a schope.

[4] The Latin word *amussis* means a carpenter's rule.
[5] A brothel; from the Anglo-Norman; the modern French *bordel*.

Hec scopa, idem.
Hoc oranum, a treasurry.
Hoc gazafilacium, a hord-hows.[1]
Hec prosenica, est domus mendicorum.
Hoc vinarium, est locus ubi vinum reponitur.
Hec lapidisina, est domus latamorum, vel est ubi lapides ceduntur.
Hoc toloneum, a tol-boythe.
　Qui mausoleum producit, aut canopeum,
　Seu toloneum, non reor esse reum.
Hoc asilum, est domus refugii.
Hoc refectorium, a fermory.
Hoc brasinium, a malt-hows.
Hoc oratorium, est domus orationis.
Hoc triclinium, est domus trina sessione f[acta].
Hoc cellarium, a seller.
Hic papilio, -nis, i. tectorium.
Hoc fanuficium, a pantry.
Hec paraula, locus ante aulam.
Hoc apendicium, a pentys.[2]
Hoc repositorium, est locus ubi aliquid repo[nitur].
Hec apoteca, a spycer schope.
Hoc macellum, bochery.
Hoc armentorium, locus ubi fiunt arm[a].
Hec caula, schep-cot.
Hoc mirrepolium, est domus unguenta...
Hec mirreteca, est repositorum ung....
Hoc armamentorium, est repositorium.
Hoc columbare, dowf-hows.
Hec menia, -orum, sunt muri civitatis.
Hoc genitorium, a bu-hows.
Hoc argasterium, ubi aliquid opus fit.

Hec antica, a hek.[3]
Hec postica, a postyrn.
Hoc posticum, idem est.
Hec postis, } a post.
Hec postellus, }
Hec fultura, idem est.
Hec litura, a mortare.
Hic fundus, a grund.
Hic murus, a walle.
Hoc antemurale, a harchcame.
Hoc promurale, defencio ante murum.
Hoc signaculum, a bretys.[4]
Hoc saxum, }
Hec petrilla, } a stone.
Hec petra, }
Hec calx, -cis, lyme.
　Pars pedis est hic calx, lapis ustus dicitur hec calx.
Hoc plastrum, a plastyr.
Hec arena, sand or gravylle.
Hic palus, a palys.
Hec basisassis est future columpne.
Hoc periperium, est superficies parietis.
Hec archus, a vowt.
Hoc laquiare, a post-band.
Hec trabia, a balk.
Hec trabicula, idem est.
Hec stipes, a stok.
Hic tignuus, vel hoc tegimen, a sparre.
Hec capula, a cuppylle.
Hec doma, a hows-rof.
Hoc tectum, idem est.
Hec grunda, a eskyng.[5]
Hec sugrunda, a bem-fellyng.
Hoc lodium, a lovyre.

---

[1] A treasury; the Anglo-Saxon word. See before, p. 58.

[2] A pentise, or shed over a door.

[3] *Hek.* A *heck-door,* in the north, is a door of which the lower part only is panelled, and the upper latticed. The word, which is not very common in this sense in old writers, occurs in the Townley Mysteries, which were written in the North (p. 106)—
　Good wyff, open the *hek,* says thou not what I bryng.
It is explained in the glossary as "the inner door between the entry or lobby, and the house or kitchen."

[4] A bretasche.

[5] *Eskyng.* A pentise is called an *eaking* in Lincolnshire.

A NOMINALE.

Hoc lucaner, -ris, idem est.
Hic caminus, a chymney.
Hoc epicausterium, idem est.
Dic epicausterium scriptoris esse cathedra.
Est epicausterium fornax ubi dequoquis ollas.
Ast illud longum que fumus ab ede recedit.
Hoc pinnaculum, a pinnakyl.
Hic cunius, a weg.
Hec pinna, est summitas cujuslibet rei.
Sit tibi montis apex, dicas pinna quoque templi.
Hoc pavimentum, a pament.
Hoc guttatorium, a guttar.
Hoc stillicidium, a drope.
Hec tectura, thak.
Hoc tegimen, idem.
Hoc tabellatum, a burd-wogh.[1]
Hec calx, } anterior pars do-
Hoc frontispicium, } mus.
Hoc hostium, a dore.
Hec fenestra, a wyndoe.
Hoc fenestrale, a fenestralle.[2]
Hec porta,
Hec janua,
Hee bifores, -rium, } a ȝatt.
Hee fores,
Hec valva, a wekyt.
Hee valve, -arum, faldyn-ȝates.
Hoc limen, -nis, thryswold.
Hic cardo, -nis, penultima corrupta, a har of a dore.[3]
Hec vertibra, idem.

Hec cera, } a lok.
Hec serula, }
Hic clatrus, a barre.
Cardo sus est foribus si cardonis sit generalis,
Et si cardonis est herba nociva colonis,
Cardonis est herba multum fullonibus apta.
Hec clavis, } a key.
Hec clavicula, }
Hec clava, a mese.
Hic clavus, a naylle.
Clava ferit, clavis aperit, clavus duo jungit.
Hoc pessulum, a snek.[4]
Hec mastiga, a snek-bank.
Hic gumfus, a dor-bande.
Hec haspa, a hespe.
Hic vectis, a slott.[5]
Hec grapa, est foramen in quo quiescit vectis.
Hoc clitorium, a clekyt.[6]
Hic huncus, a crok.
Hec cava, a guttyr in the herthe.
Hec fistula, est instrumentum in quo aqua currit.
Arbor aqueductus est fistula, musica, morbus.
Hoc aquaductum,
Hoc guttarium, } a guttur.
Hoc aqueductile,
Hic aqueductus, a cundyth undyr the erthe.
Hec barcaria, i. ovile, a schep-cott.

---

[1] *Burd-wogh,* a wall, or partition, of boards—a wainscot. We meet with the Anglo-Saxon *bord-weall,* used in much the same way. It may be here remarked that the distinction between *wall* and *wogh,* in English, was the same as between the original words in Anglo-Saxon, namely, the latter was applied peculiarly to the walls of a house, and the former to a wall of enclosure, or separation, in general. Thus, in the following lines, Gower, telling the story of Pyramus and Thisbe, informs us that they lived so close together, that the walls of their houses, and those of their court or yard, adjoined to each other—

Amonge the which, two there were
Above all other noble and great,
Dwellend tho within a strete
So nigh to gider as it was sene,
That there was nothing hem betwene,
But wowe to wowe and walle to walle.
Gower, Conf. Amantis, vol. i, p. 324, ed. Pauli.

[2] A fenestral was a window formed of a frame of paper and cloth, instead of glass.

[3] *Har,* a hinge. In the dialect of Durham, a *har* is the hole in a stone in which the spindle of a gate rests.

[4] *Snek,* a latch of a door.

[5] *Slot,* the bolt of a door.

[6] *Clekyt,* a cliket, or latch-key.

NOMINA VESTIMENTORUM.

Hec vestis, a clethyng.
Hoc indumentum, idem est.
Hoc mutarium, a chaungyng-cloth.
Hoc stragulum, ray.
Hic pannus, clothe.
Hec lanugo, -nis, walkyng.
Hec camisia, a sark.
Hec interula, idem est.
Hee bracce, -arum, brek.
Hec tunica, a cot.
Hec supertunica, a furd cott.
Hec dupliteca, a doplyt.
Hec toga, a gown.
Hec clamis, a mantylle.
Hec acupicta, a jak of fens.
Hec instita, a rochyt.
Hic superus, idem est.
Hec armiclausa, a clok.
Hec tribrica, the strapuls of a pare brek.
Hoc lumbare, a brek-belt.
Hoc braccale, idem est.
Hor colobium, a taberd.
Hoc colobium, i. vestis collobia parvula dena.
Hoc colarium, a colar.
Her manica, a slefe.
Hec lucina, a gore.[1]
Hoc mancupium, a spare.
Hec fibula, a lase.
Hor pannideusium, a boton.
Hoc armiclausum, a clespe.
Hoc mominlum, a naglott.
Hec consuetura, a seme.
Hec fimbria, a heme.
Hic lumbus, a burdyre.

Hoc stropheum,
Hec zona, } a gyrdylle.
Zona dic stropheum, palmam dic esse tropheum.
Hoc cimicinctum, a saynt of sylk.
Hoc textum, est idem.
Hoc plusculum, a bokylle.
Hec lingula, a tung.
Hec stipa, a stoythe.
Hor pendulum, a pendand.
Hec mardacula, a spar-belt.
Hoc mercipium, a pawtnere.[2]
Hic cultellus, a knyff.
Hoc acumen,
Hec acies, } a neg.
Hec sindula, a blayd.
Hoc manubrium, a heft.
Hec spirula, a vyrille.[3]
Hoc tenaculum,
Hic spirasmus, } a tang.
Hec vagina, a schethe.
Hoc cupicium, a hod.
Hoc leripipium, a typitte.
Hec tena, a coyfe.
Hic pilius, a cape.
Hoc flameolum,
Hoc multiplicium, } curchyfe.
Hoc sudarium, a sudary.
Hec tricatura, a trussure.
Hoc peplum, a wympulle.
Hoc craticulum, a kelle.

* * * * [4]

Hic affricus, the sowth-est wynd.
Hic circius, est ventus borialis sub aquilonem versus occidentem.
Hic aquilo, septentris; ventus boralis, idem est; ventus aquilonaris est sibi conjunctus versus orientem; ventus

---

[1] *Gore*, a hem, or gusset. In Walter de Biblesworth, it is given as the interpretation of the Anglo Norman or French *geroun*. See before, p. 172.

[2] *Pawtnere*, a purse.

[3] *Vyrille*, a gimlet, or wimble.

[4] Unfortunately a leaf of the original MS. has been torn out here, making a rather extensive lacuna, as the manuscript is written in three columns.

A NOMINALE.   230

collateralis est intermedius inter bariam et subsolanum.
Hec *nubes,* a clowd.
Hic *fulgur,* leyfnyng.
Hic *tonitrus,* a thonderyng.
Hec *nix,* snawe.
Hec *glacies, -ei,* yse.
Hec *grando,* halle.
Hoc *gelu, indeclinabile,* frost.
Hec *pruina,* a rym-frost.
Hic *ros, -ris,* a dewe.
Hec *pluvia,* a rayne.
Hoc *confragum,* a plays where the whyrwynd metes.
Hoc *bivium,* a gayt-schadyls.[1]
Hec *aqua,* watyre.
Hec *tectis, idem est.*
Hec *limpha etiam idem est.*
Est aqua doctrina, populus, dolor, ac elementum.
Hoc *mare,* } the see.
Hic *pelagus,* }
Hoc *fretum,* a whalle.
Hoc *flumen,* } a flod.
Hic *fluvius,* }
Hic *fons, -tis,* a welle.
Hic *rivus,* a revyre.
Hic *rivulus,* a bek.[2]
Hic *virarium,* a vever.
Hec *gurges, -tis,* a strem.
Hec *fovea,* } a dyke.
Hec *fossa,* }
Hoc *stangnum,* a dame.
Hoc *filandrum,* a gossomyre.
Hic *vel hec dies,* a day.
Hec *nox, -tis,* a nyght.
Hic *quadragesima,* a lentyn.
Hoc *natale,* 3ole.
Hoc *pascha,* pasc.
Hoc *carnibrevium.*

Hoc *ipopanti,* candylmesse.
Hec *pentetoste, -tes,* whysunday.
Hec *estas,* somyre.
Hic *yems,* wyntyre.
Hoc *ver,* groyng-tyme.
Hic *bisextus,* lep-3ere.
Hec *terra,* } erthe.
Hic *humus,* }
Hoc *saxifragium,* a qwarylc[3]
Hoc *vallis,* a daylle.
Hic *mons, -tis,* a hylle.
Hic *collis,* the top of a hylle.
Hoc *pratum,* a medowe.
Hec *via,* a way.
Hic *vicus,* a strett.
Hec *ripa,* a bank.
Hec *insula,* a nylle.
Hec *gleba,* a clott.
Hec *rupes,* a roche.
Hoc *inclusorium,* a pyn-fold.
Hic *campus,* } a feld.
Hic *rus,* }
Hoc *firmamentum,* a fyrmament.
Hec *aera,* a nakyre.
Her *boraga,* a nox-gang.
Hic *selio, -nis,* a butt.
Hec *virgata,* a rod-lande.
Hec *puppis,* a schyppe.
Hec *navis, idem est.*
Hic *lumbus,* a bott.
Hic *malus,* a mast.
Hoc *velum,* a saylle.
Hic *rudens,* a cabylle.
Hic *funis,* a cord.
Hic *funiculus, idem.*
Hic *remus,* a nore.
Hec *antenne, -arum,* gret cabyls.
Hoc *columber,* a are-hole.[4]
Hec *ancora,* a nankyre.

---

[1] Cross-roads; the word signifies literally, a separation or divergence of roads; "gate-schadylle, *compitum.*" Prompt. Parv.

[2] A small brook; still in use in the north.
[3] A quarry.
[4] *i. e.,* an air hole—a small unglazed window.

Hec troclea, a wyndas.
Hoc rete, }
Hec plaga, } a nett.
Hic hamus, a hok.

NOMINA LUDORUM.

Hic ludus, a play.
Hoc hastiludium, a justyng.
Hic armilustras, a turnament.
Hec acies, a scheltrone.[1]
Hec pila, a balle.
Hoc pedum, a clubbe.
Hoc pirrum, the chekyre.
Hec pirga, the poynt of the chekyre.
Hoc scaccarium, idem est.
Hic talus, a dyse.
Hec decies, idem est.
Hec alea, the menȝe.
Hec tuba, a trumpe.
Hec fistula, a pype.
Hec buccina, a beme.
Hic idraicus, a wadyr-pype.
Hec cithera, }
Hec lira, } a harpe.
Hec fides, a harp-stryng.
Hoc plectrum, a wrast.
Hoc timpanum, a tymbyre.
Hic psalmatus, the sytalle.
Hec vitula, a rybybe.
Hec simphonia, a symphony.
Hec paupita, a sawtre.
Hoc psalterium, idem est.
Salterium dicitur organicum fore librum.

DE VITE ET MATERIIS IPSIUS.

Hec vitis, a vyne.
Hec vitula, idem est.
Hoc vitulamen est planta vite inf . . .
Et vitis radix, sunt fructus vin . . .
Pampinus est folium, botrus flos vin . .

---

[1] The sheltron was a square, or division of soldiers, a squadron.

Hec vinea, est locus ubique usitatus.
Hec venosa, idem est.
Hec labrusca, est vitis silvestris.
Hic palmes, a brawnch of vyne.
Hoc sincetum, est ramus pretentus a vite.
Hic botrus, flos vitis.
Hic racemus, a raysyn.
Hic bubastus, est vitis vel uva in agro.
Hic spado, i. circulus vitis.
Hec uva, }
Hec uvula, } a grape.
Hec uvapassa.
Dant uvapassa clibano simeraria plebe,
Uva precerra, vel precox tibi primatura, ubi preco
Quo quando vel precox tibi prematura sunt uva.

Hec precocia, idem est.
Hec corda, est uva serotina.
Cordus, -a, -um, i. serotinus, -a, -um.

DE CIBIS GENERALIBUS.

Hic cibus, }
Hec esca, } mete.
Hic dapis, -pem, -pe, idem est.
Nobilitas viles frons generosa dapes.

Hoc manna, awngyls fode.
Hoc jantaculum, a dynere.
Hoc auncinium, }
Hec imranda, } a myd-dyner under-
Hoc merarium, } mete.[2]
Hec cena, a sopere.[3]
Hec musta, idem est.
Die mustam cenam, mustumque latens odorem.

Hoc obsonium, a rere-sopere.
Hoc convivium, a fest.
Hec dieta, est cibus moderatus, etc.
Estque dieta cibus moderatus, iter quoque diei.

Hoc corrodium, leveraye.

---

[2] A meal between the dinner and supper.
[3] A second supper, taken late in the evening.

DE PANIBUS ET PARTIBUS EORUM.

Hic panis, brede.
Hic lifus, a lofe.
Hoc colifium, hard-bred.
Hec placenta, wastylle.
Hic artocapus, a symnylle.
Hec torta, a cak.
Hec nebula, oblys.[1]
   Est nubis nebula tenuis panisque rotundus.
Hec lesca, a schyfe.[2]
Hec colirida, a dor-cake.[3]
Hoc crustrum, a crust.
Hoc frustrum, a lumpe.
Hoc minutal, a cantylle.
Hec mica, a crwme.
Hec pasta, doght.
Hec pasmacta, i. parvus panis.
Hec buccella, a morsylle.
Hic morcellus, idem est.

DE SPECIEBUS LIGUMINIS.

Hoc ligumen, potage.
Hoc olus, -ris, wortes.
Hec porreta, porray.
Hec vita, ⎫
Hoc sepulatum, ⎬ sew.[4]
Hec sorbuncula, idem est.
Hoc pulmentum, browys.[5]
Hoc adipatum, idem est.
Hoc amigdalatum, almund-mylke.[6]
Hoc risi, indeclinabile, ryse.

Hoc puls, ⎫
Hec aplauda, ⎬ a mese.
Hoc ferculum, ⎭
   Fercula nos saciant, prelatos fercula portant.
Hec polenta, grewylle.
Hoc brodium, brewe.
Hoc pomarium, appul-juse.
Hoc jurcellum, jursylle.[7]
Hoc sarabracium, sarabrase.
Hoc lattum, lorray.[8]
Hoc mel, hony.
Hic garus, a fysc-browe.[9]
Hoc oleum, oyle.
Hoc omlaccinium, charlyt.[10]
Hoc morticum, a culys.

DE CIBIS GENERALIBUS.

Hec assa, ⎫
Hec assatura, ⎬ rost.
Hec carbonella, a colope.
Hec frixa, idem.
Hoc crimium, crowkoun.[11]
Hec frixura, fryd met.
Hoc frixum, idem est.
   Frixa nocent, elixa juvant, assata cohercent.
Hec artocrea, a pye.
Hic pastellus, a pastethe.
Hic artocasius, cibus factus ex pane et casio.
Hec tarta, a tartt.
Hec flata, a flawn.
Hoc opacum, idem est.

---

[1] A small round loaf, as it is explained in the verse.

[2] *Schyfe,* or *shire,* a slice.

[3] *Dor cake.* The *collyrida* was a sort of cracknell, or crisp cake, somewhat resembling biscuit.

[4] Pottage.

[5] Broth.

[6] See before, p. 227.

[7] Jussell was a favourite dish, composed of eggs and grated bread, boiled in broth, and seasoned with sage and saffron.

[8] *Lorray,* or *lorré,* was a dish, in ancient cookery, for which receipts are found in most of the cookery books.

[9] Literally, broth of fish.

[10] Charlet was a dish, in mediæval cookery, of which the principal ingredient was minced pork.

[11] Perhaps the dish called in the early treatises on cookery *crayton,* or *criton*—a preparation of chickens.

Hoc fertum, a podyng.
Hoc omasum, idem.
Hoc laganum, same cake.
Hec salsucia, a sawstyre.
Hec hilla, idem est.
Hee delicie,
Hec lauticia, } dautyths.
Hee galanticie,
Hoc frixum, a froys.[1]
Hoc strutum,
Hec tripa, } a tripe.
Hec perra, a flyk.
Hic petaso, -nis, idem est.
Hec petasiculus, half a flyk.
Hoc succidium, sowse.
Hoc tucetum, hagas.
Hec carnes borine, beffe.
Hec carnes porcine, pork.
Hee carnes ovine, moton.
Hee carnes vitule, veylle.
Hec caro, -nis, man's flesche.
Carnes carnifices, carnem vendunt meretrices.
Hec ripa, a wyn-sope.
Hic ipa, a watyr-sope.
Hec offa, a ale-sope.
Est crateris vipa, scutelle dicitur offa,
Sed limphe proprie dicitur ipa fore.

DE LECTIS ET ORNAMENTIS EORUM.

Hec torena, est lectus regis.
Hoc plumale, a fedyr-bed.
Hoc cooportorium, a coverlyd.
Hoc toral, -lis, idem est.
Hec lodex, -icis, a blankytt.
Hoc linthiamen, a schett.
Hic carentirellus, canvas.
Hoc linthium, a tapytt.

Hec tapeta, idem est.
Hec culcitra, a matrys.
Hoc cervical, a peloware.
Hec curtina, a curtyn.
Hic lectus, a bed.
Hoc stratum, idem est.
Hoc grabatum, media producta, idem est.
Est lectus stratum, fertur via regia strata;
Mobile fit stratus ad quod depressus habetur.
Hic lectulus, i. parvus lectus.
Hic thorus, idem est.
Dicas esse thoros, paliaria, brachia, lectos.
Hoc lectiferum, est lectus stratum vel locus ubi lectuli sternuntur, vel stramenta lectorum.
Hec bojenila, i. lectus.
Hoc concubile, est lectus concubinarum.
Hoc concubiculum, idem est.
Hic genialis, est lectus qui in nupciis sternitur.
Hec sponda, est exterior pars lecti.
Hoc fultrum, est pes lecti.
Lectus servorum, discumbentium grabatum.
Cum soleas in eas caput inclinari gravatum,
Disce graba signare caput, venit inde grabatum.
Hec lectica, est lectus vel thorus, vel currus quod dicitur lectus, vel est curtina circa lectum.
Hec spinge, -arum, sunt lectuli in [quibus] sunt posite efigie.
Hoc torrium, est quidam lectus.
Hoc stramentum, letyr.
Hoc stratorium, idem.
Hoc stabum, idem est.
Hic punicanus, est lectus circumclusus tapicoleribus rubeis.

---

[1] A froise was a sort of pancake. The word is still used in the dialect of the eastern counties. It appears to have been a favourite dish with the monks; for Gower, (Conf. Amant., vol. ii., p. 92,) describing the troubled sleep of Sompnolence, says—

Whan he is falle in suche a dreme,
Right as a ship ayem the streme
He routeth with a slepy noyse,
And brustleth as a monkes *froise*,
Whan it is throwe into the panne

Hoc punicanum, idem est.
Hoc crepodium, a credyle.
Hec bamba, est lectus.
  Sit cooportorium lecto lecturaque crinis,
  Sit tectorem domibus regimen ca' sic verge,
  Armaque craterras quoque simul capulas.
Hec amphicapa, est tapeta ex utraque parte villosa.
Hec sipha, idem est.
  Amphicapam dicas gemma de parte villosa,
  Sicut historiis simplex est sipha trapeta.
Hoc subsiterium, est tapetum sub pedital.

Hec curtina, a curtyn.
  Dicas curtinas quasi rerum corda tenentes;
Hoc conopeum, est curtina adinst . . .
. . . repium recium texta ad ardendos culices et muscas.
Hoc auriale, a cord or a pelowe.
Hoc cervical, idem est.
Hoc pulviner,
Hoc cervicarium, } a coschyn.
Hic pulvinus,
Hoc limphum, } *est po . . ex line et*
Hoc limpheolum, } *lana contextus.*

A PICTORIAL VOCABULARY.[1]

(OF THE FIFTEENTH CENTURY.)

NOMINA PERTINENCIA HUMANO CORPORI.

Hoc caput, An^{ce} a hede.
Hoc occiput, An^{ce} the last parte of the hede.
Hoc interciput, An^{ce} the myd parte of the hede.
Hoc cinciput, An^{ce} the forme part.
  Cinciput anterior capitis pars dicitur esse;
  Occiput et partem designat posteriorem:
  Ast mediam partem dicas interciput esse.
Hoc frontisipium, An^{ce} a forhed.
Hic vertex, An^{ce} a natrelle.[2]
Hoc discrimen, An^{ce} the seed of the hede.
  Sit tibi discrimen divisio, glabra, periclum.
Hic crinis, ⎫
Hic pilus,   ⎪
Hic capillus, ⎬ idem sunt, *An^{ce}* a here.
Hec coma,   ⎪
Hec sesaries, ⎭
  Sesaries hominum, sed crines sunt mulierum;
  Hujus vel illius bene dicitur esse capillus.
Hoc cranium, An^{ce} a hern-pane.
Hoc cerebrum, An^{ce} a brayne.
Hec facies, An^{ce} a face.

Hec maxilla, ⎫
Hec mala,   ⎬ idem sunt, a scheke.
Hec gena,   ⎭
Hic ffrons, -tis, An^{ce} a forhed.
Hic ffrons, -dis, An^{ce} brawnche.
  Frons, -dis, ramus, frons, -tis, pars capitalis.
Hoc cilium, An^{ce} a here of the hie.
Hec bucca, ⎫
Hec ffaux, ⎬ *An^{ce}* a scheke.
  Ad navem malus spectat, malus est viciosus,
  Faux est mala, malum vicium, malum quoque pomum.

Hoc supercilium, An^{ce} a bro . . . .
Hoc intercilium, An^{ce} betwyn the browes.
Hic oculus, An^{ce} a nye.
Hec palpebra, An^{ce} a nyelede.
Hec pupilla, An^{ce} the balle of the ye.
Hec abbcies, ⎫
Hec abbedo, ⎬ *An^{ce}* the qwyt of the ye.
Hic nasus, An^{ce} a nase.
Hic naris, An^{ce} the nese-thyr . . . .
Hoc interficium, An^{ce} the bryd of the ne.
Hec piruela, An^{ce} the cop of the no . . .
Hec cartilago, An^{ce} a grystyl.
Hoc tempus, An^{ce} a tempylle.

---

[1] This very curious vocabulary is preserved in a manuscript in the possession of Lord Londesborough, which I think is of the latter part of the fifteenth century. The illustrative sketches, which occupy the margins and what would have been otherwise blank places in the manuscript, are here given, with the inscriptions attached, of the same size, and as nearly as possible fac-similies, of the original.

[2] The hatrelle. See before, p. 185.

A PICTORIAL VOCABULARY.

Hic cirrus, A^{ce} the cop of the hede.
Hoc pus, snot.
Hic polipus, idem.
   Polupus est naris fetor, et in equore piscis.
Hec mustilago, A^{ce} a mulere . . .
Hic mentum, A^{ce} a schyne.
Hec barba, } a berd.
Hoc genorbidum,
Hoc os, ossis, A^{ce} a bone.
Hoc os, -ris, A^{ce} a mowth.
   Os, oris, loquitur, corio vestitur os, ossis.
Hec lingua, A^{ce} a tung.
Hec glossa, idem est.
   Est membrum lingua, designat et hec igonis.
Hoc labium, A^{ce} a lyp *super os*.
Hoc labrum, An^{er} a lyp.
Hec gingiva, A^{ce} a gome.
Hoc omestrum, A^{ce} a mygerne.
Hec auris, } a ere.
Hec auricula,
Hoc tolera,[1] A^{er} a ere-sop.
Hec febra, A^{ce} a weyne.
Hec mandebula, a scheke-bone.
Hic dens, -tis, A^{ce} a thothe.
Hoc maxillare, a wal-thothe.
Hic molaris, idem est.
   Ventes molares, lapides die esse molares.
Hec veruca, A^{ce} a wrothe.[2]

Hic gelbus, An^{ce} a wen.
Hoc collum, An^{ce} a nek.
Hec gula,
Hoc guttur, } a throthe.
Hic jugulus,
   Est gula pars colli, vicium gula restat edendi.
Hec fontinella, A^{ce} the nek-hole.
Hic isiofagus, A^{ce} a wesawnt.
Hoc pupillum, the blak of the ye.
Hoc brachium,
Hic lacertus, } a harme-hole.
Her ulna,
   Brachia die ulnas, panni mensura sit ulna.
Hic vultus, -tus, -ui, A^{ce} a schere.[3]
Hec spina, } a ryg-bone.
Hoc spondile,
Hec spina, A^{ce} a thorne.
   Me pungit spina, pars est in corpore spina.
Hec acella, A^{ce} a harm-hole.
Hic subricus, idem est.
Hic ricus, -ci, A^{ce} a kod-lomb.
Hic ricus, -cus, -ui, A^{ce} the nest of the ye.
   Hic ricus per -ci peculas fera dicimus esse,
   Hic ricus dans -ui pars ultima constat ocelli.
Hic cubitus, A^{ce} a helbowe.
Hic umerus, A^{ce} a schuldere.
Hec arteria, A^{ce} the hole of the throt.

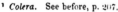

[1] *Colera*. See before, p. 207.
[2] *Wrothe*. A wart is still called a *wrat* in some of the northern dialects.
[3] The word *schere*, in the sense of countenance or mien, is not a very common word, but it occurs more than once in the romances of Gawayne, edited for the Roxburgh Club by Sir Frederick Madden.

Hec ura, A^{ce} the knot of the nek.
  Opptulio os uvam, fert vitis fertilis uvam.
Hic armus, A^{ce} a schuldyr.
Hic humerus, } *idem sunt.*
Hec scapula,
Hoc platum, A^{ce} a schuldyr-bone.
Hic stomacus, A^{ce} stomake.
Hec jecur, A^{ce} a maw.
Hec manus, -nus, -ui, A^{ce} a hand.
Hec palma,
Hoc ir, } the palme of the hand.
Hec rola,
  Palma manus, palma arbor, victoria palma.
Hic digitus, A^{ce} a fyngyr.
Hic articulus, A^{ce} a too.
  Est manuum digitus, articulusque pedum.
Hic junctura, A^{ce} junctur.
Hoc fren, A^{ce} the sckyn of the brayne.
Hec pellis, A^{ce} the sckyn of a best.
  In capitis cerebro fren est tenuissima pellis:
  Pellitur a carne pellis, carnis cutis heret.
Hoc corium, A^{ce} ledyr.
Hic pollex, A^{ce} a thumb.
Hic allux, A^{ce} a grete too.
  Est manuum polles, sed dicatur pedis allux.
Hec unguis, A^{ce} a nayle of a man.
Hec ungula, A^{ce} a claw of a best.
  Unguis non brutis datur, sed ungula brutis.
Hoc tergum, A^{ce} a bak of a man.
Hoc tergus, } a bak of a best.
Hoc dorsum,
Hic venter,
Hoc uterus, } a wombe.
Hic alvus,

Hic umbelicus, A^{ce} a nawylle.
Hec nates, A^{ce} a botok.
Hic lumbus, A^{ce} a hepe.
Hoc femur, idem est.
Hic vel hec clunis, A^{ce} a hepe-bone.
Hic torax, A^{ce} a brest-bone.
Hoc pectus, A^{ce} a brest.
Hec mamilla, A^{ce} a lytyl pap.
Hec mamma, A^{ce} a pap of a woman.
Hoc uber, A^{ce} a pap of a best.
  Nos hominum proprie mamillas dicimus esse,
  Ubera et pecudum, sed mamme et mulierum;
  Cujus mamillas dixisti, dicque patillas.
Hoc latus, A^{ce} a syde.
Hec costa, A^{ce} a rybe.
Hec costa, A^{ce} a baksterys slomb.
  Pars lateris costa, res pistoris quoque costa.
Hec pubes,
Hic lanugo, } *An^{ce}* schere.
Hoc pecten,
Hoc femur, } a they.
Hoc crus,
Hic penis, } *idem sunt.*
Hic priapus,
Hic testiculus, a balok-stone.
Hic piga, A^{ce} a balok-cod.
Hec vulva, A^{ce} a cunt.
Hic cunnus, idem est.
Hic tentigo, A^{ce} a kykyr.
Hec caturda,[1] *A^{ce}* a bobrelle.
Hec munda,
Hec matrix, } a schyn that a schyld
Hec steria, ys consevyd in.

[1] *Caturda* was used in the Latin of the fifteenth century to indicate a part of the female sexual organs, either the *labia pudendi*, or the *nymphæ*.

A PICTORIAL VOCABULARY.

Hec cavilla, A^ce a hankyl.
Hoc extum, A^ce a gret paugh.
Hoc viscus, A^ce a bowelle.
Hoc nytunum, A^ce a bowelle.
Hoc trutum, A^ce a tharme.
Hec struta, A^ce a startere of nete.
Hoc intestinum, } a nestarme.
Hic colus,
Hec diafragma, A^ce a mydred.
Hoc cordis, A^ce a hert.
Hic splen, A^ce the mylt.
Hic ren, -nis, A^ce the nerys.
Hoc epar, -ris, A^ce the lywer.
Cor sapit, et pulmo loquitur, fel cohgit iram,
Splen ridere facit, cogit amare jecur.
Hic pulmo, A^ce a long.
Hoc burbulum, A^ce a umblye.
Hec elia, A^ce flank.
Hoc cepum, A^ce talow.
Hec pinguedo, A^ce fatnes.
Erba sit hec fragus, hoc fragrum sit tibi fructus,
Hic fragrus, -gi, pomplex cernatur huberi.
Hic fragus, A^ce a hame.
Hec fragus, A^ce a strebery-wyse.
Hoc fragum, A^ce a strebery.
Hic talus, A^ce a hele.
Hic talus, A^ce a dyse.
Ludo cum talis, terram tango quoque talis.
Hic sanguis, } An^ce blode.
Hic cruor,
Sanguis alit corpus, cruor est a corpore sumptus;
Extractus venis cruor est, in corpore sanguis.

Hoc fel, A^ce the galle.
Hoc sperma, -tis, A^ce mankynd.
Semen quod seritur, set progenies quoque sperma.
Hoc alatum, A^ce a rofom.[1]
Hic condulus, A^ce a knokylle.
Hoc stercus, } a torde.
Hec meda,
Hoc genu, A^ce a kne.
Hic poplex, A^ce a hame.
Hoc internodium, } a kne-hone.
Hoc vertebrum,
Hec tibea, A^ce a leg.
Hec tibea, A^ce a trompe.
Tibia dat sonitum, me portat tibia totum.
Hec sura, A^ce a schyn-bone.
Hic nervus, A^ce a senow.
Hic pes, -dis, A^ce a fothe.
Hic poder, A^ce the fylthe of the fothe.
Hic callus, } An^ce the harde of the
Hec planta, } fothe.
Signat callus plantam collumque bovinum.
Hic sudor, A^ce swete.
Hec arcacis, A^ce slepe of the fothe.
Pes patitur arture, Ar* my fothe ys a slepe.
Hoc apostema, -tis, A^ce a postemet [2]
Hec glaucoma, A^ce a gome.
Hic articulus, A^ce a too.
Hec vola, A^ce the holle of the fothe.
Est vola pars palme, pars ale, pars pedis una.
Hic pollex, A^ce a thombe
Hic inder, A^ce a lyk-pot.[3]

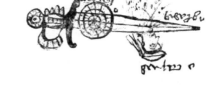

[1] *Rofom.* In the Devonshire dialect the waist is called *rofoam.*
[2] An aposteme, or abscess.
[3] The second cut at the bottom of this page, representing a hand, sword, and head, are drawn upside-down in the original, as here shown.

Hic medius, A^{ce} the long-man.
Hic medicus, A^{ce} the leche.
Hic auricularis, A^{ce} the lytyl-man.[1]
    Pollex, index, medius, medicus, auricularis.
Hec vesica, An^{ce} a bleder.
Hic musculus, A^{ce} a muskylle.
Hic musculus, A^{ce} a lytyl mus.
    Est musculus piscis, parvus mus, pars tibiales.
Hec solia, A^{ce} the sole of the fote.
Hoc solium, A^{ce} a kynges sete.
    Sub pede sit solia, solium quoque regia sedes.

NOMINA ECCLESIE NESSES-SARIA.

Hoc altare,
Hec ara, } a hawtere.
Hoc superaltare, A^{ce} a superaltori.
Hec crux, A^{ce} a crosse.
Hec imago, A^{ce} a ymage.
Hic lichitus, for a eyle-pott.
Hoc vixillum, A^{ce} a banyre.
Hic calix, A^{ce} a schalys.
Hec paterna, A^{ce} a patyn.
Hoc corporarium,
Hoc corporale, } *A^{ce}* coperas.

Hec fiola,
Hic urcius, } a cruet.
Hec osta,
Hic panis, } a nobely.[2]
Hoc sacramentum, An^{ce} the sacrament.
Hoc sacrium,
Hoc sacrificium, } sacrifyce.
Hoc turibulum, A^{ce} a sensere.
Hec aserra, a schyp that zychel ere in.
Hoc thus,
Hoc incensum, } *An^{ce}* ensence.
Hec candela, A^{ce} a candelle.
Hic almoriolum, A^{ce} almery.
Hic lampas, A^{ce} a lawmp.
Hic lichinus, A^{ce} meche.
Hic mergulus, A^{ce} herne in the lamp.
Hoc olium, A^{ce} oylle.
Hic cerreus, A^{ce} a torche.
Hic cerulus, a lytyl torche.
Hoc candelebrum,
Hoc candelarium, } a candylle-styk.
Hoc crisma, -tis, A^{ce} a crem.
Hoc crismatorium, A^{ce} a crismatory.
Hoc vestiarium,
Hoc vestibulum, } a vestri.
Hoc missale, A^{ce} a myssale.
Hoc gradale, A^{ce} a grayelle.
Hoc troparium, A^{ce} tropere.
Hoc callendarium, A^{ce} a calendere.

---

[1] These popular names of the fingers seem to be of considerable antiquity. The following curious lines are quoted by Mr. Halliwell (Dict. of Arch. Words) from a MS. of the fifteenth century in the University Library, Cambridge, Ff. v. 48, fol. 82):

  Ilke a fyngir has a name, als men thaire fyngers calle.
  The lest fyngir hat *lityl man,* for hit is lest of alle ;
  The next fynger hat *leche-man,* for quen a leche dos o3t,
  With that fynger he tastes alle thyng how that hit is wro3t;
  Long man hat the mydilmast, for longest fynger hit is;
  The ferthe men calls *towcher,* therwith men touches I-wis;
  The ufte fynger is the *thowmbe,* and hit has most my3t,
  And fastest haldes of alle the tother, forthi men calles hit ri3t.

A Nominale in MS. Reg. 17, C. xvii, fol. 39, r°.

gives the following list, very similar to that in our text:

  Hic pollex, A^{c} thowme.
  Hic index, A^{c} lic-pote.
  Hic medius, A^{c} lang-fynger.
  Hic medicus, A^{c} leche.
  Hic auricularis, A^{c} lytyl-fynger.

Mr. Halliwell has printed a modern nursery rhyme, (Nursery Rhymes of England, fifth edition, p. 155,) in which names very similar to these are still used, namely, *thumbkin, foreman, longman, ringman,* and *littleman.* In Norfolk the fingers are called popularly, *Tom-thumbkin, Will-wilkin, Long-gracious, Betty-bodkin, Little-tit.*

[2] i. e., the oblay, or offering.

A PICTORIAL VOCABULARY.

Hoc ymnare, A^{ce} a ymnere.
Hec leges, }
Hec legenda, } a legend.
Hic legendus, }
Hec letenia, } a leteny-boke.
Hec laturia, }
Hoc psalterium, A^{ce} a sawtere-boke.
Hoc antifonarium, a amphanere.
Hoc primarium, A^{ce} a premere.
Hoc mertilogium, A^{ce} a mertelage.
Hoc manuale, a crystynnyng-boke.
Hoc passionari[um], A^{ce} a passionari.
Hoc regestrum, A^{ce} a regestyr.
Hoc ordinale, A^{ce} a ordynal.
Hoc portiforum, A^{ce} a portes.
Hoc touale, A^{ce} a toual.
Hoc temperalium, A^{ce} a temperal.
Hec casula, A^{ce} a chesypyl.
Hec alba, A^{ce} a hawbe.
Hic amictus, A^{ce} a amyte.
Hec zona, } a gyrdylle.
Hoc tropheum, }
Hic phano, *-is*, A^{ce} phanun.[1]
Hec capa, A^{ce} a cope.
Hoc superpelicium, a syrples.
Hec dalmatica, a tonykyl.
Hic ffons, *-tis*, A^{ce} a funte.
Hic gradus, *-dus*, *-ui*, A^{ce} a grese.[2]
Hic baptismus, A^{ce} crystyndome.
Hec pixis, } A^{ce} a box.
Hoc alabastrum, }
Hec campana, } a belle.
Hec campanicula, }
Hoc campanile, A^{ce} a stepyl.
Hoc camparium, idem est.
Hoc tintinabulum, a lytyl belle.

Hic batillus, A^{ce} a clapyr.
Hoc centilogium, a wedercok.
Hoc calasisorium, A^{ce} a hers.
Hoc fferetrum, }
Hoc sandapulum, } An^{ce} a bere.
Hec libetina, }
Hic loculus, }
Est loculus bursa, parvus locus, et lubitina.
Hec sera, A^{ce} wax.
Hoc vitrum, } An^{ce} glas.
Hoc ilum, }
Hoc orologium, A^{ce} a horologe.
Hoc oritimum, A^{ce} a cloke.
Hoc organum, A^{ce} a orgon.
Hoc osculatorium, A^{ce} a paxbrede.
Hoc manutergium, } a hand-clothe.
Hic towalus, }
Hic certofagus, }
Hoc sepulcrum, } An^{ce} a grafe.
Hoc bustum, }
Hec tumba, } An^{ce} a tumb.
Hoc monumentum, }
Hoc poliandrum, A^{ce} a byryel-ston.[3]
Hic ysopus, A^{ce} a sprenkylle.
Hoc aspersorium, idem est.
Hic stallus, A^{ce} a stalle.
Hoc mausolium, } An^{ce} a grafe.
Hic tumulus, }
Hoc pulpetorium, A^{ce} a pulpyt

---

[1] A standard; the gonfanon.

[2] A step. In the directions in the will of Henry VI., for the building of the colleges at Eton and Cambridge, we read, " Item, the height fro the streete to the enhancing of the ground of the cemetery, 7 feete di., and the same walle in height above that, 5 feete di., with *greeces* out of the way into the same pane, as many as shalle be convenient "—" And from the provostes stalle unto the grecce called Gradus Chori, 90 feete," &c.

[3] *Byriel*, or *byriels*, was the old name for a tomb.

Hec corda,　⎱ a rope.
Hec funis,　⎰

Hec lanterna,　⎱ a lanterne.
Hec lucerna,　⎰

Hoc lectrinium,　⎫
Hic ambo,　⎬ a leyterne.
Hic discus,　⎭

Hic obstratis, A^{ce} a pannyng.

Hoc velum, A^{ce} a veyle.

Hoc simutorium,　⎱ a schererd.
Hoc atrium,　⎰

NOMINA ANIMALIUM DOMESTICARUM.

Hic dextrarius, A^{ce} a stede.
Hic emissarius, a corsowyr.
Hic sucarius, A^{ce} a trotore.[1]
Hic palafridus, a palfrey.
Hic gradarius, A^{ce} a hawmlore.[2]
Hic mannus, A^{ce} a hakeney.
Hic cabo, A^{ce} a stalon.
Hic caballus, A^{ce} a capulle.
Hic viridus, A^{ce} a thyl-hors.
Hic spado, A^{ce} a gelt hors.
Hic equus, A^{ce} alle maner hors.
Hec equa, A^{ce} a mare.
Hic pullus, A^{ce} a schekyn.
Hic pullus, A^{ce} a fole.
Pullus, -a, -um, A^{ce} bluk.
　Pullus equs, pullus galline, pullus et ater.

Hic asinus,　⎱ a has.
Her asina,　⎰

Hic saginarius, A^{ce} a pal-hors.[3]
Hic taurus, A^{ce} a bole.
Hic mulus, A^{ce} a mule.
Hic et hec bos, A^{ce} a box.

Hec vacca,　⎱ a cow.
Hec vaccula,　⎰

Hic bucculus,　⎱ a bullok.
Hic juvencus,　⎰

Hec buccula,　⎱ a hekfere.
Hec jurenca,　⎰

Hic vitulus, A^{ce} a calfe.
Hic vervex, A^{ce} a ram.
Hic aries, A^{ce} a wedyr.
Hec ovis, alle manner a chepe.
Hec verbica, A^{ce} a hew.
Hec adasia, A^{ce} pyllyd hew.
Hec erna, A^{ce} a hew-lambe.
Hic agnus, A^{ce} a wedyr-lombe.
Hic agnellus, a lytyl lambe.
Hic titirus, A^{ce} a bel-wedyr.
Hic equiferus, A^{ce} a wyld hors.
Hic aper, A^{ce} a wyld bore.
Hic verres, tam bore.

Hic porcus,　⎱ a hoge.
Hec nefrenda,　⎰

Hec porca,　⎫
Hic et hec sus,　⎬ a sow.
Hec scrofa,　⎭

Hec porcula,　⎱ a geldyd sow.
Hec nefrenda,　⎰

Hic porcellus, A^{ce} a pyg.
Hic caper, a get buk.
Hec capra, A^{ce} a gothe.

Hic edus,　⎫
Hic capriolus,　⎬ a kyd lomb.
Hic edulus　⎭

Hic leporarius, a frefownd.[4]
Hic odorincicus, a stanyel.

---

[1] *Trotore,* a trotter.
[2] *Hawmlore,* i. e. an ambler.
[3] *Pal-horse,* evidently a packhorse.
[4] *i. e.,* a greyhound. The use of the letter *f* in this word is rather singular, and reminds us of the words *fynger,* for hunger, and *fyrst,* for thirst, which were forms of the dialects of the Welsh border in the fourteenth century.

Hic caniculus, a qwelpe.
Hic catulus, idem est.
Hec catula, a byche qwelpe.
Hec lacesca, A^{ce} a hyche.
Hic molossus, A^{ce} a bond-doge.
Hic catus, ⎫
Hic mureligus, ⎬ a catt.
Hic pilax, ⎭
Hic catellus, A^{ce} a cytlyng [1]
Hic bubalus, A^{ce} a bogelle.[2]

NOMINA ANIMALIUM FERORUM.

Hic leo, An^{ce} a lywn.
Hec leena, ⎫ a leonys.
Hec leonissa, ⎭
Hic cervus, A^{ce} a hert.
Hic servus, A^{ce} a serwant.
   Hic cervus per c. scriptum sit bestia silve;
   S. si scribatur servus, famulus vocitatur.
Hec cerva, A^{ce} a hynde.
Hic cervulus, A^{ce} a hertes calfe.
Hic damus, A^{ce} a do buk.
Hic vel hec dama, A^{ce} a doo.
Hic hinnilus, A^{ce} a fowne.
Hec fferina, -ne, A^{ce} venisyn.
Hic lupus, A^{ce} a wulfe.
Hec lupa, A^{ce} a femel wulfe.
Hic ursus, A^{ce} a bere.
Hec ursa, idem est.
Hic leopardus, A^{ce} a lebard.
Hec leoparda, idem est.
Hic vulpes, A^{ce} a ffox.
Hec simia, A^{ce} a hape.
Hic cuniculus, A^{ce} a conyng.
Hec cunicula, idem est.
Hic furo, -is, A^{ce} a foret.
Hic olefans, a olefawnt.

Hic sirogrillus, ⎫ a scurelle.
Hic scurellus, ⎭
Hec mustela, a wesylle.
Hic lepus, A^{ce} a hare.
Hic rato, A^{ce} a ratun.
Hic sorex, idem est.
Hic mus, A^{ce} mowse.
Hic vel hec talpa, A^{ce} a molle.
Hic castor, ⎫
Hec melota, ⎬ a brok.
Hic taxus, ⎭
Hec taxus, a hew-tre.[3]
   Hic arbor taxus, hinc taxum dico melotam.
Hic fetrunctus, ⎫ a sulmard.
Hic pecoides, ⎭
Hic ericius, ⎫ a hurchyn.
Hic irmacius, ⎭
Hic dromidarius, A^{ce} a dromedarye.
Hec ffera, A^{ce} a wyld-best.
Hic camelus, A^{ce} a schamelle.
Hic lepusculus, A^{ce} a leveret.
Hic ffeber, ⎫ a otere.
Hic lutrissius, ⎭
Hic grillus, A^{ce} a pryket.[4]
Hic unicornus, a unicorne.
Hic gurrex, A^{ce} a water-mowse.
Hic roonideus, A^{ce} a red-mowse.
Hic cornu, indeclinabile, A^{ce} a horne.
Hec ungula, A^{ce} a claw.
Hoc palare, A^{ce} a dewlap.
Hec crista, ⎫ a mane.
Hec juba, ⎭
   Hic Jubar rex fuerat, jubar hoc lux, hec juba crista.
Hec cauda, ⎫ *A^{ce}* a tayle.
Hic dica, ⎭
Hic colimellus, A^{ce} thoyse.[5]
Hec ceta, A^{ce} a brystylle.

---

[1] A kitten.
[2] *Bogelle,* a beagle.
[3] A yew-tree.
[4] A *pricket* is, properly, a buck in his second year. The Prompt. Parv. has, "Pryket, beest, *capriolus.*" But in our text it must be either an error for *cryket,* which is the equivalent of the Latin *grillus,* or a form of this word peculiar to one of the provincial dialects.
[5] *Thoyse,* the tusk of a boar.

NOMINA AVIUM DOMESTI-
CORUM.

Hic gallus, A^{ce} a cok.
Hec gallina, A^{ce} a hene.
Hic pullus, A^{ce} a cheke.
Hic ancer, A^{ce} a gander.
Hec auca, A^{ce} a gose.
Hic ancerulus, A^{ce} a guslyng.
Hic capo, -is, }
Hic altile,   } a capun.
Hic pavo, A^{ce} a pocokk.
Hic anas, for drake.
Hec anata, a heynd.
Hic columbus, }
Hec columba,   } a dowe.
Hic pipio, A^{ce} dow-byrd.
Hic palumbus, }
Hec palumba,   } a stok-dowe.
Hic ancipiter, a goshawke.
Hic erodius, a gerfawkyn.
Hic nisus, A^{ce} a sperhawke.
Hic capus, A^{ce} a muskyte.
Hic acensorius, A^{ce} a hoby.
Hic aluctor, A^{ce} a merlone.
Hic aluctus, A^{ce} a stamel.
Hic basterdus, A^{ce} a laner.
Hic signus, }
Hic olor,   } a swane.

NOMINA AVIUM FFERORUM.

Hic regulus, A^{ce} a wrenc.
Hic vultur, A^{ce} a grype.
Hic passer, A^{ce} a sparow.
Hic carduelis, A^{ce} a goldfynche.

Hec alauda,   }
Hec antelucana, } a larke.
Hec serris,   }
Hec filomena, A^{ce} a nytynggal.
Hec alcedo, A^{ce} a colmow.[1]
Hic sturnus, A^{ce} a sterlyng.
Hic irundo, A^{ce} a swalow.
Hic vespertilio, }
Hec lucifuga,   } a bake.
Hic corvus, A^{ce} a crow.
Hic cornix, A^{ce} a rewyn.
Hic niticorax, A^{ce} a nyte-rawyn.
Hec monedula, }
Hic nodus,   } a roke.
Hec ffrigella, A^{ce} a rodok.
Hec lonefa, A^{ce} a donek.[2]
Hic bubo, A^{ce} a howylle.
Hec aquila, A^{ce} a egyle.
Hec ulula, A^{ce} a semow.
Hic onux, A^{ce} a not-hak.
Hic castrimergus, a wodcok.
Hic conturnix, A^{ce} a curlowyr.
Hec qualena, A^{ce} a quayle.
Hic milvus, A^{ce} a potok.[3]
Hec pica, A^{ce} a pye.
Hic citacus, a popynjay.
Hic garulus, }
Hic gratulus, } a jay.
Hec ipipa, A^{ce} a wype.
Hic calendula, a plover.
Hic maviscus, }
Hic sturdus, } a mawys.[4]
Hic campestris, a feldfare.
Hic pelicanus, A^{ce} a pelycan.
Hec ardea, A^{ce} a herne.
Hec Ardea, the name of a towyn.
  Ardea nomen avis, et nomen dicitur urbis.
Hec sigonia, A^{ce} a storke.

[1] More usually written *colmose*, the A.-S. *colmase*, the sea-mew.

[2] *Donek*, or *dunnock*, the hedge-sparrow. A hedge-sparrow is still called a *dunnock* in the north of England, and a *doney* in Northampton-shire.

[3] A puttock, or kite.

[4] This is still preserved as the name for the singing thrush in the eastern counties.

A PICTORIAL VOCABULARY.

Hec ibis, A^{ce} a suyte.
Hic populus, a schevelard.[1]
Hic aspergo, a cormerawnt.
Hic pitus, -ti, A^{ce} a sethe.
Hic onocratulus, A^{ce} a betore.
Hec talendiola, A^{ce} a holste.
Hic filicus, A^{ce} a telle cok.
Hec filica, A^{ce} a telle hen.
Hic perdix, A^{ce} a partryk.
Hic utericius, a mor-cok.
Hic mergus, A^{ce} a cote.
Hic mergulus, A^{ce} a dokare.[2]
Hec agredula, a tetmose.
Hic cuculus, A^{ce} a cocow.
Hic turtur, A^{ce} a turtylle.
Hic merulus, A^{ce} a thyrstylle-cok.
Hic merula, idem est.
Hic ornix, } a fesant.
Hic ffesanus,
Hic umnis, A^{ce} a scheldrak.
Hic frigella, A^{ce} a roke.
Hic selido, a kynges fychere.
Hic icter, A^{ce} a wodake.[3]
Hic tradus, a wagstyrt.
Hic strix, -cis, A^{ce} a schryche.
Hoc grus, Au^{ce} a crane.
Hoc rostum, A^{ce} a bylle.
Hec ala, A^{ce} a whynge.
Hec vola, pars quedam ale.
Hec vola, a parte of the harme-hole.
Hec vola, the lowest parte of the fote.
Est vola pars palme, pars ale, pars pedis inna.
Hec pluma, A^{ce} a fedyr.
Hec penna, A^{ce} a pen.
Hic calamus, A^{ce} a canc.
Hoc ilum, i. medulla penne.

NOMINA PISSIUM AQUARUM RECENCIUM.

Hic crocodolus, A^{ce} a codlyng.[4]
Hec murena, A^{ce} a lamprey.
Hic salmo, A^{ce} samwn.
Hic lucius, A^{ce} a lus.[5]
Hic dentrix, A^{ce} a pyke.
Hic lupis, idem est.
Hic luaculus, a pykrelle.[6]
Hic alosa, A^{ce} a leche.
Hic ganerius, A^{ce} a stekelyng.
Hic mullus, A^{ce} a bulhyd.
Hic fundulus, A^{ce} a flex-peng.[7]
Hee spunere, -arum, A^{ce} a spyrlyng.
Hec menusa, } a menys.
Hic serullus,
Hic morus, A^{ce} a haddok.
Hic capita, A^{ce} a dar.[8]
Hic turtur, A^{ce} a gurnard.
Hic gobio, A^{ce} a gobon.[9]
Hec anguilla, A^{ce} a helle.
Hec truca, A^{ce} a tryotht.
Hec rocia, A^{ce} a roche.
Hec poca, A^{ce} a pyche.
Hic echinus, } a tenche.
Hic ectinus,
Hec frisgula, A^{ce} a chevender.[10]
Hic murex, A^{ce} a breme.
Hec murenula, A^{ce} a lampren.
Hec perca, A^{ce} a perche.
Hic guttulus, A^{ce} a gojon.
Hec sepia, A^{ce} a troyte.

---

[1] A water-fowl, the *anas clypeata* of naturalists.
[2] *Docare,* the diver, or didapper.
[3] *Wodake,* the woodhock, or woodpecker.
[4] The Prompt. Parv. has, "Codlynge, fysche, *morus.*"
[5] A luce, or pike.
[6] A young pike.
[7] *Flex-peng.* The Latin word *fundulus* is generally interpreted a *gudgeon.*
[8] *Dar,* the dare, or, as it is now more usually called, the dace.
[9] *Gobon,* the *whiting.*
[10] *Chevender,* the cheven, or chub.

NOMINA PISCIUM MARINORUM.

Hec aurata, A^{ce} a sedow.[1]
Hec setus,
Hoc setearum, } whalle.
Hec epimera, -e,
Hic tumalus, } a sperlyng.
Hic sardellus, A^{er} a swerd-fyche.
Hec ostria, A^{ce} a hoystyr.
Hec ostra, A^{ce} a hoyster-chelle.
   Ostra notat testam, clausum notat ostria piscem.
Hic ausculus, A^{er} a muskylle.
Hee telie, -arum, idem est.
Hec conca, A^{cc} a cokylle.
Hic bulbus, A^{ce} a wylke.
Hic cancer, A^{er} a crabe.
Hic polupus, A^{er} a lobstar.
Hic conchilus, A^{cc} a astsyche.
Hic saltilus, A^{cr} a hobstere.
Hic meganus, A^{cr} a makrel.
Hoc allec,
Hec gerra, } a heryng.
Hec ragadia, A^{ce} a ray.
Hic uronoscopus, a thornbak.
Hic garus, A^{cr} a schate.[2]
Hic morus, A^{ce} a haddok.
Hic merlinggus, A^{er} a merlyng.
Hic mugilus, A^{ce} a mowel.[3]
Hec rosina, A^{ce} a se-hors.
Hic sepio, A^{er} a leenge.[4]

Hic panus,
Hic squylla, } A^{ce} a hake.
Hic congruus, A^{ce} a cungur.
Hoc pecten, A^{ce} a playse.
Hec ffoca, A^{ce} a floke.[5]
Hic molanus, A^{ce} a melet.
Hic turbo, -is, A^{ce} a but.[6]
Hec rubella, A^{ce} a rochet.[7]
Hec rugella,
Hoc rustiforum, } a horn-keke.[8]
Hec solia, A^{cr} a sole.
Hic canis, a doke-fyche.[9]
Hec ffingia, A^{ce} a stok-fyche.
Hoc rasorium, A^{cr} a rasowyr.
Hic dolfinus, A^{ce} a dolfyn.
Hec balena, A^{ce} a porpeyse.
Hic rumbus, A^{ce} a sturgyn.
Hic branchia, A^{ce} a gylle.
Hec squama, a scalyd-fyche.
Hec puma, A^{cr} a ffyn.
Hoc zabulum, A^{ce} sond.
Hoc laquamen, An^{ce} rownd.
Her lactis, An^{ce} mylkere.[10]
Hec testa, An^{cr} a schylle.
Hec siren, An^{cr} a mermayd.

NOMINA VERMIUM.

Hic draco, a dragon.
Hic vermis, a worme.
Hec rana, A^{cr} a frog.

— draco

---

[1] *Sedow*, the fish called a gilthead (*sparus*).
[2] The skate.
[3] The mullet, *mugil cephalus* of Cuvier.
[4] Ling, the *gadus molva* of Linnæus.
[5] *Floke*, or *flewke* (the A.-S. *floc*), the flounder.
[6] *Turbo* means properly a whelk.
[7] Perhaps the rouget, or piper-fish.
[8] *Horn-keck* appears in Palsgrave as the name of a fish, which is said to be called also a *greenback*.
[9] i. e., the dog-fish.
[10] *Mylkere*, the milt or soft roe of the male fish.

Hic bufo, A^{ce} a tode.
Hic scorpio, A^{ce} a scarpyn.
Hic serpens, alle maner naderes.
Hic agguis, A^{ce} a water-adder.
Hic coluber, A^{ce} a snake.
Hec vispera, A^{ce} a berard.
Hic idrus,
Hec idra, } a blynd-wurme.
Hec matrix,
Hec cresta, A^{ce} a angyl.
Hic biceps, } a flyyn nedere.
Hic jaculus,
Hic calus, a slo-wurme.
Hec septipedia, a gagrylle.
Hic cacadillus, } a cocatryse.
Hic basilicus,
Hec nocticula, a glouberd.
Hic lumbricus, A^{ce} a tad-polle.
Hec salomandra, A^{ce} a cryket.
Hec lacerta, A^{ce} a newte.
Hec formica, } a pysmere.
Hec murunca,
Hic bibio, A^{ce} a hox-bame.
Hec aranea, a nedyr-copp.
Hic auriglus, A^{ce} a sylver-wurme.
Hic multipes, A^{ce} a tuentifot wurme.
Hec sanguifica, } a leche.
Hec irudo,
Hec limax, } a snaylle.
Hec testudo,
Hic pulex, A^{ce} a flec.
Hic pedicus, } lowse.
Hic pediculus,
Hic lens -dis, A^{ce} a nyte.
Her ascarida, a teke.
Hic tarinus, } a maked.[1]
Hic simax,
Hec impetigo, a ryng-worme.

Hec mica, A^{ce} a mynte.[2]
Hec musca, A^{ce} a fflye, alle maner.
Hic carembes, -tis, A^{ce} a betylle.
Hoc eruga, A^{ce} a wurt-wurme.

NOMINA MUSCARUM.

Hic apes, -pis, A^{ce} a bee.
Hic asilus, A^{ce} a drane.
Hec vespa, A^{ce} a waspe.
Hic tabanus, A^{ce} a humbyl-bee.
Hec sicada, A^{ce} a grashoppyr.
Hec sinomea, A^{ce} a hond-flye.
Hic siniflex, An^{ce} a red fflye.
Hoc crestrum, A^{ce} a brese.
Hic culex, a knat.
Hoc gamalion, A^{ce} a myght.
Hec polumita, A^{ce} a bude.[3]
Hic stabo, A^{ce} a scarbude.[4]
Hic papilio, A^{ce} a butterfflye.

NOMINA METALLORUM.

Hoc aurum, ffor gold.
Hoc argentum, A^{ce} sylver.
Hoc es, eris, idem est.
Hoc es, -ris, A^{ce} brasse.
Hoc electrum, A^{ce} pewtyr.
Hoc cuprum, A^{ce} copyr.
Hoc plumbum, A^{ce} lede.
Hoc auricaleum, A^{ce} latun.
Hoc stagnum, A^{ce} tynne.
Hoc stangnum, A^{ce} a pond.
   Est aqua stans arte stagnum, stannum dic
   esse metallum.
Hec caleps, A^{ce} stele.
Hoc fferrum, A^{ce} yryn.
Hoc metallum, A^{ce} metalle.

---

[1] Maked, a maggot.
[2] A mite. See before, p. 176.
[3] Bude, the weevil, a small insect of the beetle tribe which is destructive to grain. Tusser, as quoted by Halliwell, speaks of "bowd-euten malt;" and the word is still preserved in the dialect of the eastern counties.
[4] Scarbude, or scarnbude, a kind of beetle.

A PICTORIAL VOCABULARY.

NOMINA LAPIDUM.

Hic lapis,
Hec petra, } a stonne.
Hoc saxum,
Hic mermur, A^{ce} a merbyl-stone.
Hic et hec silex, A^{ce} a flynt-stone.
Hic scripulus, A^{ce} a lytyl stone.
Hec margarita, A^{ce} a perylle.
Hec Margareta, a maydyn.

Margarita lapis, sed Margareta puella.

Hec mola, A^{ce} a myl-stonne.
Hec acates, A^{ce} a gryn-stone.
Hec cos, -tis, A^{ce} a wat-stone.
Hic terebentus, A^{ce} a thone.
Hec gemma, A^{ce} a precius stone.
Hic jaspes, A^{ce} a precioustone.
Hic berellus, A^{ce} a berelle-ston.
Hic saphirus, A^{ce} a safyr.
Hic stupelus, A^{ce} a precius stonne.
Hic cautes, A^{ce} a salt-stone.
Hic rupes, A^{ce} a roche of stone.
Hec pumes, A^{ce} a nedyr-stonne.[1]
Hec pama, A^{ce} a grapond.
Hic jacinctus, A^{ce} a precius stone.
Hic rudus, A^{ce} a cobyl-stone.
Hoc tapacior, A^{ce} a stone.
Hic gagates, }
Hec smaragdus, } a ruby.
Hec timeria, A^{ce} a fre-stone.
Her magdalena, a balwyn.[2]
Hoc egipsum, A^{ce} a egyp-stone.[3]
Hic calculus, a ston in a mannys bleder.
Hic saxus, A^{ce} a bolok-stone.
Hec tegula, A^{ce} a til-stone.

Hec cals, -cis, A^{ce} a calke-stone.
Hic cals, A^{ce} a parte of the fote.

Pars pedis est hic cals, lapis ustus dicitur hec cals.

Hoc armum, A^{ce} grawelle.
Hec gloria, A^{ce} a scheselle-stone.
Hic carboculus, a carbokyl-stone.
Hic petro, a chyp of a stone.

NOMINA PERTINENCIA COQUINE.

Hic archimacherus, a master coke.
Hic cocus, alle maner a cokys.
Hic lixa, a swyllere.[4]
Hic dapifer, a berere of mete.
Hic tripes, a brenlede.[5]
Hic cacabus,
Hic lebes, } a cawdurne.
Hoc caduum,
Hec machera, a dressyng-burd.
Her mensacula, a dressyng-knyfe.
Hic urcius, A^{ce} a bras pot.
Hic urciolus, A^{ce} a posnet.
Hec sartago, }
Hor friesorium, } a fryyng-pan.
Hic discus, a dyche.
Hic cratus, }
Hec craticula, } a rostyng-yryn.
Hoc veru, indeclinabile, a spete.
Hic veruvertor, a spete-turnere.
Hec audena, a handyryn.
Hor ipegurgium, a gobard.
Hor micatorium, a myure.
Hec criagra, }
Hec tridex, } a fleche-hoke.

---

[1] The adder-stone.
[2] Perhaps the baleis, a sort of ruby. It seems to be the same word as *balayn* in the following passage from the metrical romance of Richard Coer-de-Lion, l. 2079.

  Her baner whyt, withouten fable,
  With thre Sarezynes hedes off sable,

  That wer schapen noble and large
  Off *balayn,* both scheeld and targe.

[3] Probably gypsum.
[4] A scullion, one who swills the dishes.
[5] The brandlet, or brandreth. See before, p. 199.

A PICTORIAL VOCABULARY.

Hec limas, a haprune.
Hoc spumatorium, a schomore.[1]
Hoc austorium, a ladyl.
Hoc motarium, a pot-styk.
Hec laxis, } a sclys.[2]
Hec aspiculna, }
Hoc calafactorium, a schasure.[3]
Hec capana, a pot-hoke.
Hoc morterium, A^{ce} a mortere.
Hoc tribulum, } a pestelle.
Hec pila, }
Hoc fractillum, a pepyr-querne.
Hic fractillus, a rage.[4]
Hec patella, a pane.
Hec scutella, a scotylle.
Hec parapcis, -idis, a plater.
Hoc assitabulum, a sauser.

Hoc onafrum, }
Hic uter, -ris, } a flaget.[5]
Hec olla, }
Hec lura, a mowth of a flaget.
Hec lura, a nek of a flaget.
Lura sit os utris, et collum luridus inde.
Hic cifus, alle manyr copys.
Hic crater, } An^{ce} a pese.[6]
Hec cateria, }
Hec urna, a cowpe.
Hec murra, a masowyr.
Hoc coopertorium, a
Hec clepsidra, a speget.
Hec urnula, a not.[7]
Hec orca, A^{ce} a cane.
Hic canterus, a colok.[8]
Hec amphora, a tancard.
Hec idria, a watyr-pot.
Hec fidelia, idem est.
Hec justa, A^{ce} a gyste.
Hoc vinum, alle maner wyne.
Hoc tementum, A^{ce} strong wyne.
Hoc villum, A^{ce} febylle wyne.
Hoc ffalarnum, A^{ce} gode wyne.
Hoc tenulentum, A^{ce} thyn wyne.
Hoc merum, A^{ce} cler wyne.
Hec sapa, A^{ce} qeketh wyne.
Hoc amuennum, A^{ce} wyte wyne.
Hoc mustum, A^{ce} moste.
Hoc idromellum, A^{ce} wurte.

NOMINA PERTINENCIA BOTULARIE.

Hic botularius, a botelere.
Hoc dolium, A^{ce} a tune.
Hic cadus, a barelle.

---

[1] *i e.*, a skummer.
[2] *Sclys*, a slice, or implement for turning meat in the frying-pan.
[3] *Sckasure*, or *shasor*, a wine cooler.
[4] In Somersetshire, a broken pan is still called a *rage*.

[5] A flask, a leathern bottle.
[6] *Pece*, or *pese*, was a common name for a drinking-cup.
[7] *Not*, or *nut*, a sort of small vase.
[8] *Collock* is the name given in the northern dialects to a large pail.

258   A PICTORIAL VOCABULARY

Hoc ciromellum, A^{ce} growte.[1]
Hoc claretum, a clerote wyne.
Hoc nectar, A^{ce} piment.[2]
Hec amurca, a lyf of wyn.
Hec servisia, alle maner ale.
Hec selea, A^{ce} stale ale.
Hec ffexs, A^{ce} dregys.
Hec spuma, A^{ce} berme.

[3]

NOMINA PERTINENCIA PANATRIE.

Hic panatrius, a pantre.
Hic panis, A^{ce} a lofe.
Hec quadra, a cantel of brede.
Hec lesca,
Hec colirida, } a schefe of brede.
Hoc peripsima, A^{ce} a paryng.
Hec mica, A^{ce} a crume.
Hic bolus,
Hic murcellus, } a musselle.[4]
Hec burcella,
Est burcella cibus quantum semel accipis ore.
Hoc salinum,
Hoc assitabulum, } a salere.
Hoc ffrustrum, A^{ce} a lumpe.
Hic sal, saltis, A^{ce} salt.
Hoc coclear, A^{ce} a spone.
Hoc candelebrum, A^{ce} a candyl-steyke.
Hoc gausape,
Hoc toral, } a burd-clothe.
Hec mappa,
Hoc sissorium, A^{ce} a trenchore
Hoc manitergium, a hand-clothe.
Hec culingna, A^{ce} a lineshark.[5]

[1] See before, p. 233.
[2] See before, p. 98.
[3] The little figure at the head of this article is curious, as showing the usual form of the loaf of bread at this period.
[4] *i. e*, a morsel.
[5] *Lineshark. Culigna,* in good Latin, signified a drinking bowl.

A PICTORIAL VOCABULARY.

NOMINA VESTIMENTORUM.

Hec vestis,
Hoc vestimentum, } A^{ce} clothe.
Hoc indumentum,
Hoc superum, An^{ce} a pryn.[1]
Hoc pelicium, A^{ce} a pylchen.[2]
Hoc scapilorium, A^{ce} a scaplorey.
Hec capa, A^{ce} a cope.
Hec sarabarda, A^{ce} a sclavene.
Hoc mantile,
Hoc mantellum, } a mantelle.
Hec seclas, -cis, idem est.
Hoc capellum, A^{ce} a hat.
Hic capellus, idem est.
Hic pilius, A^{ce} a cape.
Hec tena, A^{ce} a hewd.[3]
Hoc capucium, A^{ce} a hode.
Hec armilansa, a cloke.
Hoc colobium, a tabare.
Hec toga,
Hoc epitogium, } a gowyn.
Hec supertunica, a syrcote.
Hec roba, A^{ce} a robe.
Hec tunica, A^{ce} a cote.
Hoc ventrale, a corsete.
Hec camisia,
Hec subuncula, } a scherte.

Hec supera,
Hec instita, } a rokete or a lyste.
Hec lombesina, An^{ce} a paltoke.[4]
He bracce, -arum,
Hoc ffemorale, } An^{ce} a breke.
Hoc perizoma,
Hic fforulus, A^{ce} a huwyng.
Hoc lumbare, A^{ce} a bregyrdyle.
Hec legula, A^{ce} a lanyr.
Hoc subligar, A^{ce} a stylt-bonde.
Subliger est legula caligas quas sublygans alte.

Hoc tibiale, a strapylle.
Hec caliga, A^{ce} a hose.
Hic mancus, A^{ce} a meteyne.
Hec ffirotica, A^{ce} a glofe.[5]
Hic sotularis, A^{ce} a scho.
Hic pedulus, A^{ce} a soke.
Hic ffractillus, A^{ce} a dag of a gowyn.[6]

NOMINA PERTINENCIA CAMERE.

Hic camrius,
Hic et hec sinista, } An^{ce} a schumberleyne.
Hoc lectum, alle maner off beddys.
Hoc grabatum, a sekemannys beddys.
Hoc torum, A^{ce} a husbondes bedde.
Hec toreuma, A^{ce} a kynges bedde.

[1] *Pryn*, a woman's smock.
[2] A furred outer-coat.
[3] *Hewd*, the extremity of the riband hanging from the bishop's mitre.
[4] A paltock was a doublet or cloak descending to the middle of the thigh. It is a word which has recently been brought into use again.
[5] For *cirotica*, i.e. *chirotheca*. It is another example of the curious use of the *f*, remarked in a former note. See p. 250.
[6] The dagging, jagging, or foliating, the edges of garments, came into fashion apparently in the reign of Edward III., and prevailed more or less till the latter part of the fifteenth century.

Hoc supralectum,
Hec tectora, } a selowyr.[1]
Hoc capisterium, A^{ce} a redele.[2]
Hoc pallium, A^{ce} a palle.
Hoc tapetum, A^{ce} a schalun.[3]
Hoc coopertorium, a cowyrlythe.
Hoc torall, idem est.
  Est toral mappa, tegmen lectoque vocatur.
Hic lodex, A^{ce} a blanket.
Hoc linthiamen, A^{ce} a schete.
Hoc carentivillum, a canvas.
Hoc ffultrum, A^{ce} a matras.
Hec sponda, A^{ce} a ffedyr-bedde.
Hoc servical, A^{ce} a pelow.
Hec coma,
Hoc pecten, } a combe.
Hoc caliandrum, a wulpere.[4]
Hoc anabatum, A^{ce} a docer *ad dorsum.*
Hoc calatrale, A^{ce} a syde docer.
Hec fforma,
Hoc schabellum, } a forme.
Hoc scannum, A^{ce} a benche.
Hec antipera, A^{ce} a screne.
Hoc scopum, a matte.
Hoc utensule, howseho.[5]

Hoc stramentum, lyttere.[6]
Hic stratus, -tus, -ui,
Hoc stratum, -ti, -to, } a bed.
  Stratus vel -tum confinguntur tibi lectum.
Hoc epicausterium, a thuelle.[7]
Hic caminus, a grete fyre.
Hic caminus, a chymny.
  Emittens fumum tibi sit locus ipse caminus,
  Maximus atque rogus tibi dicitur esse caminus.
Hec fagota, a fagat.
Hoc focale, fuelle.
Hic fax, -cis, An^{ce} a chyde.

PARTES DOMUS.

Hec paries, -tis,
Hic murus, } a walle.
Hoc doma, -tis, a roffe.
Hoc festum, a roffe-tre.
Hoc festum, a holy-day.
  Pars festum tecti et dicitur esse solenne.
Hoc tingnum, a spere.
Hec trabecula, a wynbeme.
Hec trabes, a refter.
Hic postis, -tis, a poste.
Hoc luquiare, A^{ce} a post-bondde.

[1] The *celure,* or roof, of the bed.
[2] The *ridel,* or bed-curtain.
[3] See before, p. 178.
[4] *Wulpere.* The Latin word *caliendrum* signifies false hair—a periwig. A *wulpere* was perhaps a head-dress composed of false hair; probably the same word as *volupere.*
[5] *Howeho.* Perhaps this singular word signifies a chamber pot.
[6] Litter, the straw with which the bed was formerly made.
[7] The pipe of the chimney.

A PICTORIAL VOCABULARY.

Hoc sigillum, a barer of a rofe-tre.
Hec ffenestra, A^{ce} a wyndow.
Hoc lucanar, a day of a wyndow.[1]
Hoc superuminare, A^{ce} a lenterne.[2]
Hec antica, A^{ce} a porche.
Hoc ostium, An^{ce} a dore.
Hoc osticulum, A^{ce} a hatche.
Hoc limen, -nis,
Hec grunda, a hespe.
Hoc domicilium,
Hoc institucium,
Hec cavilla, A^{ce} a pyn.
Hoc manutentum, An^{ce} a haginday.[3]
Hoc findolum, a lache.
Hec sera, A^{ce} a loke.
Hec serula, A^{ce} a clyket.
Hoc pesulum, A^{ce} a hespe.
Hec ventifica, a screne.
Hec assia, -e, A^{ce} a burde.
Hec pertica, A^{ce} a pherche.
Hoc repagulum, a barre.
Hic clatravus, A^{ce} a lache.
Hic obex, An^{ce} a hoke.
Hic gumser, An^{ce} a hengylle.[4]
Hec rectes, An^{ce} a hoke.
Hec area, An^{ce} a florthe.[5]
Hec capedo, dicitur spacium inter parietes.
Hoc scannum, A^{ce} a benche.
Hoc focarium, A^{ce} a hart-stone.
Hic ffocus, idem est.
Hic focus, An^{ce} a hautere.
Hic ffocus, An^{ce} a fyir.
  Est altare focus, locus et focus ignis.
Hoc reposilium, A^{ce} a fyir-belowys.
Hec basys, the grownd pelyr.

Hic stilus, A^{ce} a smal of a pelyr.
Hic stilus, A^{ce} a poyntelle.
Hic stilus, alle maner speche.
  Est stilus unde puer scribit modus atque loquendi;
  Atque stilus media pars dicitur esse columna;
  Dico basi portare domum stilumque victis ab ipsa,
  Portat epistilium quibus est erecta columba.
Hec cobluma, An^{ce} a pylere.
Hec ffornix, ⎫
Hic arcus,   ⎬ An^{ce} a
Hec vouta, A^{ce} a wout.
Hec cardo, An^{cr} a dur-herre.

NOMINA ECCLESIASTICORUM.

Hic papa, A^{ce} a pape.[6]
Hic patriarca, A^{ce} a patriark.
Hic cardinalis, A^{ce} a cardinalle.
Hic archiepiscopus, A^{ce} a arsbyschop.
Hic episcopus, An^{ce} a byschop.
Hic legatus, An^{ce} a legat.
Hic suffraganeus, a suffrigan.
Hic decanus, An^{ce} a dene.
Hic canselarius, ⎫
Hic scriba,   ⎬ a scawnceler.
Hic archidiaconus, A^{ce} a arsdekyn.
Hic officialis, A^{ce} a offysere.
Hic comissarius, A^{ce} a comissere.
Hic rector, An^{ce} a persun.
Hic vicarius, An^{ce} a vecory.
Hic presbeter,   ⎫
Hic et hec sacerdos, ⎬ a pryst.
Hic capellanus,   ⎠
  Sacris dicatus vel sacris deditus atque
  Sacra dans, vel dux sacer esto sacerdos.
Hic diaconus, ⎫
Hic levita,   ⎬ a dekyn.
Hic subdiaconus, a subdekyn.

[1] Otherwise called a bay of a window, the space between the mullions.
[2] The lantern, or light from above.
[3] A sort of wooden latch for a door is still called a *haggeday* in Yorkshire.
[4] A hengle, or hinge.
[5] *i. e.*, a floor.
[6] This word had been nearly erased in the MS., no doubt after the Reformation. It is a curious example of the extent to which the order for erasing the pope's name from public documents was carried out.

262 A PICTORIAL VOCABULARY.

Hic acoletus, An^ce a colet.
Hic exorcista, An^ce a benet.
Hic et hec secrista, a sekyrsteyn.
Hic aquarius, a haly-water clerke.
Hic aquebachelus, idem est.
Hic abbas, An^ce a abotte.
Hic prior, -ris, A^ce a prier.
Hic supprior, An^ce a supprier.
Hic sellerarius, a selerer.
Hic subselarius, a subselerer.
Hic canonicus, a chanon.
Hic monacus, a mongke.
Hic ffrater, a frere.
Hic eremita, a heremyte.
Hic doctor,
Hic instructor,
Hic monitor,
Hic petegogus,
Hic auctor, } a mayster.
Hic imbutor,
Hic papas,
Hic didasculus,
Hic magister, -ri, -ro,
   Doctor et instructor, monitor, petegogus, et auctor,
   Imbutor, papas, didasculus, atque magister.
Hic legista, a legister.
Hic grammaticus, a grammaryon.
Hic dioleticus,
Hic arcista, } a arcister.
Hic sophista, a sophister.
Hic bacularius, a bacler.
Hic clericus, a clerke.

Hic scolaris, a scoler.
Hic teolagus, a mayster of divinité.
Hic sitarius, a sumner.
Hic apparitor,
Hic sitator, } *idem sunt.*

NOMINA DOMINORUM TEMPORALIUM.

Hic imperator, a nemperour.
Hoc diadema, lapis preciosus.
Hic rex, a kyng.
Hec laurea, corona regis.
Hoc certum, a garlant.
Hec corona, s. cleri.
   Legis est certum clerique corona poete,
   Aurea rex gestat diadema vel induperator.
Hoc septrum, regis dignitas.
Hoc solium, a kynges sete.
Hoc fiscale, a kynges porse.
Hoc sistale, a kynges tax.
Hoc gazophilacium, a tresure.
Hic dux, -cis, a duke.
Hic baro, -nis, a baron.
Hic barunculus, a baronet.[1]
Hic miles, -tis, a kny3te.
Hic armiger, a squyer.
Hic generosus, a gentylman.
Hic tiro, a yoing kny3te.
Hic dominus, al maner lordes.
Hoc dominium, a lordechyppe.
Hoc donativum, a waresun.
Hoc corrodium,
Hec armilla, } a levery.
Hec nima, a sylver rodde.

---

[1] i. e., a lesser or minor baron. Our modern title of baronet of course came in at a much later period.

A PICTORIAL VOCABULARY.

NOMINA ARMORUM.

Hec arma, }
Hec arma- } a we-
tura, } pyn.
Hic conus, a crest.
Hec galea, media producta, a galle.
Hec galea, media corrupta, a helme.
Induo me galea, galeatus duco galeam.
Hec bombecina, a acton.[1]
Hec tassis, a palett.
Hic tassis, a nett.
Hec tassis galea, hic tassis rethia monstrat.
Hec lorica, a habirjun.
Hec suamata, a plate.
Hec brachialia, An^{cr} a brasere.
Hec larva, A^{ce} a visere.
Hec larva, A^{ce} a dewylle.[2]
Hec larva, A^{ce} a selerelle.[3]
Larva fugit volucres, faciem tegit, est quoque demon.
Hic torax, A^{ce} a bryst-bone.
Hic torax, A^{ce} a bryst-plate.
Hec femoralia, A^{ce} a quischens.[4]
Hec tibialia, A^{ce} a leg-arnes.
Hic gladius, A^{ce} a swerd.
Hic anceps, A^{ce} a tow-hand swerd.
Hec gesa, A^{cr} a gysyryne.[5]
Non amat ille Jhesum qui fert ad prelia gesam.

Hec spata, A^{ce} a pleyend swerd.
Hec sica, A^{re} a baselard.
Hec soliferia, A^{ce} a fauschune.
Hec clava, A^{ce} a mase.
Clava ferit, clavis aperit, clavus duo jungit.
Hic armiturium, A^{ce} a dagar.
Hic dagardus, idem est.
Hec pugio, -onis, idem est.
Hec funda, A^{ce} a sclyng.
Hoc fustibulum, a hand-sclyng.
Hec babrilla, A^{ce} a dong-babylle.
Hic arcus, -cus, -i, A^{ce} a bow.
Hec sagista, A^{ce} a arow.
Hec catapulta, a brode arow.
Hec petulium, A^{ce} a bolte.
Hec ceculicula, a sparke.
Hec ffudes,[6] a pike stafe.
Fustes fetate poterint sudes bene dici.
Hec ffustis, A^{cr} a batte.
Hic baculus, A^{cr} alle maner stavis.
Hec lancea, An^{ce} a spere.
Hec asta, An^{ce} a schafte.
Hoc scutum, }
Hoc cliphium, } a buccler.
Hec daca, An^{cr} a pollex.
Hec petrima, An^{cr} a gune.[7]
Hoc telum, }
Hoc pilum, } a darte.
Hec tela, -e, An^{ce} a webe.
Nos vestit tela, volitant per prelia tela.

[1] The *acketoun*, or *acton*, was a sort of tunic worn under the coat of mail.
[2] i. e., a devil, or demon; a hobgoblin.
[3] This means apparently a scarecrow.
[4] More usually called *cuisses*, the pieces of armour which protected the thighs.
[5] See before, p. 196.
[6] Sic, for *sudes*.
[7] This is the first occurrence of the gun among weapons in these vocabularies.

A PICTORIAL VOCABULARY.

Hec balista, A^{ce} a arow-blaste.
Hoc mustile, } *a darte.*
Hoc jaculum, }
Hec sestus, A^{ce} a pavis.[1]
Hec parma, An^{ce} a bokeler.
Hec umbo, An^{ce} a bos-bokelere.
Hoc mangnalium, An^{ce} a gyn.
Hec brida, A^{ce} a trappe.
Hoc tribucetum, An^{ce} a pyt-falle.
Hec ffalaa, A^{ce} a lumpe of a walle.
Hoc propinaculum, A^{ce} a bretayge.[2]
Hoc superfossorium, a drawte-bryge.
Hec listia, a castylle-dyche.

NOMINA BLADORUM ET ARBORUM.

Hec seges,
Hoc satum,
Hoc bladum,
Hoc granum, } corne.
Hoc fruges,
Hic messis,

Dum seritur seges, sata dum radisibus herent,
Blada virore virent, granaria grana reservant;
Fruges dum fruimur, sunt messes quando metuntur.

Hoc frumentum, A^{ce} whete.
Hoc triticum, idem est.
Hoc essaticum, An^{ce} bere.[3]
Hoc ordium, An^{ce} barly.
Hec siligo, } *An^{ce}* rye.
Hoc ergalum, }
Hec arena, An^{ce} hotys.
Hec faba, A^{ce} a bene.
Hec pisa, A^{ce} a pese.
Hec viscria, A^{ce} a feche.[4]

Hoc viscium, A^{ce} a wyse.
Si comedes visciam non est viscium tibi magnum;
A viscio -as horum discendet utrumque.

Hec mixtilio, A^{ce} moge.
Hec avicula, A^{ce} wyld hote.
Radix, festuca, conculnio, nodus, arista,
Granum cum palia fer sufficit sit quoque scripta,
Sunt partes messis firma tellure manentes.

Hec seliqua, A^{ce} a pes-codde.
Hec filupra, An^{ce} a ben-codde.
Hic manipulus, a hand-fulle.
Hic arcomus, An^{ce} a stathele.
Hoc ffenum, An^{ce} hey.
Hoc ffenile, A^{ce} a hey-stakke.
Hec garba,
Hec merges, } *Ac^{ce}* a schefe.
Hec gelima,
Hec congelima, An^{ce} a schokke.[5]
Hoc pabulum, An^{ce} fodyr.
Hoc olus, -ris, An^{ce} wurtes.
Hec betana, An^{ce} betany.
Hec betute, -tes, A^{ce} bettes.
Hec borago, -nis, A^{ce} broges.[6]
Hoc porrum, A^{ce} a leke.
Hoc sepe, indeclinabile, a hunyn.
Porri vel sepe fertur bulbus capud esse.

Hoc allium, An^{ce} garleke.
Hic sinolus, } a schybbolle.[7]
Hec sipula, }
Hoc petrocillum, An^{ce} persely.
Hec salgea, An^{ce} sawge.
Hoc lilium, An^{ce} a lylly.
Hec columbina, An^{ce} a columbyn.
Hec violeta, An^{ce} a violet.

---

[1] The *pavis* was a large shield.
[2] The *bretasche*, or parapet. See before, p. 130.
[3] *Bere*, a kind of barley.
[4] i. e., a vetch.

[5] A shock, at the present day in the north, is twelve sheaves of corn.
[6] *Broges, i. e.* borage.
[7] A *chibbal*, or small onion.

Hoc vaxinium, An^{ce} idem est.
Hic isopus, An^{ce} isopp.
Hec ditanus, A^{ce} detany.
Hec seladonia, a seladony.
Hec igromonia, a ygromony.
Hec urtica, An^{ce} a netylle.
Hic anagalidos, An^{ce} netylle-sede.
Hec paradilla, An^{ce} a doke.
Hec secuta, An^{ce} a humlok.
Hec morella, An^{ce} morelle.
Hoc solsequium, An^{ce} a rode.
Hec pervica, An^{ce} a perwynke.
Hec malvia, An^{ce} a hok.[1]
Hec lancea, An^{ce} a rob-worte.[2]
Hec buglossa, A^{ce} lange-de-befe.
Hec ebula, A^{ce} a walle-wurte.[3]
Hoc bigustrum, A^{ce} a prymrose.
Hoc ligustrum, A^{ce} a cowyslepe.
Hec rosa, A^{ce} a rose.
Hoc ffragrum, A^{ce} a strawbery.
Hec mentica, A^{ce} a mynte.
Hic papillus, A^{ce} a heyoffe.[4]
Hec eruca, A^{ce} a schynlok.[5]
Hec eruca, An^{ce} a carlok.
Hec ruta, A^{ce} rew.
Hec ffallar, A^{ce} madyr.
Hoc venenum, A^{ce} a wede.
Hec plantago, A^{ce} weybrede.
Hec maguderis, a calstok.
Hoc olusculum, a wurt-plant.
Hic cirpus, An^{ce} a roysche.
Hic cucumer, A^{ce} a fluge.
Hec papirus, An^{ce} a bol-roysche.
Hoc feneculum, An^{ce} a ffenelle.

Hic crocus, An^{ce} safryn.
Hec zizania, An^{ce} a drawke.[6]
Hec artimatia, An^{ce} wodrofe.
Hec seniglossa, An^{ce} hertes-tunge.
Hec mandracora, An^{ce} a mandrak.
Hoc aspium, An^{ce} a gresse.
Hec salmea, An^{ce} a pepyr-gresse.
Hoc anisum, An^{ce} a culrayge.
Hec dragansia, An^{ce} a dragauns.
Hoc meretrum, An^{ce} ffenylle-sede.
Hec camamilla, An^{ce} a camamy.
Hoc papaver, -ris, An^{ce} a papy.
Hec samina, An^{ce} a saveryn.[7]
Hic jusquianus, An^{ce} a hennebane.
Hoc jurbarium, An^{ce} a silfgrene [8]
Hec letusa, An^{ce} letuse.
Hic cardo, -is, An^{ce} a nettille.
Hec avencia, An^{ce} a avans.
Hec vervene, An^{ce} vermyne.
Hec menoloca, An^{ce} a bothun.[9]
Hic suctus, An^{ce} a juse.
Hec locusta, An^{ce} a sokyl-blome.[10]
Hec arundo, -nis, } a redde.
Hec canna, }
Hec carex, An^{ce} a sege.
Hec rapa, An^{ce} a neppe.[11]
Hoc colitropium, a paratory.
Hec conseria, An^{ce} a wyld fr . . .
Hoc morsuspoli, a schykyn-w . . .[12]
Hec lentige, a nedmet.[13]
Hec eufrasia, An^{ce} a heufrasy . . .
Hoc lollium, } *An^{ce}* kokylle.
Hoc git, indeclinabile, }
Hoc pulmentum, benys and pese.

---

[1] The holyhock.
[2] Perhaps the plant adders tongue, called in Latin *bancea-Christi*.
[3] Wall-wort.
[4] Hayhofe, or ground-ivy.
[5] Rocket, the *reseda* of botanists.
[6] This word is still preserved in the dialects of the Eastern counties, where it is applied to a plant resembling darnel.

[7] Perhaps the savin-tree *(juniperus sabina)*.
[8] The houseleek.
[9] A button, or bud?
[10] *Sokyl-blome,* perhaps the honey-suckle.
[11] Catmint, or nep *(nepeta cataria)*.
[12] i. e., chicken-wort
[13] *Nedmete,* perhaps the lentil, a small kind of pulse.
[14] Eyebright *(euphrasia officinalis)*.

A PICTORIAL VOCABULARY.

Hoc cirpillum, An^ce a pellck.[1]
Hec silago, An^ce wyld rye.

NOMINA ESSCARUM.

Hoc prandium,
Hoc epulum, } *An^ce* mete.
Hic cibus,
Hec esca, } *An^ce* mete.
Hec daps,
Hoc jantaculum, An^ce a dynere.
Hec cena, An^ce a soper.
Hoc obsenium, An^ce a rryre-soper.
Hoc alleum, An^ce garleke.
Hic victus, -tus, -tui,
Hoc victuale, } *An^ce* lyfe-fode.
Hoc pulmentorium, An^ce a pulment.
Est cibus et semen pulmentum dicitur esse,
At cibus quidem sunt pulmentaria dicta.
Hoc edulium, An^ce sowylle.[2]
Hic repastus, -tus, -tui, An^ce mele.
Hic panis, An^ce brede.
Hic artocopus, An^ce a symnelle.
Hec placencia, An^ce a payman.[3]
Hoc labum,
Hoc libellum, } a wastelle.
Hec ffrugia, An^ce fresbrede.
Hic panissubcerucius, a meleres cake.[4]

Hec nebula,
Hec gafra, } a wafrun.
Hoc calenum, An^ce a ffyrmele.[5]
Hoc vitalium, An^ce charlett.[6]
Hic artocacius, An^ce a flawne.
Hec artocria, An^ce a tartelat.
Hic artocrius, An^ce a pye.
Hoc legumen,
Hoc puls, } *An^ce* potage.
Hoc polenta, An^ce grewelle.
Hoc laganum, An^ce a pancake.
Hec aplauda, An^ce a cawdelle.
Hoc adopatum, An^ce brues.
Hec carbonella, An^ce a colepe.[7]
Hec pepissa, An^ce fat fleyche.
Hoc consisum, An^ce alle maner sew.
Hoc sepelatum, An^ce a sew.
Hec pereta, An^ce leke potage.
Hoc omentum, An^ce a womclotte.[8]
Hoc extum,
Hoc esmum, } *An^ce* a trype.
Hoc brodium, An^ce a brothe.
Hoc fferculum, An^ce a mese.
Hoc fferculum, a salt stole.
Fercula nos faciant, prelatos fercula portant.
Hoc fertum,
Hoc omasum, } *An^ce* a podyng.
Hoc tucetum,
Hec ulla, An^ce a sawsyrlyng.[9]
Hoc obsoniofyrus, a jusselle.
Hec assa, An^ce a rost mete.
Hoc lactatum,
Hoc balductum, } *An^ce* a poset.
Hec perna, An^ce a flyk of bacun.
Hec promulada, An^ce grovy.

---

[1] *Pellek,* a name for wild-thyme, or, as it is popularly called in some parts, ladies' bedstraw.
[2] See before, p. 199.
[3] *i. e.,* painmain. See before, p. 198.
[4] A miller's cake. Perhaps this name alludes to the common report that the miller always stole the flour from his customers to make his cakes, which were baked on the sly. See The Reve's Tale in Chaucer.
[5] *Fyrmele,* perhaps frumity, or furmity.
[6] A dish made of minced pork.
[7] A collop, or slice of meat, or rasher of bacon, broiled.
[8] The wombelout was properly the caul which envelopes the intestines.
[9] A sausage.

Hoc ovum, An^{ce} a hey.
Hoc albumen, An^{ce} the whyte of the hey.
Hic vitellus, An^{ce} a ȝelke.
Tres partes ovi, albumen, testa, vitellus.
Hec pulpa, An^{ce} the brawn of a bore.
Hoc pomum, An^{ce} a nappelle.
Hoc pirum, An^{ce} a pere.
Hoc volemum, An^{ce} a wardyn.
Hoc perapsima, An^{ce} a paryng.
Hec pulpa, An^{ce} a meyte.
Hec arula, An^{ce} a croke.[1]
Tolle peripsima, post pete pulpam, dispernis arulam.
Hoc sinapium, An^{ce} mustarde.
Salgia, sirpillum, piper, alia, sal, petrocillum,
Ex hiis sit salsa, non est sententia falsa.
Hic nuclius, a not.
Hic nucleus, An^{ce} kyrnelle.

NOMINA INFIRMITATUM.

Hec puscula, An^{ce} a whele.
Hoc ulcus, -ceris, An^{ce} a byle.
Hec scabies, -ei, An^{ce} a scabbe.
Hec impetigo, An^{ce} a tesyng.[2]
Hec veruca, An^{ce} a werte.
Hec glabra, An^{ce} a scalle.

Hec macula, An^{ce} a spote.
Hec lentecula, An^{ce} a frekyn.
Hec lepra, An^{ce} a mesellerye.
Hec ffebris, An^{ce} a fewer.
Hec utorica, An^{ce} the chawndyse.
Hic spasmus, An^{ce} the crampe.
Hic tussis, An^{ce} the cowe.[3]
Hec exteris, -ce, An^{ce} a scunnyng.[4]
Hic catarus, An^{ce} a pore.[5]
Hec reuma, An^{ce} a chynge.
Hec gutta, An^{ce} the gowte.
Hec leantaria, An^{ce} the flyx.
Nominativo clanucus, -ca, -cum, A^{ce} berede.[6]
Hic gibbus, An^{ce} a wenne.
Hec cardia, An^{ce} a cardiakylle.
Hec squacia, An^{ce} a queynose.[7]
Hic cancer, An^{ce} a cankyr.
Hec idrepia, An^{ce} the dropsy.
Hec antrax, An^{ce} a felun bleyn.[8]
Hec porigo, An^{ce} pokkys.
Hec serpedo, An^{ce} a tetere.
Hec paucitas, An^{ce} a cattes here.[9]
Hic morbus caducus, the fallyn evylle.
Hic paraliticus, A^{ce} the palsey.
Hic mutulatus, An^{ce} a mayn.[10]
Hoc vulnus, } a wonde.
Hec plaga, }
Hic sicatrix, An^{ce} a old wownde.
Hec peruda, An^{ce} a keybe hele.
Hec vibex, An^{ce} a strype.[11]
Hec anggrena, An^{ce} dede fleyche.
Hec insanies, An^{ce} a whele
Hoc epilema, -tis, An^{ce} a playster.

---

[1] *Arula* is explained in the Anglo-Saxon vocabularies as meaning a fire-pan, or vessel for holding lighted charcoal.
[2] An old name for a ring-worm.
[3] *Cowe,* a cough. This shows the old way of pronouncing the word.
[4] A disease of the heart.
[5] A pose, or cold in the head.
[6] *Berede,* perhaps bed-rid.
[7] The quinsy.
[8] A whitlow.
[9] Huloet has, "Cattes heere, otherwyse called a telon, *furunculus.*"
[10] *i. e.,* a maim.
[11] *Strype.* The Nomenclator, a vocabulary printed in 1585, explains *vibex* by "the marke of a blowe or stripe remaining in the fleshe blacke and blewe."

NOMINA MULIERUM CUM SUIS INSTRUMENTIS.

Hec imperatrix, An^{ce} a hempryse.
Hec regina, An^{ce} a quene.
Hec duxissa, An^{ce} a dukes.
Hec cometissa, An^{ce} a cometas.
Hec baronissa, An^{ce} a baronys.
Hec domina, An^{ce} alle maner lady.
Hec psraannia, An^{ce} a barow-woman.
Hec damicella, An^{ce} a damselle.
Hec fflammia,
Hoc flamiolum, } a cherchow.[1]
Hoc reticulum, An^{ce} a calle.
Hoc splinter, An^{ce} a pynne.
Hec vitta, An^{ce} a felet.
Hoc crinale, An^{ce} a here-bond.
Hec tricatura, An^{ce} a tresewyr.[2]
Hoc monile, An^{ce} a broche.
Hic limbus, An^{ce} a rebant.
Hoc peplum, An^{ce} a wympylle.
Hoc teare, -ris, An^{ce} a bonet.
Hic anulus, An^{ce} a ryng.
Hoc certum, An^{ce} a garlond.
Hec ffebula, An^{ce} a lase.
Hoc calamustrum, a quiver.
Hec abatissa, An^{ce} a abcyse.
Hec priorissa, An^{ce} a pryoryse.
Hec monialis, An^{ce} a none.
Hec presbeterissa,
Hec sacerdotissa, } a prystes wyfe.
Hic sacerdotulus, An^{ce} a prestes sun.

Hec sacerdotula, An^{ce} a prestes dowtyr.
Hec uxor,
Hec sponsa, } a wyfe.
Hec femina,
Hec mulier, } a woman.
Hec ustrinatrix, a kylme wyfe.
Hec deciccatrix, idem est.
Hoc ustrinum, An^{ce} a kylme.
Hoc ffulicium, An^{ce} a hayyr.
Hec androchia, An^{ce} a deyry.
Hic casius, An^{ce} schese.
Hic tirus, An^{ce} nyw schese.
Hoc butirum, An^{ce} botyr.
Hoc mulsum, An^{ce} the wyte of botyr.
Hoc serum, An^{ce} the whey of chese.
Sit liquor hoc serum, defundat casius ipsum.
Hoc tolustrum, An^{ce} besning.[4]
Hec balducta,
Hoc coagulum, } a crud or a posset.
Hoc occigalum, An^{ce} a sowyr mylke.
Hic quactus, An^{ce} creme.
Hoc lacticium, An^{ce} wyte mete.
Hec sissma, An^{ce} a sches-fatte.
Hoc ralatorium, An^{ce} a scharne.[5]
Hoc coagulatorium, a scharn-stafe.
Hoc multrum, An^{ce} a mylke-payle.
Hoc multrale, An^{ce} the tyn of the mylke.[6]
Hic mulsor, An^{ce} a mylker.
Hoc lac, An^{ce} mylke.
Hoc androchiatorium, An^{ce} a deyry.
Hec aucionatrix, An^{ce} a hoxter.
Hec virago, a sturdy qwene.
Hec armifodrita, An^{ce} a scrate.[7]
Hec mater,
Hec genetrix, } a modyr.

---

[1] A kerchief.
[2] The tressure, or arrangement of the hair.
[3] The inscription to this diagram is written at the edge of the paper and partly lost, but it was evidently *casius*, *i. e.*, cheese.

[4] *Besning*, the first milk, now called the *beastings*. The Latin word should be *colustrum*.
[5] A churn.
[6] *i. e.*, a milk-can.
[7] A hermaphrodite. See before, p. 217.

A PICTORIAL VOCABULARY. 269

Hec nutrix, An*ᶜᵉ* a norys.
Hec cunia, } credylle.
Hoc cunabilum,

Hec ffassia, An*ᶜᵉ* credyl-bond.
Hec mammus,
Hec mamillo,   } An*ᶜᵉ* pappe.
Hoc uber, -ris,
Hic panniculis, An*ᶜᵉ* a clowte.
Hec virgo, An*ᶜᵉ* vergyn.
Hec puella, An*ᶜᵉ* maydyn.
Hec meretrix, An*ᶜᵉ* hore.
Hec materffemilias, a hoswyf.
Hec vedua, An*ᶜᵉ* a wedow.
Hec rustica, a fyld-wyfe.
Hec pandoxatrix, a browstere.
Hec filatrix, An*ᶜᵉ* a spynnere.
Hec colus, An*ᶜᵉ* a dysestafe.
Hic fusus, An*ᶜᵉ* a spyndylle.
Hec pellicula, An*ᶜᵉ* a ryb-schyn.
Hec nebryda, idem est.
Hoc vertebrum, An*ᶜᵉ* a aworowylle.¹
Hoc girgillum, An*ᶜᵉ* a bladys.
Hoc alabrum,   } An*ᶜᵉ* a rele.
Hoc traale, -is,

Hic virgillus, a yerwyndylle-blad.
Hic globus, An*ᶜᵉ* a clew.
Hic glomicellus, idem est.
Hec glomeracio, a hep of threde.
Hec congeries, An*ᶜᵉ* a hep of stonys.
Congeries lapidum tibi sit, glomeracio fili.
Hoc ffilum, An*ᶜᵉ* threde.
Hec lotrex, An*ᶜᵉ* a lavundare.
Hoc locium, An*ᶜᵉ* ley and nettyng.
Hoc smigma, -tis, An*ᶜᵉ* a soppe ²
Hoc stigma, An*ᶜᵉ* the dere yn a mannys hede.³
Smigma capud mundat, stigma dolore gravat.
Hoc sulfur, An*ᶜᵉ* brynston.
Hoc feratorium, } a batylledore.
Hoc pecten,
Hec textrix, An*ᶜᵉ* a webster.
Hec matatrix, An*ᶜᵉ* a hokylster.
Hec mataxa, An*ᶜᵉ* a hekylle.
Hec excudia, An*ᶜᵉ* a sungylle-stok.⁴
Hoc excudiatorium, An*ᶜᵉ* a sungylle-hand.
Hec stupa, An*ᶜᵉ* herdys.
Hec narpa, An*ᶜᵉ* schewys.
Hoc rupeste, a repylle-stok.⁵
Hoc asperum, An*ᶜᵉ* a top of lyne.
Hic limphus, a stryke of lyne.
Hec costa, An*ᶜᵉ* a rybbe.
Hoc linum, An*ᶜᵉ* fflax.
Hec sutrix, An*ᶜᵉ* a sewer.
Hec brasiatrix, a brewster.
Hec contrix, a barbowres wyfe.
Hec pronuba, a bawstrop.⁶
Hec obstetrix, a mydwyfe.
Hec pectrix, -cis, a cemster.⁷
Hec carminatrix, idem est.

¹ A whirle, or round piece of wood put on the spindle of the spinning wheel.
² i. e., soap.
³ A mark of disgrace, by burning, &c. on the head.
⁴ A swingle stock, a wooden implement for beating flax or hemp, to separate the outer coating from the fibre. *Swingle-hand* is another name for the same implement.
⁵ *Repylle-stok*, an implement for cleaning flax.
⁶ See before, p. 217.
⁷ A female who combs, a kembster.

A PICTORIAL VOCABULARY.

NOMINA TERRARUM.

Hec terra, -e,
Hec ruus, -i,
Hoc arvum, -i,
Hoc campum, -i, } An^{ce} the fyld.

Arvum, campus, ager, rus, sic diversificatur;
Dum seritur sit ager, et semen conditur illo;
Campus dicatur dum fructibus expoliatur;
Messibus est arvum tectum flore vel erbis,
Incultum rus est, veluti sunt pascua silve.

Hec carucata, An^{ce} plow-lode.
Hec bovata, a hox-gangyn lond.
Hec acra, An^{ce} a akyr lond.
Hec virgata, An^{ce} a eryd lond.
Hic selis, -is, An^{ce} a ryggyd lond.
Hic sulcus,
Hec lira, } a fforow.
Hec sulcacio, An^{ce} a balkyng.
Hec fforeta, An^{ce} a hed-lond.
Hec amsages, An^{ce} a but of lond.
Hoc pratum, An^{ce} a medow.
Hoc marescum, An^{ce} a merche.
Hoc archifenium,
Hoc croftum, } a crofe.
Hic ortus, -ti, An^{ce} a 3erd.
Hic ortus, -tus, -ui, a spryngyng.
Ortus, -ta, -tum, An^{ce} spryngyng.

Ortus origo datur, per quartam dum variatur;
Quo crescunt herbe locus est ortusque secunde;
Post ortum periit infantulus ortus in orto.

Hoc erbarium, An^{ce} a herbar.
Hoc virgultum, An^{ce} a holt.
Hic mons, -tis, An^{ce} a hylle.

Hec collis, An^{ce} a lytylle hylle.
Hic agger, idem est.
Hoc montanum,
Hic alpes, } a grete hylle.

Distant montana sic, alpes, collis, et agger;
Designant magnum cumulum terre duo prima,
Alteria bina notant parvum cumulum quoque terre.

Hec vallis, An^{ce} a wale.
Hec palis, An^{ce} a more.
Hec labina, An^{ce} a fenne.
Hec ria, An^{ce} a wey.
Hec platea, a hye wey.
Hic vicus, An^{ce} a strete.
Hec trama,
Hec orbita, } An^{ce} a paytt.
Hec semita,

Trama parva via tibi sit tranversa per arvum.

Hec venella, An^{ce} a lane.
Hec specula, a totyng-hylle.[1]
Hic fumus, An^{ce} smoke.

Hoc fimarium,
Hoc sterculinium, } a muckelle.[2]
Hoc sabulum, An^{ce} sonde.

---

[1] To *tote* was to spy, or watch. A *toting-hill* would be a mound, or hill, in a prominent position, raised or occupied for watching.

[2] A muck-hill, or dunghill.

A PICTORIAL VOCABULARY. 271

Hec *arema*, An^{ce} gravelle.
Hoc *argillum*, } An^{ce} clay.
Hec *argilla*, }
Hic *linus*, An^{ce} a sclott.[1]
Hoc *fossatum*, a se-dyke.
Hec *rypa*, An^{ce} a banke.
Hic et hec *mergo*, idem est.
   Fontis mergo, maris litus, sic ripa fluentis.
Hoc *senum*, An^{ce} a modyng strete.
Hec *gleba*, An^{ce} a clote.
Hoc *cosidium*, An^{ce} a torsy.[2]
Hec *solitudo*, a wyldernys.
Hec *meta*, An^{ce} a butte.
Hec *lapifodina*, } a ston-quarelle.
Hoc *saccifragium*, }
Hec *aurifodina*, a gold-quarelle.
Hec *argentifodina*, a sylver-quarelle.
Hec *sertis*, An^{ce} a sand-bedde.
Hec *insula*, An^{ce} a hylyn of the see.
Hec *ceclas*, idem est.
Hec *mediamnis*, a freche-water dyk.
Hec *cateracta*, An^{ce} a wey of hewyn.
Hec *cateracta*, An^{ce} a wyndowe.
   Est cateracta via dicitur celique fenistra.

Hic *travo*, An^{ce} a holle wey.
Hic *bivius*, }
Hic *trivius*, } a gate-schedelle.
Hic *quatrivius*, }
Hec *spelunca*, }
Hec *caverna*, } a denne.
Hec *cripa*, }
Hoc *volutabrum*, An^{ce} a selot.[3]
Hic et hec et hoc *specus*, An^{ce} a welbryng.[4]
Hic *scrobs*, An^{ce} a swyn-wrotyng.

NOMINA AQUARUM.

Hoc *mare*, }
Hoc *pelagus*, } An^{ce} the see.
Hoc *equor*, }
Hoc *salum*, An^{ce} salt-water.
Hec *aqua*, }
Hec *latex*, } An^{ce} water.
Hec *limpha*, }
Hec *unda*, }

Hec *aqua*, An^{ce} sorow.
Hec *aqua*, An^{ce} lernyng.
Hec *aqua*, An^{ce} folke.
   Est aqua qua fruimur doctrina, dolor, populusque.

Hec *amnis*, An^{ce} freche-water.
Hec *pluvia*, An^{ce} reyn.
Hec *nix*, An^{ce} snow.
Hoc *gelu*, An^{ce} a forst.
Hec *pruina*, An^{ce} a hore-forst.
Hic *ros*, -ris, An^{ce} a dew.
Hec *glacies*, -ei, An^{ce} hyse.
Hec *grando*, -is, An^{ce} a hayle.
Hec *fossa*, }
Hec *foria*, } An^{ce} a dyke.
Hec *cavea*, }
Hec *antra*, }

---

[1] *Sclott.* Sticky clay is still called *slot* in Lincolnshire.

[2] *Torsy.* Perhaps this is a blunder for *corsy*, and means a causeway.

[3] *Volutabrum* is explained in the Nomenclator, "A wallowing place for cattell, hores, and swine." A wide ditch is still called a *slot* in Devonshire.

[4] *Welbryng.* This word, to judge by the Latin equivalent, must mean a cave.

Hic fons, -tis, An^{ce}
  a welle.
Hec scatebra, } a
Hec scatarigo, } sprynge.
Hoc tolumen, An^{ce}
  a tumrelle.
Hoc stagnum, An^{ce}
  a ponde.
Hec lacuna, An^{ce} a playche of water.
Hoc vadum, An^{ce} a wadth.[1]
Hic rivus, An^{ce} a revyr.
Hic rivulus, An^{ce} a lake.
Hic gurges, -tis, }
Hoc rudor, } a gotyr.
Hec rudor, }
Hec cloaca, An^{ce} a prevy.

Hec catacumba, idem est.
Hec pissina, An^{ce} a wayir.
Hoc meandrum, An^{ce} a stynkyng pytt.
Hec stilla, } a drope.
Hec gutta, }
Hoc stellocidum, An^{ce} a howse-goter.
Hoc stillicidium, An^{ce} a spowte.
Hic austrus, -us, -ui, An^{ce} a drawte.
Hec sorbicio, An^{ce} a spyung.
Hec catadurpa, An^{ce} a cundythe.
Hec ledonis, An^{ce} a sulse.[2]
Hec malma, a grownd-heve.
Hic cataclismus, An^{ce} Noys-flode.

---

[1] *i. e.*, a place you can wade through, a ford.

Hic portus, -tus, -tui, An^{ce} a hawyn.
Hic cataclismus, An^{ce} helle, *ut patet per versus.*
Designant tibi delivium, baratrique profundum.

NOMINA PLANETORUM.

Hoc celum, } *An^{ce}* hewyn.
Hic polus, }
Hic paradisus, An^{ce} paradyse.
Hic sol, } *An^{ce}* the sunne.
Hic phebus, }
Hic clipsis, the clyppes of the sunne.
Hec luna, } *An^{ce}* the mone.
Hec phebe, }
Hoc pleniluniun, An^{ce} ful-mone.
Hec neomenia, An^{ce} a new-mone.
Hic aier, }
Hec aera, } the wethyr.
Hic ether, }
Hec ethera, }
Hic ventus, } the wynde.
Hec aura, }
Hec nubes, }
Hoc nubulum, } a clowde.
Hec nubula, }
Hec stella, }
Hoc astrum, } *An^{ce}* alle maner sterres.
Hoc sidus, }
Hic canis, }
Hic esperes, An^{ce} hewyn-sterre.
Hic jubiter, a day-sterre.

---

[2] *Sulse*, the flow of the sea-tide.

A PICTORIAL VOCABULARY.

Hic diaspiter,
Hic lucifer, } idem sunt.
Hic saturnus, a pestlens planyt.
Hic unus, An^{ce} a lodsman.
Hic annus, An^{ce} a ȝere.
Hic mensis, An^{ce} a monythe.
Hec quindena, An^{ce} a fortenyte.
Hec septimana,
Hec ebdomeda, } *An^{ce}* a weke.
Hic vel hec dies, -ei, An^{ce} a day.
Hoc diliculum, An^{ce} a mornyng.
Hic meredies, An^{ce} a mydday.
Hec nox, -tis, An^{ce} a nythe.
Equinoxium, An^{ce} mydnythe.
Hoc crepusculum,
Hoc vesper, -eris, } a hewyn-tyde.
Hoc vesperum, An^{ce} a hewyn-song-tyde.
Hoc ignitegium, An^{ce} curfew.
Hoc intempestum, An^{ce} mydnythe.
Hic bisextus, a lepe-ȝere.
Hic tonitrus, An^{ce} thwndur.
Hoc fulmen, An^{ce} lytenyng.
Hoc fulgur, idem est.
Hic rogus,
Hic ignis, } *An^{ce}* fyre.
Hic focus,
Hic iems,
Hec bruma, } *An^{ce}* wynter.
Hec quadragesima, An^{ce} lenten.
Hec iris, An^{ce} a reyn-bowe.
Hec ira, An^{ce} wrethe.
   Iris res mira, sed non est iris in ira.
Hic ecto, -is, vox in aera respondens.
Hec ver, -ris, the tyme gruyng.
Hec esta, An^{ce} somer.
Hec filandra, a gossummer.
Solsticium estivale, An^{ce} mydsomer.
Hic autumnus, An^{ce} hervyst.
Hic infernus, -i,
Hic tartarus, -i,
Hic orcus, -i, } *An^{ce}* helle.
Hec jehenna, -e,
Hec avernus, -i,

Hic antepos,
Hec lamea, } *An^{ce}* ffayery.

NOMINA DOMORUM.

Hoc monasterium, An^{ce} a mynster.
Hec eclesia,
Hoc templum, } *An^{ce}* a kyrke.
Hec baselica,

Hec capella, An^{ce} a schapelle.
Hoc vestiarium,
Hoc vestibulum, } *An^{ce}* a vestry.
Hoc campanile, An^{ce} a belle-howse.
Hoc atrium,
Hec aula, } *An^{ce}* a halle.
Hoc atrium, a kyrke-ȝerde.
   Atria dic aulas, eadem sumitoria dicas.
Hec camera,
Hec simina,
Hic talamus, } *An^{ce}* a schambyr.
Hec conclavis,
Hec conclave,
Hoc solarium, An^{ce} a solere.
Hoc penu, indeclinabile, An^{ce} a seler.
Hoc cubile, An^{ce} a cowche.
Hec cubicila, An^{ce} a kenelle.
Hec domus,
Hec edes, } *An^{ce}* alle maner of howse.
Her casa,
Hec casula, } *An^{ce}* a cote.

Hec casula, An^{ce} a schesepylle.
Dico domum parvam casulam tibi diminutivum,
Ac indumentum dicatur presbeterale.
Hoc dormitorium, An^{ce} a dorter.
Hoc larduarium, An^{ce} a lardyr.
Hec cansella, } a schanselle.
Hoc cansellum,
Hec panatria, An^{ce} a pantyr.
Hec botolaria, An^{ce} a botry.
Hoc penus,
Hoc dispensorium, } a spenyse.
Hec epoteca,
Hec coquina, } a kychon.
Hec pompina,
Hec affina, An^{ce} a werk-howse.
Hec tabarna,
Hec caupona, } *An^{ce}* a taverne.
Hec pila,
Hoc granatorium, } a garnyr.
Hoc granarium,
Hoc orium, An^{cr} a beyrne.
Hoc porcatorium, An^{ce} a hog-stye.
Hoc galinarium, a hen-cote.
Hoc tigurium, An^{ce} a hoywl.[1]
Hoc magale, An^{ce} a lodge.
Hoc stabulum, An^{ce} a stabylle.
Hoc bostar, -aris, An^{cr} a schepyn.
Hic carcer, An^{ce} a presun-howse.
Hoc pretorium, An^{ce} a mote-halle.
Hoc toloneum, An^{ce} a tol-bothe.
Hoc lupaner,
Hec fornix, } a hore-howse.
Hoc prostibulum,
Hoc lanifisium, a wul-howse.
Hoc tabernaculum, a tabernakyl.
Hec foruca, } a prewy.
Hec laterrina,
Hoc temtorium, An^{cr} a
Hoc pandocsatorium, a bryw-howse.

[1] A hovel.
[2] The reading of these words is somewhat

Hoc pistrinum, An^{ce} a bake-howse.
Hoc ustrinum, } a kylin-howse.
Hoc torale,
Hec scola, } *An^{ce}* a scole.
Hoc studium,
Hec sella, An^{ce} a selle.
Hoc predium, An^{ce} a maner.
Hec salina, An^{ce} a salt-cote.
Hoc diversorium, } *An^{ce}* a hyn.
Hoc hospicium,
Hec opella, An^{ce} a schoppe.
Hoc gazafilacium, a treser-house.

NOMINA ARTIFICIUM CUM SUIS
INSTRUMENTIS.

Hic cultor, } a lond-tyllere.
Hic et hec agricola,
Hic nauta, } a shypman.
Hic navita,
Hic proreta, An^{cr} a stereman.
Hic naucherus, a purs-berer.
Hec prora, An^{cr} a forstanyg.
Hec puppis, An^{ce} the in parti.[2]
Hec ratis, An^{ce} the schyppes syde.
Hec carina, An^{ce} a holle.
Prora prior navis pars dicitur, ultima puppis,
Sic latus esse ratem, ventrem dicitur esse
carinam.
Hoc naulum, An^{ce} a schyppes tolle.
Hec antemnis, a hed-rope.
Hic parastes, An^{ce} a cabylle.
Hic rudens, -tis, An^{ce} a scylle-rope.
Hec supera, -eris, An^{ce} a seylle-bonde.
Hoc velum, An^{ce} a scylle.
Hic cherucus, An^{ce} a fanne.
Hoc cachesium, An^{ce} a seyl-ʒerde.
Hec ancora, An^{ce} a ankyr.
Hoc podrum, An^{ce} a helme.
Hic remex, An^{ce} a rodyr.
Hoc amplustrum, idem est.

doubtful in the manuscript, and I am not sure
that I have read them quite correctly.

A PICTORIAL VOCABULARY.

Hic porticulus, An^{ce} a maylat.
Hic abbestus, An^{ce} a fyir-stone.
Hoc pericudium, An^{ce} a fyr-hyrg . . .
Hic acus, -cus, -cui, An^{ce} a nedylle.
Hic jaclus, a thred in a nedyl . . .
Hec troclia, An^{ce} a wynddas.
Hec coclia, An^{ce} a wyndylle.
Hec navicula,
Hec lembus, } a bote.
  Nos vestit limbus, nos vectat per mare lembus.
Hec facelus, An^{ce} a sog-bote.[1]
Hic remus, An^{ce} a hore.
Hec palmula, the brede of the hore.
Hoc columbar, An^{ce} the holle of the schyp.
Hoc armamentum, a haltakylle.[2]
Hec saburra, An^{ce} a lastage.
Hic malus, An^{ce} a mast.
Hic paterfamilias,
Hic maritus, } a husbond.
Hic tantellus, An^{ce} a congyn.
Hic vir,
Hic vel hec homo, } a man.
Hic omunculus, An^{ce} a duorow.[3]
Hic membrarius, a parchmeare.
Hic servus,
Hic famulus,
Hic verna, } a servante.
Hic satrapa,
Hoc mancipium,

Hic garcio, An^{ce} a knafe.
Hic vel hec scurra, An^{ce} a harlat.
Hic vel hec alocropa, idem est.
Hic nugator, An^{ce} chaper.[4]
Hec nuga, An^{ce} a chape.
Hic nugigerulus, An^{ce} a trifelle.
Hic sponsus, a wed-man.
Hic puer, An^{ce} a schyle.
Hic et hec latro, a day thefe.
Hic fur, An^{ce} a nyte thefe.
  Tempore nocturno fur aufert, latro diurno.
Hic suffarcinator, An^{ce} a bryber.
Hic ursarius, a ber-ward.
Hic victor, a cummer.[5]

CUPERUS CUM SUIS INSTRUMENTIS.

Hic carpentarius, a carpenter.
Hic cuperus, a cowper.
Hoc dolebrum, a brode-hax.
Hec securis, An^{ce} a hax.
Hec seculicula, a hachet.
Hec acia, a tyxhyl.[6]
Hoc aquiscium, a quyver.

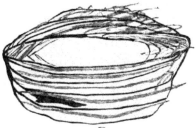

---

[1] *Sog-bote.* In the Nomenclator, *phaselus* is interpreted as signifying a pinnace.
[2] *Haltakylle,* I suppose, the whole tackle or furniture of the ship—*armamenta navis*
[3] A dwarf.
[4] *i. e.*, a japer, a jester or mocker.
[5] *Cummer,* probably a gossip, *Scottice.*
[6] *Tyxhyl,* apparently a sort of axe.

A PICTORIAL VOCABULARY.

Hoc perpendiculum, a plomet.
Hec regula, An^{ce} a rewylle.
Hoc terebrum, An^{ce} a wymbylle.
Hoc teribellum, An^{ce} a persowyr.
Hic bipennus,
Hic bidens, -tis, } a stybylle.
Hec leviga, An^{ce} a plane.
Hec seltis, An^{ce} a scheselle.
Hec strofina, a gropyng-yryn.
Hec sarra, An^{ce} a saw.
Hec vibra, An^{ce} a brake.
Hic circulus, An^{ce} a hope.
Hic aser, -ris, An^{ce} a borde.
Hic cunius, An^{ce} a sceselle.

PANDUCSATOR CUM SUIS INSTRUMENTIS.

Hic panducsator, a brever.
Hoc brasium, An^{ce} malt.
Hoc plumbum, An^{ce} a lede.
Hec fornax, -cis, An^{ce} a fornys.
Hec cuva, An^{ce} a fatte.
Hec cupa, a colle.[1]
Hec tina, idem est.
Hoc idromellum, An^{ce} wurte.
Hoc ciromellum, An^{ce} growte.
Hec fulanga, An^{ce} a try.[2]
Hec spuma, An^{ce} barme.
Hoc multrale, a payle.
Hoc colum,
Hoc infusorium, } *An^{ce}* tunnyng.
Hoc colatorium, a clenyng-sefe.

Hoc cinofegium,
Hoc sagisterium, } *An^{ce}* drafe.
Hec amurca, drowsyn.
Hec scafe, An^{ce} a bolle.
Hec scoba, An^{ce} a besum.

PISTOR CUM SUIS INSTRUMENTIS.

Hic pistor, An^{ce} a baker.
Hic clibanus, An^{ce} a rele.[3]
Hoc tersorium, An^{ce} a malkyn.
Hec pala, An^{ce} a forkyn.
Hoc furnorium,
Hec pila, } *An^{ce}* pyle.[4]
Hoc pollentridium, a bult-pele.
Polenduare, An^{ce} a bult.
Hoc taratanterum, An^{ce} a tense.
Taratantarisare, An^{ce} to bult.
Hic taratantarizator, An^{ce} a censare.
Hec pasta, An^{ce} dowe.
Hec farina, An^{ce} mele.
Hoc furfur, An^{ce} bryn.
Hoc polen,
Hoc polentum,
Hec simila, } *An^{ce}* flowyr.
Hoc ador, indeclinabile,
Hic panificator, An^{ce} a mouldere.[5]
Panificare, An^{ce} moulde.
Hoc jocabulum, An^{ce} a colrake.
Hec costa,
Hoc scalprum, } a rybe.
Hec ribra, An^{ce} a brake.[6]

 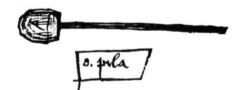

[1] *Colle,* a hogshead, or large barrel.
[2] *Try,* a corn-screen.
[3] *Rele. Clibanus* means properly the oven.
[4] The baker's peel, or implement for putting the bread into the oven.
[5] The person who makes the dough into loaves.
[6] One meaning of the word *brake* is a baker's kneading-trough. It occurs before in this page, with the same Latin, but evidently in a different sense.

A PICTORIAL VOCABULARY.

Hec massa, An^{ce} a gobet of dow.
Hoc fermentum, An^{ce} sowyr-dow.

Hic fossor, An^{ce} a dyker.
Hic murinator, a waller.
Hec merra, a mattoke.
Hec vanga, a spade.
Hec stribula, a schowle.
Hoc sinovectorium, a barow.
Hec furca, a forke.
Hec merga, idem.

Hic pomelio, a gardyner.
Hic olitor, } *idem sunt.*
Hic ortolanus, }
Hic plantator, a plantor.
Hic pomelio, venditor pomorum.
Hic pomelio, custos pomorum. Versus.
Pomelio custos, vector, vel venditor extat.

Hoc pomerium, a norchard.
Hoc pomerium, a whorde.
Hoc pomelium, idem.
Hec fals, scarpe.[1]
Hoc maxillium, a jyppe.
Hec labrusca, the bark of the vyne.
Hoc vitulamen, a branche.
Hoc sarmentum, the cuttyng.
Hec antes, a siron.[2]
Hec propago, a rote.

Hic pamplus, a vyne-leffe.
Hec uva, a grape.
Hic acinus, a ston grape.
Hic botrus, a closter.
Pampulus est folium, botrus flos, vinea totum.

Hic tector, An^{ce} a thaser.[3]
Hic contraitus, An^{ce} a crepylle.
Hec contraita, idem est.
Hoc sustentaculum, } a croche.
Hoc podium, }

Hic auceps, An^{ce} a fowlere.
Hoc viscum, An^{ce} byrd-lyme.
Hic laquius, An^{ce} a snare.
Hoc volatorium, An^{ce} a schaf-net.
Hic avigerulus, An^{ce} a pulter.

Hic messor, An^{ce} a scherer.[4]
Hec fals, An^{ce} a sekylle.
Hic falcator, An^{ce} a mower.
Hec fals, An^{ce} a sythe.
False puto vincta, meto sata, tondeo prata.

Hic auriga,
Hic vereda, } a cartar.
Hic carectarius,

[1] *Scarpe,* an instrument for pruning vines. See the verse in the next column.
[2] *Antes,* a sprout.
[3] A thatcher.
[4] A reaper. Reaping is still called *shearing* in Scotland.

*Hec carecta, An^{ce} * a carte.
Hic capsis, An^{ce} a carte.
Hec biga, } a wayne.
Hoc plaustrum,
Hic currus, An^{ce} a carte.
Hoc carpentum, An^{ce} a schare.[1]
Hoc veredum, An^{ce} a thylle.
Hic veredus, An^{ce} a thyl-horse.
Hec rota, An^{ce} a quele.
Hic cantus, -ti, -to, An^{ce} a felow.
Hic cantus, -tus, -tui, An^{ce} a song.

   Cantus, -ti, bige, cantus cantantis in ore.

Hic radius, An^{ce} a spoke.
Hic radius, An^{ce} a sun-beme.

   Est radius rote, solis, tele, geometrie.

Hec axis, An^{ce} a exylle-tre.
Hoc meditulium, An^{ce} a nafe.
Hoc epuscium, An^{ce} a cart-clowte.
Hoc retinaculum, An^{ce} a trayse.
Hoc traale, idem est.
Hec epicia, -orum, An^{ce} a berhom.[2]
Hec scutica, An^{ce} a quippe.
Hic funis, An^{ce} a rope.
Hec merga, An^{ce} a forke.
Hoc capistrum, An^{ce} a halter.
Hic inclusarius, An^{ce} a hayward.
Hic lucarius,
Hic viridarius, } *An^{ce}* a foster.
Hic forestarius,

Hic nemus, -ris,
Hec lucus, } a forest.
Hec feresta,
Hoc lucar, -ris, An^{ce} a forest-ax.
Hic parcarius, An^{ce} a parcar.
Hec indago, An^{ce} a parke.
Hoc vallum, An^{ce} a parke palys.
Vallo, -as, -i. vallum facere.
Hoc tribucetum, An^{ce} a sawtre.

Hic architenens, } a harchere.
Hic sagittarius,
Hic arcus, An^{ce} a bowe.
Hec arcitula, An^{ce} a bow-stryng.
Hec catapulta, An^{ce} a brode arw.
Hec sagitta, An^{ce} a harow.
Hoc petulium, An^{ce} a bolt.
Hoc amentum, An^{ce} a nok.
Hec cuspis, An^{ce} a bolt-hed.
Hec faretra, An^{ce} a quiver.
Hic corintheus, a bowe-howse.
Hec veltria, a lese of grehowndes.
Hic nullus, a grehownd colere.
Hoc cornu, indeclinabile, An^{ce} a horne.
Hoc defensorium, } *An^{ce}* a braser.
Hoc brachitectum,
Hec fusticula, An^{ce} a lytyl pype.
Hic agamus, a sengyl man.

Hic archimendritas,
Hic opelio, } a schepard.
Hic pastor,
Hic grex, } a flok.
Hic villus,
Hic vellus, An^{ce} a slefe.

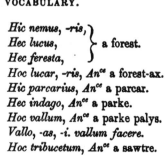

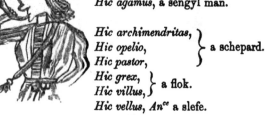

---

[1] *i. e.*, a car.   [2] A barholm, or collar for a horse to draw by.

Hoc ovile, } a fold.
Hec caula,
Hec caulamaula, a scheperdes pype.
Hoc pedum, An^{ce} a scheperdes stafe.
Hic padus, An^{ce} a scheperdes croke.
Hic palus, } a fold-stake.
Hic paxillus,
Hec cratis, An^{ce} a herdylle.

Hic pixus, An^{ce} a box.
Hoc butumen, An^{ce} a tere.
Hoc unguentum, An^{ce} grese.
Hic vaccarius, a cowhard.
Hoc armentum, An^{ce} a dryfte.
Hic equiarius, An^{ce} a hors-heyrd.
Hic capriarius, An^{ce} a gate-heyrd.
Hic edrius, i^o for a precher.

APPENDIX.

ANGLO-SAXON VOCABULARY.[1]

(OF THE TENTH OR ELEVENTH CENTURY.)

DE AVIBUS.
Aquila, earn.
Arpa, eargeat.
Acega, wudu-coc.
Strutio, struta.
Griphus, giw.
Ossifragus, herefong.
Anatis, ened.
Aneta, ened.
Larax, ened.
Ciciris,
Mergulus, scealfor.
Mergus, dop-fugel.
Fulix, ganot.
Anser, hwite-gos.
Canta, græg-gos.
Olor, swon.
Porphyrio, fealvor.

Alacid, ...
Accipiter, gos-hafuc.
Herodius, wealh-hafuc.
Alietum, spear-hafuc.
Suricaricis, mus-hafuc.
Milvus, glida.
Butzus, tysca.
Ciconia, storc.
Grus, cran.
Onocratarum, rare-dumle.
Cucu, hleape-wince.
Bicoca, hæfer-blæte.
Fusianus, wor-hana.
Rusunia, nihtegale.
Columba, culfre.
Pudumba, cusceote.
Corvus, hrefn.
Cornix, crawe.

[1] This Vocabulary, which was accidentally overlooked in printing the earlier portion of the present volume, is taken from a manuscript in the British Museum (MS. Cotton., Cleopat. A. III., fol. 76, r°), in a writing which may be of the latter part of the tenth, or of the earlier part of the eleventh century. It is preceded by a rather copious alphabetical dictionary, Latin and Anglo-Saxon, which breaks off abruptly by a mutilation of the manuscript with the letter P; and it is followed by Anglo-Saxon glosses on Latin lives of saints. The vocabulary itself, which presents some points of resemblance in its construction with that which is given first in this volume as the vocabulary of Archbishop Alfric, seems to end confusedly in a gloss of this description. It contains several curious and not very common words.

Grallus, hroc.
Cornicula, cio.
Beacita, stearn.
Mursopicus, fina.
Picus, higere.
Noctua, ule.
Ulula, ule.
Rubesca, seltra.
Sigitula, frec-mase.
Parra, cum-mase.
Parula, col-mase.
Litorius, wærna.
Tilaris, lauwerce.
Cucuzata, irþling.
Scutatus, rago-finc.
Turdella, þrostle.
Merula, osle.
Scorellus, amore.
Cardella, þistel-twige.
Turdus, scric.
Trutius, þrisce.
Birbicariolus, irþling.
Cicius, edisc-henn.
Pullus, cicen.
Sturnus, stær.
Florulus, gold-finc.
Passer, spearwa.
Gallus, hana.
Gallina, henn.
Hirunda, swealwe.
Cuculus, geac.
Tabunus, briosa.
Musca, fleoge.
Vespertilia, hreaþc-mus.
Scnifes, gnæt.
Culix, mygc.
Vespis, wæsp.
Adticus, feld-beo.
Apis, beo.
Pampilio, fif-fealde.
Crabro, hyrnetu.
Nocticorax, niht-hrefn.

Scarebius, wifel.
Blata, hræþbita.
Bruchus, ceafor.
Locusta, gærs-hoppe.
Curculio, emel.
Cicada, hama.

INCIPIT DE PISCIBUS.

Platissa, floc.
Coclea, weoloc.
Lucius, hacod.
Tinctus, sliw.
Coetus, hwæl.
Piscis, fisc.
Ballena, vel pilina, hron.
Delfin, mere-swin.
Bacharus, mere-swin.
Focus, seolh.
Porcopiscis, styriga.
Isic, leax.
Ostrea, ostre.
Geniscula, muxle.
Cancer, hæfern.
Sardina, hæring.
Lupus, bærs.
Murenula, æl.
Castorius, befer.
Ludtrius, hotor.
Anguilla, smæl æl.
Ceffalus, heardra.
Sardina, smelt.

INCIPIT DE TEXTRINALIBUS.

Textrina, telum, web.
Liciatorium, web-beam.
Fussum, spinl.
Radium, hrisl.
Cladica, wefl.
Deponile, wefta.
Nitorium,
Vertelum, hweorfa.
Colus, wulmod.

Glomer, cliwen.
Conductum, gern-winde.
Plumaria, byrdicge.
Stamen, wearp.
Subtimen, aweb.
Petica, slæ.
Apidiscus, web-hoc.
Scafus, uma.
Tala, web-gereþro.
Claus, teltre.
Fila, þræd.
Lana, wull.
Vellus, flis.
Leno, wif-þegn.
Pedissequa, þinen.
Alibrum, reol.
Calatum, toweht.
Insabula, meodoma.

INCIPIT DE HOMINE ET DE PARTIBUS EJUS.

Homo, mann.
Anthropus, mann.
Chomos, middangeard.
Michrochosmos, se læssa middangeard.
Anima, saul.
Corpus, lichoma.
Caro, flæsc.
Crementum, sæd.
Sensus, sefa.
Visus, gesihþ.
Gustus, birgncs.
Auditus, gehirnes.
Odoratus, swæc.
Tactus, hrinc.
Caput, heafod.
Vertex, hnol.
Pilus, hær.
Coma, feax.
Facies, hleor.
Capillis, locc.
Cerebrum, brægen.
Calvaria, heafod-panne.

Occipitium, hnecca.
Capitium, forewerd swira.
Cessaries, læ, wif-fex.
Tympora, þunwonge.
Vultus, anwlita.
Frons, hnifol.
Supercilium, ofer-bruwa.
Intercilium, betuh bruwum.
Cilium, bruwa.
Palpebræ, bræwas.
Oculus, eage.
Papilla, seo.
Papula, sco.
Corona, beag.
Lacrime, tearas.
Genæ, heago-swind.
Barba, beard.
Mala, ceacan.
Maxilla, ceacan.
Mentem, cin.
Auris, eare.
Pinnula, ufeweard care.
Naris, nasu.
Columpna, eall seo nasu.
Pirula, forewerd nasu.
Pennula, næs-þyrel.
Fleyma, horg.
Os, muþ.
Labium, welor.
Dens, toþ.
Abum, neoþera welor.
Gingifa, toþ-riman.
Precissor, fore-ccorfend.
Canini, hundlice.
Molares, cweorn-teþ.
Lingua, tunge.
Palatum, goma.
Faus, hyge.
Sublinguæ, under-tungan.
Toles, cyrnla.
Rumen, wasend.
Gurgilio, þrot-bolla.

ANGLO-SAXON VOCABULARY. 283

Anteriæ, ædre.
Collum, swira.
Cervex, swira.
Gula, hrace.
Humeri, eaxla.
Scapulus, sculdor.
Brachium, earm.
Subbrachia, under-earme.
Ascilla, oxtan.
Ulna, eln.
Cubitus, fæþm.
Manus, hand.
Pugnus, fæþm.
Palma, brad-hand.
Vola, hand-bred.
Artus, liþ.
Articulus, liþ-incel, lytel liþ.
Digiti, fingras.
Pollex, þuma.
Index, becnend.
Salutarius, halettend midemesta finger.
Inpudicus, æwisc-berend midmesta finger.
Anularis, hring-finger.
Auricularis, ear-clæsnend.
Ungula, nægl.
Truncus, bodig.
Torax, breost.
Pectus, breost.
Mammille, tittas.
Ubera, spana.
Lac, meolc.
Cutis, sweard.
Fellis, fel.
Pulpa, lira.
Viscus, herþ-belig.
Arvina, gelynde.
Nervi, senwe.
Vertibula, hwcor-ban.
Cartilago, gristle.
Costa, rib.
Latus, side.

Oss, ban.
Dorsum, hryg.
Terga, bæc.
Palæ, hryc-riple.
Spina, hryg-merg-liþ.
Radiolus, ribb-spacan.
Medulla, mearg.
Spondilia, hryc-rib.
Sacra spina, se halga stert.
Renes, ædran.
Lumbia, lendena.
Genitalia, þa cennendlican.
Virilia, þa werlican.
Veretrum, teors.
Calamus, teors, þæt wæpen *vel* lim.
Testiculi, beallucas.
Viscera, inilve.
Meatis, utgang.
Anus, bæc-þearm.
Nates, ears-enda.
Ydropicus, healede.
Femor, þeoh.
Femina, innewerd þeoh.
Coxa, þeoh-scanca.
Subfragines, hamma.
Puples, hamma.
Genua, cneowa.
Crura, sceancan.
Tibiæ, scancan.
Surra, scanc-lira.
Talus, ancleow.
Planta, niþeweard fot.
Pedes, fot.
Calx, hela, hoh niþeweard.
Viscera, inneþus.
Cor, heorte.
Sanguis, blod.
Cruor, dead blod.
Jecor, liver.
Pulmon, lungen.
Splen, milte.
Fel, gealla.

Stomachus, maga.
Intestinum, inilve.
Onentem, midhryþre.
Disceptum, neta.
Cecum, blind-þearm.
Ruina, lynde.
Ansa, hringe.
Cingulum, gyrdel.
Zona, gyrdel.
Ardeda, brandrida.

INCIPIT DE IGNE.

Ignis, fyr.
Flamma, leg.
Flamina, blæd.
Scintilla, spearca.
Scindula, scid.
Cinis, asce.
Favilla, ysle.
Fumus, rec.
Torris, brand.
Fax, þæcile, blysige.
Isica, tyndre.
Ignarium, algeweorc.
Lux, leoht.
Silex, flint.
Lucerna, blæcern.
Cicindilia, weocan.
Sevo, smero.

INCIPIT DE ALEA.

Alea, tæfl.
Calculus, tæfl-stan.
Aleator, tæflere.
Cotizo, ic tæfle, *tesseris*, tæflum.
Cerea, weax.
Lampas, leoht-fæt.
Candela, candel.
Papirus, taper.
Agapis, dæg-mete.
Attomos, mot.
Agonteta, ellenlæce.
Agen, beo-gang.

Alvearia, hyf.
Mel, hunig.
Apiastrum, beo-wyrt.

INCIPIT DE PLAUSTRIS ET DE PARTIBUS EJUS.

Plaustrum, wæn.
Carpentarius, wæn-gerefa.
Rota, hweol.
Themon, þisl.
Radii, spacan.
Canti, felg.
Axedo, lynis.
Jujula, iuc-boga.
Axis, eax.
Altitudo, foþer.
Tabula plaustri, wæn-gehrado.
Jugum, iuc.
Modialis, nafu.

INCIPIT DE LECTULO.

Stratum, bed.
Lectum, bed.
Sindo, scyte.
Cervical, heafod-bolster.
Pulvillus, pyle.
Armilansia, serc.
Tonica, tunece.
Sagum, hwitel, oþþe ryft.
Cappa, sciccing.
Capsula, hacele.
Ependiten, cop.
Mafors, scyfele.
Sancti monialis, nunne.
Apiarius, beo-cere.
Favum, beo-bread.
Gratis, brod.
Altor, fester-fæder.
Altrix, fester-modor.
Alumnus, foster-broþor.
Vitricius, steop-fæder.
Noverca, steop-moder.

Pupillis, steop-cild.
Albuga, flig.
Anguis, wæter-nædre.
Antidotum, drenc.
Avena, wistle.
Arvo, ierþ-land.
Agella, lam.
Agapa, ciepe-man.
Albium, mele.
Anagrippa, anlicnes.
Apotassia, fret-genga.
Alga, war.
Antulum, ceac.
Antherilus, ceac-bora.
Aucupis, fuglere.
Rete, net.
Amitis, lorg.
Rudens, rap.
Aucupium, fuglung.

INCIPIT DE LIGNIS.

Fagus, bece.
Populus, birce.
Æsculus, boc.
Abellanus, vel colurnus, hæsl.
Avilina, hnutu.
Nuclium, cyrnel.
Butrus, hos.
Robor, ac.
Glandix, æceren.
Albaspina, hæg-þorn.
Quisquilia, hagan.
Nigraspina, slag-þorn.
Moros, slan.
Fraxinus, æsc.
Acerabulos, mabuldor.
Tremulos, æspe.
Acrivolus, holen.
Beta, birce.
Alnus, alr.
Abies, sæppe, gyr.
Ulnetum, alor-holt.

Virecta, wice.
Vacedo, redisn.
Cerasius, ciris-beam.
Cariscus, wice.
Castaneus, cisten-bean.
Ramnus, colte-træppe, þefan-ðorn.
Ruscus, cneo-holen, fyres.
Taxus, iw.
Torriculum, hyrwe.
Myrtus, wir.
Malus, apuldor.
Malum, æppel.
Melarium, milisc apuldor.
Metianum, milisc æppel.
Plumnus, plum-treow.
Prunum, plyme.
Pirus, pirige.
Pirum, pere.
Pinus, pin-treow.
Amera, sealh.
Salix, welig.
Rubus, þyn.
Tribulus, brœmbel-brær.
Acinum, hind-berge.
Bacce, bergan.
Sambucus, ellen.
Timus, hæþ.
Genista, brom.
Oliva, ele-beam.
Vinea, win-geard.
Ura, win-berge.
Butros, geclystre.
Oleaster, windel-treow.
Ortus pomorum, apelder-tun.
Ortus olerem (sic), leah-tun.
Folium, leaf.
Cortix, rind.
Radix, wyrt-ruma.
Ramus, twig.
Framen, spæc.
Roboretum, æcen.
Apeletum, spracen.

Vivorna, wudu-winde.
Eder, ifig.
Fursarius, wana-beam.
Fraga, streowberge.

DE HERBIS TERRÆ.

Apio, merce.
Alium, gar-leac.
Serpulum, crop-leac.
Ascolonium, cipa.
Ungio, yne-leac.
Alba cipa, wite-tun (?).
Duricorium, hol-leac.
Porrum, por.
Cerefolium, cerville.
Nasturcium, leac-cersan, tun-c.
Ibiscum, biscep-wyrt.
Coliandrum, celendre.
Mento, minte.
Cartamo, byb-corn.
Acitula, hramse.
Acitelum, hramsan-crop.
Accitulium, iaces-sure.
Arniglosa, wegbræde.
Cinoglosa, ribbe.
Ambila, leac.
Horidanum, elone.
Napis, næp.
Pastinaca, weal-more.
Seu britia, wille-cærse.
Bibulta, billere.
Eptafolium, sinfulle.
Malva, hoc-leaf.
Marubium, hune.
Mastica, hwit-cudu.
Ostrum, wyrma.
Omagnum, wyrmella.
Papilluum, colx sege.
Parulus, sinfulle.
Scilla, glædene.
Quinquenerina, læce-wyrt.
Quinquerolium, fif-leafe.

INCIPIT DE SUIBUS.

Vistrina, stigo.
Aper, etfor.
Sus, swin.
Verrus, bar.
Majalis, bearg.
Scrofa, sugu.
Porcus, ferh.
Porscaster, for.
Forda, gefearh sugu.
Ausungia, rysle.
Perna, flicce.
Larda, spic.
Lucanica, meargh.
Bruncus, wrot.
Jus, rop.
Suesta, swina-swaþu.
Seta, byrst.
Bubullus, swan.
Extale, snædel.
Interamen, inelve.
Julium, smære-þerm.

INCIPIT DE METALLIS.

Obrizum, smæte gold.
Aurum, gold.
Aurifex, gold-smiþ.
Argentum, seolfer.
Auricalcos, grene ar, mæstlinc.
Aes, ar.
Succinum, glær.
Ferrum, isen.
Plumbum, lead.
Stagnum, tin.
Aurifodina, gylding-wecg.
Metallum, clympre.
Faber, smiþ.
Officina, smiþþe.
Follis, blæst-belg.
Cudo, anfilte.
Forceps, tang.
Carbo, col.

Malleus, hamer.
Lima, mylenstan, feol.
Cultellus, seax.
Hasta, spere.
Sicca, cultur.
Vomer, scer.
Vatilla, ferrece.
Boratorium, byres.
Rotum, vel taratrum, timbor.
Desile, bor.
Olatrum, scafa.
Runcina, locor.
Terrebellus,
Lynibor,
Pila, þoþor.

INCIPIT DE FRUGIBUS.

Ordeum, bere.
Triticum, hwæte.
Singula, ryge.
Faar, spelt.
Spica, ear.
Aresta, egle.
Calmum, windels-treow.
Parirus, flea-wyrt.
Ululatus, wulfa-geþot.
Grues, gryt.
Juvencibus, risc-þyfel.
Imbilium, leoht-leap.
Botre, æþro.
Peana, lecþ.
Coluber, snaca.
Stiba, handle.
Axima, stoc.
Mosiclum, ragu.
Subsiciva, æscapo.
Exigia, gesanco.
Grabra, gat.
Vordalium, læste.
Gergenna, sticca.
Cornas, geap.
Misarius, steda.

Equa, mire.
Equus, hors.
Cabullus, hengest.
Burdus, seamere.
Peducla, lus.
Ascarida, hnitu.
Ladasca, pie.
Ursie, sweor-hnitu.
Mulus, mul.
Asina, eosol.
Camellus, olvend.
Arimentarius, hierde.
Arimentum, hiord.
Bora, oxa.
Antile, heahfru.
Vacca, cu.
Foetus, melc.
Vitulus, cealf.
Taurus, fearr.
Vecta, enwintre.
Laudaris, steor.
Volio, fald.
Aubobulcus, oxna-hyrde.
Priveta, þri-wintre steor.

INCIPIT NOMINA SECUNDUM ORDINEM
LITTERARUM.

Acris, from.
Alacris, snel, bliðe.
Anxius, sorgiende.
Appetitus, gitsung.
Astu, fæcne.
Adridens, tyhtende.
Alitus, æþm.
Aveit, aweg fereþ.
Aquile, segnas.
Adelinas, toheald.
Adrogans,
Agem,
Adsciti, gegaderade.
Augustum, brad.
Buccum, dysig.

Balus, emb-rin.
Bona, stoppa.
Bodonicula, amber.
Urcius, hand-wyrm.
Briensis, teter.
Balsis, isen-feter.
Bulla, sigil.
Balsus, wlisp.
Blessus, stamor.
Batuitum, gebeaten.
Broel, ensc.
Broelarius, edisc-weard.
Buculus, rand-beah.
Byrseus, lypen-wyrhta.
Caprea, ra.
Capre, gat.
Caper, hæfer.
Edum, ticcen.
Hircus, bucca.
Titula, gata-loc.
Titurus, gata-hierde.
Calcar, spura.
Cuspis, gad.
Catesta, gæleþ.
Venator, hunta.
Venabula,
Molosus, roþ-hund.
Unfer, grig-hund.
Bruccus, ræce.
Celox, ceol.
Capsis, cist.
Colonus, gebur.
Cistula, spirte.
Colobium, hom.
Cacabum, citel.
Lenes, hwer.
Lancona, cille.
Sartago, breding-panne.
Olla, greova.
Patella, patella.
Camos, swol.
Scalpellum, bræd-iseu.

Capitium, heafod-smæl.
Condicio, redin.
Clavicularius, cæg-bora.
Cicur, manþwære.
Crocus, gæle, geolo.
Camisa, ham.
Calta, ræde-clæfer.
Sarcio, ic supe.
Sarcidis, geseped is.
Oscida, totrida.
Omelias, spræce.
Ortodoxos, wuldorlic.
Gnix, blere.
Calvus, calo.
Recalbus, up-feax.
Procuratio, scir.
Patrocinium, mund-byrd.
Parsus, geroscod.
Plumacium, lang-bolster.
Pistrinum, cofa.
Pistrilla, lytel cofa.
Pristris, dæge.
Panis, hlaf.
Paxmatium, brad-hlaf.
Sparsum, daag.
Sparsio, dages hlæfþe.
Tinipa, gebyrgen.
Palagra, œcilma.
Pironis,
Pastula, ong-seta.
Papula, wearte.
Punctus, brord.
Pugillaris, gyrdel-bred.
Plutecus, apa.
Pendera, fugclint.
Pansa, scaffot.
Paranimphus, dryht-mon.
Pronuba, hadswæpe.
Sponsus, bryd-guma.
Sponsa, bryd.
Thalamus, bryd-bur.
Nuptiæ, iemung.

Sibba, fere-soca.
Sarcum, weod-hoclu.
Scalprum, bor.
Sternutatio, fnora.
Tussis, hwosta.
Serina, mere-men.
Soccus, slype-scos.
Subtalaris, stæppe-scos.
Sandix, wyrt.
Stirillum, buccan beard.
Stabula, siota.
Saginatum, iemæsted.
Tinctorium, telgung.
Tyro, cempa.
Tibialis, ban-rift.
Tricilo, scora.
Torax, feolufor.
Tenticum, spindel.
Trulla, scofl.
Soporatus, gewyrsmed.
Titillatio, kitelung.
Scabellum, windfona.
Sella, sotol.
Subsellium, scamol.
Stomachus,
Sambucus, saltere.
Stronius, drop-fag.
Balidus, dunn.
Salamandra, wæter-nædre.
Scutum, sceld.
Scutarius, sceld-wyrhta.
Sandix, wad.
Stiria, gecele.
Sinus, wellere.
Singultum, gescea.
Sceda, teah.
Salum, sege.
Simfoniara, belune.
Senecen,
Talumbus, gescald-wyrt.
Varix, ompre.
Millefolium, gearwe.

Urtica, netele.
Scirpia, læfer.
Foenum, heg.
Stipula, healm.
Tentorium, ieteld.
Taber, syl.
Tegurium, lytel scyte.
Tapeta, reowu.
Tabetum, cecin.
Toxi, pang.
Triligium, þrielig hrægil.
Tus, inbærnis.
Tibicen, pipere.
Tubicen, bemere.
Tillinguæ, tuddor.
Tertiana, lencten-adl.
Tridens, mettac.
Tubulo, fealo.
Talpa, pund.
Tolia, cyrnel.
Volvula, hymele.
Ulmus, helm.
Vincus, mistellam.
Vadimonium, borg-wed.
Votibus, esteful.
Ultro citro, hider and þider.
Vestiarius, hrægl-weard.
Exnado hior, collecti.
Exenodochia, susceptio.
Peregrinorum, ymnum lof.
Ypoteseo bassio, scirnis.
Nicalalbum, milisc æppel.
Passtellus, hunig æppel.
Aratrum, sulh.
Arva, yrþland.
Juger, ioc.
Seyes, æcer.
Sulcus, furh.

INCIPIT DE DOMIBUS.

Domus, hus.
Aulea, heall.

Vestibulum, cavertun.
Camara, hrof.
Paratica, first.
Partica, win-beam.
Tignus, ræfter.
Trabs, beam.
Paries, wah.
Laquear, ræsn.
Tignaris, hrof-wyrhta.
Pavimentum, flor.
Obstupum, feor-stuþu.
Valva, duru.
Sponda, hobanca.
Spondeus, benc.
Postes, dur-stodl.
Limen, þerscwald.
Superliminare, ofer-dyre.
Spatula, bed.

INCIPIT DE MENSA.

Mensa, beod.
Discus, disc.
Catinus, scutel.
Parabsidis, gabote.
Varsalis, sealt-fæt.
Vas buteri, buter-stoppa.
Butirum, butere.
Lac, meolc.
Verberatum, fliete.
Lactudiclum, geþrofen fliete.
Lac coagolatum, molcen.
Verberaturium, þwiril.
Sinum, cyrin.
Caseum, cyse.
Calmaria, ccalfre.
Calmum, molegn.
Calmilla, lim.
Serum, hwæg.
Calviale, calwer-briw.
Pultum, briw.
Coclear, cucere.
Clerius cibus, wyrt-mete.

Quadripertitum, cocor-mete.
Vivertitum, ron-mete.
Calipeatum, hæting.
Obestrum, beost.
Juta, awilled meolc.
Ocastrum, gemenced æg.
Offa, sticce.
Cachar, lira.
Serviunculos, forglendred.
Reunculos, lundlaga.
Pincerna, byrele.
Taberna, win-ærn.
Vinum, win.
Mustum, neowe win.
Merum, hluttor win.
Dulcisapa, awilled win.
Vinum conditum, gewyrtod win.
Defrucatum, gesweted win.
Defecatum, ahlutrod win.
Mulsum, medo.
Celia, calo.
Cervisa, swatan.
Pollis, grut.
Sandix, wyrt.
Prandium, under-mete.
Cena, æfen-mete.
Viciolum, cruce.
Vescada, mundlan.
Manile, lævil.
Alucolum, treg.
Maniteorium, hand-lind.
Matile, sceat.
Tabulamen, þille.
Patera, hnæpp.
Cucumus, popei.
Pecten, camb.
Melledulci, leoht-beor.
Ciatum, steap.
Fiola, bledu.
Ciatus, bolla.
Delumentum, þweal.
Poculum, wegi.

Antulum, ceac.
Annona, non-mete.
Oxigia, sun-treow.
Cacista, hwite-clæfr.
Cuba, tunne.
Doleum, byden.
Colicus, eofor-þrote.
Callus, war.
Clamidis, godweb.
Frigus, cæle.
Calor, hæto.
Choors, tun.
Corus, þreat.
Sella, sylla.
Pella, radol-felt.
Carpella, sadol-boga.
Cicer, bean.

Coreum, hyd.
Cassidile, pung.
Corvis, mand.
Cornicen, horn-bora.
Culinia, coc.
Coquina, cycene.
Cacobatus, hrum.
Comicus, scop.
Melopius, hleot-wyrhta.
Conquilium, weoloc.
Celeps, hægsteald-man.
Calcarium, scoh.
Cancer, stalla.
Concern, hafern.
Cartilago, leoces heafod.
Cliens, geþofta.
Detracto, ic forsace.[1]

THE END.

[1] The remainder, in the MS., appears to belong rather to the glosses which follow, than to the Vocabulary, and it is therefore omitted here.

Lightning Source UK Ltd.
Milton Keynes UK
UKHW011001020119
334667UK00007B/644/P